“THE GENIUS OF THE PLACE”

"The Genius of the Place"

Essays on History and Continuity in Philadelphia

BRIAN CHARLES BURKE

Philadelphia 2024

ISBN 978-1-7369414-2-3 (hardcover)
ISBN 978-1-7369414-3-0 (paperback)

For information, contact briancharlesburke@verizon.net

Consult the genius of the place in all;
That tells the waters to rise, or fall;
Or helps th' ambitious hill the heav'ns to scale,
Or scoops in circling theatres the vale;
Calls in the country, catches opening glades,
Joins willing woods, and varies shades from shades,
Now breaks, or now directs, th' intending lines;
Paints as you plant, and, as you work, designs.

Alexander Pope

Omne tu/lit punc/tum // qui / miscuit / utile / dulci.
He has won every point, // who has mixed the useful with the sweet.

Horace, *Ars Poetica*

Contents

Estates in the City

East Park

West Park

Introduction

ALEXANDER POPE, in his poem, "Consult the genius of the place in all (1731)," encouraged the lords of English manors to observe the lay of their lands and to follow it in their designs:

> Consult the genius of the place in all;
> That tells the waters to rise, or fall;
> Or helps th' ambitious hill the heav'ns to scale,
> Or scoops in circling theatres the vale . . .

In William Penn's "Greene Country Town," naturalists like John Bartram, William Hamilton, and George Logan consulted nature more than most; but business men like Samuel Powel and David Franks created a "genius of the place" more attune to their business than to Mother Nature's. In either case, naturalists or business men, they improved their properties according to their time and taste. In this improvement, they complemented Pope's advice by that of the ancient Roman poet Horace, who suggested mixing nature's beauty with man's use:

> *Omne tu/lit punc/tum // qui / miscuit / utile / dulci.*
> He has won every point, // who has mixed the useful with the sweet.

Their particular genius mixed the virtues of plants with those of their own industry. Gardens planned by Bartram, Hamilton, Logan, and also the Fairmount Waterworks best illustrate this mix (see chapters

5, *James Logan's Cato as a Model for his Grandson George*; 11, *Bartram's Garden*; 19, *Fairmount Altogether*; and 20, *Building an Acropolis on Fairmount.*

Following Pope and Horace's advice, each essay in this book takes something that anyone can see in Philadelphia and tells stories about the Philadelphians associated with it. Bartram, Hamilton, and Logan joined nature with use extraordinarily. In all cases, however, the stories in this book reveal a particular "genius of the place" that characterizes the genial individuality of Philadelphia's urban landscape.

Eleven essays reveal this genius in the estates that have made up Fairmount Park. They all start with that of the park itself. When the Fairmount Park Commissioners were making plans, they asked the Olmsteads, the designers of New York's Central Park, for advice. They received a virtual copy of Pope's poem in reply: "consult the genius" of the Schuylkill river valley, they were told, just as nature has given it to you—don't change it. Do all you can to let this lily radiate its own beauty. Following this advice, they created a beautiful green line along the river.

On the other hand, the Commissioners did not follow through by consulting the genius of the properties, whose beauty their owners made useful with out-buildings, cultivated fields, orchards, and gardens. With the exception of Henry Pratt's garden and Edward Burd's glen, the Commissioners preserved the main building, and then they wiped away what their owners had built around them. They patched together each one of these estates without considering its individual mix of use with beauty. In stripping away everything that made the blood flow to and from the main building, they removed clues, which historians need for their reconstructions. As a result, the main buildings stand splendidly alone, like artifacts preserved in a museum. These eleven essays reinvest these buildings in some of their original personality.

The Fairmount Park Commission was doing in one sweep what time in its ever-rolling stream is always doing. It's what so commonly happens in the passage of time that we could almost say that time rolls everything away on its own. On the other hand, we know quite well what bulldozers are for! Without any help from the municipality, houses and neighborhoods throughout the city have changed so radically that they reflect almost nothing of the original "genius" of their places. Over the course of time, for example, Samuel Powel's townhouse on Third street has lost its connection to his in-laws' family compound, most notably to the Bingham Mansion that filled the rest of the block with its beautiful garden (see chapters 12, *Samuel Powel, Lord and Landlord*, complemented by 15, *The Epoch of Ann and William Bingham.*) The Powel House, however, does not stand splendidly alone, as do Belmont, Woodford, and all the other historic houses in Fairmount Park. In fact, just the opposite: the Powel House is surrounded by all the buildings built, over time, on its block of South Third street.

On the other hand, Powel's country house, just east of the Park in Powelton, was demolished. The ninety acres of its property bear no trace of Powel's or, especially, his nephew John's genius for mixing beauty with use (see chapter 12, *Samuel Powel*..., complemented by 13, *John Hare Powel—Balancing Beauty with Use at Powelton*). The Pennsylvania Railroad turned thirty of its ninety acres into a rail yard along the Schuylkill River; and it developed the remaining sixty into Powelton, a fashionable neighborhood.[1] On the Schuylkill River, below Fairmount, which divides park from city, the present condition of the rail yard shows just how much industry can make the beautiful ugly.

In Samuel Powel's legacy, his townhouse survives instead of his country house. This survival provides an exception to the rule, following which most of the essays in this book describe the country houses of men, whose townhouses have not survived. With special value as real estate in the city, the sale of townhouses gave their owners special profit. Samuel Breck and William Hamilton, on the other hand, lived solely in their country houses.

The histories of some families give their houses a special genius. As exceptions, some men built, not as individuals, but as associations:

Chapter 6, Philadelphians' 'Poor Power' to Celebrate Penn's Treaty,
Chapter 7, Philadelphians' and the Cincinnati's Washington Monument,
Chapter 19, Fairmount Altogether,

Chapter 20, Building an Acropolis on Fairmount,
Chapter 28, The Girard Avenue Bridge.

In these chapters, two monuments, a reservoir, a museum, and a bridge do not reveal individual genius, but they do reveal the lives of the private or municipal associations that created them. A further exception, chapter 30, *Fairman Rogers on Lansdowne Drive*, tells a story about the life of an aristocratic Philadelphian whose coach and four put the beauty of Lansdowne Drive to good use.

Two chapters describe the later history of a family's estate (chapter 1, *Gulielma Springett and Hannah Callowhill: William Penn's Two Wives in and out of Historical Memory*; and chapter 16, *The Family Ties of Francisville*). In both cases, their estates evolved into neighborhoods. Chapter 1 describes the evolution of the Penns' proprietary estate into Fairmount; and chapter 16, the evolution of the Francis private estate into Francisville. Only street names remain as clues to their origin. Sometimes street names can tell some good stories. In general, however, all thirty-one essays derive their stories from what we can observe, even if it is just the name of a street like Callowhill in Fairmount or Orchard in Francisville.

Some churches or municipal buildings tell stories of national importance:

Chapter 2, Carpenters' Hall, The Nation's Birthplace,
Chapter 3, Independence Hall,
Chapter 4, The Old Penn Mansion, Liberty House,
Chapter 8, St. Joseph's Escaping Notice,
Chapter 9, Christ Church and its Bells,
Chapter 19, Fairmount Altogether,
Chapter 20, Building an Acropolis on Fairmount.

These stories reach beyond individuals' genius to that of the American people and the ways in which Philadelphians encouraged its growth and enshrined its memory. Philadelphians' institutions have had national significance. Following these streams of people, even the Girard Avenue Bridge (chapter 28) connects all the people who have crossed it, as they connect one side of the park to the other.

In whatever chapter and from whatever perspective, this book tells a lot of stories: mostly about people but all of them about the city of Philadelphia and its people. In them, we see Philadelphians designing their lives in different times, with different values; from them, the genius of the city emerges to tell us its own story.

FOUNDATIONS

CHAPTER 1

Gulielma Springett and Hannah Callowhill

William Penn's Two Wives in and out of Historical Memory

PHILADELPHIANS MAY REMEMBER that Callowhill, as in Callowhill street, was originally the maiden name of William Penn's second wife. This family name and the location of its street tell an interestingly complicated story. The complication rolls up Penn's two wives into one story and one property shared by the two.

The story involves the two families whose daughters married William Penn (1644–1718). From the second family, he married Hannah Callowhill; but,—let's start at the beginning,—from the first family, he married Gulielma (Guli) Maria Springett (1644–1694). She gave him seven children, only three of whom survived into adulthood: one daughter, Letitia (1678–1745), and two sons. The first he named Springett (1674–1696) after his wife's family; and the second, William, Jr. (1679–1720), after his own.

Young Springett Penn could look forward to being the first-born male heir of the family's estate, but, two years after his mother's death, he died at age 22, too young and too soon to receive this inheritance. William Penn's love match with Guli Springett had marked a bright, hopeful period of his life. In addition, Springett had been, his father lamented, "a most affectionate, dutiful child . . . a sober young man, my friend and companion," by whose loss, he lost "all that a father could lose in a child."[2] His brother, William, Jr., however, resolving that his mother and brother's name, at least, would not be lost, named his son Springett, II.

William, Jr., next in line to inherit the estate upon his father's demise in 1718, also died too soon, since he survived his father by only two years. His demise passed his right to Springett, II, but the Springett offspring were no longer sole heirs; because,—here is the second part of the story,—their father married Hannah Callowhill in 1696, two years after Guli Springett had died. In 1699, Hannah gave birth to the first of six children, three of whom survived as heirs: John (1699–1746), Thomas (1702–1775), and Richard (1706–1771). To Hannah Callowhill, he had also willed his estate when he died in 1718. The Springett family name, that at first burned bright in expectations, ended in eclipse.

William Penn, Jr. contested his father's will; and Springett, II pled the case after his father's death. He failed in his plea, and died in Dublin, Ireland, in 1731. Now Hannah Callowhill's sons were the sole male heirs to William Penn's name and fortune. They had outlived Guli Springett's sons and had the final say, but the name Springett was not entirely lost. The proprietary estate was named Springettsbury Manor to honor Springett II's uncle and grandmother.[3]

The first plan for Philadelphia had made room for Springettsbury Manor. In Thomas Holme's "Portraiture of the City," 1683, five east-west lines of blocks extend south from the center square,—on which City Hall has been built,—but only three extend north. Holme, the surveyor, in accordance with William Penn's desire to benefit his family, cut the city short on its northern border to make room for this proprietary manor. It was a desirable location. North of the city, the land rose from a valley along Vine Street to the first hills of the Piedmont Plateau, an appropriate eminence for Philadelphia's eminent family. Callowhill was the first street north of Vine, the northern border between the old city and Springettsbury.

Thomas Penn (1702–1775) lived in Philadelphia from 1732 until 1741. He raised the profile of the Springetts' eponymous estate by building its manor house, "pleasingly situated on an eminence with a gradual descent, to a handsome level road, out through a wood, affording an agreeable vista of near two miles."[4] This lord of the manor,

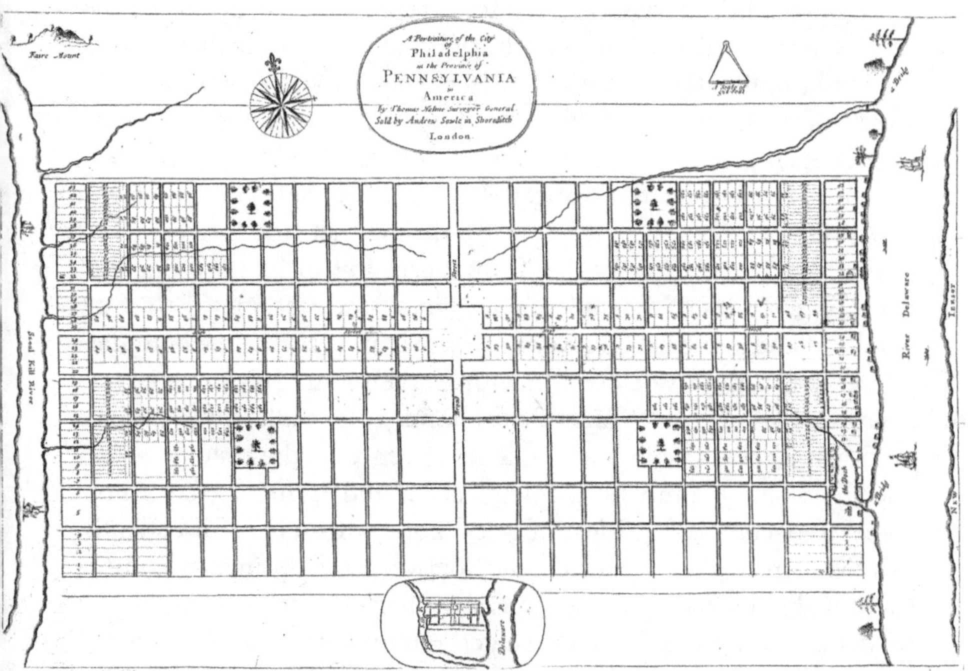

Thomas Holme's "Portraiture of the City of Philadelphia," 1683

having left the democratic Society of Friends, joined the Church of England with its aristocratic ethic—and its assumptions. He, therefore, made his house and gardens imposing, because, he asserted, a "person must appear as the first man of the place he resides in."[5]

The American Revolution ended the Penn family's legitimacy as proprietors. By the 1850's, Springettsbury Manor, democratically renamed, Springettsbury Farm, was 'improved', that is, turned to profit, by clear-cutting, paving streets, and building houses.[6] The old manor turned farm, became a suburban neighborhood, now called Fairmount, naming the area after the first rocky hill of the Piedmont Plateau up the Schuylkill. This hill has been such an important landmark that Thomas Holme's map pictures "Faire Mount" on its upper left-hand corner. Thomas Penn's family knew "Faire Mount" as the place where they might enjoy pic-nics, but they did not name their estate after it. Springettsbury, not this picturesque rocky hill, memorialized the family.

Callowhill has survived as the name of the first street north of Vine, the southern border of Springettsbury Farm.[7] It is ironic that Callowhill street indirectly memorializes Springettsbury Manor. One of the streets of the improved neighborhood, Springet street, did memorialize the Springetts, but that name was soon changed to North street, the northern border of Springettsbury Manor, now the first street south of Fairmount avenue.[8] It is also ironic that North street refers not to the name of the manorial property but to its northern border. These streets of the city neighborhood, the first ones within the northern and southern boundaries of the manor, define the boundaries of the Penns' private domain without mentioning its name.

In the heritage of William Penn's family, the Callowhills, not the Springetts, have won distinction. Reminiscences of the history of Philadelphia's oldest family in Callowhill street and Springet street unfold some of its complexity. Most of us do not know—and, consequently, can not care,—about the difference between the Springetts and the Callowhills. William Penn's namesake did care, and he tried to preserve his mother's, Gulielma Springett's, family name for posterity.

CHAPTER 2

Carpenters' Hall, "The Nation's Birthplace"

CARPENTERS' HALL STANDS at the end of an alley called Carpenters' Court, several hundred feet south of Chestnut street, below Fourth. Down the alley from the sidewalk in Independence Park, passers-by can see this two-story Georgian brick structure, built in 1770. Its red brick walls are dotted with black brick headers in Flemish bond. The hall is about fifty feet long by thirty wide. A centrally located cupola brings together its four pavilions, each thirty feet by ten. Around the doorway of the front pavilion, Doric columns support a classical pediment, and enclose Doric pilasters, supporting a fan light above double doors (*Inquirer*, November 28, 1865).

The fame of this building as the nation's birthplace requires an explanation. Visitors to Philadelphia, who have heard about Independence Hall, expect to visit this American shrine first. Wasn't Independence Hall, they ask, the nation's birthplace? They have a surprise when another building claims the title—at least

Aerial view of the cruciform design of Carpenters' Hall (1770), that Robert Smith copied from a court house in Lancaster

The Doorway of Carpenters' Hall
Doric columns enclose Doric pilasters around the door.

in the first steps of bringing the nation to birth. In 1774, Carpenters' Hall opened its doors to the first meeting of America's Founding Fathers. These two claims cause some confusion, but they tell a story worth telling.

In the beginning, Carpenters' Hall and Independence Hall had different functions, and neither one could have made any claim to national significance. Liberty was only just starting to twinkle in the eyes of Americans, when the Carpenters' Company was serving the ancient function of a trade guild, educating apprentices, regulating their masters' trade, and ministering to either one of them in need.

The Seal of the Carpenters' Company, with one carpenter's square and three compasses

Two of the first members of this guild most notably helped to build the city. Edmund Woolley (circa 1695–1771) was one of its founders. He designed the State House long before it won the title of Independence Hall, the second birthplace of American Liberty. Robert Smith (1722–1777) designed Carpenters' Hall not too long before it became the first birthplace of American Liberty. When Woolley designed a government house, and Smith, a guild hall, neither man could have anticipated the eventual fame of his building. In either case, Philadelphia carpenters, with a square and compasses like the ones on their seal, were marking out a distinguished place for themselves.

Because of their different origins, both buildings served different purposes for the first two meetings of the Continental Congress. The delegates to the First Continental Congress had good reason to ask the Carpenters' Company to open the doors of its hall to their meeting on September 5, 1774, but they were not unanimous in their decision: one delegate, Joseph Galloway, as Speaker of the Provincial Assembly, had offered his—so to speak, his—State House (eventually Independence Hall) for the meeting; but the majority of the delegates chose Carpenters' Hall, which had already hosted a meeting of discontented citizens. (John Adams called its location at the end of an alley a "long entry where gentlemen may walk.") Historian Charles Peterson has recognized the practicality of this choice:

> There were both social and business implications. Resistance to Britain was being organized on a broad basis and those marshaling public sentiment were courting the favor and support of the tradespeople and mechanics. In Boston, the boycott against British goods had been originated and carried thro' by two venerable orders of men styled "Mechanics and husbandmen."[9]

The majority made a wise decision. In 1774, the State House represented the conservative aristocracy of men like Galloway, who would have opened its doors to the meeting. Eventually, Galloway had banked too much on his conservative and aristocratic capital to keep up with America's revolutionary fervor.[10]

For the first meeting of the Continental Congress, therefore, Carpenters' Hall suited a people's movement better than King George's

State House. In 1774, "Mechanics and husbandmen" might have called the State House Dependence, not Independence, Hall, since it de-pended on the *status quo*. It had not yet earned its title.

THE FIFTY-SIX DELEGATES to the first Continental Congress, from twelve of the thirteen colonies—Georgia, the exception—met between September 5 and October 26, 1774. This sagacious conclave impressed the young Solomon Drowne (1753–1834): "My blood thrilled through my veins at the agreeable, pleasant view of so many noble, sage patriots met in the great cause of liberty" (Peterson, 102). At first, however, they met without, necessarily, a meeting of their minds. During their first meetings, two famous scenes helped both to inspire them and to bring them together as Americans. The first day, they focused on how many votes each colony should have in making decisions—just one for each colony, they debated, or more in proportion to population. Aristocratic Virginia thought that she should hold sway: "Virginia will never consent to waive her full representations, and if denied it, she would be seen no more in that Congress."[11] The meeting was not starting well.

The next day, Patrick Henry of Virginia inspired these fifty-five delegates to unite as Americans and not just as colonists. He reminded them of their danger:

> Fleets and armies and the present state of things show that the government is dissolved. All America is thrown into one mass; where are your landmarks, your boundaries of colonies? We are in a state of nature. All distinctions are thrown down; all America is thrown into one

Patrick Henry addressing the First Continental Congress, from a painting by Clyde O. De Land

> mass. The distinctions between Virginians and Pennsylvanians, New Yorkers and New Englanders are no more. I am not a Virginian, but an American.

After violence has reduced the British colonies to a "state of nature," Henry proposes a new national community. His face glowing with emotion, his earnest, deeply grey blue eyes flashing, his voice declared immortal words, "I am not a Virginian, but an American." His exhortation, it has been said, helped to tip the balance of the fate of humanity. Such resolve would bring concord from discord in any age.

In another effort to focus, the delegates on the second day proposed that the next meeting be opened with prayer. To some objection made to this proposal, the pious but sensible Sam Adams said "that he was no bigot, and could hear a prayer from any gentleman of piety and virtue if he was at the same time a friend to his country." The motion was seconded and passed (*Inquirer*, January 18, 1877). Next morning, the Reverend Duché of Christ Church started the third day with

The First Prayer in Congress, a scene "worthy of the painter's art" (painted by T.H. Matteson and engraved by H.S. Sadd)

Scripture. He read Psalm 35, the passage appointed for that day in the lectionary of his church:

1. Plead my cause, O Lord, with them that strive with me: fight against them that fight against me.
2. Take hold of shield and buckler, and stand up for mine help.
3. Draw out also the spear, and stop the way against them that persecute me: say unto my soul, I am thy salvation. . . .

To the delegates, this psalm pleading "my cause" in war came as the outstretched hand of a benevolent providence. They were living amid rumors of war. September 1, the British had removed powder from an armory in Boston; and on the 6th, violent resistance had started when five thousand mostly unarmed civilians prevented twenty-five judges appointed by the crown from presiding in the court of Worcester, Massachusetts. In response to the reading of Psalm 35, delegates like Patrick Henry, George Washington, John Jay, Samuel and John Adams listened intently to Reverend Duché's prayer. "Here was a scene," John Adams reflected, "worthy of the painters' art."[12]

Unity bore fruit. Before adjourning on October 26, the First Continental Congress resolved to boycott British imports starting on December 1, 1774: "We do for ourselves and for the inhabitants of the several Colonies whom we represent, firmly agree and associate under the sacred ties of virtue, honor and love of our country." Back in 1765 and 1768, citizens in Boston and New York had agreed to boycott British imports, but in 1774 fifty-six delegates from twelve colonies stood firm in agreement. They wisely advocated the boycotts that "two venerable orders of men styled Mechanics and husbandmen" had adopted.

Men more influential than the young Solomon Drowne admired their firm resolve. In England, William Pitt, Earl of Chatham, called it a "sacred tie." In an address to Parliament, he praised "the dignity, firmness, and wisdom with which the Americans have acted." Even in the "celebrated writings of antiquity," he said, no other people, "can stand in preference to the general Congress at Philadelphia." "I trust," Pitt concluded, "that it is obvious, that all attempts to impose servitude upon such men, to establish despotism over such a mighty continental nation, must be vain, must be futile." Patrick Henry's call to unity and the divine providence of Reverend Duché's reading and prayer had united the First Continental Congress.

AFTER THE HIGH DRAMA of the American Revolution, the American people continued to live out their story in Carpenters' Hall. This story found an unlikely hero in the 1790's, when Philadelphia served as the capital of the United States and the wealth of the new nation poured into Chestnut street. In 1791, for the security of their new tenant, the First Bank of the United States, the Carpenters moved out of their own hall. After seven years, the bank built its permanent home in 1798—America's first classical bank building that is still on Third street above Chestnut. But since Carpenters' Hall had been braced with a secure vault, the Bank of Pennsylvania soon moved in.

In the early morning of September 1, 1798, theft sharpened the edge of the story, when $162,821 was stolen from the Bank of Pennsylvania's vault. The bank directors demanded swift justice. Pat Lyon (1769–1829), a blacksmith, had a mechanical genius as a locksmith that had secured his employment to fit and repair the locks to their vault. His genius also made him their prime suspect and the first man to be arrested.

While an outbreak of yellow fever raged throughout the city, Lyon languished in prison for three months. Crime, eventually, will out: Isaac Davis, a carpenter, with his accomplice, an employee of the bank, confessed to the crime. The directors, too eager to retrieve their money, had too swiftly imprisoned a suspect. The human story of Pat's suffering—the plight of a humble mechanic bulldozed by arrogant plutocrats—had a poignancy in Americans' special version of human drama. It thrilled "their hearts with an incident of the unfaltering honesty and vindicated integrity" of the common man (*Inquirer,* November 28, 1865).

In the afterglow of his vindication and, nine years after his successful lawsuit against the directors, Lyon promoted his virtue as a common man. Before his death in 1829, he commissioned John Neagle to paint a portrait of him as a blacksmith at the forge. To one side of the forge, Neagle included the steeple of a building, either the Walnut Street Jail or Carpenters' Hall. (Either building told part of his story.)

John Neagle, *Pat Lyon at the Forge* (1829)

Lyon had become a gentleman and he could have asked to be portrayed as such, but he appreciated his roots and he wanted to celebrate them. He had vindicated his integrity as one of the humble mechanics of the city, nature's nobleman unjustly accused by his betters. Carpenters' Hall might represent either nature's noblemen or privileged plutocrats. Lyon chose the "unfaltering honesty and vindicated integrity" of nature's noblemen.

THE CARPENTERS' COMPANY had shared its history with a succession of people and institutions in Philadelphia. The Library Company (1773–1788), the First Bank of the United States (1791–1797), the Bank of Pennsylvania (1796–1797), the United States Custom House (1802–1817), the Second Bank of the United States (1817–1821), the Music Fund Society (1822), and the Franklin Institute (1825) rented its hall before acquiring their own buildings. Each one of these institutions went on to build a fine home, all of which survived into the twentieth century. These distinguished associations ended in 1838 when an auction house and a primary school became the final tenants: 'Oh, how the might have fallen!' lamented one newspaper:

> These sublime apartments, which first resounded with the indignant murmur of our immortal ancestors, sitting in secret consultation upon the wrong of their countrymen, now ring with the din of urchins conning over their tasks; and the hallowed hall below, in which the august assembly to which they belonged daily convened, is now devoted to the use of an auctioneer! Even now, while I am penning these lines at his desk, his voice stuns my ear and distracts my brain, crying 'How much for these rush-bottom chairs? I am offered $6: nobody more? Going! going, gone!!!' In fact, the hall is lumbered up with beds, looking-glasses, chairs, tables, pictures, ready-made cloth, and all the trash and trumpery which usually grace the premises of a knight of the hammer (*Public Ledger*, October, 1844).

In 1857, the officers of the Carpenters' Company remedied this stinging indignity by embracing their past. Their old hall had played a distinguished part in the Revolution and in the later history of the country and the city. They decided to preserve it and open it to the public, because it had become, as one newspaper said, "a venerated

Carpenters' Hall about 1870, with its title in the eaves

memento of the past." Rid of "the trash and trumpery" of commerciality, it could tell its own story that was "instructive, valuable and full of interest." Carpenters' Hall was not just a part of history, it was history. They announced this distinction by illuminating the entrance to the building with a special bit of modern technology: gas jets over the door spelled out "The Nation's Birthplace." Above this title, they also placed a half circle of thirteen globes to represent the thirteen original States (*Inquirer*, July 6, 1865). Perhaps because the gas jets brought some difficulty or danger, the officers eventually contented themselves with tucking their title under the eaves.

Inside the Hall, they displayed some relics of their history. Glass cases on the eastern and western walls, contained satin banners bearing the Carpenters' Arms. In celebrating the adoption of the Constitution, their ancestors had carried one of these banners in the Grand Federal Procession on the Fourth of July, 1788. They had carried the other one in the parade, February, 1832, celebrating Washington's birthday. Flanking the door on the north, in two massive gold frames, they hung a roll of the members of the Society, from its foundation.

Centrally located, stood a desk, with two antique high-backed chairs, probably of the period of the First Congress in 1774. On the wall behind them, gilt letters announced the building's fame:

Within these walls
Henry, Hancock and Adams
Inspired the
Delegates of the Colonies
With nerve and sinew for the
Toils of War,
Resulting in our National Independence.

The company celebrated this opening on September 5, 1857 with a proper ceremony and a properly jovial dinner:

> A very jovial company surrounded the tables, and although most of the company were old "boss" carpenters who had retired long since on their well-earned means, they could not forget the old days of the tin kettle and the dinner basket, and after getting their fill of the roast pig,

> *à la mode* beef, and champagne, they beat a retreat from the table as hurriedly as though the one o'clock bell had just rung (*Historical Magazine*, November, 1857).

Roast pork with beef, braised *à la mode*, and washed down with champagne, provided hearty fare. The diners' hearty good will also characterized and celebrated the spirit of the Company as much as the formal ceremony.

THE CARPENTERS' COMPANY represents a special continuity in the history of Philadelphia. Through its three hundred year history, it has served as a guild in educating its members, and in ministering to their needs. In addition, extraordinarily, it has preserved its first building as a relic of the Revolutionary War, maintaining it, and sharing the interest of its American story. Preserving, maintaining and sharing, it has benefitted and represented Philadelphia beyond any expectation of the men who built it.

CHAPTER 3

Independence Hall

How Philadelphia's History Found a Home

IN 1774, THE DELEGATES to the First Continental Congress did not at first meet in the building that we now call Independence Hall, because they identified it as the State House of His Majesty King George. At that time, it had nothing to do with being independent, because it depended on the King. After Americans had won independence from the King, they celebrated it by calling his State House their Independence Hall. Back then, that celebration required a change in name, which now, in turn, needs an explanation.

What does hall mean? If someone asks me to attend a meeting in the hall, I need to understand his reference, because the word can refer to three different parts of the same building. Way, way back,

among Norsemen in the early Middle Ages, Beowulf's mead-hall was a single large room in its own building. Gradually, it remained a large room, but with smaller rooms off of it. Finally, this large room shrank to a corridor that led to the rooms. Disconnecting each part from the whole, hall can refer to the larger room or to the smaller corridor—quite a contrast, but one certainly did lead to the other. One step further, connecting all three parts together, hall can refer to the sum of the larger room, the smaller rooms and the corridor that connects them. I could be attending my meeting in a room, a corridor or a building.

Americans' Independence Hall in King George's State House followed this evolution. To be specific, in the early nineteenth century, the building that our ancestors first called the State House and that we now call Independence Hall at first had one room that our ancestors called the "Hall of Independence." Independence Hall first referred to one room in the State House and, finally, to the whole building.

This change in name may seem to represent no more than an evolution in architectural terminology, but this evolution marked a revolution in American thought. In the first fifty years of the United States between 1776 and 1826, the name evolved until it revolved back to its origin. In other words, as the history of the State House was rolling out, evolving, to 1826, it gradually started to roll back, to revolve, back to 1776. As history evolves, revolutionaries, renouncing all that same old, same old, go back to beginnings. In the first decades of the nineteenth century, a few Americans were starting to realize that they had a past worth going back to and monuments in that past that were worth both preserving and bringing back to the present. As most other Americans were making a mad dash forward, these few turned around to go back. History. and especially its relics, are fragile—they can exist only when some men, at least, take time to look back to the past with enough appreciation that they preserve them.

Why should these few have cared about a State House? All the states had one, in which they conducted the every-day business of enacting laws and acting on them. These buildings represented the state's power and dignity, but they rarely became icons like the State House in Philadelphia. So what's so special about Philadelphia's old State House? Today, the question may seem embarrassingly ignorant or cynically unpatriotic, but in young America around the year 1810, Philadelphians needed to ask and answer it.

By 1800, Philadelphia had ceased being the capital of the state or of the country. In that year the "old State House" only provided a home for city government. The city rented out its second floor to Charles Wilson Peale for his museum—some called it his collection of stuffed alligators (*United States Gazette*, September 14, 1827). As years passed, however, a few Philadelphians, at least, had a long memory. They remembered that our Founding Fathers had signed America's Declaration of Independence in a chamber in this old State House. For example, the *United States Gazette* reported a celebration of the Fourth of July in 1824:

> The Democratic Society will meet in the room of the State House in which forty-eight years ago our independence was declared. Colonel Forrest will then read the Declaration of Independence and Thomas F Gordon Esq. deliver an oration.

At this meeting, Philadelphians acknowledged and commemorated the momentous declaration that their ancestors had issued from their State House in July of 1776. History had relevance, because they remembered and celebrated it.

They celebrated the event; but they did not celebrate the building or the room in which it took place by giving either place a separate name. They did acknowledge, however, that there was a "room of the State house in which forty eight years ago our independence was declared." The focus of American history would become sharper when Americans could celebrate their independence on a specific date, in a specific place, with a specific name. Dates, places and names—some may complain that that's all we learn when we study history in school,—but they do clarify our focus and set a foundation, on which to build meaning.

Down in Washington, DC, in the summer of 1824, Americans, in general, found a special focus for their patriotism. President James Monroe, in preparation for the semi-centennial of the United States in 1826, had officially invited the Marquis de Lafayette (1757–1834) to visit. After Lafayette had survived his mentor, George Washington, by twenty-five years, his return in 1824 sparked all the gratitude that Americans had felt for Washington as their *Pater Patriae* and first president. The celebration of their semi-centennial, therefore, went hand in hand with the celebration of Lafayette.

Up in Philadelphia, "very numerous and respectable" citizens met in the "State House Yard to make arrangements for the reception of General LaFayette" (*Inquirer*, August 20, 1824). He had just arrived on August 15 from France. Almost fifty years before, in 1777, Lafayette, age 19, had met George Washington, age 45, in Philadelphia's City Tavern. Washington cultivated his friendship with fatherly concern and used his services in the Continental Army. President Monroe had issued the official invitation, but Philadelphians thought that this Frenchman, with his "republican feelings," would appreciate "effusions of gratitude emanating directly from the people, and not produced by official influence." These "people" lived in Philadelphia and not in Washington.

Philadelphia was competing with Boston and New York to extend the grandest welcome to the nation's illustrious guest. It hired the

Currier and Ives, *The First Meeting of Washington and Lafayette* (1876)

neoclassical architect William Strickland to build a triumphal arch for his entrance.

GRAND CIVIC ARCH
ERECTED IN CHESNUT STREET
OPPOSITE THE HALL OF INDEPENDENCE

A classical triumphal arch!—what entrance could be grander? Furthermore, to continue outdoing Boston and New York, Philadelphia had a famous place, the "Hall of Independence," in which to receive this illustrious guest. Just in case the "Hall of Independence," in itself, did not announce its significance grandly enough, the city hired William Strickland to decorate it.

The *Inquirer*, at first, referred to this "Hall of Independence" as "the Room in the State House, in which the Declaration of Independence was signed, to be fitted up, under the direction of Mr. Strickland as a

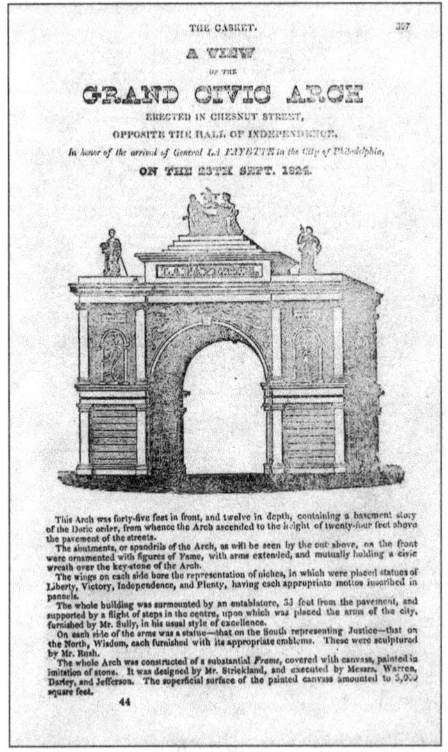

THE CASKET. 387

A VIEW
OF THE
GRAND CIVIC ARCH
ERECTED IN CHESNUT STREET,
OPPOSITE THE HALL OF INDEPENDENCE.
In honor of the arrival of General LA FAYETTE in the City of Philadelphia,
ON THE 28TH SEPT. 1824.

This Arch was forty-five feet in front, and twelve in depth, containing a basement story of the Doric order, from whence the Arch ascended to the height of twenty-four feet above the pavement of the streets.

The abutments, or spandrils of the Arch, as will be seen by the cut above, on the front were ornamented with figures of Fame, with arms extended, and mutually holding a civic wreath over the key-stone of the Arch.

The wings on each side bore the representation of niches, in which were placed statues of Liberty, Victory, Independence, and Plenty, having each appropriate mottos inscribed in pannels.

The whole building was surmounted by an entablature, 33 feet from the pavement, and supported by a flight of steps in the centre, upon which was placed the arms of the city, furnished by Mr. Sully, in his usual style of excellence.

On each side of the arms was a statue—that on the South representing Justice—that on the North, Wisdom, each furnished with its appropriate emblems. These were sculptured by Mr. Rush.

The whole Arch was constructed of a substantial *Frame*, covered with canvass, painted in imitation of stone. It was designed by Mr. Strickland, and executed by Messrs. Warren, Darley, and Jefferson. The superficial surface of the painted canvass amounted to 3,000 square feet.

44

A picture of William Strickland's "Grand Civic Arch" in *The Casket*

Levée Room for General Lafayette" (*Inquirer*, August 20, 1824). Three months later, it referred to the room as the "Hall of Independence" (November 16, 1824), and, finally, in announcing the levée, it called it "Independence Hall" (July 20, 1825). Even today, with a bit of quaint archaism, we may refer to the State House, knowing that we really mean Independence Hall.

Strickland constructed the Grand Civic Arch and decorated the "Hall of Independence," but the event spoke for itself. Lafayette reminisced that 1776 marked an era:

> Within these sacred walls, by a council of wise and devoted patriots, and in a style worthy of the deed itself, was boldly declared the independence of these vast United States, which . . . has begun, for the civilized world, the era of a new and of the only true social order founded on the Unalienable rights of man, the practicability and advantages of which are every day admirably demonstrated by the happiness and prosperity of your populous city.

"Within these sacred walls," American independence declared a new era. Now observe, Lafayette asserts, the prosperity of Philadelphians and see the fruits of this independence. Quoting Vergil, the Great Seal of the United States alluded to the *Novus Ordo Saeclorum*, "new order of the ages," that started in 1776. In 1826, when the "very numerous and respectable meeting of the citizens of Philadelphia" anticipated the importance of Lafayette's visit, they also resolved first of all that it would mark an "epoch" in their country's history:

> Resolved, That the opportunity now offered to the people of America, of rendering personal honour to General LaFayette, by his arrival on our shores, is to be regarded as one of the most interesting epochs in the annals of our country (*Inquirer*, August 19, 1824).

On the names for the date and place—July 4, 1826, the fiftieth year of the Declaration of Independence, issued from Independence Hall—Philadelphians constructed a meaning, which Lafayette confirmed. As a symbolic interpretation, they had built a "Grand Civic Arch," through which he would pass. On it, sculptors had placed statues of "Liberty, Victory, Independence and Plenty" in niches around its portal and statues of Wisdom and Justice on its entablature. He then attended a reception in the "Hall of Independence," which Strickland had decorated with democratic symbols. So many symbols! How could anyone have missed the meaning? Once in the Hall of Independence, the Philadelphians clasped hands with Lafayette to share and confirm their "effusions of gratitude" for the work of the Founding Fathers and, especially, for the work of his mentor and their first president.

In his speech, Lafayette confirmed that their work in 1776 had established "the only true social order founded on the Unalienable rights of man." George Washington and the other signers of the Declaration of Independence founded this new social order; and Lafayette provided the link between their foundation in 1776 and its "practicability and advantages, . . . every day admirably demonstrated by the happiness and prosperity" of Philadelphia in 1826. If anyone wishes to know the blessings of 1776, just take a look at the citizens of Philadelphia, busy with their "pursuit of happiness" in 1826. The date, time and place—July 4, 1826, and Independence Hall in the old State House—had special meaning for Lafayette and the citizens of Philadelphia. In an unbroken chain, the event of July 4, 1776 set the foundation of their history; and the names that they gave to its home in 1826 clarified its celebration.

CHAPTER 4

The Old Penn Mansion, Liberty House

A HOUSE USUALLY TAKES the name of its current resident, but it claims a special place in history, when it bears the name of someone famous. The Penn Mansion claimed its name, because William Penn lived there from 1699 to 1701 in his second visit to Philadelphia. Penn rented it for these three years. George Washington and John Adams might also have added their names to its fame, but they only boarded. Put together, these associations have made this house "not less unique than it is antique," one historian wrote.[13]

For a common name, Philadelphians have focused on its construction by referring to the Penn Mansion as the Slate-Roof House. In the

The Old Penn Mansion

Slate-Roof House, however, Penn gave to human liberty a document of greater significance than his lease or its slate. By this document, he declared the liberties that gave the Liberty Bell its name and inspired the famous declaration that made the Pennsylvania State House Independence Hall.

Whatever its name, Penn Mansion or Slate-Roof House, it was more significant than all other residential buildings in Philadelphia. Its loss by demolition in 1867, consequently, surpasses that of all other residential buildings in the city. On the other hand, the memory of a building does not disappear as soon as a wrecking crew has finished its work. The same historian who claimed it as uniquely antique also foresaw that the descendants of those who demolished it would "be called upon to chronicle the evidence of a change in this respect." After the wrecking crew has packed up and left, memory exercises a dynamic influence, because it speaks more eloquently than brick walls or even a fine slate roof.

Samuel Carpenter built the Slate-Roof House in 1687, when Philadelphia had just left the infancy of its fifth year.[14] Its location told a story of the growing city. For the life-blood of its commerce, Philadelphia crowded along Front street, on the Delaware River. Quests for profit abroad broke the boundaries of Penn's ideal for a "Greene Country Towne" at home. Carpenter, whom the annalist Watson called "one of the earliest and greatest improvers of the primitive city," made his fortune on Front street. Having already built his first home there, he enhanced the pastoral scene of the Slate-Roof House by building it on a lot in back of Front, facing Second. A little north of Dock Creek, it looked west toward the "greene" of Penn's "country towne."

Facing west, the Slate-Roof House also put a little green in its spacious backyard. This yard extended "halfway to Front street, enclosed by a high wall, and ornamented with a double row of venerable, lofty pines, which afforded a very agreeable *rus in urbe* or rural scene in the city."[15] The wall and double row of pines blocked out the trade up Front and preserved some green in back. In the drawing at the top of this chapter, the artist put some pines in background as reminders of Penn's "venerable" ideal of *rus in urbe*. Taking these directions on the compass to represent morality in the City of Brotherly Love, Penn's residence was turning away from Philadelphians' mercantile profit toward their pastoral peace.

Penn would also have appreciated living in Samuel Carpenter's mansion, because it resembled a fine home in England. Forming three sides of a quadrangle with two wings or bastions, it characterized Jacobean homes of the 17th century, illustrated by an H plan in Stephen Primatt's book, *City and Country Purchaser* (1667). In the 18th century, Palladian standards built houses around a central pavilion with a facade of the Ionic Order. Carpenter's mansion, by contrast, appears quaint, almost mediaeval. Whatever its style, as the largest private residence in Pennsylvania, it served as Penn's Executive Mansion.

The location and construction of the Slate-Roof House fulfilled Penn's expectation for an English house in a pastoral scene. One month after arriving, his pregnant wife Hannah made this house a home by giving birth to John Penn (1700–1747), called "the American," because he was the only member of the family born in Pennsylvania. While Hannah ran the household, Penn wrote a constitution for his pastoral utopia. He issued this Charter of Privileges, also known as the Charter of Liberties, in 1701. It functioned as Pennsylvania's constitution until 1776. By this foundation for his "Holy Experiment," Penn sounded a clarion call for democracy in America.

The fame of the Charter of Liberties has reverberated through American history. In 1751, fifty years after William Penn issued it, Isaac Norris, as the President of the Pennsylvania Assembly,—whose father, by an appropriate coincidence, had purchased the Slate-Roof House in 1709,—celebrated its jubilee by commissioning a commemorative bell for the State House. On it, he inscribed *Leviticus*, chapter 25, the second clause of verse 10: "And ye shall hallow the fiftieth year, and

PROCLAIM LIBERTY THROUGHOUT ALL THE LAND
UNTO ALL THE INHABITANTS THEREOF."

This bell has had a famously varied history of proclaiming liberty, but it might first have claimed the title of the Liberty Bell because it celebrated the liberty proclaimed by Penn's charter of 1701. It hung in the tower of the State House, which became known as Independence Hall, after it rang out the birth of the Declaration of Independence. As the home of the liberties that inspired the Founding Fathers to declare independence, the Slate-Roof House also inspired the name of Independence Hall.

Philadelphians have revered the Slate-Roof House, not only because William Penn lived in it, but also because he sent out his declaration of liberties from it. They could have,—perhaps should have,—named it Liberty House. By contrast, its subsequent history creeps to anticlimax. Penn sailed back to England in 1701, never to return, leaving his secretary, James Logan (1674–1751), in the Slate-Roof House and in charge of business.

In 1703, Samuel Carpenter sold the mansion to William Trent of Trenton for £850. In 1709, when Trent offered to sell the building for £900, Logan reported the sale to Penn: "William Trent designing for England is about selling his house, (that he bought of Samuel Carpenter,) which thou lived in, with the improvement of a beautiful garden. I wish it could be made thine, as nothing in this town is so well fitting a Governor. His price is £900, our money, which it is hard thou can'st not spare. I would give £20 to £30 out of my own pocket that it were thine—nobody's but thine."[16] (By a comparative standard, a skilled carpenter who made 5 shillings a day in 1698 needed to save all his shillings for 3600 days, about ten years, to accumulate £900.[17]) Logan, who knew Penn and his finances as well as anyone, took it "hard" that his employer and friend could "not spare" £900.

In 1709, Penn did not purchase his old home; but Isaac Norris (1671–1735) did. His son, Isaac Norris, Jr. (1701–1766), who married Logan's daughter Sarah in 1739, lived there until 1741 when he and Sarah moved to the family's suburban estate, Fairhill, which his father had purchased in 1718. From 1741 until 1864, the younger Norris and his heirs rented out the property, giving the name Norris alley to its side street. One of their first tenants was the distinguished firm of Levy and Franks, David Franks and his uncle Nathan Levy (*PG*, June 27, 1751). After Nathan's death dissolved the partnership, the building saw a succession of ever more humble uses throughout the next one hundred and ten years.[18]

On Second street, this relic of Philadelphia's earliest history experienced the pattern of urban development sooner than other neighborhoods to the west. West from Second street, the increasing and then decreasing value of these neighborhoods foreshadows the construction and destruction of many similar buildings.

But Alas! The Slate-Roof House—of all houses!—the home of American liberties—not just a house but a shrine—slumping to a slum! If only Philadelphians had renamed the Slate-Roof House the Liberty House, as they gave the State House the dignity of calling it Independence Hall! This new name might have made their children more aware of its significance.

ALTHOUGH THE SLATE-ROOF HOUSE had no more illustrious tenant than William Penn, proclaiming brotherhood in his Charter of Liberties, it later served as a very respectable boarding house for men like John Adams and George Washington. Before *hoteliers* provided lodging to visitors in hotels, genteel ladies sometimes found such work acceptable in their homes, after their husbands' death left them "in circumstances too slender" to maintain respectable widowhood. One epoch in this history has special interest, because it had its chronicler. Alexander Graydon (1752–1818), in *Memoirs of his own Time*, records his memories of his mother's guests at the Slate-Roof House. She took over from a woman who had given "some celebrity" to the house "by the style of her accommodations."

According to her son's recollection, Mrs. Graydon signed the lease for the house in 1764 or 1765 and stayed there for eight or nine years. He got the dates wrong, because the *Pennsylvania Gazette*, September 11, 1766, advertised a Mr. Garner as the new hosteler of this "commodious house lately occupied by the widow Graydon, commonly known by the name of the Slate House." Graydon records what he saw of his mother's guests as a young man: "She had the honor, if so it might be called, of entertaining strangers of the first rank who visited the city. "A biographical sketch," he suggests, "of the various personages, who became inmates of this house, might, from the hand of a good delineator, be both curious and amusing." He delineated from life, for example, "the steady and composed demeanor" of the Baron deKalb, which "bespoke the soldier and philosopher; the man who had calmly estimated life and death, and who, though not prodigal of the one, had no unmanly dread of the other." Many men worthy of memory ate their meals at his mother's table.

Naturally, he saw these boarders through the bright eyes of his youth. In a brief idyl, for example, they found a special charm in the pretty daughter of the aristocratic Lady Moore: "A sprightly Miss, not far advanced in her teens, who, having apparently no dislike to be seen, had more than once attracted my attention." This pretty Miss of Quality caught his eye and then his heart: "For I was just touching that age when such objects begin to be interesting and excite feelings, which disdain the invidious barriers, with which the pride of condition would surround itself." In the very same building where William Penn declared democracy, young Graydon dared not to declare it to his mother's aristocratic guest.

And yet, young hope sprang eternal: "Not that the young lady was stately; my vanity rather hinted, she was condescendingly courteous; and I had, no doubt, read of women of quality falling in love with their inferiors: Nevertheless, the extent of my presumption was a look or a bow, as she now and then tripped along through the entry." The equality of democracy gave scant liberty to a young man's "presumption" on the imperious quality of beauty,—not to mention the imperious quality of Quality!

Not all the visitors 'tripped sprightly' through the front entry. In an episode of the memoirs, Dr. John Kearsley (1684–1772), a distinguished physician and the architect of Christ Church, enjoyed some horseplay after an evening with the boys. "Mounted on horseback, he rode his horse into the back parlor, and even up stairs, to the great disturbance and terror of the family.

> *Quadru/pedan/te soni/tu // quatit /ungula / domum*
> (Virgil's *Aeneid* 8. 596, "With quadrupedal sound,
> the ungulate shakes the home")

Young Graydon absorbed a microcosm of worldly experience in his mother's boarding house. In helping Lady Moore's daughter to recover from this ungulate upset, he might have imparted that Stoic firmness which he had learned from the old Baron, "calmly estimating life and death," and though "not prodigal of the one," having "no unmanly dread of the other." How much more impressed might his "sprightly Miss" have been, if he had ornamented high courage by deep learning in the spondaic consonants of Vergil's onomatopoeia. After the edifying tableau of William Penn composing his Charter of Liberties, Mrs. Graydon's guests offer a "curious and amusing" sequel.

In such close proximity to the harbor, the commercial bustle of Front street moved back to Second, which, gradually but inevitably, turned its residences into shops. In 1785, "Bond and Wilson" advertised their drug store in the Slate-Roof House, at the corner of Norris' alley and Second street: "Drugs and Patent Medicines, also early and marrowfat peas, with most other useful seeds for the kitchen garden" (*Pennsylvania Packet*, April 6, 1785). To accommodate this pharmacy, with its early and late,—marrowfat,—peas, the Norris family had opened the north wing with a door and a shop window.

In the 1820's, newspaper advertisements indicated an increased presence of trade,—and its dangers,—on Second and Norris' alley. December 7, 1830, for example, the *United States Gazette* reported a fire in the cellar of the Slate-Roof House, where Michel Charles Bouvier (1792–1874), a cabinetmaker, stored and seasoned rare woods, especially mahogany, for his craft. By 1830, Mr. Bouvier perhaps occupied the store of the druggists. He might have stored his lumber in its cellar. About the same time, the Norrises altered the building to

The Slate-Roof House about 1830

In the north wing on the left, a door and show window make room for a shop. Two shops with windows and separate doors fill the courtyard between the wings.

accommodate more of this commercial activity. To complement the store and its shop window in the north wing, they filled in the empty space between the wings with two more stores, each with its own entrance and window. Their construction in wood frame proved as flimsy as the rest of the building was solid. Whatever the stock and trade of these stores, their commercial presence made the building unattractive as accommodations for the "strangers of the first rank who visited the city." Because it also made it a less attractive investment, the Norris family put the building up for sale in 1831 (*National Gazette*, April 7, 1831). They had improved the property by the addition of the two stores in preparation for this sale.

Finally, as if to make the final humiliation of this shrine a little grotesque, theatres had plastered its north wall with placards,—barely visible in the photograph,—advertising their offerings: Hamlet, The Bould Boy of Glendale; Joe Jefferson, an old Philadelphia boy, starring in Rip Van Winkle; and the Grand, Magnificent, Spectacular Drama, Entitled The Black Crook.

After the Norrises failed in their effort to sell the old Penn Mansion, it finally descended to Sally Norris Dickinson, the great granddaughter of Isaac Norris. She also put it with the building next-door, on the south, up for sale; but no one was willing to pay her price of $45,000. On her demise, it passed to her sister, the widow of Dr. Logan, and then to the widow's son. In 1864, he sold it to Charles Knecht, who intended that it be the site for the new home of the Chamber of Commerce.

At this crucial moment, the debate about preservation set a pattern for all the others that would follow. An author in the *Evening Telegraph*, November 24, 1866, defined the two horns of this dilemma:

> The spirit which watches with jealous care over the spots made sacred by the lives and deeds of the illustrious dead, is one of the surest tokens of a deep and wholesome intellectual culture. Yet it is a spirit in which the American people, as a mass, are sadly deficient.

Are our "hearts and souls and minds," he lamented, to be "wholly given up to the grasping after wealth and pleasures that have but a momentary existence?" "Grasping after wealth"—just the acquisitiveness that has consistently blighted the pastoral idyl of William Penn's "Holy Experiment"!

Charles Knecht was "deficient," but not "so sadly deficient"—or at least not so insensitive to public opinion—that he paid no attention at all to "the illustrious dead." The Chamber of Commerce shed one crocodile tear and made the city an offer:

> Resolved, that the Board of Directors of the Philadelphia Chamber of Commerce tender to the city of Philadelphia, as a free gift, the old William Penn mansion; . . . provided the city will agree to remove the same and place it for preservation on the grounds of Fairmount Park.

This self-serving beneficence was transferring the old Penn mansion for "free" to the city, which would then remove and preserve it in the Park. At least the Chamber of Commerce could have offered to help in the transfer. Suggesting "preservation on the grounds of Fairmount Park" indicates that they had been listening to some plans for preservation. (This plan for preservation eventually saved the Letitia Penn House and moved it to the Park.)

Mayor McMichael (1807–1879), whose statue at the north end of the Sedgley estate in Fairmount Park commemorates his work for the Park, considered this possibility, but he did not consider it feasible. At the end of the 17th century, it seemed, masons had prepared mortar "so carefully and skillfully" that it had acquired "the hardness of stone, and adhered to the bricks so tenaciously as to render them virtually a solid mass and made its removal, either piecemeal or whole, an impossible achievement." As an alternative to reconstructing the entire building, the mayor suggested that "enough material might be saved from the structure, when demolished, to construct in the park a building smaller than the original but on the same general plan." Even gathering up and reconstructing rubble was "deemed impossible or inconvenient, on account of its solid construction." Preserving the Penn Mansion was "impossible" and "inconvenient," or just impossibly inconvenient.

In Philadelphia's callow adolescence,—or in the glow of its commercial growth,—its citizens did not value their past enough to pay for its preservation: "And so the old Penn Mansion," the author con-

A photograph of the old Penn Mansion before its demolition

cluded, "with all the rich and interesting associations, must be swept into the past." Another reporter described its final demolition:

> *Improvements on Second street*
>
> The antiquated and time-honored buildings on Second street below Walnut, are now in progress of demolition. A board fence encloses them, and only one gable end of the old Penn Mansion remains, while those below are being leveled to the ground. These ancient buildings will soon have passed away (*Inquirer*, July 25, 1867).

The same reporter announced its passing five days later: "The Penn Mansion . . . is among the things of the past" (*Inquirer*, July 30, 1867). "Swept into the past," but not entirely forgotten!

After laying its corner stone in October, 1867, some Philadelphians boasted that their Chamber of Commerce Building would be "an ornamental to that section of the city, as well as supply a necessity that has long been felt" (*Evening Telegraph*, November, 1866). Their boast was short-lived: a fire,—its origin, for some a "mystery," but for others "cosmic retribution"—destroyed the building on December 7, 1869 (*Daily Telegraph*, December 8, 1869). A reporter praised the second building as "emblematic of the progress of improvement and necessity resulting from the commercial advancement of an association which has aided so largely the business prosperity of Philadelphia" (*Evening Telegraph*, August 5, 1877). It stood until 1976.

The heritage of the Slate-Roof House continued to call for commemoration. In 1924, the Pennsylvania Historical Commission and the Colonial Society of Pennsylvania commemorated Penn's mansion with a plaque at the southeast corner of Second and Sansom (aka Norris Alley), but thieves eventually stole it (*Philadelphia Inquirer*, November 9, 1924). In 1926, people planning the Sesqui-centennial answered its call. The States' Committee of this 150th anniversary of 1776 built a replica of the Slate-Roof House as its headquarters on the fair grounds at League Island Park (*Inquirer*, October 10, 1926).

In 1976, when the site of the Slate-Roof house stood empty, some people started to answer the call. By 1982, the Tricentennial of Penn's arrival gave them a special opportunity. In planning for this celebration, the Friends of the Independence National Historical Park raised $1.4 million to acquire the parking-lot on the site of Penn's mansion. They transformed it into "Welcome Park," in allusion to the ship, *Welcome*, that brought William Penn to Philadelphia in 1682. *Welcome* referred both to the name of the ship and to the welcome that the park would extend to visitors.

The 90 × 150 foot park celebrates Penn and his time by a representation of Holme's plan of the city in the pavement, and a chronology of Penn's life on a wall to one side. A tree decorated each one of the four squares in the plan, and a relatively small copy of Calder's colossus stands in the center square, with Penn's prayer for the city inscribed on its pedestal. A bronze model of the Slate-Roof House stands on a pedestal between lines on the map representing Walnut and Chestnut streets, just where it would be located on the map. Thomas Hine observed that the park does not welcome as much as it should: "It is," he wrote, "easier to admire than to like" (*Inquirer*, July 14, 1983). It does extend its own welcome to visitors and an introduction to their tour of Philadelphia, but it may be a bare one without a guide to explain its meaning.

In Philadelphia, the memories of a few buildings have so echoed and reechoed that they called for either re-creation or memorialization in the twentieth century. The Bicentennial of 1976 recreated the Graff House, in which Thomas Jefferson wrote the Declaration of

Independence, and the City Tavern, in which he discussed its principles with other Founding Fathers. It also celebrated Benjamin Franklin by creating Franklin Court,—at a cost of $4.75 million,—with a "ghost house," outlining his home by steel beams, and a museum beneath it. By contrast, the site of the Slate-Roof House got its park that celebrates the life of William Penn at a cost of $1.4 million.

Weigh in the balance the success of these efforts. By contrast, the celebration of Benjamin Franklin in Franklin Court outweighs that of William Penn in Welcome Park. The architectural firm of Venturi Rauch and Scott Brown designed both, but they had greater success in Franklin Court. That success should come as no surprise, since they had more than three times the funding! The Slate-Roof House, because it may be called Philadelphia's "Liberty House," deserved more funding and effort than Franklin's home, in which he did nothing very special.[19]

Both the widow's mite and the gold shekel offer their own tribute. Whatever combination of mind and muscle in either the bronze or in the gold, expecting the memorial to give "the surest tokens" of "deep intellectual culture" expects too much. By both these efforts to make up for the destruction of old shrines, Philadelphians have proven that they have not wholly surrendered their "hearts and souls and minds" to "grasping after wealth and pleasures." To honor William Penn, they have created a park representing his city plan in its pavement, his home in a bronze model, and his statue in a copy of Calder's colossus. Welcome Park commemorates Philadelphia's first and greatest benefactor and his home in which he framed its laws for "Brotherly Love."

CHAPTER 5

James Logan's Cato as a Model for his Grandson George

In 1728, James Logan (1674–1751) set aside his duties as secretary to the Penn family for a life of refined leisure at Stenton, his estate of 500 acres. When Logan's American and native American friends approached his home, they could observe the elegant simplicity of his

James Logan's Stenton (1728)

Quaker ethic. Not especially intent on architecture, however, he found his own special fulfillment in books. At Stenton, he enjoyed, his obituary said, "that leisure among his books, which a man of letters so earnestly desires" (*Pennsylvania Gazette*, November 7, 1751).

Four years later, by 1732, this "man of letters" made a personal statement by means of a translation of Cicero's essay *De Senectute*, "On Old Age." This Latin essay also has the title *Cato Major*, "Cato the Elder," the old Roman, by whose fictional voice Cicero lent his essay a special *auctoritas*. In the eighteenth century, moralists often signed their tracts with this name, because it carried moral authority. James Logan and his grandson George took Cato (234–149 BC) seriously.

"I translated that piece," Logan explained, "in the Winter of 1732 for my own diversion for I was exceedingly pleased with it." At age 58, Logan might have been pleased with "it," that is, with Cato's thoughts about old age. More than these thoughts about man's final passage through life, Cato's satisfactions with life as a farmer probably pleased Logan so "exceedingly" that he felt inspired to make an appreciative, interpretive translation of the whole essay. More clearly than the facade of Stenton, James Logan's *Cato the Elder*, in this case, his interpretation of Cato's allegiance to nature, reveals the face of the ethic that inspired him and anticipated his grandson's life:

I follow Nature,
my most excellent Guide,
as my God,
and submit to his Power
in all things.
(Naturam optimam ducem,
tamquam deum sequimur,
eique paremus.)[20]

—James Logan's translation of
Cato's profession of faith
from Cicero's essay *Cato Major*,
published by Benjamin Franklin in 1744

Cato, who famously said *Rem tene, verba sequentur*, "Hold meaning, words will follow," chose his few words carefully. Logan, on the other hand, recognizing the importance of this allegiance to nature, does not let Cato's brevity pass without his own elaboration. He uses eighteen words to translate Cato's nine. In dressing Cato's spare Latin in his own expansive English, the Roman's *optimam ducem*, literally, "the best guide," becomes "my most excellent guide;" and *eique paremus*, literally, "and <I/we> obey it," the Roman's three words, becomes eight, "and submit to his power in all things." To top it off, he magnifies Nature's "most excellent" guidance and his own 'submitting' to "his power" by the climactic "in all things," which does not correspond to anything in the Latin. Logan submits "all things" to Nature, that "most excellent guide," to whom he also gives male gender and power. Referring to Mother Nature's "power" as "his" quite extraordinarily contradicts her classical nature as Mother, not just a mother but the Mother.

James Logan's grandson George lived his life in accordance with nature. When George was born in 1753 two years after his grandfather James had died, he had the wisdom of the *Cato Major* as his birthright. These two generations, grandfather James and grandson George, interpreted and emulated Cicero's classic standard. Their commitment to learning allows us to set up James Logan's translation of Cicero's *Cato* as a standard by which we can appreciate his grandson George Logan's life. With an appreciation of books, families like the Logans have the luxury—and the luck—of incorporating them into their lives. In a lucky and luxuriant bloom, James Logan's *Cato* flowered in George Logan's life.[21]

Dr. George Logan (1753–1821) read many philosophers in his day who would advise him to follow nature as a guide. The French *philosophe* Rousseau, for example, had set it in the foundation of an education: "Observe nature, and follow the path that she traces for you" (*Observez la nature, et suivez la route qu'elle vous trace.*) Unlike Grandfather James, however, Rousseau observed the propriety of keeping Nature's gender feminine.

George took a definitive step in pursuit of Nature when he decided to set aside his vocation as a physician and take up that of a farmer. He had just married Deborah Norris (1761–1839) in 1781 and was reestablishing roots at home after medical study at the University of

Dr. George Logan (1753–1821), in a portrait by Gilbert Stuart

Edinburgh. In returning to the land, he was going against the grain of his contemporaries. Quakers have been humorously characterized as first taking up William Penn's Holy Experiment to do good on the land, but ending up in lucrative employment to do well in trade. Men ambitious for worldly success found it on Front street, where trade made them wealthy. The Logans were ahead of this game. George's father and grandfather had done so well in land and in trade that he could go back to the land to do good. William Penn's Holy Experiment thrived in his life. "The farmer's calling was older than the physician's," George Logan's biographer has observed, "—older and just as noble, just as ennobling."[22]

Cicero's Cato called this obligation to cultivate the land, not just noble but sacred. In his pagan faith, farmers were working for "the Immortal Gods." Referring to farmers as "these men," James Logan's Cato joins stewardship with a Christian commitment to improvement:

> Nor,
>   if you ask one of these men,
>   for whom it is he is thus laboring,
> will he be at any loss to answer thus,
>   'I do it,' he will say, 'for the Immortal Gods,

who,
    as they bestow'd these Grounds on me,
require at my Hands
that I should transmit them improved to Posterity,
who are to succeed me in the Possession of them.'[23]

Cicero's Cato only mentions passing it on and makes no mention of improvement. With no allegiance to the pagan creed of Cicero's Cato, James and George Logan acted as Christian stewards of the land by working to pass it on "improved to posterity" (see the literal translation in the footnote).

To work for improvement, George, at first, joined men like Richard Peters (1724–1828), George Washington's friend and confidante, as a member of the Philadelphia Agricultural Society. He had inherited membership in this élite as a legacy from his family. This society, however, did not best serve his democracy of stewardship. Almost thirty years younger than Peters, George felt called to serve a practical purpose in his own generation. In the summer of 1788, he formed a new society with a more democratic membership. His creation, the "Philadelphia County Society for the Promotion of Agriculture and Domestic Manufactures," accepted only farmers as members. George summarized much of his experimentation about agronomy in lectures to the members of this society. He became its mentor and guiding light. Years later, when its young members heard him deliver an address on the errors of husbandry in the United States, it seemed to them, his biographer has observed, that "they were listening to a veritable Cato the Elder" (Tolles, 314).

George experimented on his fields at Stenton to develop practices useful to all the farmers of Philadelphia County. In 1797, after almost two decades of farming, and one decade of guiding the Society, he published fourteen of his experiments "to ascertain the best rotation of crops together with some particular and general observations on the same calculated to promote the agricultural interest of the United States" (*Aurora General Advertiser*, February 28, 1797). He intended that his experiments at Stenton benefit, not just his community, but "the agricultural interest of the United States." George Logan was ambitious to share his improvement.

Experimenting with crop rotation, James Logan's Cato does not omit manure in its cycles:

> What need I mention . . . of the advantages of manure?
> (*Quid de utilitate loquar stercorandi?*[24])

Cicero's Cato mentions its "utility" (*utilitate*), which Logan's Cato raises to its "advantages." Cicero's Cato adds that he has already written about it in his *De Agri Cultura*, a book that James Logan had in a volume *De Re Rustica*.

For a scientific farmer like George Logan, manure meant more than dreck. George's wife, Deborah Norris Logan, in her *Memoir of Dr. George Logan of Stenton*, recalls her husband's use of gypsum as manure and his "happiness" in reading authors, useful "in agricultural and political science":

> He was also one of the first who used gypsum as a manure, and its success at the beginning was wonderful. Perhaps at no period of his life did he experience greater happiness than at this, his intervals of leisure being employed in reading authors of the greatest utility in agricultural and political science, and he was one of the foremost and most zealous advocates in whatever he thought would promote the public good.[25]

In addition to gypsum, George investigated marle as manure and he reported his findings at a meeting of the Philadelphia County Society:

> It would take a small volume, to give the complete history of every species of marle, and recite what authors have said respecting it. Pliny speaks of marle as a species of improvement known to the Greeks, but more peculiar to Britain and Gaul. He calls it the fat of the earth (*Independent Gazetteer,* January 23, 1790).[26]

Marle proved too hard to find and then extract from the ground. He experienced, as his wife said, no "greater happiness" than when he was delving into the classics of agronomy and sharing the fruit of his research with farmers in the Philadelphia County Society. On the other hand, as his wife also intimated, he had chosen gypsum as his favorite fertilizer, in addition, of course, to dung.

How he loved gypsum! Taking Benjamin Franklin's trick of tracing names or sayings in gypsum on a hillside, he took a boyish delight in surprising George Washington by a practical gypsum joke (Tolles, 97). 'General Washington,' he probably said, as he and GW walked around Stenton, 'aren't those your initials growing on the hillside? Even Mother Nature is celebrating you!'

Working for the benefit of his Philadelphia County Society in recommending gypsum as fertilizer, George focused on science, taking the joys of farmers for granted. His grandfather's interpretation of a passage from the *Cato Major* had anticipated this focus on practicality. In this passage, he translates the mention by Cicero's Cato of the "pleasures of farmers," as "the pleasures of a Country-Life." This focus on "country life" anticipates objectivity, which James then emphasizes by changing the subject of Cicero's sentence from "the pleasures of farmers" to "the Life of Nature":

> But I am now come to speak to the Pleasures of a Country Life,
> *Venio nunc ad voluptates agricolarum,*
>
> with which I am infinitely delighted.
> *quibus ego incredibiliter delector;*
>
> To these Old Age never is an Obstruction.
> *quae nec ullā impediuntur senectute*
>
> <u>It is the Life of Nature</u>,
>
> and appears to me the exactest Plan of that which a wise Man
> ought to lead.
> *et mihi ad sapientis vitam proxime videntur accedere.*
>
> Here our whole Business is with the Earth,
> *Habent enim rationem cum terrā.*
>
> <u>the common Parent of us all</u>.

On his own, James Logan adds "Country Life," "the Life of Nature" and "the common Parent of us all" to the praise by Cicero's Cato of the life of a wise man in nature. Elsewhere, he has also added the "advantages" of manure to the mention in Cicero's Cato of its utility, and "improving" land to Cicero's mention of just passing it on. These advantages, improvement, and praise of land embellish the wisdom of James Logan's Cato's. James' glorification anticipates George's experimentation. George's experiments with manure, for example, made fields gloriously fertile.

IN 1788, WHEN GEORGE gathered the farmers of Philadelphia County, he gave them a double purpose by naming their society the "Philadelphia County Society for the Promotion of Agriculture and Domestic Manufactures." His own farm at Stenton produced both "domestic manufactures" and "agriculture." 'Improve, improve,'—this call to Americans by men like George Logan inspired Thoreau's reply—"Simplify, simplify." And yet, Logan saw no contradiction between the two. By improving a farm to produce all that its community needed, Logan both improved and simplified American life.

To begin with, George's grandfather had improved Cicero's statement about the use of a farm:

> As for me, I must own, I think it impossible
> (*Meā quidem sententiā haud scio*)
>
> that any other kind of Life whatever can exceed it.
> (*an nulla beatior possit esse.*)[27]

Cicero's Cato asserts that no life could be "more blessed" than that of a farmer. James must have known Horace's homage to the blessedness of cultivating ancestral acres:

> *Beatus ille, qui procul negotiis,*
> *ut prisca gens mortalium,*
> *paterna rura bobus exercet suis.*
> (Horace, *Epodes* 2)
>
> Blessed that man, who far from business,
> as the old-fashioned race of mortals,
> works his paternal fields with his bulls.

Working his "ancestral fields" makes Horace "blessed." This sacred duty takes him "far from business." Logan's improvement starts with a secular purpose. He disregards Cicero and Horace's moral and religious commitment by saying, very vaguely, that no other life "can exceed it."

Further in the Latin, the "salutary" (*salutaris*) farm of Cicero's Cato, by its "fulness and supply" (*saturitate copiāque*), produces all that man needs for his "living" (*victum*).[28] Logan's Cato takes the twenty-eight words in this Latin sentence and expands them in his interpretation to eighty-three:

> For besides that Mankind cannot possibly subsist without it,
> there is not only a vast Pleasure derived from viewing and
> considering the Particulars I have mentioned,
> (*Neque solum officio, quod hominum generi universo cultura*
> *agrorum est salutaris,*)
>
> but it also fills the Heart with Joy to behold, how by proper Care
> and Management every thing is produced in Abundance,
> (*sed et delectatione, quam dixi, et rerum omnium,*)
>
> that can be subservient either to the Support and real Necessities
> of human Life, even to the Pleasures and Delectation of it,
> (*quae ad victum hominum,*)
>
> as well as what is required for the Service of the immortal Gods.
> (*ad cultum etiam deorum pertinent.*)[29]

Logan's Cato, the agronomist, interprets the "duty" (*officio*) and culture of fields (*cultura agrorum*) as "proper Care and Management." He interprets producing all things needed for the sustenance of men (*victum hominum*) as producing "every thing . . . in Abundance, that can be subservient . . . to the Support and real Necessities of human Life." In the eighteenth century, James and his grandson George reinterpreted and expanded the potentials of a farm that Cicero knew in antiquity. By their cultivation of fields, they rose on the shoulders of their ancestors, instead of just maintaining a family cult. 'Happy,' not 'blessed,' describes American citizens, because secular, not religious, virtue has made them happy.

George's wife Deborah gives a demure version of this dynamic accomplishment. She took "harmless pride" in what she calls her "domestic manufactures, rightly so called" because they were done at home. She describes a georgic idyl of the distaff:

> Domestic manufactures, rightly so called from being indeed the production of the farmers' families, were a favorite object of their encouragement; and this gave scope to the ingenuity and industry of their wives and introduced us in a social and pleasant manner to one another's acquaintance. I have not forgotten the agreeable interchange of visits, the beneficial emulation, and the harmless pride with which we exhibited specimens of our industry and good management to each other. The spinning-wheel was going in every house, and it was a high object of our ambition to see our husbands and their families clothed in our own manufactures (a good practice which my honoured husband never relinquished), and to produce at our social dinner parties the finest ale of our own brewing, the best home-made wines, cheese, and other articles which we thought ought to be made among ourselves rather than imported from abroad (D. N. Logan, 44).

The Logans' idyl truly sprang from the earth because they made it self-sufficient. Deborah took "harmless pride" in these accomplishments: her husband always wore clothing home-spun on her wheel; and he enjoyed "the finest ale" of her own brewing and "the best home-made wines, cheese and other articles." The home-spun and home-made made the Logans home-bred aristocrats. A wine merchant on Front street like Stephen Girard made his fortune by selling French wines. George and Deborah Logan made theirs by not buying them.

George publicized the importance of farm-based industry for the nation's economy. In 1799, after visiting Holland and Flanders to study their cultivation of flax, he published what he had observed. He concludes by encouraging this crop throughout the United States for political reasons:

> FOR the Farmers of the United States to manufacture their own linens was at all times a desirable object and has become of greatest importance from the present price of this article and the probability of its advancing on account of the present state of Europe (*Aurora General Advertiser*, April 12, 1799).

Near his farm, Mennonites in the neighboring community of Germantown had been growing flax and spinning its fibers into linen for a century. With Logan's help, farmers throughout the country would adopt the methods of these hard-working Germans. Complementing farming with manufacturing, American farmers also completed their country's independence.

Both George Logan and Cato found joy in a life on their farms, but the two thousand years between them made a difference in their joy. Cato enjoyed a blessed life because he kept his family cult independent. George Logan enjoyed an idyllic life, because he kept his farm financially independent. He advertised the nature of this independence. "A pleasant Country Seat," a farm that he put up for sale in 1802, also included a "Water Mill . . . conveniently situated for the Manufacture of Snuff, Chocolate or the Spinning of Cotton" (*Aurora General Advertiser*, March 18, 1802). A farmer on this property might became an industrialist by improving his farm, not by exchanging it for a mill in the city, where a blessed or an idyllic life was harder to win. As a poet has said, "God made the country, and man made the town." God bless!—George's ideal farm improved his country's economy by bringing it to a single, simple focus.

George Logan also turned his reading in political philosophy to serve "the public good." Signing this letter to the *Inquirer* as Cato, he distilled his reading, in this case, to serve good government:

> This is universally true, that no nation ever continued happy whose chief magistrate was its absolute master and no nation miserable, whose supreme power was properly checked and divided. . . . The commonwealth does not belong to them, but they belong to the commonwealth. Tacitus says with great truth: *Nec umquam satis fida potentia ubi nimis est*: "Power without control is not to be trusted." Every nation has most to fear from its own magistrates; because almost all nations have suffered more from their own magistrates (*Inquirer*, January 3, 1789).

When magistrates' "spirit of selfishness destroys all," no nation can remain "happy" (Tolles, 94). Their selfishness steals the wealth of the commonwealth from the commoners. Logan's self-sufficiency would flourish best in a democracy of a community.

Addressing the farmers of his Philadelphia County Society in 1790, Logan attributed selfishness to profitable counting houses and domestic prosperity to prolific fields:

> The faithful page of history manifests that the best men, the most able statesmen in all ages, have uniformly declared agriculture to be a certain support to the happiness and prosperity of any country.

By contrast, England, in securing profitable monopoly to her "merchants and manufacturers," has caused unjust war and taxation:

> England labors under a debt of near 300 millions, one third of which was incurred during the late war, to secure to her merchants and manufacturers a monopoly of the American trade. . . . The burthen of taxes has been imposed on the people, in order to pay the interest of it to a few monied men, a sixth part of whom are foreigners. . . . Nature herself has prescribed the bounds beyond which no government can proceed without sooner or later destroying itself.

With the authority of the "Laws of Nature and Nature's God" in 1776, Jefferson justified Americans' Declaration of Independence from the grasp of England's mercantile greed. In 1790, Logan refers to "Nature herself" prescribing "the bounds beyond which no government can proceed without sooner or later destroying itself." George Logan takes the ideals of Nature seriously. It was inspiring him in 1790, as it had inspired Thomas Jefferson in 1776.

Logan goes on to allude to the immoral baggage of mercantile greed: the slave trade "found to be highly injurious," and "the horrid cruelty and tyranny" which India has experienced" from a company of mercenary merchants" (*Independent Gazetteer*, March 6, 1790). Continuing Penn's ideal of a Holy Experiment for his Greene Country Towne, he cherished the vision of America as "an agricultural Eden, peopled by a happy, independent, prosperous yeomanry" (Tolles, 306).

By the end of the 1790's, George's pursuit of nature bore fruit. In 1799, he published his address on "Natural and Social Order of the World" that would produce "universal good." He was fulfilling his vocation to promulgate peace by this address that he had delivered before the Tammany Society:

LATELY PUBLISHED.
AT THE OFFICE OF THE AURORA
AN ADDRESS
ON THE
NATURAL AND SOCIAL ORDER Of THE WORLD,
AS INTENDED TO PRODUCE UNIVERSAL GOOD;
Delivered before the
TAMMANY SOCIETY
at their anniversary,
On the 12th of May, 1798.
Faire le bien c'est le recevoir.
By Dr. George Logan
(*Aurora General Advertiser*, February 9, 1799)

LOGAN'S CATO HAS ALREADY mentioned farmers as working for "the immortal gods." He complements this service, by alluding to Cincinnatus as the model Roman senator, both farming for the immortals and serving Rome for mortals. In the classic image that brought the Senator together with the farmer, a delegation of Roman Senators brought him the call to duty as he was plowing his field:

> In those Days the Senators, that is, *Senes*, or Old-Men of the State,
> dwelt in the Country, and lived on their Farms;
> *L. Quinctius Cincinnatus* was at his Plow,
> when he was called to take upon him the supreme Office of Dictator.

Logan's Cato fills out the description of Cincinnatus in Cicero (see the literal translation in the footnote). Having said that Cincinnatus "was called" to serve as dictator, he elaborates his praises of "those brave old men" and their "highest Trusts and Charges." He also mentions separately the use of "*Viatores*, or Way-Men" to explain the process of summoning senators from their farms:

> So *Curius*, and many others of those brave Old Men,
> were called from time to time off their Farms,

A Delegation of Senators summon Cincinnatus from his plow to the service of Rome.

In 1783, Washington's generals took Cincinnatus as their model, when they called their fraternal organization the Society of the Cincinnati.

> to take upon them the highest Trusts and Charges in the State or War.
> And from hence it is, that the Serjeants[30] or Messengers
> that wait on the Senate, first had, and to this Day retain,
> their Name of *Viatores*, or Way-Men.[31]

George Logan fit the image of Cincinnatus by working as a farmer and a senator. He was, so to speak, summoned from his plow to serve in the State Legislature in 1785 and in the United States Senate in 1801. In 1798, most famously—perhaps infamously—he answered his own call of duty without being summoned, when he traveled to France as an American ambassador to stem the tide of war between France and the United States. Since he answered this call without an official commission, many people regarded him as a naively officious busybody or even a traitor. And yet, he was following his own inner light as a

Quaker so conscientiously that he felt compelled to serve. To finance this mission of unselfish patriotism, he sold some of his own land:

> BUILDING LOTS TO BE LET, On Ground Rent for ever,
> A Number of Lots situate on Stenton hill, adjoining to the village of Germantown, a Plan of which may be seen and the Terms made known, by applying to Dr. George Logan, on the premises; or at the Office of the subscriber, No. 124, south Fourth-street, Abraham Shoemaker (*Independent Gazetteer*, September 1 &12, 1797).

After Logan's cordial but unofficial reception in France, he sent a letter to Deborah announcing his return. She, in turn, published it in the *Philadelphia Gazette*:

> Deborah Logan requests you to give the following a place in your paper.—Stenton, Nov. 5, 1798. Extract of a letter from Doctor Logan, dated Bourdeaux, September 9, 1798, to his Wife.
>
> "I have the pleasure to inform you that I embark this day on board the ship *Perseverance* for Philadelphia, and shall bring with me dispatches for our government, calculated to restore that harmony, the loss of which has been so sensibly felt by both countries."

He elaborates the points of this "harmony":

> "All American vessels in the harbors of France have, been released—
> all American prisoners have been set at liberty;
> and the most positive assurances have been made
> that France is ready to enter on a treaty for the amicable
> accommodation of all matters in dispute.—
> American citizens are treated with respect in every part of France, and
> the appearance of a reconciliation between the two republics affords
> the highest satisfaction to all classes of citizens in this country."
> GEORGE LOGAN (*Aurora General Advertiser*, November 10, 1798)

Back in Philadelphia, George found the nation's capital preparing for war. As a well-know Jeffersonian, he received a chill welcome from the Federalist administration, which branded his mission as the "temerity and impertinence" of "officious interference" (Tolles, 184). Washington, the former President, had been happy enough to visit Stenton when farmer George was recommending gypsum as fertilizer. Now, up from Mount Vernon to organize the army, he maintained an aristocratic *froideur* when Logan visited. Adams, the incumbent, entertained him with tea, but remained reticent through their interview. George was not embarrassed. He had done his duty, both conscientious and patriotic.

"We announce, and with sincere sorrow . . . ," the *Inquirer* begins its notice of the death of George Logan (April 10, 1821). "Sincere" anticipates its praise of Logan's life in pursuit of excellence. After an education, it continues, both "classical and professional," George trained as a physician, but he went back to the earth, combining his "occupations as a scholar and a farmer." While on the farm, he obeyed "the impulses of the warmest and purest patriotic and philanthropic zeal." This "zeal" took him to "patriotic" service in state and national legislatures and to "philanthropic" research in agriculture. Cultivating Stenton's fields or his nation's politics, he sought the best both for his neighbors and their countrymen. George lived the life that his grandfather had described in his inspired adaption of Cicero:

life,
    employed
        in the Pursuit of useful Knowledge,
        in honorable Actions
        and the Practice of Virtue;
in which,
    he,
        who labors to improve himself from his Youth,
    will in Age reap the happiest Fruits of them.

CHAPTER 6

Philadelphians' "Poor Power" to Celebrate Penn's Treaty

Abraham Lincoln famously memorializes heroism in his *Gettysburg Address*; but he also memorializes humility in its celebration. "In a larger sense," as he said, we can all appreciate, we can all sympathize, and we can all even empathize, with his humility. We realize, as he also says, the "poor power" of the words we speak and inscribe to celebrate the deeds that men do. Our memorials inevitably fail in memorializing deeds worthy of memory.

Lincoln was memorializing the Civil War giving a "new birth" to freedom, which Americans in their separate states had been bringing to birth for eight score years before even the four score and seven that he counted as the age of their union. Put simply, a lot was happening before 1776 to give birth to freedom. A lot was also happening to delay it. In the early seventeenth century, Massachusetts' theocracy was making all men subject to the Lord's house and Virginia's aristocracy was making all black men subject to their master's. Both states had set up oligarchies like those in Europe. The oligarchs had made pilgrimages across the sea so that they might have the freedom to deprive other men of theirs. The road to utopia has no end. Men are still trying to make government "of the people, by the people, for the people."

Four score years after the Massachusetts Bay Colony and the Virginia Company had been tightening the grip of their oligarchies,

William Penn (1644–1718) established utopia between the two. Enlightened by the Christian humanism of the seventeenth century, this late comer set a better keystone in the arch by obeying his inner voice of the Holy Spirit. He arrived at what Philadelphians now call Penn's Landing in October of 1682; and, in May of the next year, he went up to the Indian Treaty Ground on the Delaware River for a powwow with Chief Tammany: "Great promises passed between us, of kindness and good neighborhood," he wrote to the Society of Free Traders, "and that the Indians and English must live in love as long as the sun gave light." After the inhabitants of Virginia and Massachusetts had been waging war with the aborigines, William Penn gave freedom a new birth.

Penn's fame spread round the world. Montesquieu (1689–1755) praised his "Holy Experiment" as rivaling and even surpassing the fame of antiquity: "What has appeared to us, as extraordinary in the institutions of Greece, has actually taken place amongst the dregs and corruption of modern times. A virtuous legislator formed a people among whom probity appears as natural as courage among the Spartans" (Montesquieu, *Spirit of Law* [1748]). Native peoples and Penn acted as "virtuous" men by their light of peace, and not as soldiers by the fires of war. Their virtue has consistently challenged,—it has proven,—his descendants' "poor power" to live up to his deeds or even to set up its monument on his Treaty Ground.

In 1824, Richard Peters (1743–1828), Peter Stephen Du Ponceau (1760–1844), and Roberts Vaux (1786–1836), with other prominent Philadelphians, formed The Penn Society. Peters had served in the Revolutionary War and had been appointed to the bench by George Washington, but in the 1820's he, like many of the Founding Fathers, was nearing the end of his life,—he died in 1828. He and the members of this society were not living in a crucial epoch like the one that immortalized George Washington or William Penn. As Philadelphians, they appreciated Penn's creation of his City of Brotherly Love, because it had watered, more purely than any other colonial city, the seed bed of American freedom. They were not doing what Penn had done, but they recognized their duty to celebrate it. In November of 1824, they held a banquet. A newspaper reported its celebrating "the landing of WILLIAM PENN, on the shores of America, being the 142d Anniversary of that Memorable Event" (*National Gazette*, November 29, 1824). Before that banquet, Du Ponceau, a distinguished linguist and philosopher, delivered an epideictic, that is, a celebratory, oration.

This learned gentleman set Penn's ideal in a Virgilian hexameter:

Igneus */ est ol/lis //* ***vigor*** */ et cae/lestis / origo,*

"Empyrean fire,"—an interpretation of ***igneus . . . vigor*** in the context of its line,—"and celestial origin belong to those <men>." With these words, Anchises, in the sixth book of the Vergil's *Aeneid*, reveals to his son Aeneas the "celestial origin" and heavenly inspiration of ancient Roman heroes. "It is unfortunately too true," Du Ponceau explained, "that greater respect is paid to the memory of those who have distinguished themselves by the destruction and subjugation of their species than those whose constant aim has been its preservation and improvement." "Empyrean fire" inspires men to work for freedom, and not for slavery. With fitting hyperbole, Du Ponceau praised William Penn's fame as "only bounded by the extremities of the earth." Roberts Vaux brought this Empyrean down to earth: Penn's fair treatment of the Indians enlarged "the circle of human happiness."[32]

After Du Ponceau's oration, Vaux suggested that "a plain obelisk fixed on the hallowed spot" preserve forever the memory of the compact (*The National Gazette*, December 14, 1825). The chaste simplicity of obelisks, pointing up to eternity, inspired many monuments in the neoclassical taste of that time. In 1825, a letter to the editor of *The National Gazette* (April 13, 1825) suggested that an obelisk honor the memory of George Washington. Bostonians were busy erecting a lofty obelisk to commemorate the Battle of Bunker Hill.[33]

In 1827, The Penn Society completed their obelisk: a short shaft, just over five feet in height: appropriately Quaker in its humble plainness. It bore inscriptions on its north and south sides:

Treaty ground of William Penn, and the Indian Nations, 1682,
Unbroken faith
William Penn, Born 1644, Died 1713.

On its east and west sides:

Pennsylvania, Founded, 1681, by Deeds of Peace
Placed by The Penn Society, A.D. 1827,
to mark the site of the Great Elm Tree.

These inscriptions allude, first to the place, second to the event, and third to the principle behind the event. As to the place, "The Great Elm Tree," under which Penn is said to have made the treaty, blew down in 1810. Its rings indicated its age to be at least 283 years old, ancient in age, immortal in fame, as Richard Peters, the ancient and honorable president of the society celebrated it in verse:

All hail to thee, highly favoured tree,
Adorning our land,—the home of the free!
Most worthy was he,
Who first honour'd thee,
And thou, like him, immortal shall be.

The Penn Society intended their obelisk to stand at the roots of its magnificent ramification.

As to the event, "Unbroken faith" alludes to Voltaire's description of Penn's Treaty: "It is the only treaty between these people and

Penn's Treaty Tree

Christians," he wrote in the first of his *Letters on the English* (1734), "which was never sworn to and never broken" (*C'est le seul traité entre ces peuples et les chrétiens qui n'ait point été juré et qui n'ait point été rompu*). Like Montesquieu, Voltaire admired peace-loving Quakers. In his famous novel, Candide meets a Quaker, who is the rarity of a good man.

The allusion to the principle, "By deeds of Peace," quotes a phrase from John Milton's *Paradise Regained*:

> They err who count it glorious to subdue
> By conquest far and wide . . .
> But if there be in glory aught of good,
> It may by means far different be attain'd,
> Without ambition, war, or violence;
> ***By deeds of peace***, by wisdom eminent . . .

This phrase recalls Du Ponceau's reference to those inspired by "empyrean fire" to preserve and improve mankind. "By deeds of peace" had its own currency. Throughout the eighteenth century, advocates of freedom like Thomas Hollis (1720–1774) had taken it as their motto.

With the authority of such famous Europeans as Montesquieu and Voltaire, Du Ponceau was not wrong in claiming that "the extremi-

"BY DEEDS OF PEACE"
—William Penn Medal, 1775

ties of the earth" alone limited the fame of Penn's Treaty; but he was "unfortunately" correct in lamenting the fame of war overshadowing that of peace. A Quaker's hand to make peace, for example, might have restrained a patriot's hand to fire "the shot heard round the world;" but the 220 foot obelisk at Bunker Hill overshadows, in height and fame, the five foot one at Penn Treaty Park.

The Penn Society gave Penn's Treaty its obelisk, but they neglected one half of their duty: they purchased the obelisk for the "hallowed spot," but they did not purchase the "hallowed spot" for the obelisk. By contrast, the Bunker Hill Monument Association, before raising the obelisk itself, wisely purchased a whole hill for its site. The Penn Society placed their monument in the front yard of the man who had inherited the Treaty Ground. By later calculations, it stood fifty-one feet north-west of the site of the Treaty Elm. Fourteen years later, one newspaper reported no progress,—"the William Penn Society does nothing" (*The National Gazette*, July 20, 1841),—confirmation of man's "poor power" to memorialize.

The outlook for the obelisk went from poor to poorer. November 13, 1843, *The Public Ledger* reported "some fears entertained by the residents of Kensington that the ground on which the Penn Treaty

"*Thomas Hollis*" by Giovanni Battista Cipriani (1767)

monument is erected . . . will change owners without the reservation of the right to keep the monument in its present position." "For some reason," The Penn Society "had dropped the subject of purchasing the ground,"—perhaps, to excuse them, because the owner was unwilling to sell,—but the monument continued on its location "by sufferance only." The owner, at least, suffered the obelisk the dignity of standing in his yard; but the obelisk suffered the indignity of mischievous boys defacing it and piles of lumber hiding it. "Friendless and alone, poverty stricken and dejected," a newspaper later lamented, it stood in "a scene of dirt, old carts, stray chickens, broken-down fences, and a shanty or two" (*The Times*, January 25, and November 13, 1892).

The monument survived by sufferance to endure its suffering, but in 1890, the unthinkable became reality when the Treaty Ground became realty. The *Philadelphia Inquirer* published this menace to the mortal memorial of immortal memory:

FOR SALE.
PENN TREATY WHARF . . .
TUESDAY, MARCH 11, 1890,
AT 12 O'CLOCK NOON, AT THE
PHILADELPHIA EXCHANGE.

The next day, *The Times* reported that "the old Penn Treaty Wharf" had sold for $31,500.00 to Lisle Stokes, a real estate agent. After three score and nine years, Philadelphians finally had to complete the project of The Penn Society or lose the ground, and maybe even the obelisk, forever.

Finally, the city of Philadelphia rescued the monument from oblivion by acquiring the Penn Treaty Wharf and improving it as a park. The newspaper report called the park a "gem among the city's pleasure grounds" (*Inquirer*, May 7, 1893), opening with grand fanfare on October 28, 1893. This date marked the 211th anniversary of the landing of William Penn, sixty-nine years after 142nd anniversary, celebrated by The Penn Society in 1824.

Nothing in the design of this "gem" paid any special tribute to the historical significance of the site. As though in any common square, the city installed "a large and graceful fountain with two iron basins, the top basin supported by three figures and surmounted by another which holds the spray, in the centre of the park." The three figures might have represented the Goddess of Peace and Friendship uniting Chief Tammany with William Penn, but no catalogue of garden ornament included that sculptural group. The obelisk remained in the northwest corner, like a grandparent at a family party, sitting quietly to one side and contemplating the young folk having a good time.

THE PERIOD OF SIXTY-SIX YEARS between 1827 and 1893, in which The Penn Society's obelisk had a precarious existence, ended happily: a few Philadelphians first set up the obelisk, a few more watched over it through years of neglect, and yet a few more finally helped to establish its park, after a real estate sale threatened oblivion. Five months after the opening of the park, an article in the *Philadelphia Inquirer* set values of deed and monument in proper balance: the "justice and humanity," which are "the most important factors on which to build a friendship with the natives" show Penn's Treaty to be "a monument more lasting than any made with hands" to his "wisdom and benevolence" (October 8, 1893).

Between dogmatic theocracy up North and arrogant aristocracy down South, William Penn's "justice and humanity" set a golden keystone in the arch, but it did not prevent civil war between the two extremes. It also did not prevent either William Penn's family or his City of Brotherly Love from falling far short of his ideal. Philadelphians have demonstrated a paradigm of the "poor power to add" to what heroic men do. The history of their successes and failures should make them alternately proud and humble.

CHAPTER 7

Philadelphians' and the Cincinnati's Washington Monument

PHILADELPHIA'S WASHINGTON MONUMENT (1897) crowns the Benjamin Franklin Parkway in Fairmount Park. Its sculpture represents heroes and heroism of the American Revolution and American rivers as they knew them. Far away from the heroes' original neighborhood around Independence or Washington Square, their memorial may seem out of place. The contrast of the Squares with the Park as locations for the monument tells a story about Philadelphia's history.

The Washington Monument with the Museum of Art in the background

In addition to the history of its location, the history of funding the Monument also brings together two Philadelphia stories. These stories can explain its fit in different locations: the Society of the Cincinnati started their fund in 1810, and then Philadelphians started another in 1824. The Cincinnati wanted it to crown Independence Square until almost the end of the project.

In the Centennial, that is, the hundredth Anniversary of the United States in 1876, the *Philadelphia Times* observed that the Philadelphians' fund had more historic interest than that of the Cincinnati (November 9, 1876). Eventually, this fund bore the name of William Purves (1809–1886), treasurer of the Philadelphia Savings Fund Society (PSFS), and trustee and attorney of the monument fund. Philadelphians, having started the fund in a meeting at the Merchants' Coffee House on October 1, 1824, solicited subscriptions for the purpose of raising the monument. In response to this meeting, the *United States Gazette* reported that the "projected monument" seemed "appropriate":

> *The Projected Monument*
>
> The temporary Arch erected before the Hall of Independence to grace the reception of the great and good La Fayette has been very properly taken down and removed, its occasional purpose having been accomplished. It now remains for the citizens of Philadelphia aided by the spontaneous gratuities of those of the state to redeem the pledge which has been given to our illustrious Guest, for the erection of a more permanent and appropriate Memorial of the Revolution, whose approaching jubilee has been thus opportunely anticipated. Perhaps the long contemplated Statue of the Father of his Country may yet be elevated in Washington Square, before the occurrence of our fiftieth Anniversary (*United States Gazette*, October 15, 1824).

Philadelphians had a duty to "redeem the pledge" to their "illustrious Guest" that they would build a "Memorial of the Revolution . . . the long contemplated Statue of the Father of his Country." Its dedication would give them "the honor and benefit" of his attendance (*Inquirer*, April 13, 1825). The writer anticipated that the monument "may yet be elevated in Washington Square, before the occurrence of our fiftieth Anniversary" in 1826. Putting the statue in place would take, he speculated, just a year or two. How fondly men dream! The Philadelphians did not send Lafayette another invitation. In 1826, they could not have imagined how long "the long contemplated" project would take.

By 1826, however, these Philadelphians had accomplished a lot. They had valued their heritage enough that they preserved the State House as the place where the Founding Fathers had debated independence and signed its famous declaration. To honor this significance, they gave the State House a new name, Independence Hall. In the next step of commemoration, they were planning a monument to George Washington, the most revered of their Founding Fathers. Raising the money took a long time: seventy years would pass before President McKinley unveiled the monument in what would have seemed in 1826 a remote place outside the city. In all those years, their project evolved within the history of Philadelphia and the history of art. Good things are worth the wait, but with the unveiling in 1897, the locality and art of the Washington Monument had caused conflicts in the debate and some surprises in the final result.

At the time of the Philadelphians' plans in 1824, the men of the Pennsylvania chapter of the Society of the Cincinnati had already been collecting the funds to raise another monument to Washington. Back in 1810, they had started their own project. Their society represented a special cadre of patriots. In 1783, Washington's generals had formed a fraternity, the first of its type, "to promote," they profess, "knowledge and appreciation of the achievement of American independence." These patriots did not need a visit from Lafayette to remind them of their past or their duty to celebrate it. They had inherited this duty as the honor and the burden of their birth.

For a very long time, the Society of the Cincinnati's project to commemorate their ancestors' revered commander-in-chief remained separate from the Philadelphians' to redeem their ancestors' pledge to Lafayette. Out of practicality, the two projects did finally join forces, or, at least, funds; but their different methods also had different goals. The Society of the Cincinnati keeping their council with aristocratic reticence, did not divulge their plans until they had collected enough money to make them feasible. It also insisted to the end on retaining full control and taking full credit. Their insistence on full control created some controversy for Philadelphians about the location of the monument and some difficulty for the sculptor as he balanced his art with their history.

After the Philadelphians' disappointment of not being able to invite Lafayette to dedicate the statue on a second visit, they eventually set aside their pairing of him with Washington. They focused instead on their plan to raise a statue to Washington. Unlike the Cincinnati, they publicized their project, because they needed to collect money from the public. The Cincinnati happily received donations from the public, but they held tenaciously to their purpose of inscribing their name, and theirs alone, on the monument.

The Philadelphians started as modestly as their endowment. In 1825, six months after their failed pledge to Lafayette, the *Inquirer* suggested "a moderate sized obelisk or a column with fountains or *jets d'eau* at its base" (*Inquirer*, April 13, 1825). Nothing too much—the obelisk would be "moderate sized." In 1827, observing even greater moderation, and certainly not planning any *jets d'eau*, the Penn Society memorialized Penn's treaty with the Native Americans by an obelisk just over five feet high. Neoclassical tastes of the early nineteenth century favored obelisks. Cemeteries, for example, have preserved forests of them.[34] In 1848, twenty years after the very moderately sized obelisk honoring William Penn, the Federal government honored Washington with one very im-moderately sized—the highest in the world, 555 feet. What a contrast of thrifty Quakers with Federal spendthrifts!

Evolving epochs of "historic interest" gave different motivations for raising a statue of Washington. Enthusiasm about inviting Lafayette for its dedication in 1824 and raising it for the semi-centennial in 1826 gave way to celebrating the centennial of Washington's birth in 1832. Seeking popular support, unlike the aristocratic Cincinnati, the Philadelphians appointed delegates of the "Wards, Districts and Townships" to appoint "suitable persons as their collectors" (*Inquirer*, March 4, 1833). Doing their part, the stone masons of the city offered to furnish a cornerstone for the monument, suggesting that they might dress it on their float in the parade celebrating Washington's birthday. After that parade, celebrating Washington's hundred and first birthday, February 22, 1833, they set it in Washington Square (*Philadelphia Times*, November 9, 1876).

In the hope of giving the cornerstone its monument, William Strickland designed one. With Independence Hall, not Washington Square, in the background, Washington's equestrian statue rises above two levels: on the second, bound fasces separate three figures on each side, with water flowing into basins on the ground. Strickland's classical design did not inspire anyone to raise sufficient funds to make it a reality; and the cornerstone waited in vain for its monument. The seed had been planted, John Sartain later reflected, but it never germinated.

Without publicizing their activity or publishing any design, the Cincinnati had been busily raising their own endowment. After gathering in 1810, their distinguished committee men, Major D. Lennox, Judge Richard Peters, Major W. Jackson, Mr. Charles Biddle and Mr. Horace Binney, had collected $3,576.59 by 1819. By 1825, they added $2,522.85, bringing the total to $6,099.44. Horace Binney (1780–1875) acted as a trustee of the fund from 1810 until his death in 1875, when it amounted to $107,300. "The growth of the fund is due in a great measure to the zealous efforts of Mr. Horace Binney, whose honored

William Strickland's design for a monument to Washington in Independence Square, published by John Sartain

name will long be known in the annals of Philadelphia." Binney was ever active in undertaking projects for the public good. At the age of fifteen, as a student at Harvard, for example, he had started its Hasty Pudding Club.

The Cincinnati continued to accept a contribution from the public with the understanding that it funded a monument "regarded solely as a tribute of the Society of Cincinnati to the memory of Washington." By the centennial of their society in 1883, they intended to have $150,000, at which time they would proceed with plans for the monument (*Philadelphia Times*, May 24, 1880). In 1871, Mr. Purves entrusted $30,302 to the Pennsylvania Company, which this company, in 1888, gave to the Society of the Cincinnati. In the 17 years intervening, it had accrued to the sum of $79,255.62. The company, at no charge, had increased the fund by $48,951.68 (*Times*, May 17, 1897). The patriotic Philadelphians, who had been canvassing and collecting since 1824, felt that honoring Washington had priority and allowed no resentment toward the Cincinnati if they wanted to claim the credit. "For the greater good," they might have said.

In the years between the planning in 1880 and the unveiling in May of 1897, some Philadelphians were working for the greater good, but others felt some resentment of the aristocrats' stubborn insistence on full control. They objected to both their choice of the artist and the location of "that monument." The *Inquirer* in June of 1880 announced the objections to the choice of the artist:

THAT MONUMENT

A STORM BREWING OVER THE COMMITTEE'S CHOICE

Having considered a number of submissions, the Cincinnati had chosen the design of Rudolf Siemering (1835–1905), a German sculptor from Berlin. Without any serious look at his design, some Americans could not endure the thought of a German designing their American monument: his selection by the Cincinnati, they said, was "humiliating to American art . . . and an insult and mortification to our people" (*Inquirer*, June, 1880). 'So!,' they might have said, 'American artists are not good enough for those aristocrats?' Even thirteen years later, they still lamented "foreign design, foreign construction, rather representing a foreign autocrat than presenting an original work of art" (*Inquirer*, June 6, 1893). Such mutterings did not reflect any careful judgment. In an editorial, the *Inquirer* expressed its support for Siemering's selection: "The committee did quite right to select the foreign design, not because it was foreign, but because it was the best, and very much the best" (June, 1880).

Objections to the choice of the artist became less pertinent as Siemering's bronze literally settled into its stone foundation. Debates about the location of the statue took their place: should it be Independence Square or the Green street entrance to Fairmount Park. Always firmly set in their awareness of history, the Cincinnati had chosen Independence Square. Since they had started the project, paid most of the money, and commissioned the artist, it made sense to respect their choice. Some, however, so favored the location in the park that they did not defer to the Cincinnati. In the face of this fierce opposition, the *Inquirer* joked that anyone who had "the brazen effrontery" to try to benefit the city should be forewarned. The city should appoint, it added, a committee "to fix the proper amount of punishment" for such benevolence (*Inquirer*, March, 1892).

The Cincinnati had focused on Independence Square as the site for their monument from the time that they started its endowment in 1810. On the other hand, some patriotic citizens, with a different concept of history, considered a very large nineteenth century monument, even one honoring George Washington, inappropriate in an eighteenth century square. From 1776 to 1876, art had evolved to a point that the aesthetic of 1810 did not fit 1880. "Nothing could add to the glory of Independence Square," they held; and, in 1890, a monument to George Washington or to any other man would desecrate the place, which American memory had hallowed.

In or out of Independence Square, the Cincinnati's monument had significance that deserved a special site. Long before the Benjamin Franklin Parkway connected City Hall with the Philadelphia Art Museum, the Green street entrance to the park offered a worthy alternative. Itself the most significant entrance to Fairmount Park, it had, for a long time, needed a landmark. After the Fairmount Park Art Commission had already installed statues of Abraham Lincoln and U.S. Grant down the river drive, the statue of Washington could function as the starting point of this parade of history. Not everyone agreed: "There was a time when it was the fashion to erect monuments in the park," but "a rural park is not the proper place for a monument" (*Inquirer*, June, 1892). In the minds of these critics, monuments functioned best in their historical milieu—in this case, Independence or Washington Square—that gave them context. How could a "rural park" give any context to George Washington?

To some, Siemering's monument was out of place in Independence Square; and to others, out of place in Fairmount Park. Neither site could please everyone. As a facetious solution, the *Inquirer* published a cartoon showing the monument suspended from a balloon so that it could be simultaneously everywhere and nowhere.

The Cincinnati persevered; and the debate 'raged' on:

IN A GREAT RAGE OVER THE MONUMENT
Historian Keyser Predicts Trouble if the Cincinnati Persist in their Plans.
Others Say That Violence Will Not Be Resorted To
(*Inquirer*, June 6, 1893).

The suggestion of violence probably continued the *Inquirer*'s facetious commentary and its cartoon which pictured Siemering's equestrian statue of Washington floating over the city. Another cartoon pictured the General on his horse in a "battle of Independence Square" (*Washington under fire!*, *Inquirer*, February 28, 1892). Launching their own salvos, proponents of the Green street site exaggerated the size of the monument to make it seem an incongruous hulk, looming over Independence Hall:

THE TRUTH ABOUT THE MONUMENT
Desperate Efforts To Mislead the Mayor and the Public

DISTORTED STATEMENTS EXPOSED
The Height, Forty-four Feet Above the Ground, Not Over Seventy
One-Thirty-Seventh of the Square Area All That Will Be Required

"For a mere show piece," the article explained, "the end of a boulevard would have been an appropriate site, but this is an historical statue." Any large statue might have served as a focal point at the end of a boulevard, but not Rudolf Siemering's. The writer concludes with a final boast, "There is no grander historical statue on the face of the globe" (*Inquirer*, March, 1892). How could such grandeur and historical significance merely decorate an entrance to the park?

At the eleventh hour, without any explanation, the Cincinnati finally agreed to the Green street entrance as their site (*Inquirer*, December, 1895). In the face of such considerable opposition, these aristocrats were conceding to popular opinion. Their tenacity, they might have realized, had become pertinacity. In an argument impossible to win, they had made their point. The descendants of George Washington's Generals had argued for history; but the monument now provides focus at the end of a long boulevard, far from the location that would befit its historical representation.

To CELEBRATE THE VASTNESS of the American continent, Rudolf Siemering surrounded the heroes of 1776 by their native inhabitants, whom he set at the four points of the compass above America's rivers with their characteristic flora and fauna. Each one of the four pairs of thirteen steps, alluding to the thirteen original colonies, divide these natives that represent the rivers bounding George Washington's country: the Hudson and Delaware on the east side, and the Ohio and Mississippi on the west. He had studied pictures of native Americans that provided models for the male figure representing the Hudson, having bagged his prey, and the female representing the Delaware, spreading her nets.

On the west side, Siemering did not portray his river gods as Native Americans. Both gods, the male representing the Mississippi and the female, the Ohio, look away from their scene with romantic distraction. By contrast, no longer just hunting and fishing, like the Hudson and the Delaware, the male is spearing an alligator and the female, a large snake—it's dangerous out there in the Wild West! On the other hand, the chaste Ohio alludes to the *Venus Pudica*, chaste Venus, by bringing her hand across her breasts. This allusion to classical art and the romantic tradition of adventure distinguishes these two river gods from the settled ones back East.

Siemering has separated the podium supporting the statue of Washington, into two areas. At the east and west ends, two comple-

Above left: The Hudson River
Above right: The Delaware River
Right: Venus Pudica

mentary groups portray the goddess America. In an essay published in 1880, long before its unveiling in 1897, John Sartain has called these "two large groups of noble design."

> Each group consists of three figures, besides numerous accessories, the prominent one at each end being America. In one she sits between a soldier, who eagerly offers her his sword, and a recumbent field laborer asleep, whom she eagerly endeavors to awaken. Her hair flows free and

The Eastern side of the podium representing America victorious

> she is animated, as in the presence of pressing danger. In the corresponding group, at the opposite end, America sits, calm and grand, majestic in serene repose, a Phrygian cap on her head, sceptered, while men in military costume are placing at her feet wreaths, flags and other trophies.

Two bas relief panels cover the north and south sides of the pedestal, one which Sartain mistakenly, back in 1880, thought would depict an army on foot, led by Washington on horseback; the other a subject "not so intelligible," he said, and "which might be changed with advantage to some other subject, say to Washington resigning his military command to the civil authorities. He thought that only this relief should be changed (*Inquirer*, July 20, 1880). He had good reason to be skeptical about both reliefs.

Sartain anticipated this main difficulty in the design. In the relief panels on the north and south sides of the podium, Siemering faced a dilemma: representing Revolutionary history in his usual dramatic narrative, while, at the same time, including the original members of the Society of the Cincinnati. Above or below each panel, he lists the names of the figures, twenty-one above the south panel and fifteen above and below the north panel. These numbers double and triple the usual number of figures in his other relief panels on German monuments.[35]

Siemering first intended that the southern panel continue his theme of the vast American continent by giving it the title "Westward the Star of Empire Takes its Way." In the center, Benjamin Franklin turns back to face Thomas Jefferson—neither man a member of the Cincinnati. The left and right sides of the panel give clues to the difficulty that Siemering found in balancing his artistic bent for drama with his duty to his patrons to portray their ancestors.

The southern relief panel, "Westward the Star of Empire Takes its Way"

The left side represents a family bringing up the rear of the westward march: a woman carrying a large sack on her shoulders and her son pushing his brother in a wheelbarrow. Such a familial scene fits the sentimental representation of *das Volk* in Siemering's other monuments. In addition, however, the artist also pleased his patrons: he pictures two members of the Cincinnati, Benjamin Lincoln (1733–1810), the first United States Secretary of War (1781–1783) and John Sullivan (1740–1795), an original member of the Society and the first president of its New Hampshire chapter.[36] These two men loom over this family, without any connection to it or to "the star of empire" taking "its way."

The right side of the relief even better demonstrates Siemering's dilemma. It portrays Richard Dale (1756–1826), the great grandfather of the Chairman of the Trustees of the Cincinnati's endowment. Seemingly, Siemering had no pictures of John Paul Jones (1747–1792) and John Barry (1745–1803), the next two names in the parade, because he portrays them with helmets covering their faces, but shouldering oars, at least, to indicate that they are sailors. This sequence of three Pennsylvania members of the Cincinnati, unique to the monument, alludes to a Dale family story that was important to Richard Dale's great-grandson.

Siemering was portraying what the Cincinnati had asked for, at the price of cluttering and confusing his two reliefs. Sartain politely called them "not so intelligible." The Cincinnati's list rules—better, perhaps, ruins—the relief panels. It compromised Siemering's dramatic articulation. Other monuments in his work do not display this capitulation to names.

This facelessness alludes, at least, to a good story. Richard Dale, Senior, was the only original member of the Cincinnati, who was not one of Washington's generals. He had served so nobly as first lieutenant to Captain John Paul Jones on the *Bonhomme Richard*, especially in its famous naval battle with HMS Serapis, that he became a member by special request of Washington himself. Siemering pictures him with a sword, in allusion to the sword of honor presented to Jones by King Louis XVI, and willed, in turn, by Jones to Dale: "My good old Dick," Jones said, "is better entitled to inherit it than any other person, because he did more than any other to help me win it." Siemering was pleasing Richard Dale, the great-grandson, by this allusion to the story about his family's fame and its treasured heirloom. Having made such concessions to please the Cincinnati, Siemering did not include his original title, "Westward the Star of Empire Takes its Way." In this case, he sacrificed his theme to a portrayal of his patron's ancestor and an allusion to his fame. After this allusion to the navy, James Clinton (1736–1812), dressed in buckskin with his dog, does fit both the sculptor's theme of the westward march and the Cincinnati's list. After the French and Indian War, Clinton commanded a corps of men, known as "Guards of the Frontier."

Siemering has also omitted the titles that he intended for the northern panel, *Sic Semper Tyrannis* and *Per Aspera ad Astra*, which represents an army on the march, but without Washington in the lead, as Siemering thought. These titles still fit, but he probably omitted them since he had already omitted the first one. Henry Knox (1750–1806), Washington's Senior General, who succeeded Benjamin Lincoln as the second United States Secretary of War (1785–1789), leads the parade, just as he also mustered Washington's generals for their fraternity. As the revolution was ending in 1783, he founded the Soci-

The northern relief panel

ety of the Cincinnati and wrote its charter. William Smallwood (1732–1792), the first president of the Maryland chapter of the Cincinnati, follows Henry Knox, as also William Moultrie (1730–1805) president of the South Carolina branch of the Cincinnati.

THE INQUIRER'S BOAST may still be correct: "There is no grander historical statue on the face of the globe than Philadelphia's Washington Monument" (*Inquirer*, March, 1892). How many other sculptural programs in nineteenth century America bring together as many figures as successfully? Whatever is lacking arose from the patrons' insistence on the inclusion of their members in the relief panels, and the problem that this insistence gave the sculptor. The Cincinnati held out until almost the end on a historical location for the monument and even when they conceded to the site in the park, they still had their way in cluttering the relief panels with their own charter members. As a result, people visiting the monument stare in vain at these panels, as they try to identify some theme. Rudolf Siemering should be there to explain the themes that he wanted; while the descendants of Richard Dale and other Cincinnati could tell them the family stories that they had asked for and gotten.

CHAPTER 8

St. Joseph's Escaping Notice

Along with Penn and his fellow Quakers, men of all faiths had left the old world for the new so that they might have freedom to practice their religion. While William Penn was living in the Slate-Roof House, he made religious freedom the first priority in his Charter of Liberties. In a long sentence, he based this grant on two assumptions: **no people** can be "truly happy" without "freedom of their *consciences*," and **Almighty God**, "the only lord of *conscience*," "enlightens" their minds. Having set God's fatherly spirit and man's true happiness in the foundation, Penn did "**grant and declare**" religious choice to people according to their "*conscientious persuasion*."

> First,
> **because no people** can be truly happy,
> though under the greatest enjoyment of civil liberties,
> if abridged of the freedom of their *consciences*
> as to their *religious* profession and worship,
> —**and Almighty God** being (sic) the only lord of *conscience*,
> father of light and spirits,
> and the author as well as object of all divine knowledge, faith, and worship,
> who only
> does enlighten the minds
> and persuade and convince the understandings of people,—
> **I do hereby grant and declare**
> that no person or persons inhabiting in this province or territories,

who shall
confess and acknowledge one almighty God,
the creator, upholder and ruler of the world;
and profess him or themselves obliged
to live quietly under civil government,
shall be in any case molested or prejudiced in his or their person or estate
because of his or their *conscientious persuasion* or practice,
nor be compelled
to frequent or maintain any *religious* worship, place, or ministry
contrary to his or their mind,
or to do or suffer any other act or thing
contrary to their *religious persuasion.*

In 1731, three decades after Penn issued his Charter of Liberties, Father Joseph Greaton, S.J. built a Catholic chapel in Philadelphia that would put Penn's grant to a test. Sent from Maryland as a Catholic missionary, he escaped notice by entering Philadelphia dressed as a Quaker. Just south of Walnut street, below Fourth, he built a chapel and residence in one building. Tucked between Willings Alley and buildings on the southeast corner of Fourth and Walnut streets, just 18 by 28 feet, it looked more like a residence than a chapel,—again, all to escape notice. In the earliest days of Christianity, house churches had always been a means of escaping notice. Inevitably, however, the masses that this Catholic priest regularly celebrated on Sundays did not escape notice. July 25, 1734, Governor Patrick Gordon reported to the Council that a Popish priest was openly celebrating a Romish rite in violation of the Royal Charter.[37]

The Council tabled his report, without further discussion. As long as no liberal defender of freedom of conscience published a defense of Penn's Charter of Liberties, no conservative defender of the Royal Charter needed to deny it. *Qui tacet consentit*—silence implies consent. Silence also preserved Penn's brotherly love. Because discussion might provoke discord, a tacit spirit of live-and-let-live preserved this religious practice in the home of a priest, in which, by the way, he celebrated Romish rite.

Eventually Penn's sons did speak up, but not to confirm their father's liberties. Having joined the Church of England after his death in 1718, they did not support his religious ideals. In 1738, one of them wrote to James Logan, Patrick Gordon's successor as governor: "It has become a reproach to your administration that you have suffered the public celebration of the scandal of the Mass." Local newspapers continued to report the excesses of religious bigotry in Europe, which many of the enlightened in Philadelphia might also, by then, have attributed to the Penn family.

Throughout the eighteenth century, local newspapers in colonial Philadelphia maintained tacit tact in making no mention of Roman Catholicism in the city. Private reports must have existed, and, by chance, one appeared in a newspaper. Tamoc Caspinina,[38] "a gentleman of foreign extraction, who has lately resided in Philadelphia," published a series of letters in the *Pennsylvania Packet* in 1772.

He admired Philadelphia as the city of Brotherly Love: "Liberty," he declared, "is the genius of Pennsylvania" (*Pennsylvania Packet*, March 30, 1772). One letter, dated January 14, 1772, reported his meeting with the Rev. Harding, who succeeded Father Greaton in 1750 and served until 1771: "Mr. H. appears to be a decent well-bred Gentleman; and I am told, he is much esteemed by all denominations of Christians in this city, for his prudence, his moderation, his known attachment to British liberty, and his unaffected, pious labors among the people to whom he officiates (*Pennsylvania Packet*, September 7, 1772). Tamoc Caspinina appreciated the practice of the biblical exhortation, *Philadelphia Maneto*, "Let brotherly love remain!" (*Hebrews* 13.1). In Philadelphia, the "prudence, moderation," and attachment to "liberty" of "Mr." Harding kept brotherly love afloat.

Brotherly love kept afloat and even flowed free, as America's democratic tolerance broke through the ice jams of Britain's colonial intolerance: "There were, some years ago," an editorial observed in 1782, "many Protestants in this country, who thought it impossible, or at least highly improbable, that a retainer to the Roman Catholic Church could be saved. But happily they are at length ashamed of their folly, and begin to acknowledge that the Supreme Spirit is equally father of all mankind, and regards only the purity of the heart, not the particularity of profession." Finally!—Americans were catching up to William Penn's "purity of heart," when they realized that the "particularity" of their democratic "profession" acknowledged "all mankind" as children of the same "Supreme Spirit." Free of European bigotry, they were starting to profess religion purely without prejudice: "An inhabitant of the United American States," he continued, "now labors under far fewer prejudices in these matters than the English—he can look at a Frenchman or a Spaniard or an Italian without imagining that he discovers the mark of the beast in his forehead" (*North American Intelligencer*, May 29, 1782).

In the late eighteenth century, a philosophical glow bathed this Philadelphian in optimism. By the nineteenth, swarms of Roman Catholic immigrants made many native Protestants suspicious of their threat and prone to discover the "mark of the beast" on their foreheads—more likely, the mark of the beast on their own.

St. Joseph's worked hard to flow into the mainstream. For its first entrance into these currents, it claimed the name of Washington and the patriotic spirt of the American Revolution. According to an oft-repeated, time-honored, account, George Washington and his staff visited the church for a performance of the *Te Deum* celebrating the American victory at the Battle of Yorktown.[39] Martin Griffin, in one chapter of his history of the church, has denied the claim—"Washington not at St. Joseph's." His denial is valid, in itself, but a notice in the *Pennsylvania Packet*, July 10, 1779, provides a clue to its origin, and partial validity:

> On Sunday, the 4th of July, being the Anniversary of the day which gave Freedom to the vast republic of America, the Congress, the President and Council of the State, with other civil and military officers, and a number of principal gentlemen and ladies, attended at the Roman Chapel, agreeable to invitation from the Minister Plenipotentiary of his Most Christian Majesty. A *Te Deum* was performed on the occasion, to the great satisfaction of all present.

The report's mention of the "President" may suggest the presence of George Washington, but John Jay presided at that time in Philadelphia, and Washington had charge of the Continental Army in New York State.

July 4, 1779, even without America's *Pater Patriae*, St. Joseph's set a watermark in the history of religion. The French ambassador, honoring America's alliance with his country, and as the minister of "his Most Christian Majesty," Louis XVI, sent "the Congress and the President," an invitation in French, with English translation. Naturally, he invited them to celebrate by the rite native to his country. Whether George Washington did or did not attend makes little difference. In welcoming the French as allies, Americans were creating a multicultural community, in which narrow parochialism could not have a place.[40]

Narrow parochialism also had no place in St. Joseph's open-handed generosity. After the cholera epidemic of 1797 had left many children orphans, the church built an orphanage, which the Legislature incorporated on December 18, 1807. Remarkably, the society established to support this charity publicized one of its meeting in 1808: "The members of the Roman Catholic Society of St. Joseph for Educating and Maintaining Poor Orphan Children, are requested to attend a stated meeting on Tuesday the 19th at 6 o'clock P.M. at St. Mary's school room" (*Aurora General Advertiser*, January 14, 1808). Twenty-five years later, the ladies of St. Joseph's were also organizing a Christmas fair to raise money for the orphanage: "*Orphans Fair at the Masonic Hall.* An exhibition and sale of useful and fancy articles will be held by the Roman Catholic Ladies Association of St. Joseph's Orphan Asylum, on the 17th, 18th and 19th day of December" (*National Gazette*, November 25, 1833). Another notice of the fair explained the benefits of charity: "For contributions in money or in kind the reward will be the self-felt gratitude which is ever pleasing, together with the rich harvest always reaped where good actions are sown" (*National Gazette*, December 13, 1833). Put simply, charity benefits the giver as much as the receiver.

St. Joseph's flow into the mainstream inevitably met some snags.

Just before the turn of the eighteenth century, a disturbance outside the church after Sunday services ominously foreshadowed the riots in 1844 that would betray Philadelphia's brotherly love.

In his Charter of Liberties, Penn granted Pennsylvanians freedom to "confess" one almighty God according to their conscience, as long as they would "profess" their obligation "to live quietly under civil government." Unfortunately, European discord about the national allegiance of religion was reaching across the ocean. Under its malevolent influence, American religious faith started to infringe on civil government. The blight that our ancestors crossed the ocean to escape was blighting their children.

Radical Irish-Americans spawned this blight, when they coerced all their fellow Irish-Americans in St. Joseph's to sign a petition for the repeal of England's Alien Bill. They first posted their "request" in the courtyard of the church: "The natives of Ireland who worship in this church are requested to remain in the yard after Divine service until they have affixed their names to a memorial for the repeal of the Alien Bill." Congregants would "remain" in the courtyard "until" they turned their faith into a political allegiance. "Intentions of the most atrocious nature," the *Inquirer* labeled this mix of politics with religion that had, it charged, the "unparalleled effrontery to assault the members of the Catholic Church during divine service" (*Inquirer*, February 11, 1799). Later in the nineteenth century, hot-headed Irish Catholics would create trouble throughout Philadelphia.

St. Joseph's Total Abstinence Society did seek to alleviate one problem particular to the Irish, when it welcomed Father Matthew of Cork, the famous champion of temperance, during his crusade in North American. Not limiting its work to winning over people to the cause of temperance, it had also participated, in 1841, in a parade of mourning at the untimely death of President Harrison: "A meeting of the Pennsylvania Catholic Total Abstinence Society and Beneficial Association of St. Joseph's Church, Rev. Mr. Barbelin in the chair . . . planning a parade of mourning for William Henry Harrison, deceased April 4, 1841 (*Public Ledger*, April 14, 1841). In the Centennial of 1876, this society included a statue of Father Matthew in a remarkable fountain at the main axis of the fair grounds. What better way to celebrate the cause of sobriety than by offering all visitors a drink of water! St. Joseph's charity was stepping forward to cure a great social ill, while also proudly proclaiming a mix of Irish nationality with morality and patriotism.

By the 1820's, in an appeal to "fellow citizens of every religious persuasion," St Joseph's solicited contributions for a new church to replace its first one-story home: "It has been the good custom here and in other parts of our country, for Christians of one denomination, to contribute funds toward the erection of churches for another . . . Kind and mutually liberal sentiments are thereby excited between the various professors of the common Faith and Hope, and the most effectual tribute is paid to the cause of Christianity in general, and to public morals and order" (*National Gazette*, April 24, 1824). It also raised money by a fair at the Masonic Hall, "its proceeds to be in aid of the fund for the erection and completion of the new church" (*National Gazette*, March 28, 1839). Fairs at the Masonic Hall also flowed into the mainstream, because fraternal orders, like the Masons, opened a common ground for "public morals and order."

In 1838, more than one hundred years after Father Greaton build the first humble chapel, the laying of the cornerstone for the new building marked progress in the life of both St. Joseph's and of the United States. The little church in Willings alley was finding its place in the life of Philadelpia. The account in the *Public Ledger* glowed with enthusiasm: "The ceremonies were interesting and to many entirely new. Mr. Ryder in a truly eloquent discourse explained the ceremonies of the occasion, pointed out the causes for gratitude, which Catholics had to God, for their liberties in this country, and their duty and willingness to pray for defense of that liberty." Representing the "interesting" event to the common man, the writer gives the officiating priest Mr. as a title.

The text in the cornerstone started with a Latin blessing, *Quod Felix faustum fortunatumque sit, Deique in gloriam bene vertat.* "May it be lucky, favorable and fortunate, and may it turn well to the glory of God." The full text adds sacred and secular times and persons to the blessing:

In the Pontificate of Gregory Sixteenth
THIS
Corner Stone of the new St. Joseph's Church
is laid this fourth day of June;
Being Whitsun Monday, in the year of our Lord,
one thousand and thirty-eight,
Of the Independence of these United States the
Sixty-Second;
In the Administration of Martin Van Buren,

eighth President of the United States;
Joseph Ritner, Governor of the State of Pennsylvania;
John Swift, Mayor of the city of Philadelphia;
Right Rev. Henry Conwell, Bishop of the Diocese . . .

After noting the architect and the builders, the text commemorated old St. Joseph's:

> **endeared** to the Catholic community as the cradle of their faith,
> **consecrated** by the labors of venerable pioneers of religion,
> **illustrious** as the nursery of many distinguished priests,
> **and ever memorable** as the first temple, in which the hymn of thanksgiving was chanted to the God of armies in the presence of Washington and his military staff for the blessings bestowed upon the infant republic in her struggle for right and liberty
> (*Public Ledger*, June 8, 1838).

The National Gazette had also included St Joseph's time-honored claim to the fame of George Washington, when it reported the first patriotic service at the old building, "where first the anthem of thanksgiving for the success of our revolutionary struggle was sung in the presence of Washington and his staff and representatives of the Allied powers of France and the United States" (*National Gazette*, May 5, 1838). Substitute Jay for Washington, and the report is entirely correct.

One year later, St. Joseph's installed an organ in its new building. A newspaper account of this installation gave an introduction to the church, before it went on to describe its new musical instrument. It assumed that many Philadelphians knew nothing about the presence of Roman Catholics in their city—Who are these people and where is their church?, many might have asked.

> This church, which stands back from the north side of Willing's Alley is remarkable for its quiet reclusion, and by no means calculated to attract the attention of strangers. Perhaps there are thousands in the city who are not aware of its existence, although it was founded prior to the Revolution. The congregation has always been equally remarkable

> for its quiet and unobtrusive labors in well doing by receiving the poor and needy, and administering consolation to the afflicted to the extent of their ability, contenting themselves with a very humble edifice, until their resources enabled them to construct a new one without encroaching upon their labors of love and charity. In the construction of their new Church they have displayed the same moderation and prudence by erecting a comfortable and substantial building, avoiding all unnecessary and costly ornaments (*National Gazette*, December 24, 1839).

The author does not set St. Joseph's apart for its distinction in religious history,—not even for the apocryphal visit of George Washington! The phrase, "founded prior to the Revolution," gives short shrift to the history of its foundation. On the contrary, it emphasizes the congregation's good character, not its history. St. Joseph's "very humble . . . quiet reclusion" could have described the synagogue in Philadelphia or the activities of any minority that had the tact and the good sense to keep a low profile. Passing over its pursuit of religious liberty, for which St. Joseph's was known in the first epoch of its history, the account highlights its charitable work, well publicized in the second: "remarkable for its quiet and unobtrusive labors in well doing." "Well doing" determines St. Joseph's antiquity, home, and respectability.

MODERATION AND PROPRIETY could not prevent discord, especially as shanty sons of Saint Patrick bore the stigma of being the drunks, carried off to jail in Paddy wagons. As their numbers increased and their voices grew more raucous during the 1840's, organizations like St. Joseph's Catholic Total Abstinence Society and Beneficial Association could no longer even hope to remedy or conceal their degradation and drunken shenanigans. Descendants of the Scots-Irish Protestants, in the majority, revived the resentments toward the Irish Catholics that their ancestors had felt back in the British Isles.

In this volatile atmosphere, relatively small issues blew up to violence. A debate about the translation of the Bible for use in public schools became so rancorous that it caused riots, the Bible Riots. "The narrow and bitter bigotry," Eleanor Donnelly observed, "of these 'Natives,' as they were called, was fired by the indiscreet zeal of some hot-headed Catholics, and furious religious riots ensued."

Brotherly love held its head in shame during the Bible Riots of 1844. Outside the city, in the nearby town of Kensington, a mob burned down the Irish Catholic Church of St. Michael. In the city, Philadelphia police prevented violence before it could begin: "All the avenues leading to St. Joseph's Church in Fourth near Prune (Locust), and in Willings Alley, have been guarded by troops, who suffer no person to enter the space unless they live within the square. This precaution is rendered necessary by threats of destruction which have been made in reference to this building" (*Public Ledger*, May 9, 1844). In another account, the leader of the mob acknowledged that Father Barbelin, the priest of St. Joseph's, was French, and not Irish: "Oh! no," he said, "that little Frenchman won't hurt anybody!" and his gang passed on.

THE MOB'S SPARING Father Barbelin (1808–1869), the "little Frenchman," made a story worthy of this man of God; but blockading the neighborhood around his church explains its the survival more readily than fellow feeling. On the other hand, this story does indicate that he had a popular following. After the riots, Philadelphia felt ashamed of its betrayal of brotherly love. Religion as loving benevolence, instead of poisonous old-world allegiance and bigotry, appropriately celebrated kindly Father Barbelin.

A photograph of Father Felix Barbelin

In addition to serving as the priest of St. Joseph's Church during the riots of 1844, Father Barbelin also founded its hospital in 1849, and its college in 1851. He brought St. Joseph's to the three-fold functions of a church, school, and hospital. At the unveiling of the Father Barbelin Memorial, J. Duross O'Bryan, Esq. delivered the eulogy. As one of the good Father's old students, he emphasized his teacher's devotion to children: "No child that ever happened within the fairy circle of his company but was reluctant to depart and anxious to return. Sunday school was crowded, always, not because attendance was compulsory, but rather because children wished voluntarily to go." In pastoral duties, "if misfortune came or trouble brooded in a household, his voice was ever heard assuaging grief and alleviating distress. His presence seemed to bring sunshine with it." Father Barbelin's devotion sanctified the site of his labors: "Upon this spot and within these walls, cluster the memory of the happiest days of our lives" (*Inquirer*, June 6, 1870).

"May this memorial," the speaker concluded, "stand a beacon to guide us from the shoals of this life to the deep waters of God's love." As the mother of all Catholic institutions in the city, St. Joseph's has also stood as a beacon to all Philadelphians,—but a beacon that has often hidden its light to survive. In September, 1959, President Eisenhower signed a bill which drew the church out of hiding. He authorized the Interior Department to purchase the seven properties, east of the south corner of Fourth and Walnut streets, and just north of the lot on which Father Greaton had built his church in the middle of the block (*Inquirer*, September 16,1959). When it demolished these buildings and turned the empty lot into a garden, the church stood open to view. This work of faith no longer needed to escape notice but to attract it.

Speech Delivered at the Unveiling of the Father Barbelin Memorial

This monument is made of Italian marble, an unostentatious but enduring form, of modest simplicity. Love clings to this form, and through the dim vista of years, while recollection can illumine the way, discovers its object in the features of love. No words can supply, no language express so fully and completely to this congregation, the virtues which adorned the character of Father Barbelin as this sculptured relief, his placid meek and saint-like countenance that we knew and loved from childhood. His life arises to our view, pure and unsullied as the stone from which it speaks.

He possessed and exercised in an extraordinary degree the faculty of entrancing the attention of children and of supplicating their love. No child that ever happened within the fairy circle of his company but was reluctant to depart and anxious to return. Sunday school was crowded, always, not because attendance was compulsory, but rather because children wished voluntarily to go. He held the young imagination by instructive histories. The love thus begun never ceased: it continued throughout his life, and as the children grew up they sought his company and his counsel. In him they found the most disinterested friend and the sagest advisor.

If misfortune came or trouble brooded in a household, his voice was ever heard assuaging grief and alleviating distress. His presence seemed to bring sunshine with it. Father Barbelin's virtues were of the class that sought not the flare and light of public notice. By his patience, his mildness and above all, by his angelic purity of life, he taught by his example that to be good and to do good was in the power of everyone, even the humblest.

Such was the life of Father Barbelin. Beautiful beyond description in its candid innocence, grand and majestic in its powerful simplicity. In sincere and heartfelt attestation of his worth, in gratitude for his services, in love and veneration for his memory, this assembly has gathered. The occasion must give rise to strange and peculiar feelings. Upon this spot and within these walls, cluster the memory of the happiest days of our lives. With St. Joseph's Church and Father Barbelin, our own existence has hitherto been closely connected. One link is broken.

May this memorial keep alive in our hearts the recollection of our happy association with him. May it stand familiar while life is with us, and remind us by his life to amend the defects of our own. May it be as a father, receiving his prodigal son, extending a welcome to erring ones to return to the Church. May it stand, unimpaired by storm, uncrumbled with time, a beacon to guide us from the shoals of this life to the deep waters of God's love (*Inquirer*, June 6, 1870).

CHAPTER 9

Christ Church and Its Bells

> Most of our streets need cleaning.
> June bugs will soon be in season.
> The tendency of rents is slightly downward.
> Christ Church's bells chimed last evening.
> Strawberries are now comparatively cheap.
> (*Inquirer*, April 2 & May 28, 1870)

IN THE EIGHTEENTH and nineteenth centuries, Philadelphians so readily recognized Christ Church with its tower and steeple that grocers selling strawberries on North Second street advertised themselves as its neighbors. If citizens did not look up to its steeple, they heard its bells clearly enough that the *Inquirer* reported their chiming as a routine item in the day's news. These chimes were as much a part of urban life as the streets that needed cleaning, through which they walked, and the crazy June bugs that they batted aside. Down the Delaware, passengers on ships might catch sight of the steeple and perhaps hear its bells, before they even set foot in the city. Without appreciating the history of an Anglican institution like Christ Church, with its tower, steeple, and bells, contemporary Philadelphians still enjoy their sight and sound.

We can see and hear a lot about life in Philadelphia
and some of its idealistic callings,
if we learn some chapters in their history.

THE BITTER RESENTMENT in the first chapter of this history may surprise us. In the 1690's, Quakers in Philadelphia shuddered at the very thought of an Anglican church, especially one flaunting a tower with bells.[41] They would not have allowed it to exist, but their king had given them a charter that stipulated his subjects' right to establish this, his national church. The Quakers should have prudently taken 'live and let live' as their rule. Let William Penn's Holy Experiment experience a church that some of them might have called worldly and wicked. And yet, they tried to disregard this stipulation and its experience.

Quaker magistrate Edward Shippen arrested the man who submitted the request to establish Christ Church: "They are bringing priests and swords amongst us," he cried, "but, God forbid, we will prevent them" (*The Times*, November 17, 1895). He shrank at the thought of priestcraft and its wars blighting the Quaker City. Hadn't Quakers crossed the ocean to escape this wickedness? His action expressed their fervent—but futile—hope for a utopia. In this sense, Quakers' short-lived utopia came to an end when the Anglicans built Christ Church in 1695. It had enjoyed thirteen years of contented isolation, before the Anglican church of the spiritual and worldly establishment moved in and started its inevitable take-over. *Sic transit gloria mundi*, even "the glory" of the Society of Friends' vision of holiness.

Philadelphia Quakers could find some consolation in living for fifty more years without seeing the worldly vanity of a lofty church tower—a campanile. After sixteen years, however, they did have to put up with the clanging of a bell. Before the vestry of Christ Church could build a tower and steeple for a proper "ring of bells," it set one in the crotch of a nearby tree by 1701, and in a belfry by 1709. Picture the stark and painful contrast, on either side of Second and Market streets, between the simple Quaker meeting to the south, and Christ Church to the north. While the Quakers wait in godly silence for the voice of the Holy Spirit, they have no choice but to hear the bell's call to worship. Seeing this nest of priestcraft across the street gave offense enough, but hearing its cacophony . . . ! It sounded as a tocsin of all that they had suffered back in London.

With the passage of time, Quakers found some solace in sharing civic life with the parishioners of Christ Church. Even though these

Anglicans had imported their religion, its architecture and litany from the old world, Quakers did not need to import old-world bigotry in meeting the competition. They were all equal under the law of William Penn's "Great Experiment." Except for the most contentiously doctrinaire zealots, happy communal life gradually mitigated the sting of jealousy.

In the second chapter of this history, during the 1750's, another generation of Quakers, more cosmopolitan than parochial, less defensive, and firmer in Philadelphia's Brotherly Love, could join with other citizens in welcoming the following notice:

SCHEME

Of a LOTTERY for raising *One Thousand and Twelve Pounds, Ten Shillings*, to be applied for finishing the STEEPLE to CHRIST-CHURCH, in Philadelphia, and the residue towards purchasing a Ring of Bells.

Benjamin Franklin, on the committee to raise money by lottery, published this notice in his newspaper, *The Pennsylvania Gazette*. He concluded with an appeal to the civic pride of all Philadelphians: "We hope that a work of this kind, which is purely ornamental, will meet with encouragement from all well-wishers to the credit, beauty and prosperity of Philadelphia" (February 13, 1753). By the middle of the enlightened eighteenth century, who could have indulged in such doctrinal pettifoggery as to trace back this "purely ornamental" steeple to pagan wickedness?! Philadelphians had something to be proud of: by 1753, they had gotten past the parochialism of Quaker orthodoxy.

Time vindicated Benjamin Franklin's claim that the tower, steeple and bells would ornament Philadelphia to its "credit, beauty and prosperity." The tower and steeple complemented the interior of the church, which had been built, extraordinarily, in the Doric Order. It was, the *United States Gazette* boasted, "one of the chastest models of Grecian Spire that is known to exist, and the first architectural ornament of our city, for which we are indebted to Robert Smith, by whom it was erected in 1752." Nothing in London could surpass its beauty: "The steeple of the BOW CHURCH, in London is reckoned the finest spire there; but is inferior to this, both in originality and design,

Christ Church

and in beauty of elevation—it is only superior to it in height, rising as it does from a very lofty tower" (*United States Gazette*, May 5, 1826).[42]

Before more chapters in the history of the bells of Christ Church, Philadelphia has a special bell that deserves its own chapter, because its fame has resounded beyond all others. In 1751, the Pennsylvania Assembly celebrated the fiftieth anniversary of William Penn's Charter of Liberties by commissioning the Whitechapel Foundry in London to cast a commemorative bell for the State House. After its arrival, it cracked and was recast twice, before it was hung in the State House tower on June 7, 1753. This bell already had distinction in 1751, but it went on to win a distinct fame and a special name as the Liberty Bell.

The same year,—with less historical significance,—the vestry of Christ Church met on February 22 to review a report for the purchase of a "ring of bells." From the money raised by the lottery, as advertised in *The Pennsylvania Gazette*, they paid the same foundry in London £560, 7s and 8d (560 pounds, 7 shillings and 8 pence[43]) to cast eight bells. The tenor bell weighed 1800 pounds, 280 pounds less than the State House bell. The remaining seven weighed less in proportion; but, in sum, all eight weighed 9,000 pounds. Captain Budden transported them in his ship, the Myrtilla; and Nicholas Nicholson installed them in the tower (*The Times*, March 28, 1885). Both men provided their services free of charge.

Annually, the bells have performed two tasks, one sacred, the other secular. Their chimes herald the birth of Jesus at midnight on Christmas Eve, by tradition, the hour of His birth; and they toll the old year out and ring the new year in on New Year's Eve. A newspaper reported their heralding of Yuletide, after the State House bell struck midnight: "As the State House bell tolled the hour of midnight, from the belfry of old Christ Church, rang forth the sweet chimes of those glorious old bells, which long before our freedom was born, waked at Christmas midnight the sober citizens of ancient Philadelphia" (*The Times*, December 25, 1875). Long before "our freedom was born" in 1776, "sober citizens" listened happily for the State House bell tolling midnight, as the downbeat to the "sweet chimes" announcing Christ's birth. A motley group of citizens, some in rags, others in fine linen, gathered on Second street to hear the eight bells of Christ Church welcoming Christmas. They greeted the first peal with a loud "Hurrah."

Secular, but with its own wistful enchantment, a "muffled peal" tolled on New Year's Eve from 11 to 12 P.M., followed by a "clear peal" from 12 P.M. to 1 A.M. The bells of Christ Church have tolled the old year out and rung the New Year in as long as they have hung in its tower. "It is a very solemn sound, the New Year's chime, a sad leave-taking of the dead past" (*The Times*, December 17, 1893). "Of earthly sounds," this chime rings the old year out most solemnly, because it belongs only to this earth. It sounds a solemn dirge for the dead past, the passing of all that sons of earth can hope to possess (*The Times*, December 27, 1891).

Sons of earth can, at least, follow great events. The tenor bell of Christ Church followed the lead of the State House bell in one classic, historical duet. By tradition, the State House bell shared its most iconic peal,—the one that gave it its new name,—with the bell of Christ Church on July 8, 1776, when they joined to summon citizens to a public reading of the Declaration of Independence: "when the State House bell rang out, the bells of Christ Church began ringing in unison" (*Inquirer*, November 17, 1895). A house of God taking up the brave peal of the State House gave its nod to our Founding Fathers' honorable undertaking. Whatever the intangible aura between man and God, this historic heraldry gave Americans two tangible icons. Declaring independence, the State House became Independence Hall; and ringing the call to liberty, its bell became the Liberty Bell. Christ Church and its bells shared this glory, without changing their names. The numinous aura of independence and liberty has pervaded Philadelphia ever since.[44]

After July 8, 1776 cast its intangible spell and created tangible icons, July 9, 1776, dawned as just another day. History had taken its course and the bells of Christ Church greeted the morning with streets still in need of cleaning, and the prices of strawberries and rents still rising or falling. The church continued one service outside liturgy, but very much attune to the common man. The chimes of its eight bells gave him such pleasure that the vestry decided to offer them to the many farmers crowding the streets on Friday night before market day. In 1826, an "old gentleman," who recalled the installation of the bells way back, he thought, in 1756, reminisced about this entertainment. The church made them available to country folk "for practice or for pleasure" on those evenings "without a special permit from the church Wardens, Mayor of the city, governor of the state, or president of the union" (*United States Gazette*, April 21, 1826).

Alongside the broad sweep of humanity in this reminiscence, the Father of our Country kneeling in prayer makes a piously civic icon. To sell their produce in Philadelphia, farmers were driving heavy Conestoga wagons, drawn by teams of four or six horses, and stringing them along Market street near their stalls in the market. After they had settled in, but before they got some sleep in their wagons or in neighborhood hostelries, they assembled to hear the music of Christ Church bells, which rang out a merry chime for their enjoyment (*Inquirer*, August 19, 1865). Perhaps also, men chosen to ring "for practice or for pleasure" might have been associated with churches out in the country. They needed no "special permit" from the usual hierarchy of authority: "church wardens" all the way up to the "president of the union." The tower and its bells, which Benjamin Franklin recommended as "purely ornamental," ornamented the city as entertainment for farmers before market days; but they also might have served President Washington on any other day.

In addition to their use in the community, the bells had official duties. On June 4, 1774, they rang in celebration of the King George the Third's birthday for the last time.[45] After the birth of the new nation, they did not ring to celebrate's the birthday of its Chief Executive, but they did ring to do *post obitum* honor to the birth of George Washington. The Mayor of Philadelphia, like the President of the Union, could issue a "special permit" for their peal, but the vestry had gradually tightened its purse strings and put a price on it. One year, the Mayor paid the church for this celebration (*United States Gazette*, February 22, 1837). It lasted all day, all over the city: "At sunrise, a national salute of 13 guns was fired at the Navy Yard, and the bells at Christ Church commenced ringing a merry peal, which was repeated at short intervals throughout the day. At sunset a similar salute was fired, the bells ringing a closing peal . . ."

A debate ensued: Who would pay? Public opinion held that matters of petty finance should not determine honor to George Washington, "the greatest and most noble man that ever adorned the world," but Christ Church insisted on payment (*Public Ledger*, February 19 & 20, 1846). Their insistence on payment gives a clue to some financial trouble. February 23, 1846, both the Christ Church bell and the Liberty Bell rang for George Washington's birthday, but the Liberty Bell cracked in the work. A slot was carved along the crack and secured by two rivets. Appropriately, this most famous of all American bells had rung for the last time in honor of George Washington.

INTO THE EARLY NINETEENTH CENTURY, the sight and sound of Christ Church identified Philadelphia as much as Independence Hall and the Liberty Bell do today. Staying in the city, the *National Gazette* observed, "is to be within sight of Christ Church steeple" (July 16, 1836). Hearing its bells assured citizens that they were in the very heart of their home (*Pennsylvania Gazette*, May 21, 1835). Christ Church became so closely identified with Philadelphia that it started to tip the balance between its religious and civic functions. It also had provided a focus for civic, just as much as one for biblical religion. As a significant witness to history, Americans revered it as a shrine of their history.

By the 1860's, however, when Philadelphia had grown beyond the small city hovering about its port on the Delaware River, Philadelphians started to express regret that such an important shrine "for Christian and patriot alike" had such a "remote and inconvenient location" (*Inquirer*, November 29, 1860). Few people lived in the neighborhood around the church, and only a few of the faithful walked the distance to attend the church of their forefathers. Christ Church had become the mother church of all Episcopal churches in the city and by extension, in the nation, and also a shrine of American history. It could not close its doors, but tight finances made it hard to keep them open.

As income declined from pew rentals, on which churches in that era relied, the vestry decided to declare it a free church with an endowment for its maintenance. Congregants supported a free church by giving each week in envelopes, as their consciences dictate (*Inquirer*, December 29, 1888). Financial support might also come from patriotic societies like the Sons of the Revolution (SR). About the same time that Christ Church became free, descendants of men who served their country during the Revolutionary War formed the SR. In 1890, it met to celebrate an anniversary. *The Philadelphia Times* described the event:

THE PROGENY OF HEROES
SONS OF THE REVOLUTION CELEBRATE THEIR ANNIVERSARY
OLD CHRIST CHURCH CROWDED

Christ Church claimed the dignity of age as "Old Christ Church." Those attending the service are not heroes of old, but they claim dignity as "progeny," celebrating their heritage. The same bells that summoned each hero to hear the public reading of the Declaration of Independence on July 8, 1776, summon his descendants to commemorate history and to worship the god who "gave the nod to the beginnings"—*Annuit Coeptis*, as their country's Great Seal announces. The SR decorated the church to celebrate their ancestors: "The old church was bright with bunting and flags, and against the massive pillars were shields bearing the names of the distinguished men whose pews were situated immediately beneath them." Sons of the Revolution celebrate history in Christ Church as a national shrine more than as God's house (*The Times*, April 21, 1890).

ROUTINELY, CHURCH BELLS both summon the faithful to worship, and toll at their funerals. "Merrily," at midnight on December 25, they announce the birth of Christ. Solemnly, the last hour of December 31st, they ring out the old year; and, happily, the first hour of January 1st, they ring in the new. Artfully, without celebrating anything special, they ring 'changes.' Ringing changes sounds the bells in precise sequences. "It's not easy work," observed one veteran ringer, "ringing the changes" (*The Times*, January 1, 1879). The first display of change ringing in America took place in Christ Church on Sunday, June 9, 1850. "A band of English bell ringers" rang the bells in Holt's ten part peal of Grandsire's triples, containing 5040 changes. They completed their peal in three hours and fifteen minutes (*Inquirer*, August 7, 1882). Henry W. Haley led, ringing the tenor bell, with Thomas H. Lesage, treble; Charles Rahill, second; Frederick G. Wade, third; William Lobb, fourth; James Hewitt, fifth; Henry W. Haley, sixth; Edward Sawyer, seventh; Richard Dodd and John Davy, also tenor (*Inquirer*, December 18,1898). These eight bells rang precisely 5,040 changes in mathematical sequence (*The Times*, January 1, 1884). This "notable and wonderful exhibition" attracted "a vast crowd of listeners" (*Inquirer*, August 8, 1882).

With two "rings" of four bells, the eight bells of Christ Church make a chime, which is the standard number of bells needed to ring changes. Without hitting all the right notes, this chime can play the perennial Easter hymn, "Jesus Christ is Risen Today." Only a carillon can play all the notes in a full repertoire. It needs at least twenty-three bells to sound this full range. From Latin *quaternionem*, "set of four," carillon originated in sets of four bells. By the end of the nineteenth century, the carillon of the Church of the Holy Trinity was filling Rittenhouse Square with Victorian favorites like "Home Sweet Home," "The Last Rose of Summer," or Bonnie Blue Bells of Scotland." Philadelphians went uptown, to churches, like Holy Trinity or St. Marks, just east of Rittenhouse Square, to hear a sweetly sonorous repertoire, but without the romance of historical associations.

And yet, in Philadelphia, history counts! Long before Philadelphia had even thought of enjoying the pleasant amenities of its five squares, and even longer before the carillon of Holy Trinity was serenading fashionable Rittenhouse Square, the Liberty Bell and the bells of Christ Church had become symbols of the city's and the nation's history. Everyone could enjoy their chime, but some citizens appreciated them as American icons and worked to perpetuate them. In 1876, Henry Seybert (1801–1883) presented a new tenor bell for Independence Hall to the City of Philadelphia. He had appreciated the inspiration of the Liberty Bell during the dark days of the Civil War, and he made a commemorative bell to fill its place.

As a metallurgist, Seybert knew what he was doing. He cast a replacement for the Liberty Bell that incorporated symbolic metals from the past. For a beginning, his bell weighs 13,000 pounds to represent the thirteen original colonies. In the ancient custom of beating swords into plowshares (*Isaiah* 2.4), he literally melted and then melded a lot of history: the bronze of two cannons from the battle of Saratoga, one American, the other British; and of two from the battle of Gettysburg, one Union, the other Confederate. In his bell, the cannons that have divided people in war unite them in peace. At first, after this new bell seemed to lack tonal quality, it was recast. It still rings the hours from the steeple of Independence Hall, celebrating the liberty for which Americans fought in two great wars.

Like Mr. Seybert during the Civil War, business men around Second and Market listened to the bells of Christ Church during World War II. In their neighborhood, they knew that listening to these bells made them Philadelphians. Before the war, some of them had not appreciated the bells as symbols, but "they began to hear their brave and assuring sound during troubled days and started thinking of what they meant," said rector Kloman. After the war, they gave the church two bells made from metal reclaimed from enemy guns. President Truman ordered the United States Army ordnance to supply it. Metal, cast for destruction, they recast for peace (*Inquirer*, February 24, 1947). At first, also, after these bells, somewhat like Mr. Seybert's, did not sound in tune with the mellow old bells, the business men again recast with better metals in 1953 (*Inquirer*, June 18, 1953).

IMAGINE HEARING BELLS for the first time: A.D. 960, Ingulphus, the putative author of the history of the Abbey of Croyland, recorded his first impression when he heard its bells, reputedly, the first in an English campanile: *Fiebat mirabilis harmonia, nec erat tunc tanta consonantia campanarum in tota Anglia* ("They made a miraculous harmony, and there was not such great consonance of bells in all England"). *Mirabilis harmonia*—miraculous harmony! In Philadelphia, a poet celebrated the bells of Christ Church after the Civil War:

> These chimes, they tell a thousand tales,
> Sweet tales of olden time,
> And ring a thousand memories,
> At vesper and at prime (*Inquirer*, September 20, 1865).

Vesper and prime ring with a "sweet" image of bare-footed friars singing vespers at 6PM and prime at 6AM. And yet, of the "thousand tales" told and the "thousand memories" recalled, not all could have been "sweet." Let us toll, the bells sing, hours and days of men's lives:

> *Gaudeamus gaudentibus,*
> *Doleamus dolentibus.*
>
> Let us rejoice with men rejoicing,
> Let us grieve with men grieving.[46]

Hearing the chimes and seeing their tower have represented life in Philadelphia. How have some Philadelphian lived this life? Answering their call to joy and to grief,—to joy in our liberties and to grief in their defense,—has represented this life's high calling.

CHAPTER 10

William Hamilton of Bush Hill and The Woodlands

When William Penn's son Thomas (1702–1775) arrived in Philadelphia on August 6, 1732, Pennsylvanians expressed joy and satisfaction in seeing this son of their late, Honorable Proprietor. Clergymen, who had enjoyed the religious liberty established by his father, particularly expressed their "loyalty and obedience to His Most sacred Majesty King George, and duty and affection to your honorable family" (*Pennsylvania Gazette*, January 18, 1733). Fourteen years after the death of his "never to be forgotten" father, Thomas was returning to his father's "holy experiment," hoping to gain profit, but about to experience moral complications in reaping it.

Andrew Hamilton (*circa* 1676–1741), as the Penns' lawyer, family friend, and neighbor, played a special part in this welcome. He delivered the after-dinner speech, when his fellow justices of local courts entertained Thomas "handsomely." Like the clergymen, he expressed loyalty to king, country, and the especially local,—and, for him, personal,—theme of loyalty to family, "the uncommon zeal for the prosperity of your honorable family, from which, under His Majesty's happy influence, the people of these counties derive those privileges which so justly entitle them above their neighbors to the name of Freemen." Thomas thanked Justice Hamilton and his colleagues "heartily" for "the respect you express for myself, and your regard to my family" (*Pennsylvania Gazette*, September 14, 1733). As the speaker of the General Assembly, Hamilton had also assured Thomas of that body's "firm adherence to your honorable family" (*Pennsylvania Gazette*, August 14, 1732). Pennsylvanians had good reason to be loyal, because they lived in a special place. Midway between Puritans in Massachusetts and Cavaliers in Virginia, they enjoyed "privileges" of "Freemen" that Willam Penn had made possible.

'Regard for family' had special meaning for Andrew Hamilton. As the progenitor of his own family in Pennsylvania, Hamilton was, like William Penn, both acquiring land and passing on both it and its burdens to his sons, Andrew, Jr. (1713–1747) and James (*circa* 1710–1783), and especially to his grandson William (1745–1813). These three generations from 1676 to 1813 represent the sweep of history from the earliest days of Philadelphia to the early nineteenth century.

WHEN KING CHARLES II granted the vast lands of Pennsylvania to William Penn, he gave him and his family land with no cash. Whatever cash they might have they had to derive from their land. The Penns passed on this advantage with disadvantage to Andrew Hamilton when they paid him for his legal services with land from their proprietary estate. As their friend, on the other hand, they were happy to have him as a neighbor. By this transfer in 1726 and 1729, Hamilton owned half of their proprietary estate, Springettsbury, in the hills above the northern border of the city at Vine street. To his half, he gave the name Bush Hill, perhaps alluding to its deforested terrain. Eventually, he acquired enough of the property that posterity has remembered the name Bush Hill and forgotten Springettsbury, perhaps because its manor house burned down in 1784 (see Edward Burd's *Letters*, March 24, 1784). Hamilton's children and grandchild would return home to Bush Hill, if only to be buried in his family cemetery.

About a decade after Andrew acquired Bush Hill from the Penn family, he purchased a large tract of about 300 acres on the west bank of the Schuylkill River. These two acquisitions he could have counted as only two among many. On his demise, he left thousands of acres to his two sons Andrew, Jr, and James, but these two estates on the east bank and the west banks of the Schuylkill would represent the changes in the map of the city from the eighteenth to the nineteenth centuries.

As the first generation of the Hamiltons in Pennsylvania, Andrew was already dealing with the second generation of the Penns. Benjamin Franklin had never met William Penn, but he knew his reputation for integrity. Acquainted with Penn's sons, Thomas and John, he joked with a friend that, "according to all accounts, there was more of the gentleman in Billy Penn drunk than there is in both Thomas and John sober." A father passes on tangible assets more easily than intangible character.

Without this extreme contrast of drunk with sober,—and, of course, old Ben loved to make jokes,—Andrew Hamilton did pass on to his family fame and a moral example that they could only hope to match. To all Americans, he passed on his greatest legacy by his eloquent defense of John Peter Zenger in 1735 on a charge of libel, in which he established American freedom of the press. Hamilton, John Fanning Watson observed, enjoyed a reputation for "high honor and ability" throughout the city. After his death in 1741, when he left land to his sons, he could not have known how, much less, how wisely, they might use it. He left them one use that they maintained: out of all his real estate, he continued to occupy his grave on Bush Hill. However vast the Hamiltons' land, this plot, significantly and fundamentally, lay at its heart.

In his specific bequests, Andrew left Bush Hill to his first son James. To his second son Andrew, Jr., he left his large plantation of 356 acres on the west bank of the Schuylkill River. Andrew, Jr. outlived his father by only six years. In 1747, therefore, his son William, then only two years old, became the heir of his father's 356 acres. Andrew Jr.'s older brother James outlived him by thirty-six years. When James died in 1783, with no surviving son, he willed his nephew William both Bush Hill and a tract of 179 acres adjoining the 356 on the Schuylkill. As son and nephew, William inherited, in sum, a single plot of 535 acres on the west bank of the Schuylkill. Thanks to his grandfather, father, and uncle, William virtually owned what we now call West Philadelphia. The Woodlands, the name of these 535 acres, west across the river, and not that of Bush Hill, north of the city, would eventually survive. With much land east of the Schuylkill owned and settled, opportunities for major land owning were moving from east to west.

Although Bush Hill still served as the final resting place of William's grandfather, father and uncle, it had less potential, by its size, than the Woodlands. By analogy, although William's grandfather Andrew shone as a luminary in the early history of Philadelphia, William had inherited so much land from his grandfather's vast holdings that he has influenced the shape of the city as much as any other Philadelphian after William Penn. Long after Penn's surveyor, Thomas Holme, laid out the plan of old Philadelphia, William Hamilton laid out its first grand suburb in West Philadelphia. Grandfather Andrew made possible his grandson's life as William of the Woodlands, whose life as lord of the manor his grandfather could only have imagined.

Grandfather Andrew also passed on to his son James and to his grandson William one loyalty that eventually drove a wedge between them and the progress of American democracy. Because of the family's "loyalty and obedience to His Most sacred Majesty King George," James fled to New York City with the British after 1776, and died there in 1783. William, though considered by some to be a traitor to the patriot cause, was lucky, because Philadelphia did not take after blood-soaked Paris in the aftermath of the French Revolution. Family and breeding did matter and he managed to retain his property by keeping a low profile. In practice, however, democracy did not mean much to him. Since his father's death, William of the Woodlands had been following the fate of his family as landed gentry above the common herd.

William's uncle James had toured England in 1746. Like him, William set out in 1784 on his Grand Tour for two years. As the lord of such a baronial estate on the west bank of the Schuylkill, he traveled through England so that he might learn how best to play his role as the lord of the manor. He visited every grand house worth visiting, and then consulted architects about plans for his own, which he would build back home. When he returned, he lived at Bush Hill, in 1788 and 1789, while he was building the home that has survived as the mansion of The Woodlands. He cultivated The Woodlands even more grandly, and more grandly out of his time, than his uncle James had cultivated Bush Hill. Imagine the incongruity of this Anglophile lord of the manor playing the grand *seigneur* in young America. William of the Woodlands was surviving as a relic of the colonial era before 1776.

In 1790, when William started living at the Woodlands as its cultured lord, he also started managing Bush Hill as its harried landlord. These two histories started in the last decade of the eighteenth century, after he had returned from England in 1786, built his mansion from 1788 to 1789, and settled into his life as William of the Woodlands. By his association with Bush Hill and The Woodlands from 1790 until his death in 1813, we can follow him pursuing his own idyl at The Woodlands and managing his family's property at Bush Hill.

William, Landlord of Bush Hill

At first, William had the good luck of having a distinguished tenant at Bush Hill: John Adams rented it in 1790. He was serving as George Washington's Vice President in Philadelphia, while it was the temporary capital city of the nation from 1790 to 1800. Adams' wife Abigail commented on the beautiful view and gardens in her new home: "We have a fine view of the whole city from our windows; a beautiful grove behind the house, through which there is a spacious gravel walk, guarded by a number of marble statues, whose genealogy I have not yet studied." Facetiously, she mentions the possibility of studying the "genealogy" of the garden statues that probably represented classical gods and goddesses. She also had the opportunity to study the genealogy of the family's ancestors in the Hamiltons' cemetery, but she did not have much time to pursue either study. Abigail and John enjoyed their view from the hill for only a year, before they moved into town to be closer to the work and social life of the capital, often praised as the Athens of America. Perhaps they sought the safety of the city after they heard the story of William and his niece being held up by highwaymen in 1787, as they were returning home.

After his first tenant moved into Philadelphia, William advertised Bush Hill to let throughout the 1790's: "The Mansion House at Bush Hill with fifteen acres of the adjoining ground is to be rented. Enquire of W. Hamilton, The Woodlands" (*Aurora General Advertiser*, August 23, 1793). He was probably hoping for another tenant equal in distinction to John Adams, but Providence had quite another plan. It would soon take him from a feast to what he might at first have regarded as a grim taste of famine. Just after this advertisement appeared in

The caption of this picture in the *Universal Magazine*, 1787, three years before Hamilton settled into The Woodlands, designates Bush Hill as "the seat of William Hamilton."

August, Bush Hill was serving by September as a hospital in the yellow fever epidemic.

Before Bush Hill Hospital had a proper management, Philadelphians were at first calling it a house of death instead of a hospital. In historical memory, its use as a hospital in this dire time gave Bush Hill special fame in the annals of Philadelphia. Suffering and death, however, hung at first like a pall over the property; and William had to deny some rumors that the victims of the epidemic had been buried on site: "The Mansion House and Offices to be let, with ten or twelve acres of the adjoining ground. Some prejudices have been formed from a groundless report that a number of dead were, during the late fever, buried within the enclosure. W. Hamilton, at the Woodlands (*Aurora General Advertiser*, May 7, 1795). The presence of his family's burial ground on the hill perhaps sparked these rumors. He assured the public that the dead lay in the potter's fields of the city's squares.[47]

By 1795, William tried to recover from the economic crisis of the epidemic. Lowering his sights, he had success in making his uncle and grandfather's home a pleasure garden. It made sense for the general public to pay admission to enjoy as a resort what a wealthy man did not want to lease as a home. Bush Hill had a suitable location, far enough outside the city to offer pastoral pleasures, but not too far for convenient access. Many such resorts would offer a breath of country air to city-dwellers. At this time, other enterprising entrepreneurs were advertising pleasure gardens on the Schuylkill as rivals of Vauxhall Gardens on the Thames.

The first entrepreneurs started ambitiously:

> Messrs. Bates and Darley of the New Theatre, respectfully inform the citizens of Philadelphia and its environs, that they have taken the manor house and grounds of Bush Hill (the property of William Hamilton, Esq.) and are now preparing to open them by subscription, for the general accommodation and amusement of the public under the name of the PENNSYLVANIA GARDENS AND HOTEL (*Inquirer*, May 7, 1797).

These two musicians were offering "a concert of vocal and instrumental music, after the manner of the public gardens in Paris, London, *etc*. Admission, half a Dollar" (*Inquirer*, July 7, 1797). Bates, who had performed on the London stage and Darley, at Vauxhall, were soliciting subscriptions in the hope that they might have money in advance. Collecting money up front by subscriptions would put their first balance sheet in the black,—investors beware!

Their first efforts met with success. A reviewer praised their performance, its venue, and "the partiality of our fair country-women for this elegant place of amusement." His praise rose to hyperbole: "No public place in or near London equals Bush Hill in natural beauty, and Bates and Darley have given it every artificial aid, which imagination . . . and a brilliant illumination can effect. . . . It cannot fail of attracting all the elegance and fashion of the city, making Bush Hill as famous as Vauxhall of England" (*Aurora General Advertiser*, June 24, 1797). Bush Hill's Anglophile landlord was importing a bit of London's sophistication to Philadelphia!

Hamilton's delight would last no longer than John Adams' lease. Darley, parting company with Bates after one season, tried to succeed on his own: "Mr. Darley informs his friends and the public that on Monday, March 5, Bush-Hill, House and Gardens, will be reopened as a tavern under his sole direction" (*Aurora General Advertiser,* March 21, 1798). How the mighty have fallen!—in less than a year, Philadelphia's Vauxhall had become a "tavern." Darley was only making a vain effort to fend off his creditors, because his hopes in the Spring ended in a sheriff's sale by the Winter: "Sheriff's Sale, December 12, 1798; unexpired lease, a large quantity of lamps, a large organ, all the board fence containing about 100,00 feet of planks and oak posts, ornamented boxes, benches and tables, sealed and taken in execution as the property of Messrs. Bates and Darley (*Aurora General Advertiser,* December 17, 1798). Alas!—the pathetic vestiges of what had delighted "the elegance and fashion of the city;" and, of course, William Hamilton's "unexpired lease" in red on his accounts.

William Cobbett (1763–1835) reported in his memoirs that both these "diverting vagabonds" owed him money, and ended up in debtors' prison. (Cobbett, at that time, living in Philadelphia in exile from Britain, was running a bookshop.) They left prison on parole only long enough to give a performance. "When the play was over, and they began to scent the morning air," he joked, "they, like ghosts, returned to their prison house." In the drama of William Hamilton's enterprise on Bush Hill, Bates and Darley, like vampires, drained him of profit and splashed his books with red ink.

At first, having Bates and Darley as tenants must have given Hamilton genuine pleasure. One delight from his idyllic days in London was setting up in his backyard! For this Anglophile, John Adams' tenancy must have seemed dully democratic by contrast. Next Spring, back down to earth, he tried to find a tenant, any tenant, for immediate occupancy: "The mansion House at Bush-Hill, with a garden and about eighteen acres of land, to be let and entered on immediately. For terms apply to William Hamilton, The Woodlands" (*Inquirer,* April 22, 1799). After another year and finding no tenant, he advertised his ancestral home, like Darley, as a "tavern" and hoped that someone would rent it either as a Public House or a home: "To Be Let, Bush-Hill Tavern . . . either for a country seat or a Public House" (*Aurora General Advertiser,* April 2, 1802). Either alternative could save his balance sheet.

Finally, Bush Hill's "natural beauty" succeeded in attracting another theatrical entrepreneur. In 1803, for a final, literally, brilliant display, Hamilton leased the mansion and grounds to Lozout & Brown. J. E. Lozout, a pyrotechnist from France and Germany, advertised an exhibition of "Fire Works at Bush Hill." The first display dazzled spectators with "a battle between suns and stars, a piece of the greatest brilliancy." In intermissions, "an excellent band" performed pieces punctuated by an occasional "rocket blast" (*Aurora General Advertiser*, July 20, 1803). Perhaps the rockets punctuated the band's performance of Handel's "Music for the Royal Fireworks." If the band did not delight Hamilton by playing Handel, the gate, at long last, pleased him by returning a profit.

In 1805, after the fireworks, Bush Hill drew its life from the countryside. It attracted a society of cattle grazers and drovers for practical purposes: "Bush Hill Mansion House Hotel now opened as a place of entertainment, under the patronage of the Society for Improving the Breed of Cattle. Its elevated, airy and pleasant situation, and short distance from the city, render it a very agreeable place of recreation for dinner and tea parties, *etc*." (*Aurora General Advertiser*, July 3, 1811). By 1811, the society was advertising its sixth annual fair. It was also sponsoring an annual fair in November, at which cattlemen and farmers might sell horses, cattle, sheep or swine, in addition to attending the society's shows of breeding stock. "Every convenience as respects enclosures, hay, etc. will be provided. There is also a large tavern on the spot where those who attend the show and fair may be well accommodated" (*Aurora General Advertiser*, October 11, 1811). The gardens, frequented in 1797, by "all the elegance and fashion of the city," now hosted genteel farmers, the likes of Richard Peters (1744–1828) and John Hare Powel (1786–1856). What amounts of the good earth would they tramp into the "Bush Hill Mansion House Hotel"!

In the yellow fever epidemic of 1793, Bush Hill had use because it hovered just above the city. Proximity also made it a convenient place of resort, close to the city; and a meeting place for cattlemen selling their stock, midway between city and country. After the 1790's, the city that was distant, when the elder Andrew Hamilton first acquired the property in 1726, was growing closer in the 1800's,—and the country was growing farther away. Before the one final success of Bush Hill as a place of resort for fireworks, William was planning to "improve" it as a suburb of the city:

> At Bush Hill, the mansion house is to be let, with about 20 acres of adjoining lands. Also, some lots (from 3 to 5 acres each) to be let on improving leases for years, situated on the high grounds next to Francis's Lane, affording views of the city and of the Delaware. Likewise, a number of lots to be let on ground rent, on Vine and Callowhill streets, both eastward and westward of Broad street. Apply to William Hamilton, The Woodlands (*Aurora General Advertiser*, July 7, 1800).

Like a good realtor, Hamilton described the neighborhood. He had laid out lots on the edge of Bush Hill, along Francis's Lane (a boundary of Francisville and later Fairmount Avenue) to the north, and between Vine and Callowhill streets to the south. From this property, Samuel Breck reported that William's heirs derived $36,000 a year in rent, until they were forced to put the Woodlands up for sale after the they lost the lease for these rents in 1820 (*Diary*, August 3, 1820). William had taken the first steps in the development of Bush Hill as a residential and industrial neighborhood that would not develop fully until the 1850's, forty years after his death.

When William died on June 5, 1813, his obituary praised his "noble mansion," The Woodlands, as the home of his "frank, affable hospitality," his "good taste and judgement in fine arts," and his "very general knowledge of botany." This eulogy of "William of the Woodlands," concluded by mentioning Bush Hill as the site of his burial: "interred in the family burying place at Bush Hill" (*United States Gazette*, June 16, 1813). Before he joined his father, uncle, and grandfather in the family plot, their ancestral seat had given him as much predicament as profit. Perseverance in developing his family's property took its toll.

William of The Woodlands

While William endured frustrations in maintaining his grandfather's estate, he was developing the Woodlands with aristocratic aplomb. In the beginning of his ownership, when he inherited the property at age 2, The Woodlands existed only in the stars of his destiny. Twelve years later, still just a farm, its first notice in a newspaper advertised "a light bay horse" wandering astray into "the Plantation of William Hamilton in Blockley Township, in Philadelphia County." "The owner," the notice continued, "proving his property, and paying charges to the subscriber, living on the premises, may have him again" (*Pennsylvania Gazette*, May 31, 1759). Specifically, Richard Crean, "the subscriber," living "on the premises," ran the "plantation." Young William Hamilton had better things to do than to take care of strays. He was living with his uncle at Bush Hill or with his mother in town, and starting his life as a gentleman. In 1759, at age 14, he was studying to receive his "degree of Bachelor of Arts," three years later, from "the College in this city," at the age of 17 (*Pennsylvania Gazette*, May 27, 1762).

By the time he was 33, he had a sharp eye for fine horses, especially when a horse thief had stolen one of them:

> Twenty-six pounds <sterling> reward. Stolen last night from the stable of William Hamilton, on his farm between the Middle and Lower Ferries, a handsome yellowish bay horse; he is an excellent chair-horse, and trots, paces and canters under the saddle . . . Was carried off at the same time, a well finished plated bridle bit (20 shillings for the bridle), having black double reins, and head-stall fronted with green and white bindings, also a half worn saddle stitched with silver wire, and saddle cloth blue and whiter striped . . . Five pounds for securing the thief, so that he may be brought to justice (*Pennsylvania Packet*, August 25, 1778).

No time wasted to catch this horse thief: the day the horse was stolen, William wrote a notice and sent it into town for publication the next day. We can sense his outrage. He obviously loved the stolen horse and listed its talents through a long sentence, more discriminating in description than in style. Introducing this description of his horse and its tack, he refers simply to his "farm" without the dignity of a title. Of course, he did not need to describe his farm, since no one had stolen it.

In this episode, we can appreciate young William's interests. In 1778, a decade before his inspiration in England and his return home to fulfill his vision, he was raising horses on his "farm." (A young man in the twentieth century would value his car more than the home where he kept it.) As part of his reputation as William of the Woodlands, William the Equestrian was confidently advertising his fine taste in horses and his indignation at a horse thief,—"may he be brought to justice." He had set this building block firmly in the foundation of a proper lord of the manor. In the future, he would announce his position as the lord of the manor by signing notices as "William Hamilton, The Woodlands."

William Hamilton's life as a gentleman took horsemanship as one building block in its edification. After he had built it, only William Bingham in Philadelphia could rival either his edifice or his edification. For that matter, no other gentleman had concentrated as much as he had. Unlike Bingham, he was content to be William of the Woodlands and nothing else. With his hands full in cultivating his house and garden in the countryside, he did not, extraordinarily, own a house in town.

Guests may sometimes admire the grand facade of a mansion as its grandest part. Hamilton's guests, however, once past the portico and into the "Reception Hall" of the Woodlands, could marvel at two oval rooms on either side, and a Ball Room in the manner of Robert Adam. As a student of ancient Roman architecture, Adam had learned to complement every right angle with a curve, so that the eye could find no dead ends. No other home in Philadelphia could match this sophistication.

When William toured England, he learned that aristocrats worked as hard on their gardens as they did on their mansions. Before he returned home, he wrote to his secretary about his hope for a garden: "Having observed with attention the nature, variety & extent of the plantations of shrubs, trees & fruits & consequently admired them, I shall (if God grant me a safe return to my own country) endeavor to make it smile in the same useful & beautiful manner." In William's letter to his secretary, he did not mention the beauty of English gardens, but "the nature, variety & extent" of their "shrubs, trees & fruits." Back in his estate, he developed a professorial knowledge of botany with the enthusiasm of a dilettante. When Manasseh Cutler visited, William assured him that "there was not a rare plant in Europe, Asia, Africa, from China and the islands in the South Sea, of which he had any account, which he had not procured." Although this boast may seem hyperbole, Thomas Jefferson had such confidence in his ability that he persuaded the American Philosophical Society to entrust to Hamilton's care the seeds gathered by the the Lewis and Clark Expedition. Andrew Jackson Downing (1815–1852) called William's gardens and those at Gore Place "the two best specimens of the modern style . . . in the earliest period of Landscape Gardening." On the other side of the timeline, he called the Peters' gardens at Belmont "a noted specimen of the ancient school of landscape gardening" (*A Treatise on the Theory and Practice of Landscape Gardening, Adapted to North America*, 1841).

One visitor to the Woodlands at the end of the eighteenth century quipped that Mr. Hamilton was "interested only in his house, his hothouse, and his Madeira (Julian Ursyn Niemcewicz, *Under Their Vine and Fig Tree: Travels through America*). Hamilton's passions "only" filled his life and delighted his guests: together, they would enjoy the beauty and utility of his peerless garden, then a meal in his uniquely beautiful dining room, and finally the edification of consulting botanical texts, in his parlor or library, over Madeira from his cellar. Only in the company of William of the Woodlands, could Americans enjoy this enchantment, which inspired one woman to write a poem:

> Then, while within the Woodlands fair domain,
> The Muses rove, and Classic pleasures reign;
> For distant climes no longer will I sigh,
> No longer wish to distant realms to fly.
>
> (John C. Shields, *The American Aeneas: Classical Origins of the American Self*, 2001).

In addition to building an impressive mansion and planting a comprehensive garden, William also "improved" his estate, as he had done at Bush Hill,—but with a significant difference. Four years after he advertised lots for rent on the edges of Bush Hill, he advertised "building lots for sale" on The Woodlands: "The situation in point of health, beauty and convenience, is certainly inferior to none in the vicinity, being highly elevated, commanding fine views of the city, . . . enjoying every advantage of wholesome air, most excellent water, and elegant prospects" (*Aurora General Advertiser*, January 27, 1804). He improved Bush Hill for profit, but he took pride in improving The Woodlands, because he was creating Hamiltonville, an idyllic community after his own heart.

Do not underestimate William Hamilton's aspirations! Any lord of the manor should be able to view his village nestled in the valley beneath his eminence. To enhance the village that bore his name, he gave land for "a commodious and substantial School House in the village of Hamilton, on the lot granted for that purpose" (*Aurora General Advertiser*, April 1, 1812). He also gave land for a Presbyterian (Walnut Street Presbyterian) and an Episcopal church (St. Mary's), but he required that the Episcopal church build a tower on the south side of its sanctuary that he could see from his home. He had considered every refinement. "Inferior to none" described anything he did.

No Philadelphian has ever matched William Hamilton's aristocratic taste and accomplishment. He stands out as a unique example of a Philadelphia gentleman, but his life, on the other hand, typifies an epoch in the city's history. Deriving strength from his roots, he could not have attained his uniqueness without his grandfather, father, and uncle. Family histories typically trace lines of accomplishment, but the Hamiltons had a line unique in the history of Philadelphia. Andrew Hamilton's association with William Penn's family gave him advantages which he passed down to William, who could live a life like the Penns' without the stigma of their loyalty to the British monarchy. (Only the three generations of the Logans,—James, James Jr. and grandson George,—offers a parallel, but James only served as William Penn's secretary, not as prestigious a post as that of Andrew Hamilton, his lawyer.)

When William Hamilton died in 1813, he joined his father, uncle and grandfather in their burial plot on Bush Hill, but his family moved this plot, by 1850, to a vault in the yard of Christ Church. A small family cemetery had become incongruous in a neighborhood of row homes and an impediment to its improvement. Bush Hill has only survived as a name in the history of this neighborhood, now filled with respectable houses constructed after 1850. The Hamiltons left no remnant of the site of their first home.

William Hamilton's Bush Hill survives only in historical memory and in the name of Hamilton street in the modern neighborhood.[48] His spirit lives on in the growth of Hamiltonville in West Philadelphia. The mansion crowns the hill above a cemetery. The neighborhood, in its heyday, became the best suburb of the old city because of William of the Woodlands and his village stretching beneath it.

CHAPTER 11

Bartram's Garden

LIKE ALL FARMERS, John Bartram (1699–1777) hoed many a row every day, until one day he left it to look at a daisy: "I plucked the pretty flower, viewing it with more closeness than common farmers are wont to bestow upon a weed." After bestowing this uncommonly close look on a weed, he felt ashamed: "What a shame to have spent so many years in tilling the earth and destroying so many flowers and plants, without being acquainted with their structures and their uses!" When he told his wife about this new focus, she tried to nip it in the bud,—she called it his "new scheme." Only "opulent" gentlemen could indulge such fancies. She overlooked one aspect of her husband's new focus: by their natures, both "opulent" gentlemen and "common farmers" do not usually deign to "bestow" a second thought "upon a weed".

Was his wife right? Was her husband just impulsive and not inspired?

At first, who could tell?—but John knew that he had to give it a try. The following Wednesday, he hired a man to hoe his rows, while he went to Philadelphia in search of a book. He returned with a botanical text and a Latin grammar. Three months later, with the help of a schoolmaster, he had learned enough Latin to understand the language of botany. His bud started to bloom: "Then I began to botanise all over my farm" (Crèvecoeur, *Letters*). His special focus on weeds,—of course, native American ones,—allowed him to understand what made the New World uniquely new. It also made him and his house and garden uniquely famous.

This story explains the origin of Bartram's fame, but it's not the only one. When a son of the earth, like John Bartram, has gained fame, its first bloom may be as difficult to explain as the mysteriously common earth from which it grew. A mystery veils the facts behind the story just told about John Bartram's awakening to the world of plants. Its author created it as much from myth as from fact.[49] Five years after Bartram had died, Hector St. John de Crèvecoeur told this story in the next-to-last chapter of his *Letters from an American Farmer* (1782). He fictionalized it as a story told by a Russian gentleman.

In his introduction, Crèvecoeur also idealized its context: "Examine this flourishing province <of Pennsylvania>," he wrote, "in whatever light you will, the eyes as well as the mind of a European traveller are equally delighted; because a diffusive happiness appears in every part." Crèvecoeur chose Bartram, whose name he disguises as Bertram, as his model for the "diffusive happiness" that Europeans often praised, but sometimes envied and belittled. Bertram represents the best of American meritocracy; but does Bertram really represent Bartram? The real Bartram also helped to create his own myth by emphasizing, a little disingenuously, his origins as a poor, uneducated boy. This humble pose gave him an excuse for not learning Latin as well as he should have!

Later authors improved on Crèvecoeur's myth-making. His story dated the epiphany over the daisy to Bertram's first marriage which ended with the death of Bartram's wife in 1728, the same year Bartram purchased his farm on the Schuylkill River. Details of marriage and domesticity do not suit the myth of a hero, who should experience his epiphany at birth, in the cradle, or at least in youth. One hundred and thirty four years after Bartram's death, a Philadelphia clergyman properly mythologized his epiphany—or was it just his focus?

> One day, when about 16, he was hoeing and at the end of the row, he was attracted by some wild flowers in the fence corner. He picked up a bunch of daisies, the kind indigenous to American soil . . . and marveled at their general construction . . . When his work was done he asked his father what kind of books told about flowers, and was told that works on botany treated of them. He had never heard the name before, but went to his room and took all the money he had and set out

for Philadelphia, ten miles away to buy a botany. That night, as a Dock street bookseller was about to close his shutters, he was astonished at the sight of an uncouth, dusty youth, who wanted to buy a book on botany. There was not one in the colony in English, but he had one in Latin. Young Bartram bought the huge tome, and a Latin grammar for a sum of money that seemed a fortune to him, and reached home at midnight. He sat up all night studying the Latin grammar. He took the book to the field every day. . . . (*Inquirer*, March 23, 1891).

This story pulses with young American blood—no taking off from work and hiring a hand, no nagging, faint-hearted old lady, and no difficulty or tedium of language study. Just in case it has not impressed enough, the pious narrator concludes with a superlative: "I know of no example in all history where persistent effort under difficulties produced such results." Surely, the clergyman filed this story among his edifying Sunday School lessons! It lent edifying dignity to John Bartram's biography. Having won, at the end of his life, a special place in American history, he might have a beginning worthy of the end.

For the moment, however, let's set aside the dilemma between myth or fact in origins, and let John Bartram's earthy goodness sculpt stone for his home and cultivate native weeds.

BOTH THE "RUSSIAN GENTLEMAN" and the Philadelphia clergyman praised John Bartram's origins as an American natural, born for the study of nature. In the full flower of Bartram's career, Carl Linnaeus (1707–1778), the inventor of modern taxonomy, most famously, called him "the greatest natural botanist in the world." "Natural" describes an autodidact, having knowledge and understanding without formal education. Even in adulthood, Bartram had fame without much fortune, because he preferred learning to earning.

Friends helped him to learn, because he had earned their friendship. In 1729, for example, James Logan bought him a copy of Parkinson's *Herbal*. In a letter, he described the recipient of his gift: "a worthy person, worthy of a heavier purse than fortune has yet allowed him . . . No man in these parts is so capable of serving you, but none can worse bear the loss of his time without due consideration" (*The Times*, May 30, 1896). Seventeen years later, the first mention of Bartram in a Philadelphia newspaper mentions another gift: "Mr. John Bartram, Botanist, informs us that he has had two fair specimens of the English ash-color'd ground liver-wort, sent him by Dr. Dillenius, chief professor of Botany at Oxford" (*Pennsylvania Gazette*, March 27, 1746). Both friends like James Logan and Dr. Dillenius happily gave him the help that he either had deserved or earned by "serving" in the past. Their relationship with Bartram was not a one-way street of charity.

Not as famously as Carl Linnaeus, but just as significantly, William Dunlap gives John Bartram's son William (1739–1823) the title "nature's nobleman" in a passage that contextualizes its definition: "We approached an old man who, with a rake in his hand, was breaking up clods in a tulip bed. His hat was old and flapped near his face, his coarse shirt was seen near his neck, as he wore no cravat or kerchief. His waistcoat and breeches were both of leather, and his shoes were tied with leather strings . . ." Did George Washington or Thomas Jefferson wear a "cravat" when they were breaking up their clods? For that matter, did Washington or Jefferson ever even break up clods? Maybe they did, but nature's nobleman certainly did, but he did not wear a cravat while he was doing it. Beyond the simplicity and rusticity of Bartram's clothing, Dunlap goes on to describe his conversation: "He entered into conversation with the ease and politeness of nature's nobleman. His countenance was expressive of benignity and happiness" (Dunlap, *Diary*, May 9, 1797). The "benignity and happiness" of nature's nobleman speak with a native eloquence of goodness that outshines the learned eloquence of mere words.

Linnaeus' praise of the father as the "natural botanist," and Dunlap's slightly left-handed praise of the son as "nature's nobleman" describe a family whose clothing and bearing, education and conversation bespoke earnest simplicity and sincerity. Such men would also cultivate a garden sincerely and earnestly but simply without brilliance. Such men also would win more friends than profit. John, especially, had won friends on both sides of the Atlantic and enjoyed fame, and some remuneration that these friendships brought. Who knows, for example, what profit he might have reaped from Dr. Dillenius' gift of "two fair specimens of the English ash-color'd ground liver-wort." Most significantly, both for fame and for profit, his friends secured his appointment as botanist to King George III in 1765, for which he received a stipend of fifty pounds a year. It financed expeditions for botanical research and collection.

WHAT SORT OF GARDEN did nature's nobleman and the natural botanist cultivate? Highfalutin' folk dwell in high places; and nature's noblemen make the most of what's left below. By their nature, they cultivate daisies on the lowland that the upscale folk upstream might scorn. In advertising Philadelphia to investors, William Penn had praised it as high and dry, because his surveyor, Thomas Holme, had placed the city above the marshes at the confluence of the Schuylkill with the Delaware. For his family's estate, he had reserved even higher ground north of the city, along the Schuylkill river. His friends and the wealthy men of the eighteenth and nineteenth centuries lined up their estates on ground higher yet above his. Nature's noblemen enjoyed no such upward mobility. In 1728, without the resource to purchase land in the Penns' neighborhood upstream, John bought a

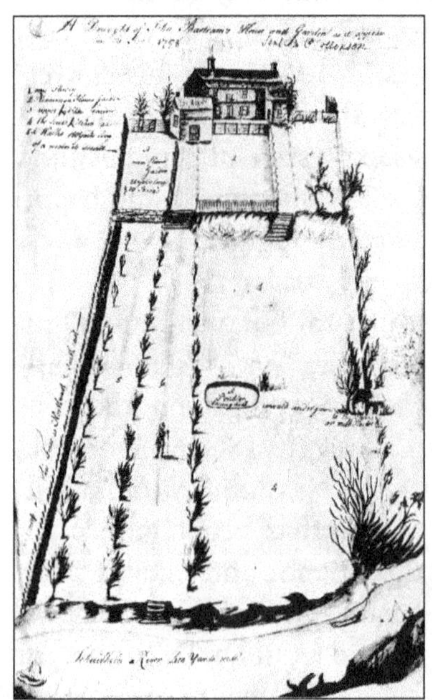

Bartram's map of his garden in 1758

farm of 112 acres downstream, far below the high ground. He then got down with his neighbors to share the hard work of reclaiming its marshes as meadows.

A good farm has fertile fields that made it worthy of its title. But a nice farm has something pleasant, even if it is just a kitchen garden to one side of the main house, with a few flowers for color. For his garden, John reserved about six acres in back but mostly in front, of his house. In 1758, William drew a map, which probably represented what he thought his family's nice garden should look like: a kitchen garden, next to flower gardens, both in front of the house, separated by a terrace, and then an allée of trees surrounding its main path, passing by a pond, on its way down to the river. Both George Washington at Mount Vernon on the Potomac, and his friend, Richard Peters at Belmont on the Schuylkill, planted an allée of trees,—it was a must in a garden of any pretension.

Crèvecoeur, of course, idealized Bertram's garden: "small but decent . . . bearing the marks of perfect order and regularity, which in rural affairs, always indicate a prosperous industry." Ten years after John's death, when Manasseh Cutler visited William in 1787, he found just the opposite of "perfect order": "everything is badly arranged for they are placed neither ornamentally nor botanically, but seem to be jumbled together in heaps" (*The Times*, April 19, 1891). In the same year, George Washington visited to buy some plants. He left with some plants for Mount Vernon, but with a low opinion of the garden, which, he said, "was not laid off with much taste." In whatever degree, perfect or imperfect, tasteful or tasteless, the Bartrams' garden represented "evidently a labor of love, hardly the product of mere bought labor" (*Harper's*, February, 1880). "Evidently," also, John and William had better things to do than to emulate their wealthy neighbors up stream.

The man, whom Linnaeus praised as "the greatest natural botanist in the world," and his son, whom Dunlap left-handedly praised as "nature's nobleman," designed a house and garden that have survived to explain their titles. Even in 1770, and especially after 250 years, house and garden need some explanation. The garden no longer grows to explain how the famous botanist cultivated it. Archeologists need to dig it up to explain that. The house still stands, true to the nature of the botanist who built it and the nobleman who lived in it. Sons of the earth can admire it.

For the homes up the Schuylkill, on the lofty banks of its cultured neighborhood, the late Renaissance architect Palladio set a standard. Mount Pleasant and Cliveden in Germantown best exemplify his design. He based much of his architecture on the classical orders, Doric, Ionic, and Corinthian, but especially, on the Ionic. In the suburbs of Venice, he usually designed villas with the Ionic order, appropriately suburban between the rustic simplicity of the Doric and the urban luxuriance of the Corinthian. With stone hewn by his own hands,—and help from his sons and hired hands,—John set up a central Ionic column flanked on each side of the porch by Ionic pilasters. Complementing these hand-carved columns, the windows have hand-carved baroque surrounds. One outbuilding incorporates into its wall fragments of a Doric entablature, with a quaint triglyph and metope. Palladio sometimes combined the Doric with the Ionic order. From the earth, John Bartram hewed a masterpiece of eighteenth century folk art, the likes of which exists nowhere else.

From the earth also, John hewed his religious beliefs which he literally hewed on the stone beneath the window sill of his study:

It is God Alone Almyty Lord
the Holy One by Me Ador'd
John Bartram 1770

As a devotee of God's *flora*, he did not acknowledge Him in the Son and Holy Ghost of the Trinity. Over the door of his greenhouse, which he built in 1761, he had also inscribed two lines from Alexander Pope's, *Essay on Man*, Epistle 4:

Slave to no sect, who takes no private road,
But looks through Nature up to Nature's God.

To continue the quotation, Bartram portrayed himself as the man who "pursues that chain which links the immense design, / Joins heaven and earth, and mortal and divine." This man of the earth was following the great chain of being from earth through heaven, but his earthy roots kept him from following the great chain of the Holy

Spirit from the Epiphany through history. He had expressed his Unitarian belief in his Quaker Meeting so consistently,—and probably, so insistently,—that it disowned him in 1758.

He advertised the positive belief of his Unitarian heterodoxy beneath the window sill of his study.

John Bartram was so accomplished and so beloved that although his son William could never outshine his brilliance, he could also find security in its afterglow. One notice in the *Pennsylvania Gazette* in 1785 indicated this profit: "Whereas William Bartram, of the township of Kingsessing, and that of Pennsylvania, being duly sensible of the signal indulgence shown by his creditors, in forbearing to distress him, thinks it his duty, in this public manner, to acknowledge the same, and to make them all compensation in his power . . ." (*Pennsylvania Gazette*, April 27, 1785). Eight years after his father's death, William was acknowledging financial trouble. On the other hand, the family name and its friends allowed him to enjoy their "signal indulgence." Since no further notices appeared, we can assume that he satisfied his creditors. Publishing a popular book of his *Travels* in 1791 gave him some financial stability. The Bartrams' spirit continued to protect his garden and inspire its patrons.

William left the commercialization of the garden to his brother, John Bartram, Jr. and John Jr.'s daughter, Ann. The following advertisement appeared in the Spring of 1810:

KINGSESSING GARDENS,
Near Gray's Ferry, four miles from the city.
JOHN BARTRAM AND SON,
Have to dispose of, as usual, at the lowest prices,
VARIETIES OF
TREES, ORNAMENTAL SHRUBS &
FLOWERING PLANTS
& PARTICULARLY . . . . .
They likewise put up for exportation, Growing Roots and Seeds of Trees, Shrubs and plants in the best order

(*Aurora General Advertiser*, April 7, 1810).

Renaming their property Kingsessing Garden established a little independence for John, Jr. and his son. Significantly, William's name does not appear as sharing in this venture. He was not a savvy man of business and faced the constraints of his restraint.

The Bartrams' ideals, thankfully, found patrons. With the death of John's granddaughter, Ann Bartram Carr (1779–1858) in 1858, the third and last generation that cultivated the family garden had departed, but John's spirit still hovered over the place. In 1850, eight years before her death, Andrew M. Eastwick (1811–1879) purchased her family's garden. Eastwick, having spent some of the happiest hours of his youth in the garden, resolved to preserve it (*Inquirer*, May, 1888). But, alas!—five years after his death, the property was again in danger of "improvement," the word used in the nineteenth century to describe clearcutting a property and spreading a housing development over it. In the 1880's, some visitors came away with dire foreboding: "There is little doubt now that the once famous garden will soon be entirely obliterated. It is certain that the house will soon be demolished" (*Inquirer*, November, 1884).

Thomas Meehan (1826–1901) stood up to the plate. After training at Kew Gardens in London, Meehan had served for a few years as Eastwick's chief gardener. Naturally, he was the best man to take up Eastwick's resolve, even though he had gone on to edit horticultural magazines, establish his own nursery, and serve as vice-president of Philadelphia's Academy of Natural Sciences. Taking a job that established public policy, he served on Philadelphia's Common Council from 1877 until 1888.

As he served on the Council, he kept Bartram's Garden in mind, because his seat on the Common Council served his plan to preserve it. Of course, he was not the only person to believe that all Philadelphians had good reason to do so: "There are but few more delightful and romantic spots in and about Philadelphia," said *The Times*, "which at the same time possess an intense historical interest, than Bartram Park" (October 5, 1895). For many Philadelphians, the history of their city consisted only of echoes, ever more faint as time passed. The places themselves needed to be preserved so that the echoes might not fade. "Philadelphia has done better than any other community," but the task could never be finished (*The Times*, November 10, 1895). Bartram's Garden forged one link in the chain that linked Philadelphia's citizens to their past.

To add fuel to this plan, critics of Fairmount Park had complained consistently that only the wealthy with access to carriages could appreciate its beauty: "Poor people had neither the time nor the means to visit Fairmount Park" (*Inquirer*, May, 1888). Every citizen should have easy access to parks, they argued, because they provide a "breathing place to the people" (*Inquirer*, January, 1890). The city was starting with Bartram's Garden to provide parks throughout its neighborhoods.

In 1884, Meehan helped to introduce an ordinance for small parks that included Bartram's Garden as one of three properties. Friday March 13, 1891, almost seven years after Meehan's ordinance, the city took the famous garden into its park system. "The action of the city," *The Times* reported, "was not taken a moment too soon to save what is left of the old place . . . a wreck, a comparative ruin, a wreck of its former self" (March 14, 1891). One hundred and sixty-three years after John Bartram first bought his 112 acre farm, a small part of his labor of love took on new life for the people of Philadelphia.

"I KNOW OF NO EXAMPLE in all history," said the pious clergyman of John Bartram's origins, "where persistent effort under difficulties produced such results." The history of Bartram's Garden echoes the clergyman's superlative: The City of Brotherly Love can boast of no example in all of its history where the spirit of a single man and his family has similarly preserved its heritage. Crèvecoeur can also define this heritage: "Examine this flourishing province <of Pennsylvania>, in whatever light you will, the eyes as well as the mind of a European traveller are equally delighted; because a diffusive happiness appears in every part." "In every part," especially down river below the grand estates of William Penn's affluent neighborhood, the spirit of "brotherly love" has flourished.

John's descendants joined in the John Bartram Association to preserve the memory of their heritage and to meet at their ancestor's garden each year on June 2, his birthday. When they met in 1893, the

Inquirer announced their first reunion in "Bartram's Park" as that of the "The Four Hundred" (June 9, 1893). "The Four Hundred" alludes to Mrs. Astor's exclusive list of the four hundred élite families of New York City. John Bartram would have been amused and touched by his descendants' claiming his name as a badge of honor.

ESTATES IN THE CITY

CHAPTER 12

Samuel Powel, Landlord, and Lord of the Powel House and Powelton

In eighteenth century Philadelphia, the distinguished Powel family had three sequential Samuels, father, son and grandson:

> Samuel Powel (1673–1756), *obiit* age 82, "the rich carpenter,"
> Samuel Powel (1704–1759), *obiit* age 55, "the great builder,"
> Samuel Powel (1738–1793), *obiit* age 55.[50]

Samuel Powel (1738–1793), the third generation, rose on the shoulders of his father and grandfather to become the man whom history remembers as the mayor of Philadelphia, both before and after the Revolution, and the master and legendary host of the distinguished Powel House, 244 South Third street. His career was as distinguished as his home and its table, but he could never have boasted of being a self-made man. He enjoyed his privileged life and its success, because his father and grandfather had made him a member of Philadelphia's landed gentry.[51]

At the age of 17, May 25, 1756, Samuel matriculated at the recently founded College of Philadelphia.[52] Three years later, at the age of 20, having graduated, he continued his pursuit of knowledge by joining serious young Quakers in their "Society Meeting Weekly in Philadelphia for Their Mutual Improvement in Useful Knowledge." Very soon, having received his inheritance, after his father's demise, he set

Angelica Kauffman (1741–1807) painted this portrait of Samuel Powel in 1764, when he was 26 years old.

out to find more improvement on a Grand Tour in October of the next year. Extraordinarily, he toured for seven years, from 1760 to 1767, "lolling," he admitted, "in the lap of ease." "Rich, attractive and well spoken,"—one historian's description,—Powel paid his respects to such notables as George III, Pope Clement XIII, and The Sage of Ferney (Voltaire). Before his tour culminated in the pilgrimage to Rome, he was privileged to join the entourage of the younger brother of King George III. Among his mementos, he brought home his portrait by Angelica Kauffman.

Down to earth, with a little modesty, Powel conceded that his "good fortune" had surpassed his "merit" (Tatum, 10–11). Funded by his father and grandfather's wealth, he could have spent his life as a refined *dilettante*, "lolling in the lap" of "good fortune." And yet, his uncle advised that ten years' education and edification had quite satisfactorily improved this grandson of a wealthy carpenter. Perhaps Kauffman's portrait can give one clue for his motivation to return:

young Samuel Powel had building plans in hand. Once back home, he turned from improving himself to improving Philadelphia.

His grandfather, "the wealthy carpenter," and his father, "the great builder," and had laid foundations for these improvements both for Samuel and for Philadelphia. They had accumulated wealth in real estate, purchased with their profits from building and commerce. Before he was born, the *Pennsylvania Gazette* was announcing the arrival of ships at "Samuel Powel's Wharf" (September 5, 1734 and November 4, 1736). Most of their ninety properties in the city were south of Market street. In that area, Powel's father had built houses on Pine street, east of Second (*The Times*, September 12, 1899).

Once back in Philadelphia, Samuel started to tend the fortune that had financed his Grand Idyl. The *Pennsylvania Gazette* advertised his collecting rents from "sundry lots on Third and Laurel street between Walnut and Spruce" (May 24, 1770) and "sundry lots on Front and Third street" (December 26, 1771). Now he had the opportunity to appreciate the privilege of being "Philadelphia's largest landlord" (Brobeck, 424), as he collected the rents that had funded the education and edification of his privilege. (Picture the young dandy portrayed in Angelica Kauffman's portrait walking about the city with his rent book!) In eighteenth century Philadelphia, land made lords of landlords.[53]

Powel owned property at "Third and Laurel street," but he bought a house across the street for his family home after he married Elizabeth Willing (1743–1830) in 1769. By this purchase, he was taking his place in the enclave of Elizabeth's family, the Willings. An extraordinary woman, his wife Elizabeth, as a friend of George and Martha Washington, would leave her mark on the nation's history. Her father, Charles Willing (1710–1754), built the first house of this enclave on the block of west Third street between Walnut and Spruce. He had acquired this property from William Penn's family. Naturally, the alley that led to his home came to be known as Willings Alley. There, Charles lived with his wife and their eleven children. Across the alley, to the south, one of his daughters,—Elizabeth's older sister,—Mary Willing Byrd (1740–1814), and her husband, William Byrd III (1728–1777), lived in the house adjoining the Powels' for the first year of their marriage (1761–1762). Powel's brother-in-law, Thomas Willing (1731–1821), Charles' oldest son, had taken over as the head of the family after his father died at the age of 44 in 1754. Samuel's home now claims special fame as the Powel House, but it started its life as just one building, and not a particularly important one, in the Willings' enclave.[54]

In 1766, the notice of its sale advertised this property as 396 feet deep, the full length of the block between Third and Fourth streets. It also mentioned a brick stable, two stories high, 26 by 20 feet, facing Fourth (*Pennsylvania Gazette*, October 15, 1766). Powel had a cobblestone stable yard laid down in 1770 (Tatum, 85). He was making his property as useful as it was beautiful. By 1931, when Miss Frances Wister, with her Philadelphia Society for the Preservation of Landmarks, saved Samuel Powel's house from becoming a parking lot, the parcel of land that it occupied was 30 by 180 feet, less than half its original size.

Samuel and Elizabeth's home set a high standard for domestic elegance, but her niece, Anne Willing Bingham (1764–1801), and her husband, William Bingham (1752–1804), the wealthiest man in Philadelphia, outclassed any competition. In 1788, almost ten years after the Powels had moved into their home, Bingham built his mansion and surrounded it by a beautiful three acre garden that filled the block. It so stood out as the most impressive home in the city that Thomas Birch made it the center piece of one of his *Views of Philadelphia* in 1800. On the right, an octagonal tower attached to Powel's house sticks out between two trees.

The garden now in the side and back yards of the Powel House recalls the gardens of the Bingham mansion in the eighteenth century, but we would be mistaken in imagining Powel making his property only beautiful. In 1787, he published a notice in the *Pennsylvania Gazette* that gives us a different impression: "Strayed from the stable yard of the subscriber, in Fourth-street, between Walnut and Spruce-streets, on Wednesday evening, a red COW, supposed to be about nine years old . . . also a dark brown COW, almost black, about five years old, . . . whoever will deliver them to the subscriber, shall have FOUR DOLLARS Reward, paid by Samuel Powel" (*Pennsylvania Gazette*, June 20, 1787). What use are pretty flowers, if his kitchen needed fresh milk? Perhaps to mark the two sides of his *rus in urbe*, "country in the city," Powel built a brick wall to screen his house, up front on Third, and a wooden fence to keep the cow from getting loose, in back on Fourth.

In the eighteenth century, the country was so much closer to the city that it was sometimes virtually in it. Powel probably sent his two cows out to his own pasture without taking them far from their stable. In 1781, he advertised land, just south of Cedar, that is, South street, Philadelphia's southern boundary: "To be let, for the season or a term of years, about eighteen acres of very good pasture ground. Enquire of Samuel Powel" (*Pennsylvania Packet*, July 14, 1781). Five years later, having probably subdivided his tract of eighteen acres, he advertised "sundry lots of pasture ground, to be let, one of which is now nearly ready for mowing, adjoining to South street in the city. Enquire of Samuel Powel" (*Pennsylvania Packet*, June 8, 1786). In 1796, John Hill's "plan of the city of Philadelphia and its environs" shows open land south of Seventh and Cedar streets. Cows grazed on those fields, even if they did not belong to Samuel Powel.

POWEL'S BACK YARD, with its two dairy cows in the barn, next to the kitchen garden with its cabbages and asparagus (Tatum, p. 114), put a little country in back of his townhouse, but his friends were building mansions out back in the real country on the banks of the Schuylkill. In November, 1775, he joined them when he paid his brothers-in-law, Thomas Willing, and Tench Francis (1730–1800), husband of the elder Anne Willing (1744–1781), £1,675 for 97 acres on the west bank of the river, just north of the Market street ferry. He owned another property in Roxborough, for which he had planned a house "with a draftsman's precision" (Maxey, p. 21); but he made the nearer property his own by naming it Powelton. It was just far enough from the city to serve as his country retreat. From 1775 until his death in 1793, he improved it by putting up fences, spreading manure, plowing fields, stacking hay, draining marshes and clearing trees from the banks of the river. In 1786, he also constructed a barn (*Collection of Powel Family Papers* in the Library Company of Philadelphia). His beautiful townhouse on Third street only just started to be as useful as his farm across the river.

The cornucopia from the townhouse on Third and the farm across the Schuylkill was supplying the festive board of Samuel and Elizabeth Powel, the distinguished couple that history books celebrate. In addition to keeping his cornucopia overflowing, Powel held positions that qualified him to invite the notables of his day to enjoy it. Historians have attributed to him the distinction of being the last colonial mayor before the Revolution and the first mayor after it,—a paradigm of political aplomb. Newspapers of the day did not at first report his mayoralty in 1775. They did report his election as one of two alderman, just beneath the mayor in authority, in 1774 and 1775, but not at first his election as mayor. Aldermen had elected Samuel Rhoads to be the Mayor, according to the reports in the *Pennsylvania Gazette* (October 5, 1774). Samuel Powel, again, according to the *Gazette*, was elected an alderman in 1775, and Samuel Rhoads, again, elected Mayor (*Pennsylvania Gazette*, September 27, 1775). Just a week later, October 4, 1775, the *Gazette* reported Powel's election as mayor. Rhoads had withdrawn,—it was not uncommon for elected mayors to refuse the honor, or perhaps, the onus (Stern, 46),—and Powel was stepping in and up to fill the gap. By October, with the Revolutionary War begun and the Second Continental Congress meeting, Powel must have recognized this new and very special commitment.

The connection between Samuel's political and personal life tells stories about the life of the upper class during the Revolution in Philadelphia. Even a family dinner included a Founding Father, because Elizabeth's brother, Thomas Willing, attended both the First and Second Continental Congress in 1774 and 1775. George Washington, when he attended these congresses, dined consistently with the Powels. John Adams, after he had dined there on September 8, 1774, famously,—and a little facetiously,—wrote home to Abigail that he had partaken in a "most sinful feast." The sumptuous flow from the Powels' cornucopia impressed this unworldly Bostonian!

In the parlous times before and after 1776, associating with patriots like Washington and Adams did not make Powel immune to suspicion. His landowning class in Philadelphia had to make a difficult transition from colonialism to independence. Though never a Tory, Powel, with his friends and relatives, like James Wilson, Thomas

Willing, and Benjamin Chew, were members of the ruling élite that the common man suspected of loyalist sympathies (Tatum, p. 24). Imagine his dilemma. During his European idyl, for example, he purchased fine furnishings in London, which he shipped over to Philadelphia and displayed in his home. In the boycotts of British goods during the 1760's, local Philadelphia craftsmen resented this Anglophile patronage. For them, it represented too much Anglican favoritism and too little American patriotism (Tatum, p. 114). Such were the mutterings on the street. At his ease, in the Powels' parlor, however, George Washington sat on English mahogany chairs, just like the ones that he enjoyed in his parlor at Mount Vernon.

During the American Revolution, the citizenry of Philadelphia focused suspicion, specifically, on Samuel Powel, as the man who had been collecting all those rents. Chevalier de Chastellux, one of the Powels' guests when he was serving on Rochambeau's staff, mentioned it: Powel's "attachment to the common cause has hitherto appeared rather equivocal" (Tatum, 26). Francis Bailey (1744–1817), editor of *The Freemen's Journal*, suggested an obvious means of demonstrating loyalty. By "A CARD," that is, a public notice and request, in 1781, he skirts impertinence by reminding "the gentlemen" procuring "subscriptions" in support of the Revolution that they should wait "particularly" on Samuel Powel:

> A Citizen presents his compliments to the gentlemen who had the honor of being appointed by congress to procure a subscription, loan, &c., and he begs leave to remind them, that there are some gentlemen of large estates, which have suffered nothing by the war, and which are greatly improved in value by the arrival of these virtuous and distressed citizens: Such, for instance, is Samuel Powel, esq.[55] These may require to be waited on particularly, for as some of them may, or at least ought to be solicitous to shew that they are not enemies to us and our cause, their subscriptions will probably tell.

A community, which by its etymology shares munificence (community), requires that wealthy men, particularly, give "munificently" so that they may enjoy the re-muneration, not of money, but of reputation and trust. These men had a duty to buy war bonds, so to speak, especially when others' misfortune 'greatly improves' their good fortune. They cannot be neutral. They must contribute to show that they are not "enemies to us and our cause." Munificent contribution, Bailey continues, costs them very little:

> If they only subscribed the present advance of their rent rolls, it would do something, though nothing out of their pockets. At any rate, they would do wisely to show some proof of their attachment to us in the present unpromising state of British affairs, lest we be forced to recollect that their conduct subjects them to a suspicion of being on the list of Pennsylvania associators mentioned by Lord George Germain.

With luck, ships tossing about on the seven seas bring wealth; *terra firma* stays put and stays profitable. Samuel Powel collects rents on so many properties that his munificence would require no more than an expense out of pocket in monthly accounts. He would not need to draw anything from capital. In concluding, Bailey progresses from telling the government how to do its job to a few words about Powel's upper class privilege: Beside . . .

> the gentleman whom I mentioned, has one of the largest city estates—has no children—has traveled for improvement—has had a liberal education—and has not been reckoned a violent whig. Each of these consideration ought to have some weight with him: all of them ought to produce liberal effects: I therefore entreat that you would not neglect waiting on Mr. Powel, the sooner the better, as his example may be of consequence (*The Freemen's Journal*, August 8, 1781).

Liberally educated, landed, and liberated from even the usual expenses for children, Samuel Powel has no excuse not to contribute liberally. First an alderman and finally a mayor, he must set an example. It's up to him to show his colors, and "the sooner the better."

Passing the test of the common citizens set for him in their *Freemen's Journal*, and, especially, that of the oligarchs in their Landholders' dinner parties, Powel won the first election for Mayor after the Revolution: "Saturday last, the Aldermen of this city held a meeting, for the purpose of choosing a MAYOR, when Samuel Powel, Esquire, was unanimously chosen" (*Pennsylvania Packet*, April 13, 1789, & *passim* from April 20 to December 31, 1789). In 1790, the Aldermen unanimously re-elected him, but he declined because he had chosen instead to serve as a state senator (*Independent Gazette*, April 17, 1790). After his first year in the legislature, his fellow Senators unanimously chose him as a successor to Richard Peters, the Speaker of the House, and master of Belmont (*Aurora General Advertiser*, February 1, 1792).

While the Founding Fathers were meeting in Philadelphia to plant the foundations for a new country, Powel was also busy entertaining them and planting his country estate across the Schuylkill. And yet, he did not seize every opportunity to entertain. May 1, 1784, The Feast of Saint Tammany, George Washington traveled to Philadelphia for a meeting of the Society of the Cincinnati. In the company of Robert Morris, he then attended this Feast of the Sons of Tammany on the property of Edward Pole, a dealer in fishing rods and tackle, and one of Powel's neighbors on the Schuylkill. All the "sons" received Washington with many toasts. One of the them wrote a poem to celebrate the event:

> Ye vet'ran chiefs, who this day meet,
> To celebrate each gallant feat . . .
> Fair freedom ev'ry soul inspir'd;
> The good, the wife, th'unletter'd swain
> Then join the dance, begin the song,
> Nor yet forget to whom we owe,
> The blessings which from freedom flow,
> But all who love bright Liberty
> Join Washington with Tammany
> (*Independent Gazetteer*, May 8, 1784).

The "vet'ran" coterie of Washington's generals in the Society of the Cincinnati and every "unletter'd swain" joined "the dance" and drank the toasts. Powel did not host an entertainment as popular as this one, which usually ended in drunken disorder (*Independent Gazetteer*, May 20, 1786). The august presence of George Washington probably restrained the high spirits of this particular feast,—at least until he left.

Powel was always ready to celebrate with respectable dec. About a year later, when Pennsylvania approved the Federal Constitution in

1787, he wrote a letter to Washington to tell him the good news and mention the offer of Philadelphia as the location for the new capital: "So foederal are we that an invitation has been handed to the Convention signed by the Landholders of Philadelphia County, offering the said county as the seat of the future Government. This measure was taken at a very respectable meeting." Without the *mobile vulgus* of Francis Bailey and the Sons of Tammany, but with the "very respectable" landed gentry, Powel was making this offer. He went on to include the common man in support of the Constitution: "All Ranks of People here rejoice in the Event of this Evening's Deliberations, which was proclaimed thro' the City by repeated Shouts & Huzzas. The Convention will sign the Ratification Tomorrow Morning" (December 12, 1787).

Powel also led a "very respectable" parade of the farmers. As President of the Philadelphia Society for Promoting Agriculture, he joined "all ranks of people" by leading the society's unit in the celebration of the Constitution by The Grand Federal Procession, July 4, 1788. Behind him, one of his fellow members carried its flag, which showed Industry represented by a Ploughman, guiding a plough drawn by oxen, followed by the Goddess of Plenty, bearing a cornucopia in her left hand and a sickle in her right—with a view of an American Farm in the background. Underneath, the flag bore the motto, "Venerate the Plough" (*Pennsylvania Gazette*, July 9, 1788). In 1789, the men who venerated "the plough," also put it, along with a sailing ship, on the escutcheon of the city of Philadelphia.

Three years earlier, in 1785, he had been a founding member of this society. As a leader among "Landholders of Philadelphia County," he shared a patriotic duty to improve agriculture with men of this class. Their membership distinguished them with a "mark of social eminence."[56] Like George Washington, an honorary member, they venerated the plough and found better methods for its forging and use, without actually ploughing fields themselves. Resting on mahogany chairs at home, Powel and Washington discussed farming as much as politics. "In a shared enthusiasm for agricultural pursuits," one historian has observed, "George Washington and Samuel Powel were a matched pair."[57]

As members of the Philadelphia Society for Promoting Agriculture, both men took an interest in improving local produce, which included one of the country's first commercial vineyards, founded by Pierre Legaux in 1787, in nearby Spring Mill, about five miles up the Schuylkill (*Inquirer*, November 8, 1896). Its shareholders included such distinguished men as Alexander Hamilton, Aaron Burr, Johns Hopkins, and Robert Morris. August 16, 1793, Legaux, "the Vine-Dresser of Spring Mill," invited George Washington, President of the United States; the Governor of Pennsylvania, Chief Justice McKean; and Samuel Powel, President of the Philadelphia Society for Promoting Agriculture, to enjoy his first vintage (*Aurora General*, June 3, 1801). This distinguished company enjoying a bit of merrymaking at *Monsieur* Legaux's *vendage* offers a vintage image of Americana. Appropriately,—but sadly,—this harvest festival would be one of the last events of Powel's life.

Just a month later, in September, 1793, Samuel came to an unfortunate end. This misfortune indirectly involved George and Martha Washington. Back in 1787, Samuel and Elizabeth had visited George and Martha at Mount Vernon. After the visit, Elizabeth wrote an eloquent letter thanking Martha for her "sense of the elegant Hospitality exercised at Mount Vernon, where the good Order of the Master's Mind, seconded by your excellent abilities, pervades every Thing around you, & renders it a most delightful Residence to your Friends." Elizabeth emphasizes the "good order" of George Washington's mind preparing their hospitality. Six years later, 1793, the Washingtons urged the Powels to seek refuge at Mount Vernon from the yellow fever epidemic in Philadelphia. Unfortunately, Samuel stayed at home, and contracted the disease. In a belated effort to flee, his carriage took him out of the city, but he only got as far as the farm house of his tenant at Powelton. September 29, Samuel Powel died in one of its bedrooms. His idyllic Powelton at least served as a refuge for his last breath at the age of 55.

In 1787, when Ann Willing Bingham was living in Paris with her husband William, she received a letter from Thomas Jefferson, in which, in contrast to the "empty bustle" in Paris, Jefferson lists the "tranquil pleasures" of living in Philadelphia: "the society of your husband, the fond cares for the children, the arrangements of the house, the improvements of the grounds fill every moment with a healthy and an useful activity." Care for family and "improvements" in property make life "heathy" and "useful" in Philadelphia. Since Americans inhabit vast open spaces, they naturally consider use and improvement of land as their special virtues.

In the epitaph, which Elizabeth inscribed on her husband's grave in the Christ Church yard, she mentions use and improvement as the virtues of her husband's life:

> . . . he had employed the best Talents of Nature,
> Highly **improved** by Education and Reflection,
> only to make himself privately and publicly **useful**. . . .
> To all this was added a Taste for Science, for the Fine Arts
> And for all the **Improvements** of Civil Life.

Samuel Powel "**improved**" himself and then his city, "to make himself privately and publicly **useful**."

In the twenty-first century, Philadelphians are lucky that Powel's house has been preserved. When they visit it, they can savor Elizabeth and Samuel's luxury as a jewel in the crown of the city's domestic life back in the days of our Founding Fathers. And yet, they did not enjoy their luxury in splendid isolation. They enjoyed it because it drew upon vital connections to the use and improvement of Philadelphia and its countryside.

CHAPTER 13

John Hare Powel: Balancing Beauty with Use at Powelton

BY THE TIME John Powel Hare reached the age of 20, his parents, Robert Hare and Margaret Willing Hare, had reared him, the University of Pennsylvania had educated him, and his family's accounting firm, Willing & Francis, had employed him. In themselves, his very respectable family, education, and career would not have made him, by his 25th year, a fitting subject of a heroic portrait by the most famous portrait painter in England. His middle name holds the clue to this fate: John Powel Hare had the middle name of his wealthy and distinguished uncle, Samuel Powel (1738–1793).

Sir Thomas Lawrence portrayed this handsome young man with Byronic panache, because John Powel Hare, by putting his middle name last, became his uncle's adopted son, John Hare Powel. In 1808, his maternal aunt, Elizabeth Willing Powell (1743–1830), the widow of Samuel Powell, made him the heir of her late husband's great fortune. The name and wealth of his aunt and uncle raised him to American nobility,—without Tory embarrassments. Unlike the Hamiltons or the Chews, the Powels celebrated and improved their American heritage by their loyalty to the patriotic cause of 1776. John's uncle, Samuel Powel, serving as mayor of Philadelphia before the Revolution, had so preserved his wealth and his reputation as a patriot that he served as mayor after it.

John Hare Powel (1810) by
Sir Thomas Lawrence (1769–1830)

As soon as John H. Powel became a gentleman in 1809, this former accountant saw profit in setting aside his balance sheets, and going off to England,—but not merely to the life of the idle rich. He would live as impractically as he pleased, but it was his pleasure to become a model of practical impracticality. At first, at least, John Hare Powel could afford to see red ink in his accounts that would have brought a cold chill to John Powel Hare. In character, he coined the gold, his biographer said, of "truth and honor," valuing men for their "heart and individual worth."[58] He balanced the useful with the beautiful.

In Lawrence's portrait, the firm gentleness of John Hare Powel's countenance promised that he would live as heroically,—and as romantically,—as this portrait portrayed him. Until the 1830's, at least, he could afford the role.

WHEN JOHN POWEL VISITED his father's family in England he came to love the English. On the other hand, when he worked with Thomas Pinckney, the United States' ambassador to England, he came to hate the duplicity of their diplomats. Pairing domestic joy with diplomatic dismay, he passed on a rule to his children: "Trust the English, but distrust their diplomacy." In his personal life, he imported the best from England so that he might enjoy the best American life in Philadelphia.

After spending 1809, '10 and '11 in England, he returned to Philadelphia in time to serve in the War of 1812. By then, he knew what he was fighting for. After the war, he was "ardently attached to military life;" until "his mother's tears and his friends' entreaties induced him, with great reluctance, to give up this cherished prospect for active military life." This ambitious young man devoted himself to whatever good cause he saw.

Back home, Colonel Powel started a new life as an agriculturist at Powelton, his family's estate on the west bank of the Schuylkill River, a short walk north from the Market Street Bridge. In 1800, his aunt built the core of the house, which he would inhabit and eventually embellish. For the moment, however, he had no need for a stately mansion or a gentleman's farm in pursuing his dynamic goal "to promote agriculture as the best foundation for the progress and power" of American democracy. This agriculturist got close to the earth.

For about ten years, from 1815 to 1825, Powelton enjoyed its golden age. By day, John worked to run his farm; and, by night, he studied and wrote about it. In a contribution to *The National Gazette*, December 22, 1824, he got to the roots of the best fodder: "I am convinced that a small quantity of Indian corn should be added, for the most economical and successful application of beets, or any roots in America, for the nourishment of cattle. I have for some years caused my animals to be fed three times a day." Making careful choices like this one for fodder, he raised stock for quality, and he consistently opposed "the tendency to produce animals chiefly remarkable for size." County fairs have too often taken "great size for excellence." Whatever tall tales Americans may tell, the biggest bull is not necessarily the best.

To raise the best, he bred stock from the healthiest breeds that he could find. While the Bartrams and the Hamiltons were exporting uniquely native *flora* from America and importing *exotica* over the seven seas, John Powel was importing to Powelton the best grazing *fauna* from Europe and exporting it, so to speak, throughout the country. Philadelphians read in the news about the arrival of these ungulate aristocrats from England: "In the packet ship Algonquin, Capt. Dixey, have arrived a bull and a cow of the short horn, Durham breed, and two South Down sheep. They were selected by one of the most experienced graziers in England, and have been imported at great expense by John Hare Powell, Esq." (*United States Gazette*, November 16, 1825). Few American farmers could boast of such "great expense" to purchase the expertise of "the most experienced graziers in England." Powell was probably the man who submitted this report of his accomplishment to the newspaper; or he was, at least, happy to see it. He was also happy to share, at no charge, this prize breeding stock in neighboring counties.

From about 1815 to 1823, he worked to establish himself,—and others,—in his new calling. This work came to fruition in 1823 when he announced the formation of "The Pennsylvania Agricultural Society": "Sir—I have the honor to state, that the Pennsylvania Agricultural Society will hold their first annual exhibition, in Chester County, where it will give them great pleasure to receive the officers and members of your society. I am, Sir, very &c. yours, John Hare Powell, Cor. Sec'ry (*National Gazette*, October 13, 1823). In these years, he bred stock, planted crops, and shared the fruit of his labors in friendships throughout the state, so that he might lay the foundation of this society for the advancement of agriculture. Through it, he worked for the good of all American farms.

The year 1825 crowned the golden years of Powelton's pasture, when its pastor won nineteen silver trophies for his stock at the third annual meeting of the Pennsylvania Agricultural Society, October 19th, 20th and 21st, 1825, at Prospect Hill in Philadelphia. The announcement in the *National Gazette* listed prizes by their dollar value in silver plate. Powel won the two most valuable, one piece of plate worth $50 for "the best bull, not less than 1 year old," and another for "the best thoroughbred improved Durham short horn bull" (*National Gazette*, October 31, 1825). These and other trophies, also awarded for best cow, heifer, ram and ewe, he considered "among the treasured heirlooms he had to bestow upon his children."

Powel called these prizes "the proudest triumphs of his life," because they recognized and rewarded his work to improve agriculture.[59] Another account of the meeting added a couple of personal details: Mr. Powel's service as a member of the Society and also his contingent to the Exhibition were very "valuable." Whoever might have been in his "contingent,"—managers and farm hands or friends sharing his interest,—Powel had been seeking out and entertaining kindred spirits. The account also reported that he was "unfortunately obliged to return home in the morning, in consequence of a fall, from which, however, no serious consequences are apprehended" (*National Gazette*, October 22, 1825). This fall would not be the only one to change his plans.

Powel established the Pennsylvania Agricultural Society as a rival to PSPA in an effort to reach a wider audience: "all officers shall be PRACTICAL FARMERS." In 1823, a farmer protested: "I've tried three times for a premium on swine, but they were given to rich farmers . . . it is a confounded shame, that the state should spend ten thousand dollars to give rich farmers its silver plate (Simon Baatz, *Venerate the Plough* [1985], 45). Powel was elected president of Pennsylvania Agricultural Society in 1829, but having been elected state senator in 1827, he spent most of his time in Harrisburg.

In 1825, Powel also entered the arena of genteel agricultural polemics. People could easily have picked him as a target. In addition to the admiring looks, imagine the invidious stares at a man whose "expenditures," his neighbor John Milnor said, "so far exceeded the returns" that he "never derived a profit" from raising cattle. Powel published a pamphlet answering some of the petty criticisms of Colonel Timothy Pickering (1745–1829), who in his old age had turned his contentious wrangling from political to pastoral. This man, formerly Secretary of State and of War under George Washington, had tried unsuccessfully to gain wealth, and he envied the man to whom it had come without effort: "I am not," grumbled Colonel Pickering, "the adopted heir to a great estate."[60] Secure in his pastoral seat, Powel viewed such wrangling with equanimity: "Such discussions," his biographer said, "added great zest to his favorite pursuit, and lent excitement to the quiet details of country life." He had the leisure and capacity to enjoy some disputes even over petty details of his word choice. The title of his polemic, *Reply to Colonel Pickering's Attack upon a Pennsylvania Farmer*, announces the self-effacing modesty of calling himself a farmer.

David J. Kennedy (1816–1898), *Residence of John Hare Powel*

Also in the year 1825, Powel complemented his success as a farmer by improving the home, which his aunt had built twenty-five years before. Unlike the Ionic Order, most used by Palladio for suburban villas, the Doric, designed by William Strickland (1788–1851), displayed the grand simplicity of Powel's aspirations. The oxymoron, grand simplicity, describes Powel appropriately as the grand "Pennsylvania Farmer." One architectural historian, Charles Wood, has defined this exact reproduction of the Greek Doric order by its "bold and forthright massing and stark and simple forms." Powel's son Samuel characterized his father's taste as "stern and severe; in all his feelings, he was a republican."[61]

"Stern and severe" republican principles expressed themselves best in the simplicity of the Greek Doric.[62] In the usual manner of many gentlemen, Powel cultivated an interest in architecture. The wife of one of his descendants felt some annoyance at his wanting to take credit for the design: "how maddening to have felt that the architect was not important!" As Strickland's patron, he might have justified this presumption, because both he and the architect were copying the Greek Doric Order from Stuart and Revett's *The Antiquities of Athens.*

In 1825, Powel's 39th year marked the high point of his career in agriculture, architecture and polemics. Having enjoyed this success, he looked to politics for fulfillment. His service during three terms, 1827, '28 and '29, in the Pennsylvania Legislature in Harrisburg diverted his attention from Powelton. By 1830, he advertised the conclusion of the pastoral chapter in his life:

> *Improved Durham Short-Horned Cattle.*
>
> Mr. Powel's stock of high bred Short Horns, consisting of sixty males and females, either imported or bred by him, will be offered for sale at Powelton. . . . These animals have never been offered for sale, nor would they be sold if the owner were not about to leave America for some time" (*National Gazette*, May 5, 1830).

Powel is advertising a sale, that is extraordinary in his own commitment to the quality of its stock. If he "were not" about to go to England, he "would" not be able to put such fine stock up for sale,—a tangle of subjunctives contrary-to-fact!

John Hare Powel made this sale an event, memorable, first of all, for its idyllic setting:

> Before the appointed time of sale, the lawn near the house was well filled with respectable visitors, who came either to admire or to purchase. Among the company, we observed the Baron de Krudener, the Russian Ambassador, and General Eaton, Secretary of War. . . . The company which exceeded 1000 persons enjoyed the shade of the beautiful trees which bound the park on the North. Immediately after the sale, tables, upwards of 300 feet long, were spread under the shade of the same beautiful trees, in the furnishing of which no less taste, judgment and liberality were manifested by our host than in the management of his other affairs (*United States Gazette*, June 22, 1830).

The reporter does not mention any rough-edged rustics attending this event, although the crowd of 1000 could not have drawn exclusively from the likes of Baron de Krudener. Powel complemented the idyllic scene by setting and resetting a well-stocked table for his many guests. Other people in Philadelphia, like members of temperance and political societies, enjoyed celebrations and picnics at "the woodlands of Powelton" (*Public Ledger*, July 7, 1841). They also profited from Powel's "taste, judgment and liberality."

Powelton's sylvan scene served only as an idyllic backdrop to its stock at center stage. The reporter gives just a nod to Powel's expertise in breeding: "All seemed joined in general admiration of the beauty of the cattle . . . conveying a compliment on the taste, judgement and patriotic spirit of Col. Powel." He pointedly passes over this praise for the man to what he thinks Powel's "taste, judgement and patriotic spirit" should demonstrate: in contrast to Powel, "some of our agriculturists appear to be utterly careless or inattentive to the breed of cows, sheep, pigs and other animals." Powel was teaching by example.

Unlike "utterly careless or inattentive" agriculturists, the "respectable visitors" paid high prices for breeding. Almost uniquely, but, in this case, inevitably, Powel profited from his "patriotic spirit." The fifteen animals mentioned by the reporter sold for from $110 to $510 each. In the only lot of the sale, "two bulls and two cows sold together for $1735!"—just imagine! This sale could not have turned Powelton's accounts from red to black, but his flamboyant patriotism did have its reward. Whatever Powelton's final balance sheet, Powel did not miss the opportunity to act in his role as the gracious host, entertaining the "respectable visitors" with his usual "liberality." This liberality was staging its farewell performance. His friend Sydney George Fisher observed a definite lack of interest after 1825: Powel "goes to Europe and gets tired," and then comes home. In his mid forties, he had lost the intensity of his youth.

In the mid 1830's, Powelton was also entering another stage in the life of its city. Eighty years before, when John's Uncle Samuel purchased its site, he visited only by ferry from Market street to the west bank of the Schuylkill. By 1839, John was signing a petition for a very different neighborhood. It proposed free passage across the Market Street Bridge so that "every mechanic, every individual in the city, would be benefitted."[63] The laborer, the petition explained, should not have to sacrifice part of his wage to get to work, and the citizen should not have the inconvenience of paying a toll to enjoy "the recreation of a walk across the Schuylkill." Growing industry and trade had changed the neighborhood around Powelton: "The increase of trade on the Schuylkill . . . by means of the great system of internal improvements requires that places of deposit should be formed on the western shore for commodities of the coarser kind" (*Public Ledger*, March 6, 1839). In signing the petition, John had a special and personal awareness of what "every mechanic" walking to and from nearby lumber, coal, brick, and stone yards would mean for his farm.

By 1843, Sidney George Fisher, whose estate, for the time at least, was far out of the city, lamented that if Powelton "were 10 miles from town, it would be a delightful residence, but it looks on the coal wharves and a mass of brick buildings on the other side of the river and is so near the city that it is constantly liable to trespass and intrusion." He follows up with a judgement about John Powel's classical building project that might have applied to anyone, including eventually himself, who had built an estate without considering the inevitability of urban sprawl: "Mr. Powel was foolish to build it, as he will most probably never live there and has not income enough to keep it up in proper style."[64] Accusing John Hare Powel of being "foolish" takes the air out of his aristocratic indifference to expense and brings him back to the account books that he had first learned to keep,—and then disregard,—as a young man. Impractical management of Powelton had been taking its toll on the old money of his uncle's fortune. It seems likely that Powel really did count on profit from the sale of his stock in 1830.

Powel recognized the handwriting on the wall. He subscribed to a stock offering of 4000 shares of the West Philadelphia Railroad in 1835 (*National Gazette*, March 3, 1835). In 1836, he published a plan for laying out wide streets and avenues in West Philadelphia and Powelton (*United States Gazette*, March 5, 1836). In 1836, also, Powelton suffered a fate of becoming a resort:

> Powelton.—We learn that Messrs. Turner & Cuthbert have taken the splendid mansion belonging to Col. J. Hare Powell, with a part of the grounds at Powelton, with a view of opening it as a public house, a place of general resort. The delightful situation of the mansion and grounds will render the place desirable to our citizens, who need some point toward which they may walk or drive in a summer's afternoon. It is the intention of Messrs. T. and C. to give to the establishment character which shall ensure the company of the most respectable citizens (*National Gazette*, May 3, 1836).

This enterprise went bankrupt after one season: "Assignees' sale of superior liquors, furniture, *etc.* of the Powelton Hotel," *The National*

Gazette, announced in September of 1836. The next year, another entrepreneur tried again: "Powelton Cottage—Vincent Hammond hath taken the Powelton Cottage on the West side of the banks of the Schuylkill and fitted it up in superior style, where he intends to furnish parties and companies" (*Public Ledger*, August 22, 1837). Three years later, "gentlemen" had an opportunity to enjoy life at Powelton during the summer: "Boarding—Gentlemen are respectfully informed that they can be accommodated with handsome apartments and pleasant Summer Boarding at moderate terms by applying at the Powelton Cottage" (*Public Ledger*, June 13, 1840). Bush Hill, just across the river, had gone through similar tenants and uses at the turn of the century.

Summer boarders at Powelton in 1840 were enjoying a brief twilight before the coal wharves and other "places of deposit," which Fisher saw on the east bank, extended across the river to the west. "I will venture to say, that, within fifteen years from this time," one observer wrote in 1844, "all that beautiful tract of land will be covered with the residences of gentlemen of fortune, merchants, lawyers, doctors, and if you please, editors (*Public Ledger*, June 3, 1844). Unfortunately, not all of the ninety acres of Powelton provided homes for such respectable residents.

Five years before he died, Powel announced the sale of Powelton: "The estate called Powelton is offered for sale in blocks, or in larger portions, or entire . . . adapted to cottage residences, amidst forest trees, and commanding extensive views of the surrounding country. John Hare Powell" (*Public Ledger*, May 2, 1851). A year later, he sold the "entire" tract to the Pennsylvania Railroad (*Public Ledger*, April 19, 1852). The railroad retained 30 of the 90 acres of Powelton for a rail yard and sold the other 60 acres for residential development. In 1856, the year of Powel's death, it published a map, *Route of a Proposed Railroad from Powelton West Philadelphia to the Philadelphia Gas Works and thence to the River Delaware*. It showed the railroad's tracks running straight through Powelton.

The area of 30 acres, which has remained a rail yard, suffered the saddest fate of all the old Philadelphia estates. November 9, 1863, *The Inquirer* reported a car shop in the shape of a U, 346 feet long with wings 200 feet each, on the site of the Powelton Fair Grounds. One citizen commented on this 'ruthless' improvement: "West Philadelphia

Scene at the US Agricultural Society's Fair, Philadelphia (1856)

It pictures the embankment above the coastal plain on the river, which, to this day, is still visible west of the rail yard.

Improvements—The valuable estate called Powelton, on the west side of the Schuylkill, between the permanent and the wire bridge, when improved, will give still greater facilities to the business of that great state work. The estate, which is to be sold, is one of the handsomest in the county; but the spirit of improvement ruthlessly destroys the merely beautiful to enhance its value by converting it into the useful" (*Public Ledger*, April 30, 1851). When the city created Fairmount Park, it preserved the estates above the Waterworks, but it allowed the area below the weir to become a workshop,—a devil's workshop,—of industry.

In 1856, a magazine showed Powelton as the scene of harness racing at the United States Agricultural Fair. Powel would have been pleased to see that the State Society was making use of his estate to host the national Society. He had always hoped to extend agricultural improvement from Philadelphia to the state and the country. On the other hand, he had worried about horse races attracting gamblers who would blight thoroughbred beauty with crime.

After breaking his hip in a fall on the ice, Powel suffered a decline in his health. He did not stay in Philadelphia to observe Powelton, at first, hosting horse races, or finally, suffering 'ruthless' improvement. Like Fairman Rogers later in the century, he moved to Newport, where he died in 1856, five years after he had sold his farm.

CHAPTER 14

Benjamin Chew's Family in the City and in the Country

At about the age of forty, Benjamin Chew (1722–1810) brought his family from their townhouse on Front street to spend the summer in their newly built country house on the Germantown Road. Having come from deep roots in his father's plantation down south in Delaware, he was working to establish himself up north in Philadelphia. (The Mason-Dixon line (1767) would soon draw the line between "up north" in Pennsylvania and "down south" in Delaware and Maryland.) Urbane rusticity complementing urban sophistication established a man's place in the city's upper class.[65] After he and his family spent one summer on the Germantown road in Mount Airy, the home of his friend William Allen, he had come to enjoy the fresh air in the hills north of the city. Allen, one Philadelphia's wealthiest men, was connecting him to Philadelphia's business and social life.

Chew called his home Cliveden. Its elegance announced his rank, and its size provided a building large enough for his ever-increasing family. Bereaved of his first wife in 1755, but remarried in 1757, he was anticipating more children. Even while he was building it, three daughters did come; and by the time he finished it in 1767, the Chew family numbered five daughters from his first marriage, two sons from his second, plus the three girls recently born. Investment in family would pay off. In life, his daughters clothed his rank in elegance; and after death, they preserved his heritage.

Cliveden (1763–1767)

Cliveden's rusticity looked elegant. Neatly clad in local stone, it rose as though from the earth. A Mennonite stonecutter and mason had quarried and dressed its ashlar blocks from gray schist of the Wissahickon Valley—not the usual rubble gathered from fields. A few years before, these craftsmen had built Germantown Academy (1759) with similarly solid material. As these peace-loving Mennonites were laying foundations for an idyl of peace, they would not have anticipated that their walls would suffer the ravages of war. Ten years later, in the upheavals of empire, October 4, 1777, cannon balls from the six-pounders in the Battle of Germantown, bounced off these walls "like pebbles."[66]

The stonemasons gave Cliveden Palladian style in addition to rock-solid walls. Over in Italy, Palladio used the Ionic order to place his villas between the rural simplicity of the Doric and the urban elegance of the Corinthian. Townhouses in Philadelphia did not observe this order of the classical orders. On Third street, Chew's home would frame its front door by Ionic columns. (By contrast, visitors to the

Left: Cliveden's doorway in the Doric Order. *Right:* The three classical orders, top to bottom: Doric, Ionic, Corinthian.

home of his neighbor, Samuel Powel, passed through the Doric.) The Philadelphia Carpenters' Company recommended the Doric for both city and country by using it as the sole illustration in its *Articles and Rules of 1786* (Richards, 9). On its own, the Doric order marked Cliveden's rural setting, correctly rendered with a pediment above triglyphs and metopes.[67] Its rank in the classical orders complemented Cliveden's elegantly solid construction.[68] Just in case this solidity look stolid, Chew imported urns of Portland stone to decorate the roof. He was so proud of them that he called them "my urns."[69]

Whatever its balance of local stonework with classical order and

Mount Pleasant (1761), built a few years before Cliveden (1763–1767)

Mount Pleasant rests on ashlar blocks in its basement story. On its second and third stories, stucco, covering a rubble facade, has been scored to resemble ashlar. A brick belt course divides the second and third stories horizontally, and brick quoins (i.e. corners) accent them and their center pavilion vertically. Instead of Mount Pleasant's elegant balance, horizontally and vertically, of stone and stucco with brick—and its Palladian window in the center of the second story—Cliveden's ashlar blocks on all three stories bespeak rustic simplicity and solidity. Both buildings are Palladian, but, to point a contrast, Mount Pleasant is urbane; Cliveden, rustic.[70]

decoration, Cliveden's elegance fit into Benjamin Chew's *curriculum vitae*, because it fulfilled the promise of his aristocratic birth. He had a colonial ancestry deeper than that of the average Philadelphian. Unlike the first Philadelphians arriving in 1682, later in the seventeenth century, his grandfather was colonizing Virginia in 1622. He had descended from one of the "first families of Virginia." His distinguished origin, however, did not come without its burden. His family had taken root with an evil of European colonization, to which he became accustomed. Slaves on the four hundred acres of Whitehall, the ancestral plantation, south of Dover, Delaware, made his family's life luxurious.

Slave labor, therefore, also had its place on his *c.v.*; but, by contrast, Cliveden's eleven acres and his own career in the law did not encourage slave driving—in and around Philadelphia, at least. In addition, citizens in the City of Brotherly Love mandated a better way. In 1780, their General Assembly passed the Gradual Abolition Act, remarkably, the first comprehensive abolition in North America.

Chew chose to live in Philadelphia, north of the Mason-Dixon line, but he did not espouse its morality. This son of the Old South clung to his ancestral evil. On June 17, 1789, for example, he published a notice for the return of a run-away slave (*Dunlap and Claypoole's American Daily Advertiser*, June 17, 1789). Finally, on his demise, he bequeathed to his wife "my Man Harry, my woman Sarah, and all my Rights . . . to her Children, and the time of Service of my Boy David who is bound <to> me until he attains his Age of Twenty Eight Years" (Richards, 138). To the end, Benjamin Chew was a slave-holder.

Benjamin Chew had a flaw in his morality, but not in his intellect. His intelligence found its mentors in Andrew Hamilton (*circa* 1676–1741), and his younger law-partner William Allen (1704–1780), who had married Hamilton's daughter Margaret (1709–1760) in 1734.[71] In 1736, Benjamin started to study law in Hamilton's office after his parents moved to Philadelphia. His father, as the first Chief Justice of Delaware, had set him a high standard. In 1743, after Hamilton's death, Benjamin traveled to London to continue his study in one of the Inns of Court, but his father's death brought him back home in 1744.

Returning to his paternal roots in Delaware, Chew took his first step in an American political career by his election to the local assembly with others, in his case, from Kent County, Delaware: "Representatives, Benjamin Chew, Andrew Caldwell, James Train, and Robert Wilcocks" (*Pennsylvania Gazette*, October 11, 1750). One name in this list gives a promise of future alliance. Robert Wilcocks was a relative of Alexander Wilcocks (1741–1801), who married Chew's daughter Mary (1747–1794) in 1768 (*PG*, May 26, 1768), and who would later join his father-in-law to speculate in land and to oversee the University of Pennsylvania. Chew built his career on such alliances. Rising in the ranks, he soon served as speaker for the lower house of the Delaware counties.

After his career in Delaware, he returned to Philadelphia in 1756. Within seven years of his return, he was moving into Cliveden; and within ten, he won the special appointment of the governor of Pennsylvania to serve as "Register General for the Probate of Wills" (*Pennsylvania Gazette*, August 20, 1765). He reached his father's accomplishment when he also won the special appointment of the governor to serve as "Chief Justice of the Supreme Court" to replace his mentor and law partner, William Allen (*Dunlap and Claypoole's American Daily Advertiser*, May 9, 1774). Twenty-four years after his first election to the Delaware Assembly in 1750, therefore, he had reached the pinnacle of his career.

As he was doing public service in assemblies and courts, his private practice inherited from the law partners Hamilton and Allen, also made him wealthy and well-connected. Hamilton, especially, had become distinguished as the Penns' neighbor, and wealthy as their lawyer. As Hamilton's protégé, Benjamin also continued to serve as the friend and legal council of William Penn's sons and grandsons: John (1700–1747), Thomas (1702–1775), and Richard (1706–1771); and Richard's sons, John (1729–1795) and Richard, Jr. (1735–1811). Friendship with Richard's son John proved significant. This connection with Pennsylvania's proprietary family gave him prestige but less profit than it had given his mentor. In fact, it made him suspect of British sympathies in 1776. This liability weighed in the balance with the firm foundation that the support of the colonial first families had given him.

Having built his career and Cliveden by 1767, Chew started to look for a new address in the city. In his first marriage in 1747, he had been living on Front street. His search for space and style that reached its goal in Cliveden, also continued in the city. Stonemasons had raised Cliveden from the earth, rock-solidly on its own, but only the right neighbors could give his townhouse éclat. His search in town reached its goal on the west side of south Third street, between Walnut and Spruce, where he found all that he could want. There, on Willing's

Alley, Charles Willing (1710–1754) and his son, Thomas (1731–1821), wealthy merchants, who had also served as the city's mayors, owned a large parcel of the block.

On this property, acquired from William Penn's family, Charles Willing built his home. He lived there with his wife and their eleven children. Subdividing it for two daughters, he started to create an enclave for his family. First, he built the house to the south on Third (then #110, now #252) for his daughter Mary Willing (1740–1814), and her husband, William Byrd, III (1728–1777). They lived there for the first year of their marriage (1761–1762), before moving to Westover, Mr. Byrd's family seat in Virginia. In 1769, Willing built the house next door for his younger daughter, Elizabeth Willing (1743–1830), and her husband Samuel Powel (1738–1793), also a mayor of the city.[72]

Eventually, Benjamin Chew bought the property in which the Byrds had lived for a year. The purchase brought together some lines of his social network. William Allen first connected him to the sale. Allen, his neighbor on the Germantown road, had rented Mount Airy to him before he built Cliveden. A few years after the Byrds left, Allen purchased their home, and gave it to his daughter, Ann Allen (1746–1840) and her husband, Governor John Penn (1729–1795). After Richard Penn's death, when his son John and John's wife Ann returned to England, they sold their home to Chew in 1771.[73]

Chew, therefore, found a snug fit when he moved into this neighborhood. He had enjoyed close connections with the Penns, Willings, Hamiltons, and Allens. They represented a ruling élite, the cream of Philadelphia society. With these neighbors, he was keeping up—and fitting in—when he took Allen's judicial appointment after that man's retirement as Chief Justice of the Pennsylvania Supreme Court in 1774. He had fully transferred his family's life and status from Delaware to Pennsylvania.

Having sealed the deal with Chew, John Penn might have shared some memories, as they sat over their Madeira after dinner. Back in 1726, John's grandmother, Hannah Callowhill Penn, had given Andrew Hamilton, Benjamin's mentor, 150 acres of Springettsbury, William Penn's proprietorial estate. This land, which served as payment in kind to Hamilton for his legal services, became Bush Hill, Hamilton's family estate. The name now rings with even greater fame than Springettsbury, the Penns' property, from which it was subdivided. In 1771, Chew was also serving as friend and legal council to the Penn family, just as his mentor had in 1726. The 45 years between 1726 and 1771, however, had made the difference between a watershed event in 1726 and a simple sale of a townhouse in 1771. On shoulders and in shadows, either man might have pondered glory waning in the passage of time.

True, Benjamin Chew was living after the glorious days of Philadelphia's founding fathers, but he was certainly not about to stand in their shadow and see his glory wane. His star was rising—and radiant. He had paid a high price—£5,000—for Penn's property; and it had given him extensive grounds: 118 feet fronting on Third street, extending 396 feet back to Fourth (Richards, 14). For his money, he got more space than he could have imagined and as much style as he could have found anywhere. A high brick wall, sixty feet along Third street, enclosed his beautiful garden. An observer considered it to be one, she said, of the "greatest ornaments" to the neighborhood. "Some of the largest and most elegant weeping willows I ever saw anywhere" cast their shade over the wall (Richards, 15). In back of the garden, an orchard and a pasture extended to Fourth street. When William Birch (1755–1834) wanted to picture an idyllic street in Philadelphia, he chose the Willing compound on south Third.[74]

Chew gilt his lily. To tend the gardens of both his town and his country house, he hired a gardener at 35£ a year, plus room, board, and clothing. His gardener took a place ahead of his coachman as the best paid member of the domestic staff. Imagine the conversations of these two men, as the coachman conveyed the gardener between town and country.

Sixteen years after his demise, Chew's heirs published this description of the property in a notice for its sale:

> *Valuable Real Estate.*
>
> ON FRIDAY EVENING, The 20th inst. at 7 o'clock, at the Merchants' Coffee House, will be sold that extensive House and Lot of Ground, situate on the west side of Third street, between Walnut and Spruce streets, being part of the estate of the late Benjamin Chew, Esq.

> deceased, bounded on the north by the ground of the late Thomas M. Willing, Esq. and on the south by the residence of William Rawle, Esq.<previously the residence of Samuel Powel>, containing 88 feet, 8 inches front on Third street, and running the same width westward about 180 feet from the line of Third street to a spacious court of 26 feet in width leading into Spruce street. On the premises, stands a large and excellent house, 30 feet front, by 52 feet deep, 5 stories high, unusually finished with handsome wainscoting throughout the two lower stories, with garret rooms, &c. The back buildings, connected by a two story brick passage of 18 feet in length, are unusually extensive and commodious, running 60 feet in depth: of which buildings 40 feet are three stories high, and 20 feet two stories high. On the court, or coach way, leading into Spruce street, is erected a substantially built Stable and Coach-house, with accommodation for two carriages and four horses. A pump is on the premises, also a water cistern, and the hydrant water introduced; in short, every accommodation suitable for a large family (*Inquirer*, November 21, 1822; and March 22, 1826).

The two dates of this notice, 1822 and 1826, indicate that the Chews did not rush into a sale.

Once the Chews did sell their townhouse, they moved one piece of furniture out to Cliveden that represented their heritage from John Penn. A family tradition has maintained that Penn left a Marlborough-leg, i.e., straight-leg, camel-back sofa (1766) in the house as a gift to the Chews after he moved out. It might have seemed relatively insignificant at the time, but it has become the single most significant piece of furniture in Cliveden (Richards, 50).

John Penn's sofa is part of a larger story about Philadelphia Chippendale. As he was furnishing his home, he even brought the cabinetmaker, Thomas Affleck (1740–1795), born in Aberdeen and trained in London, to work in Philadelphia. When John returned to London, he also gave a pair of Affleck's chairs, and other furniture to John Morton of Philadelphia. Perhaps, Penn left behind the sofa for the Chews, simply because it was larger and harder to move

In 1772, Benjamin Chew could not have made too much of this gift from John Penn, because it occupied only a small part of the life that he was enjoying. In town, he lived in a high-profile location with a prestigious reputation. In addition, he had combined John Penn's townhouse in Thomas Willing's compound with Cliveden, up the Germantown road from William Allen's Mount Airy. His gardener's handiwork brought mother nature into Penn's "country towne" and made it as "greene" and beautiful as William Penn had intended. Each block in his town, he hoped, would contain gardens. In town and country, Chew's gardener impressed the élite as they promenaded; and his coachman, commuting between the two in coach or phaeton, impressed the passersby as they gawked. The property advertised his distinction—fine grounds, beautifully planted; and a fine stable, impressively—that is, expensively—equipped.

Benjamin's daughters both shared his enjoyment and increased it. The neighbors, also, Willings on one side and Powels on the other, increased their social life by sharing it. In order of social rank, the Willings took the lead in sharing. A couple of years after the Chews moved in, the Willing-Powels' family dinners included a Founding Father, because Mrs. Powel's brother, Thomas Willing, was attending both the First Continental Congress in 1774 and the Second in 1775. George Washington, when he attended these congresses, ate dinner consistently at the Powels'. John Adams has made their hospitality part of history. After he had dined there on September 8, 1774, he famously,—and facetiously,—wrote home to his wife Abigail that he had partaken in "a most sinful feast." The sumptuous luxury of the Powels' table impressed this plain-living Bostonian, whose ancestors had relished beans, after they sweetened them, of course, with a little molasses.

Eager to share, the Chews worked hard to increase. Their hospitality impressed Adams no less, perhaps even more. In their home, after he socialized in the parlor, the front room on the second floor that he called, "an elegant and most magnificent chamber" he ate in the dining room, the back room on the first floor. He described this elegant scene in his diary:

> Dined with Mr. Chew, Chief Justice of the Province, with all the gentlemen from Virginia, Dr. Shippen, Mr. Tilghman and many others. We were shown into a grand entry and staircase, and into an elegant and

most magnificent chamber, until dinner. About four o'clock, we were called down to dinner (Richards, 17).

Elizabeth Chew called this "most magnificent chamber" the Tea Room. The largest room in the house, it accommodated tea and card parties or whatever the Chews' hospitality required.

At the Powels' table, Adams, along with Washington and other Virginia gentlemen, forgot the Powels' "most sinful" feasts, while he enjoyed "turtle," he wrote in his diary, "and every other Thing—Flummery, Jellies, Sweetmeats of 20 sorts, Trifles, Whip'd Syllabubbs, floating Islands, fools—&c., and then a Desert (*sic*) of Fruits, Raisins, Almonds, Pears, Peaches—Wines most excellent and admirable. I drank Madeira at a great Rate and found no Inconvenience in it" (September 22, 1774). The Founding Fathers favored Madeira, fortified by brandy and high in alcoholic content, but Adams felt "no inconvenience" as he enjoyed it.

John Adams was not so overwhelmed that these exotic treats left him speechlessly agape—at least, in his diary. He confided to that book that Philadelphians were inferior to Bostonians in most everything except in their markets—and also, significantly, by the way, in their charities. (The Quakers could take pride in their charitable spirit.) From Philadelphia's markets, Mrs. Chew brought rare and exotic flavors for her guests. Philadelphia, at least, took the gold in gastronomy!

Could Mr. and Mrs. Chew, and especially their daughters, have sensed that their comfort and luxury would ever end? In the parlous times before and after 1776, even Penn's, Powel's or Chew's association with patriots like Washington and Adams did not make them immune to suspicion. They had shared too much a part of colonial rule to appear as solid patriots in 1776. Running this gauntlet of the common man's suspicion and resentment, all the élite in Philadelphia made a difficult transition from British colonialism to American independence. Washington himself knew that the families in the Willings' compound had been raised with broad sympathies, but that they were not traitors (Tatum, 24).

The years 1776, and especially 1777, when the British occupied

Philadelphia, represented a watermark in the lives of Philadelphia's élite. In 1776, on his last day as Justice of the Supreme Court, Benjamin Chew delivered this definition of treason:

> Opposition by force of arms to the lawful authority of the King or his Ministers is High treason, but in the moment when the King or his Ministers shall exceed the Constitutional authority vested in them by the Constitution—submission to their mandate becomes Treason (April 10, 1776).

In spite of this neat legal reasoning—perversely, perhaps, because of it—the Continental Congressmen considered him a suspicious character. With an abundance of caution, when the British occupied the city, they put him and John Penn under house arrest in August, 1777. The two men remained in isolation until June, 1778, when the British left the city. After a year, the Congress recognized that they were not guilty of treason, and released them. Chew had his freedom in law, but he recognized, with good sense, that he had to impose sensible limitations on his life in the city.

Where could he live?—not in Cliveden, in his words, "an absolute wreck" after the battle of Germantown (Eberlein, 338). Local historian John Fanning Watson reported that "Chew's house was so battered that five carpenters worked a whole winter to repair and replace the fractures." They replaced the front door that had been "filled with shot holes."[75] Plagued and impoverished by this and other cares, Chew sold Cliveden in 1779—but he repurchased it in 1797, for £8500. (It remained in the possession of the Chew family until 1972.) Even in 1797, almost twenty years later, the repairs continued: "I have bought back Cliveden," Chew wrote to a relative, "but it is in such dilapidated condition that it will take a small fortune to restore it" (Hanley, 36). Having bought it back, he brought back to good shape at great expense.

In the meantime, finding a refuge in his paternal roots in Delaware, he moved with his family to his father's plantation in 1781. He rented his townhouse to George and Martha Washington from November 1781 to March 1782. The Washingtons then moved to 190 High street, eventually the President's executive mansion. Chew's house sometimes stood vacant until the end of the war, when he returned to Philadelphia and resumed his duties as a judge. The new government had such a need of his legal expertise that it welcomed him back as President of the High Court of Errors and Appeals (1791–1808). In the ten years of his absence since 1774, his town house, after the Washingtons left, had suffered from neglect and careless tenants. With his wife's help from an inheritance, he paid £253.4.0, another "small fortune," to prepare his home for the last decade of the century, when Philadelphia basked in glory as the capital of the country. By 1791, he returned to his enjoyment of the best of life in town and country, but he had paid a high price for it. The fourteen years between 1777 and 1791 marked a bleak epoch of his life.

Throughout the last decade of the eighteen century, while Washington, D.C. was being prepared as the capital of the country, Philadelphia served as its capital in the meantime. Its social life flourished as never before or after (Richards, 64). Advocates of democracy, however, might have debated whether this flourish suited the new egalitarian America. In the long shadow of George III, some would have celebrated His Excellency George Washington and Lady Washington as monarchs. Even in this new democratic frame, Mr. President was the cynosure of his own American court. Philadelphia society happily populated levées in the morning and salons in the evening. Abigail Adams, the wife of Vice President John Adams, described one gathering in the Chews' "most magnificent" tea room, which she calls the "drawing-room."

> On Friday evening last, I went with Charles <her son> to the drawing-room, being my first appearance in public. The room became full before I left it, and the circle very brilliant. How could it be otherwise, when the dazzling Mrs. Bingham and her beautiful sisters were there; the Misses Allen, and Misses Chew; in short, a constellation of beauties? (December 26, 1790).

"The Misses Allen, and Misses Chew," the ladies from the neighborhood, enjoyed the limelight, but by the 1790's a rival had risen to become the belle of every ball she attended. Ann Willing Bingham (1764–1801), Thomas Willing's daughter and, therefore, Elizabeth Willing Powel's niece, reigned as queen. "The dazzling Mrs. Bing-

Lady Washington's First Reception in Philadelphia (Alexander Hay Ritchie, 1822–1895), at which Sophia and Harriet Chew stood among those honoring "Lady Washington" on the dais

ham" also held her own court in the splendid mansion that her husband built on the three acres along Spruce street.[76]

Benjamin's daughters shone as a "seven sisters" in the "constellation of beauties": Margaret, "Peggy," Chew (1760–1824), Juliana (1765–1845), Henrietta (1767–1848), Sophia (1769–1841), Maria (1771–1840), Harriet (1775–1861), and Catherine (1779–1831). Their father went to much expense to make their hospitality gracious and their dance steps graceful.

Peggy, Sophia, and Henrietta stood out. Henrietta's company so charmed George Washington that he asked that she keep him company as he sat for his portrait in the hope he might look a little less dour than usual.

Peggy Chew, eldest daughter of her father's second marriage, was born just when he started to plan Cliveden. In the British occupation of Philadelphia in 1777, she had charmed the British officers, especially, Major John André (1750–1780). He served as the guiding spirit of "The Meschianza," May 18, 1778, General Howe's farewell party, at which the British army celebrated his and his army's departure from

Left: Sophia Chew (1793) (John Trumbull [1756–1843]).
Right: Peggy Chew (1789) (Charles Wilson Peale [1741–1827]).

Philadelphia. He designed its triumphal arches, banners and even its invitation. This gallant chivalrously sprang from the ranks as Peggy's "Knight of the Burning Rose." Historians have considered this celebration the high point of Philadelphia's social life. While Peggy and her sister Sophia reigned among its queens, their father suffered embarrassment among patriots who suspected him as a Tory.

One of Peggy's and Sophia's admirers wrote a poem to give their charm equal praise:

With either Chew such beauties dwell,
Such charms by each are shared,
No critic's judging eye can tell
Which merits most regard.
'Tis far beyond the painter's skill
To set their charms to view,
As far beyond the poet's quill
To give the prize that's due.

After the war, Peggy returned to her father's roots in the South by marrying John Eager Howard on May 23, 1787, who became the governor of Maryland in 1788. George Washington attended the ceremony at Cliveden. The Howards took up residence at the newly constructed Belvedere, which became known as a "scene of much hospitality" and a "center of elegance and grandeur." Sophia Chew Philips did not enjoy luck like that of her sister. After her husband died in 1800, just the third year of their marriage, she spent the rest of her life in Philadelphia.

IN PHILADELPHIA, Benjamin Chew earned a place in its ruling élite. At home, he and his wife Elizabeth contributed beauty and charm to its social life. George Washington treated their daughters like his own children. In the long term, however, these women kept their hearth aglow for more than social events.

In Cliveden's first years, its substantial walls stood guard round this warmth—how much history had they witnessed! As generations passed, however, the Chew women made their own substantial contributions to their family's heritage. Throughout the nineteenth and the twentieth centuries, the old mansion owed them a debt. They corroborated their charm, by perseverance, as they preserved the hearth that had sheltered and enriched their family's life.[77]

CHAPTER 15

The Epoch of Ann and William Bingham

OCTOBER 31, 1780, *The Pennsylvania Packet* announced a marriage: "Married, on Thursday evening, William Bingham, Esquire, to Miss Willing." Between Ann Willing, age 17, and William Bingham, age 29, there was a discrepancy in age, but none in background. Both their families had built great wealth on solid foundations. The distaff side had especially complemented wealth by beauty and charm. When Abigail Adams saw Ann's beauty scintillating with charm, she described her as "dazzling." Ann's dazzle lit up more than a tea party. If the writer for the *Packet* had expatiated on his concise statement, he could have anticipated Ann and William's marriage as a radiant epoch. (What prophetic power that would have been!) By sharing their American—and particularly Philadelphian—lives with their transatlantic world, the Binghams added a unique chapter to American history.[78]

In her American, democratic realm, Ann Willing Bingham, on her own merits, had no peer. Her husband William could appreciate the proverbial wisdom, "An excellent wife is a crown to her husband" (*Proverbs* 12.4), because his wife crowned his wealth by her radiant beauty, charm and wit. She turned all heads when she entered a ballroom and kept them turning when she spoke. If William saw men turn to him when he entered his meeting room, he could also take pride in his wealth and influence putting his wife where all her charms could shine.[79]

Ann Willing Bingham's most popular portrait offers a clue to the extent of her—and her husband's—realm. When the Binghams traveled to London in 1783, Sir Joshua Reynolds painted her portrait and Francesco Bartolozzi published it in an engraving. Why did the most famous English portrait painter of his day and the engraver to the King of England celebrate her? After she had become the cynosure of all eyes in her debut at the court of King George III, why wouldn't they celebrate her beauty, especially when it gave them profit and fame? People wanted to see what this famous woman looked like. The Binghams called Philadelphia home, but William's business acumen, crowned by Ann's beauty, spread their fame beyond the Quaker City.[80]

The Binghams' family business in Philadelphia had nurtured the roots of this fame. Another clue from before William's birth, can identify these roots of his good fortune in inheriting and increasing a fortune. In the *Pennsylvania Gazette*, May 2, 1745, his father advertised the business that would spark his son's brilliant career and his daughter-in-law's scintillating charm:

> To be sold by William Bingham, within 3 doors of the Baptist-Meeting, in Second-Street, very good gun powder, by the barrel or half-barrel, green and bohea Teas, by the dozen, or small quantities; with a choice assortment of linens, cambricks, callicoes, oznabrigs, broad-cloths, green, blue and scarlet, plush, and sundry other goods, by wholesale or retail, very cheap for ready money.

William's father did not exclude any possible business,—"by the barrel or half-barrel," "by the dozen, or small quantities," "by wholesale or retail," all "very cheap,"—purchased, not with credit, but with "ready money." He advertised "very cheap" goods like "bohea," a China black tea. His stock of fabrics ran the gamut,—cambricks from Cambrai, calicoes from Callicut, down to oznabrigs from Osnabrück, coarse cloth meant to clothe slaves. If his customers needed something else, he also carried sundries,—all and sundry, to meet their needs.

But, wait!, just in case readers may have lost interest, he calls them to attention with a *Nota Bene*, "Note Well!"

> *N.B.* There is also to be disposed of by said William Bingham, five hundred acres of land at the forks of the Delaware, two thousand in Virginia, and twelve hundred and fifty on Cape May.

With good reason, reader, pay attention! The senior Bingham's purveying all and sundry continued to finance his speculation in land that he had inherited from his father, James. Along with his "very cheap" gun powder, tea, fabrics and sundries, his very large tracts of land, were establishing a fortune. This merchant, who was selling "small quantities" of "very cheap" tea, was also selling a large part of Cape May. By the third generation, these holdings, grown and well tended, included one eighth of the state of Maine. They helped to spread the wealth and fame of William, Jr. and Ann across the land and over the ocean to the court of King George III. They established a wide realm for Mrs. Bingham's reigning beauty.

One year after William Bingham, Sr. published his advertisement in the *Gazette*, he announced that he had moved "from the House (two doors below the Baptist Meeting) in which he formerly lived to a House near Black-Horse-Alley, two doors below Mr. William Bradford's, Printer, in Second Street." In either building, he lived above his store; and in his new location, he continued to sell "sundry sorts of shop goods at the cheapest rates, for ready money only" (*Pennsylvania Gazette*, August 21, 1746). In itself, his thrift was a virtue, but it also paid dividends. Even though he had not survived to enjoy them, they were richly endowing his son, forty years later.[81]

For the definition of the Binghams' realm, one letter from Thomas Jefferson provides an explanation. In 1787, when Ann and William were living in Paris on their Grand Tour, she received a letter from Thomas Jefferson, in which, in contrast to the "empty bustle" in Paris, Jefferson lists the "tranquil pleasures" of living in Philadelphia: "the society of your husband, the fond cares for the children, the arrangements of the house, the improvements of the grounds fill every moment with a healthy and an useful activity." Care for family and "improvements" in property make life "heathy" and "useful" in Philadelphia. Since Americans inhabit vast open spaces, they naturally consider the use and improvement of land as their special virtues. 'Be an American!,' Jefferson advises. Following this advice, Ann returned to Philadelphia and wrote a significant chapter in American history.

William Bingham, Jr. with his wife, Ann Willing Bingham, no longer lived above the store of his family business. In 1787, having returned from their Grand Tour through England, France and Italy, they lived on the west side of Third street between Walnut and Spruce, next to the home of her aunt and uncle, Elizabeth Willing Powel (1743–1830) and William Powel (1738–1793). William and Ann Willing Bingham represented the third generation of the Willings on this block. On the north side of the block, Ann's grandfather, Charles Willing (1710–1754) had first acquired the property from William Penn's family about 1740. The Powels had bought their property in 1769. William and Ann bought the rest of the block, south of the Powels' home. By 1786, therefore, three generations of Willings resided on this block: from north to south, grandfather Willing (1740), his daughter Elizabeth (1769) and his granddaughter Ann (1786).

The Binghams' property was by far the largest in the Willing compound. It extended "263 feet, 6 inches on Third street, 396 feet on Spruce, and 293 feet, 6 inches on Fourth" (*Aurora General Advertiser*, October 14, 1805). On this large plot, William set out to build, his biographer has said, "the finest and best furnished house in America." In building this elegant house, he used all the notes that he had taken after visiting fine mansions around England. Carriages approached the mansion by a circular driveway. Guests entered a marble entrance hall in a mosaic pattern with a white marble staircase. For parties, Ann filled it with flowers. Once inside guests admired art purchased from Italy, fabrics from France, and furniture from England.

Philadelphians called their home simply "The Mansion House." It was, Watson reported, "the admiration of that day for its ornament and magnificence." William Petty Fitzmaurice, 1st Marquess of Lansdowne and lord of Bowood in Wiltshire, England, helped his friend Bingham to design the gardens, surrounded by Lombardy poplars and "curious and rare clumps and shades of trees,"—"a woodland scene" in the city (Watson, *Annals* [1884], v. I, p. 414).[82] William Hamilton of the Woodlands had introduced the Lombardy poplar from the north of Italy. Its branches hugging a statuesque trunk, like that of the Italian cypress, evoke the gardens of Italy.

"A house fit for a queen!"—passersby might have exclaimed,—their exclamations had some kernel of truth. Once Philadelphia became the capital of the nation from 1790–1800, the Binghams' parties took on

Thomas Birch (1755–1844), *View in Third street from Spruce* (1800)

The Bingham mansion is prominent. Note the wings on either side. To the right of the Lombardy poplar, an octagonal tower provided water closets for the Powels' home.

special significance. Those in attendance at Ann and William's house, and at her aunt and uncle's next door, included, Watson boasts, "the highest in the land . . . Washington, Adams, Jefferson and other distinguished American and foreign statesmen and ministers" (Watson, *op. cit.*, v. III, 272). Unofficially, Ann, as the "the uncrowned queen of the Republican court," was conducting "her country's first and last salon in the European manner (Alberts, 213). Her democratic reign represents a short period in American democracy, after American government had freed itself from His Majesty, but before its etiquette had freed itself from His pomp. Experience in the salons of London had prepared Ann to follow Jefferson's advice and fill up the transition with her special American charm.

Bingham's country house occupied the most beautiful spot on the west bank of the Schuylkill, a small plateau between two valleys with their streams flowing into the river, but he had not built it. John Penn (1725–1795), a grandson of William Penn, had purchased this property in 1773; and on it, he had built Lansdowne, "a stone mansion of magnificent proportion," Watson has effused. Penn lived there until his death in 1795. Bingham purchased it at a sheriff's sale in 1797.

In the Palladian style, Lansdowne had a portico, which, like Palladio's *Villa Cornaro* (1553), displayed the Doric order on the first storey and the Ionic on the second. Drayton Hall (*circa* 1750) in Charleston might also have inspired this variation of the classical orders. In the *Villa Cornaro*, in Drayton Hall, and also in Lansdowne, a pediment surmounted the portico; but in Lansdowne, uniquely, bay windows projected from either end of its two storeys.

A long, tree-lined avenue approached the house. Watson described the grounds as "undulating, beautifully laid out, with fine old trees and romantic glens and ravines." June 23, 1795, after John Adams visited, he wrote back to his wife Abigail: Lansdowne is "very retired, but very beautiful." He might better have said "very retired" and "very beautiful," because Lansdowne's "very retired" location complemented its beauty. The stream in Lansdowne Glen in Fairmount Park still hints at this "romantic" wildness.

For a few years after 1797, Ann and William made Lansdowne the country seat of their "hospitality and elegance." This "wealthy and fashionable" couple entertained, as Watson has said, "the highest in the land. . . ." Watson, the annalist, praised lofty personages appropriately, but the warmth of the Binghams' "hospitality and elegance" made everyone feel at home. In September of 1797, for example, Robert Gilmor, the son of Bingham's business partner, stayed at Lansdowne. During the day, this young man hunted in the field or read in the library. One evening, he dined with the family of the British minister, Sir Robert Liston (1742–1836). With this family, he spent enough time at the dinner table to eat; then they gathered on the Doric portico and out onto the lawn, where the whole family was accustomed to play games (Alberts, 311).

Lansdowne's Palladian elegance may also cause us to overlook the good earth of its farm. How else did the Binghams put food on their elegant table? In the neighborhood, cows were grazing here and there among the pastures: "Notice: Came to the farm of William Bingham, Esq. called Lansdowne, in Blockley township, Philadelphia county, some time near the 22d of June last, a small black cow, very old, the owner is desired to come, prove property, pay charges and taker her away. Thomas Bones" (*Aurora General Advertiser*, August 18, 1800). Thomas Bones continued to manage the farm even after Mr. Bingham's death.[83]

An eye for beauty led the Binghams to Lansdowne on the west bank of the Schuylkill. The same eye, quite extraordinarily, also led them to Black Point on the north shore of New Jersey. In the 1790's, the remoteness of the barrier islands to the south discouraged visitors, but the mainland, to the north, was relatively more accessible and certainly more varied in its landscape. Streams, rivers and lakes cut through the coast, as they flowed into the ocean. The first coastal town to become a popular resort took the name Long Branch, because its stream, a tributary of the Shrewsbury River, extraordinarily, flowed south to north, into the river, instead of the usual course of water, west to east, into the ocean. The peninsula formed by Shrewsbury, as its two branches flowed into the ocean, below the Highlands and Sandy Hook, caught the Binghams' eye. Surrounded by water on three sides, it resembled Lansdowne that is also a peninsula, so to speak, surrounded by streams flowing into the Schuylkill. No other place on the Jersey shore can rival the beauty of this peninsula between the two branches of the Shrewsbury.

In 1791, Bingham purchased *Belle Vue* at Black Point, an estate of about 275 acres at the tip of this peninsula, now located in Rumson. His house survived into the twentieth century as "a large and cumbersome structure, of no particular style."[84] What a contrast with his elegant town and country houses! The previous owner must have appreciated the view, a *belle vue*, of course, because the house had a sky parlor, which Bingham equipped with a telescope, a spy glass, and concave mirrors, popular in their day, to reflect it.

He remodeled the original house by adding wings, but he was more intent on making its farm self-sufficient for his family's needs. In his first summer, he told his contractor, "the resources of the neighborhood" had not supplied his family adequately. The north Garden State's cornucopia had not flowed copiously enough for the high standards of his household. In 1792, he ordered the construction of a barn, greenhouse, milk house, ice house, and, of course, a necessary. Although the Binghams had access to beaches at Sea Bright and Sandy Hook, they did not do any sea bathing. As the first summer residents on the Rumson peninsula, they lived on a gentleman's farm,—enjoying the double pleasure of river views and sea breezes.

In both places, on the seashore in a remodeled farm house, and on the banks of the Schuylkill in a Palladian villa, Bingham had established farms. In addition to enjoying his villa on the Schuylkill, summering on the seashore was extraordinary. It anticipated the resorts in that area later in the nineteenth century. Bingham's life was consistently reaching beyond Philadelphia.

May 11, 1801, Ann Bingham, at the age of 36, died and was buried in Bermuda. In the last weeks of February, although convalescing from giving birth to her third child, she had gone out on a sleighing party. She caught cold and was too frail to shake it. When her health went into a rapid decline; William thought that a trip to Madeira would help her to recover. She did not have the strength to sail any farther than Bermuda. William returned to Philadelphia, bereft of the crown of his "excellent wife." A few years later in 1804, after he had served in the United States' Senate for six years, William died in Bath, England, at the age of 51.

Bingham's tomb in Bath alludes to his "knowledge of the interests of his country and his zeal for their advancement." It ends with two lines from an *Ode* of Horace:

> CUI PUDOR ET IUSTITIAE SOROR
> INCORRUPTA FIDES NUDAQUE VERITAS
> <*Quando ullum inveniet parem?*> (Horace, *Carmina* I, 24).
>
> (When will modesty and the sister of justice, uncorrupt faith,
> and pure truth find any man a peer to him?)

This quotation from Horace fit William Bingham who at his graduation ceremony from the University of Pennsylvania participated in a "Latin syllogistic dispute," *Utrum mens humana sit immortals?*, "whether the human soul is immortal" (*Pennsylvania Gazette*, December 1, 1768). According to the classic dignity of this allusion, William Bingham had no peer in virtue. In their American character and life, he and Ann had no peer. Their life together represents a unique American experience, so unique that it transcended the bounds of their country. Ann, especially, put American blood into British manners and brought them back to Philadelphia.

The Binghams' lives epitomized the cosmopolitan culture of Philadelphia when it served as the capital of the country in the last decade of the eighteenth century. In 1858, Samuel Breck, their neighbor at Sweetbriar on the Schuylkill, reminisced: Ann Willing Bingham "stood above competition in her day; nor has anyone of equal refinement in address or social stateliness, and graceful superintendence of a splendid establishment, been produced since in any circle of our city" (Alberts, 414). Appropriately, neither Ann nor William died or was buried in Philadelphia, nor did their children marry Philadelphians. Their lives reached beyond the geographical limits and cultural limitations of America. Ann and William helped America make the passage from British to American manners, but their children only made it one way and ended up British in Britain—falling on the European side of the classic American Anglophile dilemma.

After William's demise, his mansion stood empty until it became the Mansion House Hotel. A notice for its sale in 1810 boasted that "as to materials, workmanship and elegance, it is exceeded by none in the United States." Guests, the notice boasted, might enjoy "the most complete and elegant establishment for a public house in the United States" (*Aurora General Advertiser*, January 30, 1810). Seventeen years later, the hotel had 70 rooms "more accommodations and conveniences for a larger hotel and tavern than, it is believed, any other establishment of the same nature in the United States" (*National Gazette*, May 15, 1827).

In 1846, the building suffered so much damage from a fire that it was demolished in 1849 by Nicholas Bouvier who built a home for himself and his partner in business. In the rear of the lot he built "an extensive steam sawmill" as part of his business (*Public Ledger*, June 11, 1849).

CHAPTER 16

The Family Ties of Francisville

DURING THE LIVES of the two sons of Tench Francis (?–1758), Tench, Jr. (1745–1797) and Turbutt (1740–1782) and his grandchildren, the family estate grew into the village of Francisville. His sons' careers in law, land and retail did not leave a distinctive mark on Francisville like the one that the Bartrams left on their garden, the Peters on Belmont, or the Hamiltons on Bush Hill and The Woodlands. Though less distinctive, the lives of this family fill in its context. In the 1770's, at the beginning of this history, two portraits by Charles Wilson Peale provide clues for the life of Turbutt; and street names in Francisville also provide clues for that of his older brother Tench.

CONNECTIONS BY FAMILY and business help to tell the story of the Francis family. Tench's first son, Tench, Jr. married into the Willing family. His wife, Ann Willing, daughter of Thomas Willing (1710–1754), and their daughter, Ann Willing Francis, doubly confirm the origin of Ann street in Francisville. Family ties and the 'counting house of Willing and Francis can also confirm the origin of Charles and Powell[85] streets. Ann Willing Francis was the sister of Elizabeth Willing Powel, whose nephew and heir John Powel Hare worked in the firm of Willing and Francis. Employment and family connected John Powel Hare with the Francis family. Charles Francis, Jr., also joined this firm (*National Gazette*, March 19, 1834 & December 11, 1835).

Turbutt Francis connected with the Mifflin family, when he married Sarah, the daughter of Samuel and Rebecca Mifflin. The portrait by Charles Wilson Peale (1741–1827) of Sarah's mother, *Mrs. Samuel Mifflin and Her Granddaughter, Rebecca Mifflin Francis* (1778) portrays the maternal side of this union. The girl in the portrait, Rebecca Mifflin Francis, was the daughter of Turbutt and Sarah Mifflin Francis.[86] The title of this painting omits one clue to the importance of the Francises' connection with the Mifflins: Mrs. Samuel Mifflin's Christian name, Rebecca, indicates that her granddaughter, Rebecca Mifflin Francis, had her grandmother's name. Young Rebecca's having her maternal grandmother's name marks just one instance of all three Francis children having names from their maternal line.

In Philadelphia of the eighteenth century, the Mifflins' name opened doors. Rebecca Mifflin's husband, Samuel Mifflin (1724–1781), had gained great wealth as a merchant. Charles Wilson Peale also painted a portrait of him that celebrated this success. When Turbutt Francis married Samuel's daughter, he was making an hypergamous match.

Charles Wilson Peale, *Mrs. Samuel Mifflin and Her Granddaughter, Rebecca Mifflin Francis* (1778)

He and his wife Sarah showed particular respect to her father, by making Mifflin the middle name of their first son, Tench Mifflin Francis.

By the third and most important tribute to the Mifflins, Sarah and Turbutt Francis also gave their second son, Samuel Mifflin Francis (1776–1829), the full name of his maternal grandfather, Samuel Mifflin. Both Tench Mifflin Francis and his brother, Samuel Mifflin Francis, had reason to give their maternal grandfather special respect, both inside and outside the family. Samuel Mifflin owned one of the wharves that opened the harbor to a merchant like Tench Mifflin Francis for his stock and to the firm of Willing-Francis for their accounts.

Peale's painting celebrated this familial connection by picturing Rebecca Mifflin teaching her namesake granddaughter, Rebecca Mifflin Francis, from a book of emblems. Such books made virtues emblematic and served the Christian and classical education of the young. This painting itself served as an emblem of the close ties between the two families, but as only one of a pair. Peale's portrait of Samuel Mifflin celebrated the family's paternal wealth, and that of Samuel's wife and granddaughter celebrated its maternal virtue.

Samuel Mifflin, however, wanted his grandson, Samuel M. Francis, to bear his name as more than a middle initial. By his will in 1781, he left him property on the condition that he drop his father's name. Samuel Mifflin, the elder, wanted an heir with his name. Perhaps after Turbutt Francis' death one year later, in 1782, his son, young Samuel Mifflin Francis, at age 6, could more easily drop his father's name to become Samuel Mifflin. By wealth or well being,—who knows in what proportion?—Samuel Mifflin, Sr. gained a unique name in the family of his son-in-law, Turbutt Francis.[87] (Since much of this story has focused on family names, it may be of interest that both Tench and Turbutt are the names of fish.)

Both the Mifflins and the Francises contributed to the patriotic cause of 1776, but Samuel Mifflin, Sr. did so more generously in proportion to his wealth. The Francis family suffered in proportion to their relative lack,—and perhaps, also, in proportion to their patriotism. The British had not burned their mansion. Instead, they had so dismantled it that it remained a splendid wreck into the nineteenth century (*Times*, April 22, 1886). They dismantled it because they had heard rumors of a secret vault on the property, in which patriotic Philadelphians had hidden their valuables. The vault did exist, but the British could not pinpoint its location. Before these Philadelphians fled the British invasion, they had constructed this vault on the Francis estate,—now on north Nineteenth street below Brown,—lined it with triple brick, twenty feet below the street, and hurriedly packed it with jewelry, money, and rare stuffs. Having sealed its iron trap doors, they fled, either to serve as soldiers or to live as refugees in towns up the Schuylkill (*Inquirer*, November 19, 1898).[88] Hoping to find this treasure trove, the British carefully dismantled the Francis mansion, piece by piece. They might as well have burned it to the ground, as far as it could ever again have served as a home.

In the tradition of old Philadelphia families, the Mifflins and the Francises owned estates, both north of the city. When Samuel Mifflin, aka Samuel Mifflin-Francis, died in 1829, at the relatively young age of 53, he left land without much cash to his wife and nine children. Also in the tradition of old families, his heirs continued to subdivide their family's estate, renting its plots to generate cash and finally selling them to generate more. About 1826, when Francisville first appeared in notices of sale, it became prominent in their history.[89]

In 1826, Samuel Mifflin-Francis, at age 50, three years before his death, published the first notice of a sale: "Valuable Property in the pleasant village of Francisville, one mile from the city of Philadelphia, with three brick dwelling houses, 100 feet on Ann street and 300 feet on Powell street, the rental of the houses presently brings in $240 *per annum*, subject to ground rent of $100" (*National Gazette*, March 21, 1826). This notice in 1826 made the first mention, in a Philadelphia newspaper, of a property for sale in "the pleasant village of Francisville;" but it also indicates that the family had already been renting it privately before they were trying to sell it publicly.

The Francis family suffered loss in the American Revolution. In the industrial revolution of the early nineteenth century, they did not profit as much as other Philadelphia families. Samuel Mifflin-Francis served as President of the Union Canal Company, with the distinction of being called "the Clinton of Pennsylvania," in allusion to the development by DeWitt Clinton (1769–1828) of the Erie Canal in New York

State. Pennsylvania, unfortunately, did not enjoy the bonanza from its canals that New York had from the Erie Canal. His executive position did not made him wealthy. After his death on March 24, 1829, his widow sought a "remuneration" from his business that had not been remunerative to him in life. The Union Canal Company awarded a "remuneration" to her and her children "proportioned to her claims" (*National Gazette*, May 18, 1829). At the beginning of the nineteenth century, investors at first bet on canals with water, only to realize later that they might more profitably put their money on rails with steam. Samuel Mifflin-Francis had picked the traditional, but less lucrative, mode of transportation.

Samuel's widow, turning to the family's land as her other source of income, continued to sell subdivisions of Francisville: "A frame House and Stable on a Lot 200 × 300 feet, grape vines, fruit trees, shrubberies, ground rent of $60.00 a year; the lot may be subdivided" (*United States Gazette*, April 17, 1829). The "grape vines" recall William's Penn's plan for a vineyard on his proprietary estate, from which Francisville had been subdivided. Vineyard and Grape streets in Francisville allude to this viticulture. Over the years, ever smaller subdivisions of its large plots have congested Francisville as much as any other neighborhood in Philadelphia.

Notices for these sales continued to appear into the 1830's: "Beautiful lot in Francisville. 50 feet on Francis Street and 50 feet on Ann street by 320 feet deep; three frame dwellings fronting on Ann street, subject to ground rent of $15 *per annum*" (*National Gazette*, November 23, 1838). Ground rent of "$15 *per annum*" seems appropriate for a humble cottage.

Most of the cottages in Francisville had wood frames, contrary to the tradition in Philadelphia, the Red City, of building with brick. These small wood-frame cottages, with gardens, before and behind, made Francisville a village in the country, until brick, throughout the nineteenth century, replaced the wood; and all its buildings faced on a street in the city (*Inquirer*, May 29, 1884). Francisville had an unpretentious, humble origin. One of these wood-framed cottages has survived into the 21st century, but within a row of brick homes, and without the garden that would evoke an image of the "pleasant village" that first surrounded it.

When Turbutt Francis' children took his father-in-law's name, the support that the Mifflins gave the Francises and Francisville helped their subsequent history. Even with this infusion of new blood and a new name, their fortunes did not prosper proportionately. After the death of Samuel Mifflin's grandson, Samuel Mifflin-Francis, his widow's request for a "remuneration" from his company, and her sale of the modest wood frame cottages of Francisville reflect the family's relatively limited resource.

Hamiltonville, by contrast, profited from the wealth of William Hamilton and its location on his very large tract of land in a distinct,—and distinctive,—suburb, west of the Schuylkill River. Francisville, in a relatively small area close to the city, had neither the location, nor the wealth of its founding family that might set it apart as a prestigious community. Its name survives because its right-angled streets, projected off of Ridge Avenue's diagonal, have given it a grid pattern different from that of the city that surrounds it. By contrast, Hamiltonville provided the nucleus of a distinctive community in West Philadelphia, but it survives only as a name without distinct boundaries. Hamiltonville has distinction without distinct boundaries; Francisville has distinct boundaries without distinction.

Note: Francisville's extraordinary grid, going against the grain of Philadelphia's grid, has preserved its identity. When Tench Francis, Sr. first bought the property, it was located on the Ridge Pike, just a mile outside the old city. In surveying the land for development, his family laid out its streets at right angles off this road. This plan seemed regular, until the usual grid of Philadelphia streets eventually surrounded it and made it seem irregular. Its relatively irregular grid, separated from the regular grid of the city, allowed it to preserve the original names of its streets, named after members of the Francis family. By contrast, the names of the original streets in Hamiltonville disappeared when Philadelphia's grid pattern absorbed them. William street, for example, was absorbed by Locust street, and James street by Chestnut street.

At the beginning of the twentieth century, Philadelphia planned to drive its north-south streets through Francisville by extending 17th and 18th street (*Inquirer*, May, 8, 1906). The city never executed this plan, probably because of the considerable expense that it would have required. Poor Francisville!—it wasn't worth it.

Francisville's uniqueness does create problems. At the end of the nineteenth century, the *Inquirer* joked that trolley cars made their passengers seasick by swinging so sharply around its corners (*Inquirer*, January 31, 1892). One serious incident occurred when an unwary pedestrian got lost in its maze of streets and fell prey to neighborhood hooligans:

> SMALL-SIZED RIOT. An incipient riot . . . An attack at Francis and Orr streets on a hapless pedestrian, who, lost in the mazy way of the section, sought information as to how to get out. The crowd, all young men, ridiculed him; and, at his angry response, one of them attacked him (*Inquirer*, June 27, 1898).

Francisville still disorients pedestrians, haplessly wandering into its "mazy way," but not necessarily falling into a riot.

CHAPTER 17

Stephen Girard and His Farm

After some very distinguished Philadelphians of the eighteenth century made their fortunes on Water street as merchants, they retired to the banks Schuylkill as gentlemen. Stephen Girard (1750–1831) started his career in this pattern. At age 14, he sailed from his native Bordeaux as a mariner; and at age 26, he settled in Philadelphia as a merchant, but he never retired. When he died at age 81, he emphasized this unbroken career in the title of his will: "Stephen Girard, of the City of Philadelphia, in the Commonwealth of Pennsylvania, Mariner and Merchant, being of sound mind. . . ." He made a point of not calling himself a gentleman. "Plain in appearance, simple in manners," observed his friend Nicholas Biddle, "his long life was one unbroken succession of intense and untiring industry." "Plain" and "simple" describe his life and explain his success. Gentlemen retired to lives of refined leisure; to his death, Stephen Girard pursued the life of a merchant.

As a merchant, however, Girard balanced humility with humanity, along with the brokerage of French wine. He passed on a legacy of this humanity to Girard College, the charity school that he founded by his will. By its stipulations, the students' meals would be "plain but wholesome;" their clothing, "plain but decent;" and their lodging, "plain but safe."[90] On the other hand, a Greek peripteral temple surrounded them as they lived this plain and simple life.[91] Plain and simple, but excellent in its own way, can also describe his farmhouse in Passyunk, which has survived as the most significant relic from his

Founder's Hall of Girard College

life in Philadelphia. In its fields, orchards and greenhouse, Girard got down to the earth that gave him opportunities for its produce and productivity ever-new.

STEPHEN'S GRANDPARENTS HAD MOVED from the French countryside to the port of Bordeaux. His father, Pierre, at age 13, had followed the salt air scent to the sea. Stephen, at age 14, signed on as an apprentice officer on a ship, in which his father had an interest; and he rose to become a captain by age 23. He focused his trade on French San Domingo, now called Haiti, and its port *Cape François*, where his father had also done business. It was commonly called *Le Cap*, capital of San Domingo.

In 1776, Girard sailed up from *Le Cap* to Canada. In June, as captain and half owner, he brought the ship, *La Jeune Bébé*, from *Saint Pierre, Miquelon*,[92] back down the East Coast. After rough seas had tossed most of his casks of fresh water overboard, he sought refuge up Delaware Bay. On June 6, *La Jeune Bébé* landed in Philadelphia.

At first from necessity, but eventually because he liked the place, Stephen Girard made Philadelphia his home. While the city was weathering the political storms of the American Revolution, he sought business from his father in Bordeaux and from his brother, Jean, in *Le Cap*. Aware of potential hostility of the British toward the French, he even, for a while, set up his home and a small business in Mount Holly, New Jersey. Back in Philadelphia, he advertised his first stock in trade in the summer of 1783:

STEPHEN GIRARD,
At his STORE in Water-street, between Market and Arch-streets.
HAS FOR SALE,
MOLASSES, Sugar, Coffee, old Bourdeaux Claret, Oporto Wine, sweet Oil, Salt, Tea, writing Paper, Raisins, Geneva in cases, French Aniseed, Wire, Cloths, Tammies, Nankeens, Handkerchiefs, Linens, Gauzes, white sewing Thread, artificial Flowers, women's Caps, fishing Seines of sixty fathoms length
(*Dunlap and Claypoole's American Daily Advertiser*, July 22, 1783).

For Cape Francois,
THE Ship Polacre L'ESPERANCE, Captain Anthony Vidal:
She will sail the 15th of August next, and will take in some Freight.
For particulars enquire as above.

Girard derived his stock from the trade that he had developed with his father and brother. He imported molasses, sugar and coffee from *Le Cap*; and claret, aniseed (*Anisette de Bordeaux*) and Oporto wine from France. ("Geneva in cases" refers to gin from the juniper.) At age 33, he was developing trade in fine European wines. Especially, in "the Ship Polacre L'ESPERANCE," which he advertises for a voyage down to his brother in *Le Cap*, he had started to build the fleet of ships that would increase his wealth.

After a few years, Jean Girard came up from *Le Cap* to join his brother Stephen in a partnership. These two Frenchmen advertised a sophisticated, high-end trade:

Stephen and John Girard,

At their store in Water street, midway between Market and Arch streets—*Have for sale*

FRENCH brandy three years old, in half and quarter butts, porto wine in pipes and half pipes, claret in casks, old Frontignac wine in cases of 12 bottles each, molasses, coffee in bags and barrels, cocoa, rum, Castile soap, sweet oil in cases of 12 bottles each, Holland ginger, Zant currants in half barrels, raisins in drums, verdigreas, brimstone in boxes, fresh cargo beef in barrels, writing paper, a few tons of bar iron

(*Dunlap and Claypoole's American Daily Advertiser,* October 9, 1786).

Reversing the order of the advertisement that he wrote three years earlier, Girard first lists the fine wines of his high-end stock, and leaves the molasses and coffee in second place. Two years later he would elaborate his descriptions: "old brandy in hogsheads, high proof, and of the best quality" (*Dunlap and Claypoole's American Daily Advertiser,* July 23, 1788). In 1788, he and his brother dissolved their partnership. Jean commented on the separation: "It is amusing to have you ask me how you can make more money. You will always be the same, never content." "Never content," ambitious brother Stephen set a fast pace!

By the 1790's, Stephen Girard had accumulated enough wealth for a genteel retirement; but, as his brother observed, he could never rest "content." His part in a remarkable drama in the history of Philadelphia demonstrates that his dis-content had an impulse far different from greed. Ambition, pure, but never content, animates the benevolent expression in his portrait that does not portray a miser.

In the first scene of this drama, one of Girard's ships from *Le Cap* sailed up the Delaware Bay in the Spring of 1793. It was carrying some French refugees from the slaves' uprising led by Toussaint Louverture. The good fortune of his fellow Frenchmen to find refuge brought an unexpected misfortune to his city. This and other ships from the West Indies were transporting the mosquitoes that spread the yellow fever epidemic of 1793.

Stephen Girard, the merchant and mariner, "never content"

The plague tested the mettle of the city. Wealthy citizens fled, one newspaper observed, to take pleasure in "their opulence, insensible to the misery of their fellow citizens" (*Aurora General Advertiser*, November 4, 1808). Stephen Girard took no pleasure in opulence, and he did not remain "insensible to the misery of his fellow citizens." As always, he stood apart. His stance came naturally from his perspective: cosmopolitan in origins, and enlightened in character—above petty acquisition, and down to earth. Extraordinarily, of course, and beyond all the calculations of the natural man, his courage and humanity made him stand firm and apart.

Like a good captain of his ship, he took the helm. He paid to equip the Hamiltons' mansion, which the city had rented as a hospital, at Bush Hill, a suburb north of the city. Though in charge as an administrator, he also personally ministered to the needs of the patients. After the virulence of the disease lessened in October, one newspaper described his ministrations:

> He has acted as a father, constantly in the rooms, encouraging the sick, handing them whatever they stand in need of, covering them, wiping the sweat off their brows and performing many offices of kindness to them, at which nice feelings, in any other circumstances, would revolt (*The Independent Gazetteer*, October 26, 1793).

Sophisticated, but unselfish and down-to-earth, Girard needed less courage than might have seemed necessary, because he knew what not to fear.[93] Few Philadelphians were equally sensible, even the physicians. After the third outbreak of the fever in 1798, he despaired of their rationality: "Our doctors have for the third time," he lamented, "lost their wits;" and even their morality: he labeled the members of the Philadelphia College of Physicians "ignorant charlatans" (McMaster I, 349 & 374–375).[94]

As long as he could spare time from his public service in the seasons of plague, Girard continued to pursue his business and he built a commodious home and counting house in 1796. Before 1796, he had lived and worked at 33 North Water Street, which he gave as his address in the *Aurora General Advertiser* from July 22, 1783 until May 19, 1796. At first, with ambitious hopes for his new building, he tried to hire Pierre Charles L'Enfant (1754–1825), the famous French architect. Unsuccessful in this request—L'Enfant was too busy designing Washington, D.C.—he himself designed the building and superintended its construction. Moving from his attempt to hire an architect to doing the work by himself speaks well for his initiative: when he could not hire the best man for the work, he did his own best work instead. At Bush Hill, without, or perhaps, in spite of, physicians, his own work had been the best.

In that Spring and Summer, he was moving his home and store; and in August 16, 1796, he first advertised his new place at 23 North Water street. It had three bays and five floors, topped by a roof walk, from which he could observe activity in the harbor. One door opened to his business and another to his home—a plain post and lintel entrance, with a transom window for his business, and a classical pedimental entrance with a fan light for his home. At 21 North Water street, his adjoining counting house had two bays, two stories, and also a plain post and lintel entrance, with a transom window, like the one next door. By these doors, Stephen Girard opened his building to business, but he separated it from domesticity.

IN 1797, A YEAR after moving into his new home and counting house, he purchased two farms near the confluence of the Schuylkill River with the Delaware. On his farm, he also joined a new home with business. Wealthy merchants becoming gentlemen did not choose land in this neighborhood. They built their mansions on higher ground up the Schuyllkill, above Fairmount. In the late 1780's, this notice described a property down the Schuylkill:

> A TRACT of Land in the township of Passyunk, on the road leading to Penrose ferry, about 3 miles from the city, containing 17 acres, 109 perches and 3/4, more or less; on which is erected a Frame Barn; about 5 acres of it may with little expense, be made into good meadow; the other part is good arable land; three acres of this land has never been cleared; and being near the citv, would suit a person who attends the markets (*Dunlap and Claypoole's American Daily Advertiser*, May 9, 1789).

Girard would have welcomed the challenge of these 17 acres: "with little expense," he could make five of them into "good meadow," and with much work, he could clear three for the plow. Of course, "little expense" did not spare him much work! In this neighborhood, meadow and "arable land" suited a farmer "who attended the markets." Before 1797, he had not "attended" to farmers' business or attended their markets; but he now hoped to grow some of the goods that he had been buying.

In December of 1797, he purchased one farm of 71 acres for £4479, 18s, 11d, Pennsylvania money, from "George Cooper, skin dresser and breeches maker." The farm house, 25 feet in width and 112 feet deep, "beautiful in its ancient style of roomy simplicity," a newspaper reminisced in 1895, had "a wonderful suggestion of liberty and plainness and comfort . . . yet such as no banker of the present day would live in" (*Inquirer*, October, 1895). The writer assumes complacently that a man as wealthy as Stephen Girard, in 1895, would not live as Stephen Girard had in 1795. In 1895, at the end of the nineteenth, the greatest—and most complacent—of centuries, he considered Victorian materialism and pretension a universal value!

Merchants aspiring to become gentlemen would also not have espoused Stephen Girard's relentless work ethic. They usually retired to become gentlemen farmers, but Girard never forgot business. Having just designed and overseen the building of his home with his counting house, he happily put a new ledger for his harvests and vintages on its shelf. Memories of his grandparents' life in the countryside might have been calling him back to his roots. Along with some of this nostalgia, his new fields brought together and advanced different parts of his trade, and gave him healthy exercise that he had never had on his wharf. Far beyond some healthy exercise, his hearty life on the sea had prepared him for hard labor on the farm! In his usual schedule, he spent the morning hours over his accounts, commuted to work on his farm in the afternoon, and returned home in the evening to put in a few hours over his accounts before retiring. All together, he worked, as he said, like a galley slave.

His past trade had given him a priority: after so many years of importing wines from vineyards in France, he imported vines for his own vineyards in Passyunk. Girard was not the first to have this idea. By introducing viticulture on his proprietary estate, William Penn first tried to grow grapes. As soon as Girard acquired the farm, he asked one of his importers for vines instead of wines:

> As I have lately come into possession of two properties in the country, situated three miles from our city on the road to Fort Mifflin, I beg you will send me by return of the ship *Good Friends* some roots of muscat vines and another of good white grapes.

Muscat, and its diminutive muscatel, describe a white grape and its wine, like the Frontignac wine that he had imported. In a letter to a friend, Girard mentioned the great "pain" that he was taking to foster their growth:

> I have taken much pain with grape vines. Our severe winters are a great obstacle to their progress. . . . I have about 250 of the best sort imported

> from France and Spain, except one vine which is pretty large and raised from the seed of a grape imported in a jar from Malaga. Out of that vine, I had last several fine large grapes in full maturity (McMaster, II, 411).

Why did Girard search out a special grape vine from Malaga? From the southeast coast of Spain on the Mediterranean, it was perhaps related to the muscat grapes that he also imported. By 1812, he had a large arbor of French and American grapes (*Aurora*, June 16, 1812). Growing grape vines came naturally to him, but their growth did not come naturally in Philadelphia's "severe winters."

Oenology was just the beginning of his -ologies. He had also purchased a farm from a sale of the property of Henry Seckel, who owned it from 1791–1797. Seckel, also a wine merchant, had introduced the Seckel Pear tree, whose fruit may be the only one native to America. After tasting it, Thomas Jefferson thought that it was superior to any pear that he had eaten in Europe. He developed Mr. Seckel's pear orchard, which the Pennsylvania Horticultural Society called "second to none in the country."

Girard imported 300 fruit trees, which he hoped would be "useful to our country." In his vineyard and orchard, no one could do the work quite as well as he could: "In consequence of not having a good overseer nor gardener, all my valuable fruit trees are uniformly planted or trained by me" (Hubbard, p 511). Since no one else appreciated as he did how much he had paid to import his "valuable" investment, he was not about to entrust planting and training it to any one else.

Along with his careful work in oeniculture and pomoculture, Girard could not forget olericulture. (He took such pains with his grape vines, fruit trees and vegetables that his enthusiasms deserve their place in the ologies!) After all, muscatel and pears graced the table after his family had eaten their vegetables. "On the subject of gardening," Girard continued in his letter to a friend, "if you want some good cabbage, lettuce, celery, onions, carrots, beets, turnips, parsnips and other vegetable seed, please to let me know." Along with hearty—and heady—-coles, Girard grew even heartier roots and tubers.

Of course, a thrifty man like Stephen Girard liked roots and tubers. In October of 1793, before he was growing food for his own table, a house guest reported that his household sat down to a dinner of sweet potatoes and beets with pickled cucumbers, pears and apple pie, along with Madeira wine.[95] Roots and tubers stored well and provided excellent nourishment. In 1827, when he was provisioning an expedition at the foot of Broad Mountain on the eastern side of the Mohanoy Mountains, he sent "three barrels of potatoes, a barrel or two of beets and turnips, radishes, and a keg of white beans" (McMaster II, 437).

Girard tried hard to give each precious shoot a good shot at life, and then he raised them all to be the best: "I raise them myself from seed," he wrote in reference to his vegetables, "which I received from time to time from places in Europe; consequently it is pretty good, and I will send you what you want for your own use" (McMaster, *loc. cit.*). The Horticultural Society also asserted that he was the first agriculturist to introduce the artichoke. He sold his produce in the South Second street market. "It was of such excellent quality," the *Inquirer* boasted, "that it always sold higher than the prevailing prices."

On board ship, Girard had learned the ropes. On his farm, he grew hemp so that he could do his own rigging. As usual, he grew the best, or at least the tallest: "There is now growing on the property of Stephen Girard in Passyunk township, Philadelphia county," a newspaper reported, "a stalk of Hemp amongst others nine feet four inches high and has not yet attained its ultimate height. The stalk is four inches and a half in circumference just above the surface of the ground" (*US Gazette*, August 1, 1828).[96] He did not own his own rope-walk, but he knew the ropers, who would buy his hemp.

In addition to Girard's house guest reporting that he sat down to a vegetarian meal in 1793, Girard, in his later years, reported that he ate only ship's bread, vegetables, "pure water" and "strong coffee" without sugar or cream; and, sparingly, claret with water (McMaster, II, 411–2). On his farm, however, he never disregarded livestock. He stocked his barns with the "best breeds of sheep and cattle" imported from Europe (McMaster, v. 1, 355). Every December, he slaughtered about 200 cattle to provide cargo beef or corned beef for his fleet.[97] All his work paid dividends. The products of his farm, "though produced at a lower cost, were infinitely better than those from neighboring farms" (*Inquirer*, September, 1894). As usual, he worked hard to achieve the business man's goal: large profit with little expense.

While Girard was planting and pruning, he was also building.[98] He built, as he called it, "The Mansion House" next to the original farm house (1750), with a classical pediment above three bays, a parlor on the first floor, two rooms on the second, and, of course, cellars for storage in the basement. Along with the cellars, he made his home useful in the manner of a European farm house. By 1803, he had added to the Mansion an east wing with service rooms and a greenhouse, where he grew lemons, mandarin oranges, and other fruit trees, "all," according to the Horticultural Society, "large and beautiful." By 1831, The Place had 583 acres; and the Mansion House, 16 rooms.

After ten years of Girard's cultivating his Place, its neighborhood increased in value and prestige:

> FOR SALE
> TOGETHER OR IN LOTS
> *That elegant and highly cultivated farm, called*
> SPRING HILL
> SITUATE about three miles from the city, and half a mile from Gray's Ferry, in Passyunk—containing 70 acres divided into handsome lots, and each lot well watered with never-failing springs, except one wherein is a good well—most of the land is in grass and clover, and for a grazing or dairy farm, equal to any in the vicinity—about 12 acres is very handsome meadow. There are on the premises, a two story Brick House with a pump of excellent water at the door, and a good Spring House, a large commodious Brick Barn, with a pump in the yard
> (*Aurora*, March 10, 1809).

Spring Hill, an "elegant and highly cultivated farm," has "handsome" lots, with "very handsome" meadows; "excellent water" from "never failing springs," and "a good Spring House;" around "a large, commodious brick barn." By 1809, after cultivating his farm for eleven years, Girard's high standards gave neighboring "Spring Hill" some distinction. By contrast, he had given his farm no more pretentious a name than "The Place." "Girard's Place" was making his neighbor's place someplace to prize.

Girard's farming and building bear witness to his simplicity and practicality, which his own life can elaborate: "The sole amusement which I enjoy is to be in the country constantly busy in the work of the farm generally." In his enthusiasm, he outworked any laborer in his employ (Hubbard, 511). He so prized his work that he found it hard to delegate, but by necessity, he had to get help. The contract that he made with Jonathan Dickinson, about 1810, reflects the tireless labor and the exacting accountability that he expected of himself. Dickinson signed up to do "all kinds of carting and farming work agreeable to the directions which will be given to him by Stephen Girard." He was told just what to do. After he did what he was told, he would, of course, see more: "He will also take the greatest care of the fences, trees, fruit, carts, wagons, husbandry-implements, buildings of all kinds, horses, cattle, pigs, fowls and generally everything which grows or will be on the places and chattels belonging to said Stephen Girard." Both sentences, ending with "Stephen Girard," leave no doubt of who stands at the helm!

Dickinson—and his wife—also had to have good heads for business: "He and his wife will attend the markets with milk and all other articles which will be raised on the place . . . and will keep an account of all the money received, and pay the same every Saturday or oftener if required to Stephen Girard." Dickinson and his wife owed specific accounts of profits from the market "to Stephen Girard."

Dickinson's wife also had her own work: "Jonathan Dickinson's wife will do all the work which is generally done by an industrious farmer's wife particularly in the dairy line. She will also cook, wash and mend for the boarders. She will keep the house, hen house, milk house and all other things put under her care in a complete cleanliness." Girard does name her, except in assuming her role as the "industrious farmer's wife." Jonathan Dickinson answered to his boss, but his wife answered to him by doing what was expected of a woman in her position.

In the balance for all this work, Dickinson, his wife and children had "house room" rent free, bed clothes, firewood, and $200.00 a year. Dickinson's farm hands received $.75 a day, from which they paid for three meals, each at a cost of $.12½, in sum, $.37½ (McMaster II, 66), This price for board left them $.37½ for their day's work—about 120.00 a year. By the way, a dairymaid helping Mrs. Dickinson received $1.00 a week. Girard called his farm family's meals "good wholesome provisions, as such which are generally used in the country by frugal farmers." These hands paid half of their wage to enjoy this cornucopia.

Girard wrote virtue into Dickinson's contract: a farmer is "frugal," his wife, "industrious," and their food, "good" and "wholesome." He set such exacting moral and practical standards that he would keep his overseers and their wives in happy service for only as long as they emulated him. And if they really did emulate him, they would not serve him for long!

After Girard's demise in 1831, his estate divided his farm into "31 parcels of land, total acres, 565" (*US Gazette*, January 17, 1832), selling 60 acres immediately for $6659.81 (*US Gazette*, January 17, 1832). Until 1893, it rented the remaining parcels for cultivation. In 1906, the estate constructed houses on this property, renting them out until 1950, when it finally sold them. His farmhouse has survived as the centerpiece of a park.

Stephen Girard stood apart. His legacy has also set him splendidly apart in the peripteral Corinthian building of Girard College. These mute stones do not speak eloquently enough about the simple work ethic that raised them. That ethic planted grapes, pears and sweet potatoes as carefully and enthusiastically as it launched ships onto the seven seas and young orphans into life.

CHAPTER 18

Nicholas Biddle's Greek Facade on John Craig's Spanish Andalusia

FROM 1782 UNTIL 1790, John Craig and his brother James advertised their stock in *Dunlap and Claypoole's American Daily Advertiser.* Their first notice offered "pork in barrels" with "London particular"—a Madeira wine so particulate with pigmented particles that it looked as thick as London fog. (In England today, London particular describes pea soup in a facetious reference to London fog that is just as thick.) Along with "London market old Madeira Wine," the Craigs were building a high-end stock of wines from Spain and Portugal (July 27, 1782). Four years later, they set aside their homey pork barrels and set out "choice old red Port Wine":

Choice old red Port Wine,
Of the First Quality,
Received from the Royal Company of Oporto,
TO BE SOLD,
By James and John Craig,
Who have also for sale, London Particular, and London Market Madeira Wines, Grenada and Tobago Rum, Ginger, &c. &c.
April 21, 1786
(*Dunlap and Claypoole's American Daily Advertiser,* May 2, 1786).

To acquire wine "Of the First Quality," the Craigs formed a partnership with Francisco C. Sarmento, of the House of Sarmento and Company on the Spanish island of Teneriffe. With his help, they imported this "first quality" from "the Royal Company of Oporto" on the mainland of Portugal. One brand of their rum got its name from the Caribbean island of Grenada, which the Spanish first named after Grenada in Andalusia.

The Craigs later commissioned ships to trade directly with Spanish Teneriffe, and Portuguese Madeira (March 2, 1787). This Portuguese-Spanish connection put their business in high gear. Señor Sarmento also gave his daughter in marriage to Craig's son. When he returned home, he left his American business in the hands of his in-laws (*Inquirer*, December 11, 1794).

Like other well-to-do merchants, John Craig purchased an estate, where he might enjoy his success. In 1806, he hired the architect Benjamin Latrobe (1764–1820) to make his farm house fashionable. He died in 1807, just when he could have started to enjoy his life behind Latrobe's Federal facade on the north side of his home. Fate, however, planned on a second more colorful generation enjoying life behind the facade on the south.

In the first step toward this second generation, John Craig had been blessed by a daughter, Jane (1793–1856), a woman of remarkable character. He recognized her "brilliant capacity" for everything she undertook, and a heart "alive to every noble and virtuous sentiment."[99] This remarkable woman deserved a good match. She found a very good one in Nicholas Biddle, who took her hand on October 4, 1811. Nicholas would add a new wing to her family's home, and brighten its respectability with renown—even panache.

But before Biddle gave the Craigs' home fame, they gave it its name. With their Spanish connections, they readily took the name suggested by Nicholas' brother James (1783–1848). He was serving as a midshipman on the frigate Philadelphia, stationed off Andalusia, the region in the south of Spain. While on a mission to defeat the Barbary pirates who had been preying on merchant ships, he wrote a letter home. "Why not," James asked, "name the place Andalusia where I now am?" (Eberlein, 548). What Biddle was suggesting in his traveling fit what the Craigs' had been doing in their trading.

Nicholas Biddle, therefore, did not name Andalusia, but he gave it form and fame far beyond its evocation of sun-drenched vineyards

Andalusia's north facade, designed by Latrobe in 1806

in Spain. On the other hand, the Craigs' heritage had set its foundation. Toward the end of Nicholas' life, after his own fortunes had fallen to ruin, his wife Jane supported him with the income from her foundation. In this sense, John By his profitable deals on Front street financed his son-in-law's classical ideal on the Delaware.

"Form and fame far beyond" can describe Nicholas Biddle himself (January 8, 1786–February 27, 1844). To begin with form: he was so handsome—and so vain—that he had almost twenty portraits of himself painted or sculpted. He was also so intelligent and so profoundly educated that everything he did and—especially in his espousing classical rhetoric—everything that he said and wrote,—redounded to his fame. His special profession in speaking and writing sprang from his extraordinary devotion to the study of language. After finishing the University of Pennsylvania's classical curriculum at the age of 12, he graduated, at 15, from Princeton as a valedictorian of his class. Back to Philadelphia in 1801, he spent three years sharpening his language skills by studying law, even though he would not spend his life in legal practice—or, as he might have said, in pettifoggery.

Sartain's engraving of Nicholas Biddle, from Sully's portrait

He certainly went beyond his father and his father-in-law. Extraordinarily, in Philadelphia, America's most important port, its Cradle of Liberty, and its capital from 1790 to 1800, Nicholas did not, like his father-in-law, buy and sell; nor did he, like his father, spend his life as a legislator. He reached far beyond the average professions.

Having received an education far above average, he set sail in 1804 on the Grand Tour that would prepare him for his profession. He started and ended it as a secretary to diplomats, first in Paris and finally in London. In Paris, he worked as a secretary to John Armstrong (1758–1843), a family friend, then serving as the American Minister to France. With Armstrong, he helped to work out some financial aspects of the Louisiana Purchase. At the end of his tour in 1806, he worked as a secretary to James Monroe, then serving as the American Minister to the Court of King James. At one reception, Monroe looked on in bemused wonder as this young scholar enlightened some Cambridge dons on the nuances of Homeric and modern Greek. Working for Armstrong and Monroe, soon to serve as President of the United States (1817–1825), started his education in finance and connected him with the important people, who appreciated his extraordinary abilities.

During his time in Greece, young Biddle found inspiration in Cicero, a Latin author not particularly relevant to his travels. His anthology of Cicero's orations complemented the sights he was seeing. At times, it gave him his "only consolation" in the empty downtime while he was waiting to get somewhere.[100] (Biddle was studying ancient Greek architecture in the morasses of Turkish tyranny without the comfort and efficiency that tourists would enjoy later in the nineteenth century.) In Cicero, in addition, he found more than diversion from a traveler's tedious travail:

> I have constantly in hand Cicero's orations . . . To the writings of Cicero our attachment increases with our intimacy. I had once read them with a schoolboy's attention, more occupied with moods and tenses than beauties of style or force of reasoning. But I now read them with pleasure & fruit & in a season of more leisure. . . . To a general scholar these writings are very attractive, but to one of my profession they are all important (McNeal, 179).

"To one" of Biddle's "profession," Cicero gave "beauties of style or force of reasoning" to write and speak with as much wit as weight. This "great master of eloquence" gave him the eloquence to articulate his understanding of the world. He made Ciceronian eloquence his own. Even in conversation, Sidney Fisher observed, his speech was "ready fluent, elegant and witty . . . always choice and happy . . . flowing in free sparkling and harmonious periods." Ciceronian wit and weight, neatly articulated in periodic prose, animated whatever he professed.

With his discrimination, this "great master" of speaking identified ideals as much in their absence as in their presence. To illustrate this discrimination, Biddle quotes him addressing his friends about friendship: *Amicitiae consuetudines, . . . quid haberent voluptatis, carendo magis intellexi quam fruendo* ("I have understood what pleasure the familiarities of friendship might have, by missing them more than by enjoying them.") With this discrimination, for example, Biddle separated the manner from the matter of Cicero speeches. He called Cicero's speech, *Pro Marcello*, "an elegant specimen of courtly adulation" (208). In its pursuit of liberty, democratic America did not need "courtly adulation," but it could admire and use its elegance. Biddle emulated Cicero's "elegance" in speaking and writing, instead of his "adulation."

As they traveled together, Biddle and Cicero discriminated between the ancient Greeks' ideals, and the sordid morasses, in which they shined so radiantly. "Their wonderful genius in sculpture and in architecture shows an astonishing degree of refinement" (165)—glowing in the dark shadows of tyranny. This discrimination gave him a means of understanding culture: he separated good from bad in their interwoven warp and woof. "Of the proudest cities of Greece, enough <glory> remains," he reflected, "to indicate its position and proclaim its misfortune" (94).

As he viewed the rise and fall of civilizations—rising in the past; and, with a "melancholy satisfaction," fallen in the present,—Biddle articulated these distinctions: "Among the pleasant impressions, which I have felt, I have not been indifferent to that of bringing the veneration and sympathy of the new and only republic to the ruins of the old and thinking with a melancholy satisfaction that we may be one day as great and as miserable as they" (195). He brought home to the newly formed republic in America "a veneration and sympathy" for the first republic in Athens.

Biddle also took Cicero's statesmanship as an ideal: "To govern men, particularly by means of eloquence, seems to me the object most worthy of ambition in a free government." In his discrimination, however, he did not imitate Cicero's legal pleading or politic fawning: "The routine of an attorney, pleading, is beneath imitation" (179). His lofty soaring above politics to statesmanship would put obstacles in the way of a political career. He left the common man in his dust; and the common man was happy to brush it off and leave him aloft and alone.

Before he soared above commoners, Biddle reached one goal to which he aspired when he won the election to the Pennsylvania Assembly in 1811. On the floor, he argued for a Federal Bank. His speech showed the understanding of economics that he had gained in working on the Louisiana Purchase in Paris. This First Bank of the United States, Biddle argued, was both constitutional and crucial to the economy. The historian Fritz Redlich has called this speech "the maturest expression of banking knowledge to be found in America in that period."

Appreciating Biddle's speech, President Monroe, who had already appreciated his ability in London, made him a director of the Second Bank of the United States in 1819. At that point, Biddle set aside the academy and the assembly for the economy: "I prefer my last letter from Barings or Hope," he quipped, "to the finest epistles of Pliny or Pope." Correspondence with the Barings in London and with the Hopes in Amsterdam helped him to establish an international system of banking.

On the board of the Second Bank, Biddle was setting aside the books of a poet like Alexander Pope for the account books of a banker like Thomas Hope (1704–1779)—but not entirely. The Hopes had also done so, but not entirely: Thomas' grandson, Thomas Hope (1769–1831), had also traveled in Greece and then revived Greek architecture when he returned home. In his new job, Biddle was setting aside Pope for Hope, but his fine mind never stopped its refinement.

He also never stopped his broader profession of educating and enlightening with eloquence. In his eulogy of Thomas Jefferson's "finer intellect" in 1827, he had observed that the "exhaustless love of study . . . enables finer intellects to sustain the burthen of public duties," and, at the same time, resist the self-centered concern that "intense devotion to the business of the world is too prone to inspire." For Nicholas Biddle, a cultured man refines whatever he does by rising above it. He maintained this Ciceronian profession while he was keeping his eye on the nation's bank balance.

The directors of the bank shared his classical profession. Before he joined them in 1819, they had advertised for an architect to design "a chaste imitation of Grecian architecture in its simplest and least expensive form" (*Philadelphia Gazette*, May 18, 1818). They chose William Strickland (1788–1854) to design and build a bank with eight columns of the Doric order, inspired by the Parthenon. When Strick-

The Second Bank of the United States

land was working on this new bank in 1819, Biddle became one of its directors; and in 1824, he had been its president for two years when Strickland completed the project.

The Second Bank of the United States marked a milestone in the history of American architecture. Its Doric order gave a visible identity to the generation of Americans after the generation of the Founding Fathers of 1776. In his praise of Thomas Jefferson as the author of the Declaration of Independence, Biddle described the strength of its language as "Doric": "It is well that its stern massiveness should accord with the strong and Doric simplicity of the columns it sustains" (*Eulogium* of Thomas Jefferson). The strength of the young republic so informs the "stern massiveness" of Jefferson's language that the strong Doric columns of its language support the country.

This classical image was not new. In 1788, Doric columns had represented the Federal Edifice, which, John Van Horne has said, "translated the Constitution into visible symbols." At the end of the eighteenth century, however, the specific one of the three classical Orders—Doric, Ionic or Corinthian—chosen to support the Edifice did not mean much to the average person. For example, when the Carpenters' Company actually built a Federal Edifice in 1788 for Philadelphia's "Grand Federal Procession," they chose to build it in the Corinthian Order. What difference, the old carpenters might have asked, could it make? Weren't Corinthian columns good enough to support the building?

By 1824, students of ancient architecture like Biddle and Strickland had learned to answer this question with a resounding 'no!' Georgian architecture, with its Corinthian columns, represented an era long gone. Hadn't the Patriots of 1776 toppled the statues of King George, from whom Georgian architecture had taken its name? The Corinthian Order also evoked the corruption of the Roman Empire and Roman Catholicism. Architectural styles, popular in the eighteenth century, had come to represent unpopular ideologies: "Long stale, the Georgian, the Adamesque Federal, the Roman and the eighteenth-century French, had finally become politically unsavory." By contrast, James Fenimore Cooper attributed rustic, Doric strength to Andrew Jackson: "the virile qualities of decision, courage and patriotism, joined to simple courtesy and independence . . . the stronger image of the Doric model."[101] The Doric columns of the Second Bank represented young Americans' native strength.

In the American republic, Strickland's new copy of the old Parthenon did not shine luminously from under the dark shadows of tyranny, like its ruined prototype in Athens. But even with the vigor of the young republic as backdrop, Biddle had enough understanding to separate the good from the bad in their interwoven fabric. He took a "melancholy satisfaction" in his awareness that the old lies implicitly in the new; and that Philadelphia, like Athens, "may be one day be as great and as miserable" (McNeal,195). Even in his shiny new temple of finance, he pictured himself enclosed in a "vast marble tomb,

> 'mid vaults of damp stone and huge chests of cold iron,
> That would quell all the fancy of Shakespeare or Byron.

Athens' death had prepared for Philadelphia's life. In either city, its image inspired admiration for man's rise and, simultaneously, melancholy for his fall.[102]

In Athens, two Doric temples complement each other. Biddle first admired the "astonishing . . . refinement" of the eight Doric columns of the Parthenon. He then admired the "grand simplicity" of the Temple of Theseus (aka the Temple of Hephaestus) with six columns on the width of its rectangle. Older and smaller than the Parthenon, The Theseum taught Biddle a lesson in the melancholy of magnificence: "When I see the temple of Theseus, which teaches us to admire the grand simplicity of a great people, I feel for the decline of human greatness" (McNeal, 112).

Young America's down-to-earth virtue admired the simplicity of the Doric in both the Theseum and the Parthenon, but Biddle and his fellow bankers made a discriminating choice between the two. They chose the octastyle Parthenon as a model for their bank; he chose the hexastyle Theseum as a model for his home. Back in 1806, John Craig had already improved one wing of Andalusia. For him, Benjamin Latrobe had designed its north facade in the Federal style and his daughter had added her design for octagonal sides on its long rectangular room. In the 1830's, when the Physick-Randolphs were catching up to fashion by adding a semi-octagonal wing to Laurel Hill, Biddle was planning an extraordinary addition to Andalusia.

He chose Thomas U. Walter (1804–1887), as his architect.[103] Working together, they expanded the house in 1834–1836 with the addition of the facade of the Theseum. One historian has called Andalusia, all-together, "a satisfying blend of the Regency, <Federal>, style with the more restrained early phase of the Greek revival" (Eberlein, 513). "More restrained" may not adequately describe Biddle's dynamic addition, but its pure classicism, representing the Greek, complements that of the Federal, representing the Roman.

As an academic aristocrat, Biddle enhanced Andalusia with a Greek simplicity like that of Homeric epic. As an academic and landowning aristocrat, he cultivated his fields with Vergilian georgic. To get the best out of this cultivation, he also joined Philadelphians of a like mind and social class in the Philadelphia Society for Promoting Agriculture. At that time, Richard Peters of Belmont, one of the nation's Founding Fathers, was serving as its beloved president, an office that he would hold until his death in 1828.

January, 1822, at the society's annual meeting, Biddle delivered an address that the *Inquirer* praised as "elegant and instructive" (February 20, 1822). In it, he describes the ideal "landed proprietors" (divided here to emphasize its Ciceronian balance of two tricolons of phrase, in **bold**, within the surrounding tricolon of clause):

Landed proprietors,
well educated,
brave,
and independent
—the friends of the government, without soliciting its favors
—the advocates of the people, without descending to flatter their passions;

these men,
rooted like their own forests,

may yet interpose between the factions of the country,
to heal,
to defend,
and to save.

Biddle's rhetorical art articulates his lofty vocation in a rounded period. He refers to all hearty American sons of the earth, when he describes them as "rooted like their own forests"—an inspiringly deep-rooted metaphor. Specifically, addressing the Philadelphia Society for Promoting Agriculture, he describes landowning aristocrats as "well educated, brave, and independent." He is not referring to all hearty American farmers, who did not need to be "well educated" to take root "like their own forests." Addressing landowning aristocrats, however, Biddle's tricolon, predicating "brave and independent" on "well educated," particularly calls to mind a man like himself who could read and appreciate Vergil's *Eclogues* and *Georgics*.

Like the shepherd Tityrus in the first *Eclogue*, he writes poetry while resting under his spreading beech:

Tityre, tu patulae recubans sub tegmine fagi
silvestrem tenui Musam meditaris avena.

Tityrus, you, recumbent under the shade of a spreading beech,
Meditate the sylvan Muse with your thin oaten pipe.

Aristocrats, particularly, disdain "soliciting favors" from politicians or flattering the passions of the mob. In his own particularly brave, well educated independence, Biddle exercised the same control over America that he would exercise over its economy when he was appointed president of the national bank in 1823 (Sklansky, 158). His purpose, "to heal, to defend, and to save"—a forcefully climactic tricolon—describes the aristocrat's duty to his country. Cicero might also have expressed this eloquent expression of civic duty. Biddle took the helm as President of the Society in 1831; and, like old Judge Peters, he continued in office until his death.

In a review of this address, the *Inquirer* called it "practical, and founded in personal observation as well as speculative enquiry." Fifteen years later, the newspaper reported some "practical" fruit of his "inquiry": "Mr. Nicholas Biddle" was displaying grapes at the Horticultural Exhibition in Masonic Hall (September 20, 1837). It made no further reports of this activity, but we can imagine that Biddle approached it like a professional viticulturist.

Starting with William Penn, other prominent Philadelphians had been interested in viticulture. Biddle's in-laws, the Craigs, had based their business on importing wines from Portugal and Spain. Biddle had probably heard about Stephen Girard's entrepreneurial effort to grow his own grapes after many years of letting others grow them for him. He had also heard about Girard's frustration when severe Philadelphia winters blighted his vines.

Biddle had a solution for Girard's problem, but it was costly beyond anything that Girard's thrift would have dared. In 1835 and 1836, Thomas U. Walter, built a grapery at Andalusia, with a heating system, at the cost of $21,807 (Wainwright, 28). Biddle was exercising determination—and indulging in extravagant expense—to advance his project. He might have won a blue ribbon at the Exhibition in Horticultural Hall, but he would have had no other profit. After his death, his grapery fell to ruin.

With the moral that Nicholas derived from his travels in Greece, "ruin" can touch a chord. Like the shepherds in Poussin's painting, *Et in Arcadia Ego*, we may happen upon one of the grapery's walls that has survived in the gardens of Andalusia. It offers a melancholy witness to pure aspirations ending in failure. Biddle could not have anticipated this melancholy end to his project, but he would appreciate its pathos. Together with Poussin's elegiac painting, Shelley's poem "Ozymandias" (1817), may inspire our meditation:

> I met a traveller from an antique land
> Who said: Two vast and trunkless legs of stone
> Stand in the desert. Near them, on the sand,
> Half sunk, a shattered visage lies, whose frown,
> And wrinkled lip, and sneer of cold command,
> Tell that its sculptor well those passions read
> Which yet survive, stamped on these lifeless things,
> The hand that mocked them and the heart that fed:
> And on the pedestal these words appear:
> "My name is Ozymandias, king of kings;
> Look on my works, ye Mighty, and despair!"
> Nothing beside remains. Round the decay
> Of that colossal wreck, boundless and bare
> The lone and level sands stretch far away.

"Round the decay" of Biddle's wreck, we see no landscape "boundless and bare" stretching "far away." Andalusia's beautiful garden, like the one in which Poussin's shepherds enjoy their idyll, brings our meditation home. No man plans on his project falling to ruin, although this sad eventuality seems especially appropriate in Nicholas Biddle's garden. When other men have decorated their gardens with purpose-built ruins, we call them follies. Biddle has added a genuine ruin of his own folly to the classical paradigm of his life.

For his own purpose-built work, however, Biddle dutifully used his eloquence to inspire. In his eulogy of Thomas Jefferson, he gave background for the motto of The Philadelphia Society for Promoting Agriculture, "Venerate the Plough." Its seal depicts a plowman, with Demeter, who invented the plough, looking on. Jefferson, "our chief magistrate," had won a prize in France for his improvements on its design:

> Our chief magistrate had triumphed in the competition
> to improve that earliest and noblest instrument of peace,

which disturbs, only to bless, the bosom of the earth,
and was never yet perverted to oppression or injustice.

In language evocative of Vergil's *Georgics*, Biddle pictures the plough blessing the earth as an "instrument of peace."[104] Jefferson also described his activities, one of his biographers observed, "in tones reminiscent of an *Eclogue* of Vergil." "Have you become a farmer?" Jefferson asked a friend, "Is it not pleasanter than to be shut up within 4 walls and delving eternally with the pen? I am become the most ardent farmer in the state."[105] Strictly speaking, Jefferson's description of himself reminds us of a farmer in the *Georgics*, and not of shepherds in the *Eclogues*.

In his address at the Agricultural Society's fair in 1840, he praised peace in the georgic idyll: "The instinct of agriculture is for peace—for the empire of reason, not of violence—of votes, not of bayonets." In the *Georgics*, Vergil went one step further when he invoked Minerva, "favoring" patron of the Arcadian town of Tegea, which is welcoming to her cult; and the *inventrix* of the olive, which is pleasing to peace (*placitam Paci*). He also invokes the boy (*puer*) Triptolemus, whom Demeter first taught to demonstrate (*monstrator*) the plough:

adsis,/ o // Tege/aee, fa/uens, // ole/aeque Mi/nerua
inuen/trix, // un/cique pu/er // mon/strator a/ratri.

Be Present, Minerva, favoring Tegea, and, of the olive,
the *inventrix*, and the boy, who demonstrated the curved plough.

Without venerating Vergil's rustic pantheon of gods, but inspired by the poet's deep roots in the earth, Biddle praised Americans, who have beaten their bayonets into plough shares. Members of The Agricultural Society could not have considered themselves literal Vergilian shepherds or farmers,—neither did Vergil himself,—but they admired and emulated Vergil's pastoral and georgic ideal.

LIKE ALL OF US, Nicholas Biddle lived on the shoulders of giants; but, unlike most of us, he admired them and imitated their virtues. Having rebuilt Andalusia for Homeric epic and cultivated it for Vergilian georgic, he made it the home of Ciceronian "learning and leisure."

As he was traveling through Greece, he had idealized his great master's home:

> that seat of lettered repose,
> the resort of learning and leisure,
> which almost personified philosophy herself (McLean, 55).

With Cicero's ideal of a statesman's "lettered repose," he made Andalusia his "resort of learning and leisure." Under similar circumstances, he and Cicero found refuge in their country villas. After Cicero retreated from the Forum, he settled into life in his villa, "where he composed," Biddle declared, "those deep philosophical works which have been the admiration of all succeeding time."[106] Biddle did not rival Cicero's *De Officiis*, but after his resignation from the presidency of his bank in 1839, he rid himself of sordid rivalries and embraced literary leisure. Behind the Doric facade, Sidney Fisher described an idyl:

> . . . the resort of the intellect of the country. John Quincy Adams, Webster, and the great politicians of the nation were entertained at his dinners, when coruscations of wit and bright sallies abounding with anecdote and information were continually occurring to enliven these festive gatherings (Wainwright, 22).

Biddle loved being the center of portraits or parties. He created a sensation, wherever he appeared. Round this master of Andalusia, his coteries sparkled with "coruscations of wit and bright sallies abounding with anecdote and information." Laying the foundation of this wit, Biddle quoted Cicero recommending a wide focus of education: *non solum ut de jure civili ad eos, verum etiam de omni aut officio aut negotio referratur*—"not only should people refer their concerns to <lawyers> about civil law, but also indeed about every duty or business."[107] Lawyers or bankers—all men—might profit from this wide world.

Biddle's contemporaries, Joseph Jackson observed, viewed him "in as many lights as a cut diamond has facets." Over the populists supporting Andrew Jackson, for example, his Second Bank cast a dark shadow as "a classical temple of Mammon" (Wainwright, 46). After its collapse, Dickens famously called it "a handsome building of white marble, which had a mournful, ghost-like aspect, dreary to behold. . . . the tomb of many fortunes; the Great Catacomb of investment." Biddle himself had anticipated this sepulchral image by picturing himself "'mid vaults of damp stone and huge chests of cold iron."

Beyond his infamous defeat in the bank war of the 1830's, Nicholas Biddle's most significant legacy to American history clothed early American democracy in classical beauty and gave to American bankers an architecture that dignified their authority. The dignity of this classical beauty has survived; the education and ethos that invented it, has also survived, but tucked away in the cloisters of academe.

ANDALUSIA HAS REMAINED in the hands of Nicholas Biddle's descendants since his wife, Jane Craig Biddle, died in 1856. Fortunately, it has survived to preserve the household effects of Biddle and his descendants in an extraordinary house museum. The library, for example, still has the anthology of Cicero's orations that young Biddle read on his travels in Greece. What a pilgrimage for any Ciceronian to see this treasured volume!

Notice of a public sale has twice cast its dark shadow over this survival. The first appeared just nine years after Jane Craig Biddle's death:

> THE SPLENDID COUNTRY SEAT KNOWN AS ANDALUSIA, THE RESIDENCE OF THE LATE NICHOLAS BIIDLE Esq.,
> Will be sold at public sale, on Tuesday Morning, Nov. 7th, at 12 o'clock, at the Philadelphia Exchange. It is beautifully situated on the River Delaware, about 14 miles from Philadelphia; it contains a very extensive river front, and fronts on the railroad and turnpike, and has one splendid mansion and one of less size, a farm house, gardener's house, and extensive graperies. There are in all 113½ acres, susceptible of being divided into at least three first-class country seats (*Inquirer*, October 13, 1865).

Fortunately, no one could meet the minimum bid.

Fifty years later, the second notice appeared in a year between the deaths of Biddle's two children, Craig Biddle (1823–1910) and his sister Jane (1830–1915), who continued to live on the estate:

> ANDALUSIA BEAUTIFUL COUNTRY SEAT, 13 ROOMS, with all conveniences, 7-room tenant house, stable and other buildings; about 12 acres of excellent ground, fine lawn and orchard, old-shade trees and choice shrubbery, trolley frontage, close to Cornwall's Station, 38 minutes to Broad st., frequent trains; this property is in excellent condition and can be bought right (*Inquirer*, May 10, 1914).

By establishing a trust of $35,000, Jane Biddle hoped to preserve Andalusia as a "haven of refuge" for her family, but greed stirred up what the *Inquirer* called a "family feud" that threatened to overturn her will (*Inquirer*, July 20, 1916). Fortunately, a judge, upholding her bequest, put an end to the efforts that some members of the family had made to sell Andalusia. It has survived as a haven for their heritage.

EAST PARK

CHAPTER 19

Fairmount Altogether

PHILADELPHIANS HAVE BECOME so accustomed to the presence of Fairmount in their city that they have brought the two words of its original name, Fair Mount, together in Fairmount. Making the mount of Fair Mount just a syllable, they started to think of Fairmount avenue or its neighborhood instead of the Fair Mount. When two words double into one, their meaning fades a little. When some Philadelphians say the they live in Fairmount, they are making no reference to the hill.

When two words of a foreign language double up into one, their meaning fades even more: the Dutch phrase *Schuyl Kill*, "hidden river," indicates that Dutch explorers first saw this river "hidden" by marsh grass at its confluence with the Delaware. Philadelphians have also become so accustomed to the *Schuyl Kill* in their city that they have put these two words together in Schuylkill. Etymologies clarify meaning: Fair describing Mount clarifies Fairmount, just as *Schuyl* describing *Kill* clarifies Schuylkill. William Penn considered Fairmount so fair a mount that he made it the crowning and culminating point of his proprietary estate along the Schuylkill river.

In addition to appreciating Fairmount as fair, Penn also appreciated its position. In 1683, his surveyor, Thomas Holme, placed Philadelphia at the confluence between the Schuylkill and the Delaware rivers, but not at the southernmost tip of that confluence, because it contained low, marshy ground. (If global warming should cause water

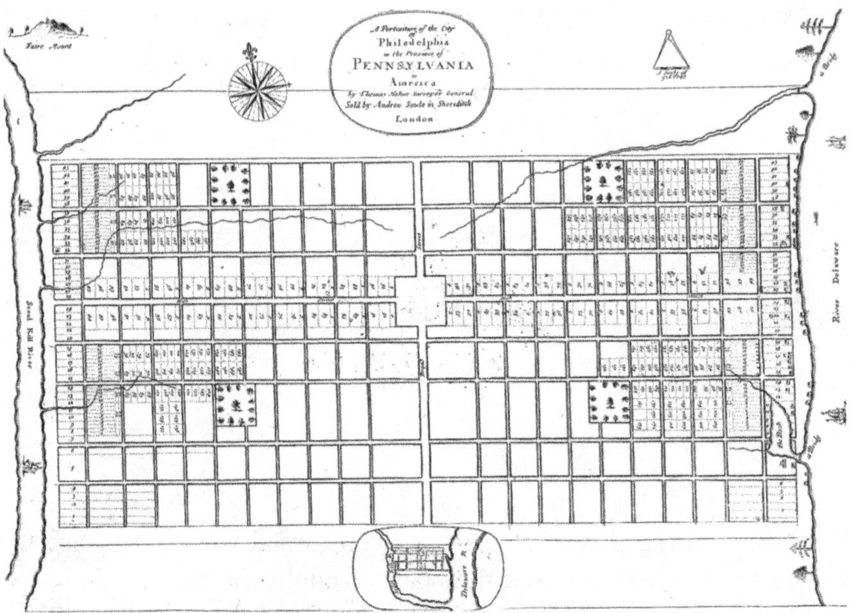

Thomas Holme's "Portraiture of the City of Philadelphia" (1683)

Holme's map pictures five blocks south, but only three north, of Center Square. *Ergo, Nota Bene*: center square is not at the center of the city. *N.B.*, also, that "Faire Mount" so significantly bounded the city that Holme pictured it as a tiny point at the upper left.

to rise in that area, Holme's caution would be vindicated.) He placed Philadelphia on the coastal plain between the two rivers, but high and dry on that plain, above the marshes. To make Penn's proprietary estate higher and dryer, he cut the northern area of the city short by two blocks so that Penn might retain possession of Fairmount, the first hill to rise above the coastal plain.

In its culminating progress—first marsh, then plain, and finally hill—Fairmount marks the third step in the topography of the city. As the first rocky promontory at the base of the Piedmont Plateau, Fairmount has a significance like that of the Capitoline Hill in Rome, which also marks the beginning of the Piedmont on the Tiber river in Italy. Like the Capitoline also, this third phase in Philadelphia's topography has experienced so much change that it tells a story like no other.

Fairmount not only has a description and a position like no other hill on the river, no other hill in Philadelphia has an original name. Like the Capitoline Hill, it takes the lead in a chain of hills, but, unlike the Capitoline, it does not have six brothers,—Aventine, Caelian, Esquinal, Palatine, Quirinal, and Viminal,—all with names and some fame in Rome's history. In 1770, when Robert Morris bought three hundred acres along the Schuylkill, including Fairmount and the hills above it, he brought them all together by calling his estate, simply, The Hills. Except for Lemon Hill, the second hill above Faire Mount, named about 1800, Fairmount stands alone in having an original name. Fairmount Park springs from Fairmount, the mother of all of its hills.

At first, Penn naturally thought that Fairmount was fair, because he saw it in its pristine state of nature. Since then, Fairmount has served so many uses that we can see little of the beauty that Penn admired. For beauty, we can look to other rocky crags up the river. For use, Philadelphians at the beginning of the nineteenth century, especially a hydrologist named Frederick Graff (1775–1847), found that Fairmount might be the place from which they could provide the city with its water.

Starting out as a carpenter in 1799 assisting Benjamin Latrobe, Graff had helped him to design the Waterworks and its garden in Center Square, where City Hall now stands. When this site and its machinery proved inadequate for pumping water from the Schuylkill River to the city, Graff took the project up river to Fairmount. (One hundred and twenty five years later, he could have gone up to Fairmount on the Benjamin Franklin Parkway.) Fairmount's position on the river and its elevation gave it a better chance to succeed.

If his pumps could only defy gravity, the rest would be easy:
If they could take water,
to the reservoir,
up the hill,
from the river,
gravity would take it,
from the reservoir,
down the hill,
to the city.

To dig the reservoirs at the top of the hill, the ruin of this Faire Mount did not take place subtly or slowly. Dynamite did it quickly and brutally. By 1812, it had first blasted enough fair out of Fairmount to make the terraces on which to put the pumps at the bottom and the reservoir at the top. Blasting inflicted utility, and left a little beauty behind. Preserving some of it in a garden offered Graff a challenge and an opportunity. When people came to visit, the terraces made for technology could also accommodate these visitors, who might admire the machines in what remained of natural beauty. The South Garden, dating from 1839, is the oldest and the only one to have survived. (The park commission laid out the North Garden in the 1860's and wiped it out in the 1920's) This garden had a very special purpose in bringing natural beauty together with human technology. Even though mostly blown away, Fairmount might still be fair with its practical American beauty.

Especially after the Watering Committee had put the equipment and the reservoirs in place, continued blasting posed a threat not

The South Garden in 1839, with five abreast on its ramp and a fountain with a jet said to reach as high as 17 feet

only to the technology on the hill but also to everyone around it. One newspaper reported a disastrous accident: "A blast was made in the stone quarry on the lower side of the reservoir at Fairmount, on Saturday last, which threw a stone weighing a thousand pounds on the top of a two story dwelling within about forty yards, doing it considerable injury" (*Public Ledger*, February 24, 1840). How could visitors enjoy the beautiful garden, when dynamite disturbed them, and then boulders flew about as a consequence?

Blasting had opened such large quarries, that some people called Fairmount what it had become, Quarry Hill. In 1860, the *Public Ledger* reported a quarry on the hill supplying stone for the construction of a mill house: "Nearly all the stone for the erection of the mill house at the mound dam, at Fairmount, has been taken from the quarry, at the base of the reservoir. This stone has been taken from below the old path that led to the reservoir, and also from under the hill, so that when the hole is filled up, the bank will again present nearly the same rugged and romantic appearance that it did before the excavation" (April 18, 1860). "The old path that led to the reservoir" refers to the one leading up the hill from the North Garden, the larger garden first pictured in Graff's design of 1839. The writer states optimistically that Fairmount would suffer no ultimate damage: the hole made by the quarry would be filled in to restore the "rugged and romantic appearance" of the hill. Fairmount would get other facelifts over the years. The results of this destruction and reconstruction still remain. As relics of the blasting, hundreds of large stones cut from the quarry still bolster terraces in the hill, especially on its north side along Kelly Drive.[108]

To make Fair-mount worthy of its adjective, the city needed to repair more than the obvious damage to its slopes. Industry had scarred the area around the hill and the lives of the people who lived there. This blight extended to the east and the west, up and down the river. To the west, up the river, Coates street, now Fairmount Avenue, came to a dead end at the river beneath Fairmount and turned up to Landing Avenue. Down river, Callowhill street led to the bridge below Fairmount. The riverboats that docked off these two streets delivered their cargoes to the surrounding coal and lumber yards, from which gas works, coal oil works, lamp black factories, and cotton mills derived their fuel or raw material (*Inquirer*, December 14, 1861). The riverboat men blighted the neighborhood.

One writer, attempting to describe these wharves and their denizens, admits that the task "defies our pen, though Dickens could make a graphic picture of it without doubt" (*Inquirer*, December 14, 1861). This area around Landing Avenue, called the Flatiron, because of its triangular shape, had a bad reputation. Calling on Dickens to describe it assumes a spectacle, both sad and shocking, since Dickens famously described nineteenth century urban blight.

Not emulating Dickensian melodrama, but mocking it, a comic ballad tells the sad fate of a daughter of Saint Patrick, Bedelia, who worked at one of the cotton mills, J. & W. Yewdall's Worsted Goods Manufactory. She was betrayed by one of the notoriously bad riverboat men:

> It is of a girl at Fairmount, that I am going to sing,
> Her cruel, sad misfortune tears to your eyes will bring;
> She loved a gallant boatman, who always dressed to kill,
> She was a cotton-dolly, and she wrought a Yewdall's mill.
>
> —*The Girl from Yewdall's Mill* by Jimmy Smith,
> sung to the air of "The Raging Canal"

After a cruel betrayal by this "gallant" has driven his cotton dolly to suicide, her ghost haunts Fairmount at midnight:

> And every night at twelve o'clock, on top of Fairmount hill,
> The ghost of Bedelia may be seen, gazing on Yewdall's mill.

This poor girl might have better sought the consolations of religion at the Church of Saint Francis Xavier (1839), right next to her workplace, at the eastern end of Fairmount. Bishop Kendrick built this church and Saint Patrick's, west of Rittenhouse Square, for the Irish Catholics working and living along the Schuylkill wharves. These poor shanty Irish needed some consolation.

The wharves and industry to the west along Landing avenue posed a threat to the beauty of Fairmount and its park. Anyone approaching the park had "a disagreeable ride or tramp" over it before he could get to the picturesque scenery (*Inquirer*, July 8, 1861). The designers

Fairmount

In this photo, Fairmount rises to the left, St. Francis Xavier to the right, and Yewdall's Mill, slightly obscure beyond the church. This area is now in front of the Philadelphia Museum of Art.

of the park did more than repair this disfiguring industry. They simply—and completely—removed it. In the 1860's, they purchased and razed the industrial properties in the Flatiron, along Coates Street and Landing Avenue. They also razed the Four Nations Hotel, Robert Morris House, and Rialto House, along with shabby rookeries passing as dwellings for the locals (*Inquirer*, January 26, 1864). The stark contrast between the east and the west sides of Fairmount,—beautiful park to the west and ugly industry to the east,—persisted into the twentieth century. Even the beautiful Benjamin Franklin Parkway did not remove this blight along the river, east of Fairmount.

After the Waterworks first made Fairmount useful in 1812, the city succeeded by the 1860's in making it fair again. The citizens took special pride in this transformation: "Public works are proverbially tasteless, but we can proudly point to our park in all its simple loveliness;" Philadelphia's *Evening Telegraph* boasted, "mankind is so inimical to nature that we can proudly boast of having done nothing to spoil the native graces of the scene (September 15, 1870). The writer is justly proud, but he does slip into hyperbole in his boast that the city has done nothing "to spoil the native graces of the scene."

Making Fairmount fairly accessible required steps up to its gazebos on the middle and upper terraces. The picture from 1839 shows a flight up from the terrace of the South Garden to a gazebo in the middle terrace. A citizen sent a letter to the *Public Ledger*, requesting another flight at the north entrance on Coates street: "Mr. Ledger, permit me earnestly to request the attention of those who have the direction of Fairmount, to the desirableness of a flight of steps from the gate to the upper terrace. The expense would not be great; it would prevent a great deal of desecration, particularly of evergreens on the slope, and would greatly diminish the rush of persons on the principal flight which is often at present so great as to threaten accidents, especially to children, and almost always annoying to ladies" (*Public Ledger*, July 8, 1839). An example of a serious accident, James Bradley, residing at 2413 Pennsylvania avenue, died from his injuries after running into one of these evergreens on his sled (*Inquirer*, January 14, 1873).

The *Public Ledger* suggested one way of protecting children, more eager for fun than safety: "The only way to prevent accidents to children," it observed, "is to have them always attended by a caretaker. No amount of stone wall or iron railing can prevent accidents to thoughtless children. We have seen little girls running down the steps on the north side of the reservoir, three abreast, when a single misstep might have precipitated them from 80 to 100 feet into the pit made by quarrying stone. We have heard that the child hurt the other day was sliding down the banks, and went over the rocks near the Coates street gate, eight or ten feet high" (July 26, 1860). Imagine this bedeviled caretaker trying to prevent children from running, then from falling, and finally trying to catch them if they did! One improvement in the 1860's replaced the steps in the South Garden by an s-shaped ramp that still rises, by a more gradual, safer and easier incline, up the hill.[109]

In the South and North Gardens, statues pleased the eye, and fountains quenched thirst; while summerhouses provided rest and shade; and benches, first called settees, provided rest under the trees. William Rush (1756–1833), celebrated as the Father of American Sculpture and one of the members of the Watering Committee, carved a wooden statue of *Water Nymph with a Bittern* (1809) for a fountain in the Waterworks at Center Square. Graff eventually transferred it to the South Garden of Fairmount, where it remained until 1872, when a bronze copy replaced it.

Rush later carved *The Schuylkill Chained* and *The Schuylkill Freed* (1825) to adorn the pediments of the two mill houses. After Rush installed these statues, more refined taste in art found them lacking: Fanny Trollope admired *Water Nymph*, with the reservation that it was "not the work of Phidias." A strident critic expressed disdain for these two allegories of the Schuylkill: "The solitary and ill-carved figures are a disgrace to the assumed character of the city for classical taste. The figures of Neptune (*sic*) chained and other groups, are positively hideous. They would better become an oyster shallop than the boasted Fairmount" (*Public Ledger*, June 22, 1839). This critic certainly did not appreciate the early folk art of the Father of American Sculpture. Indeed, they do not come from the hand of Phidias! And yet, indeed, he does come close to a degree of understanding. His reference to the possibility of their adorning "an oyster shallop" seems appropriate, since Rush started his career carving figureheads for ships.

Fountains pleasing the eye and quenching thirst suited the purposes of the Waterworks. Once Graff transferred Rush's *Schuylkill with a Bittern* to the South Garden, he used the water pressure from the reservoirs to raise its jet as high as seventeen feet. With this grand *jet d'eau* in mind, the editorial voice in the *Public Ledger* seems mistaken or at least unappreciative: "There is a sad deficiency of fountains in our squares. Fairmount offers a fine spot for a fountain of elaborate beauty" (*Public Ledger, ibid.*). Perhaps this writer, criticizing Rush's allegories, and hoping for "a fountain of elaborate beauty" is justifying the show of water pressure. Granted, the Committee conceded, *Schuylkill with a Bittern* does not rival the work of Phidias, but we "elaborate" it to spout water magnificently! Technology can boast of its own art.

Twenty-five years later "a new fountain," although not one of "elaborate beauty" was installed and remains in place: "A new fountain has just been finished at Fairmount, constructed of Berks county brown stone and supplied with water from a spring above one hundred and fifty feet distant, flowing from a rock near Coates street. The water drops into a basin that contains several cups of water (*Inquirer*, August 11, 1864). A picture of this fountain in 1883 shows a lady standing beside it with a drinking cup. This may be the same spring, to which Fanny Trollope referred many years before as "a stone basin of simple workmanship, having a cup for thirsty travelers."

By 1866, "the grounds around the Fairmount Water Works," the *Philadelphia Evening Telegraph* reported, "are now in splendid order, and present a very attractive appearance. On the north side of the reservoir, a marble fountain, eight feet high, including pedestal, filled with flowers, has been erected. Near it, a unique summer house is nearly completed—twenty-four feet across with four wings, facing each of the roads" (May 30, 1866). The "summer house" may refer to a structure mentioned elsewhere at the Green street entrance (i.e., the Hunter street entrance on the Graff plan of 1839). The design of the Parkway and its extension in Kelly drive removed these decorations and the North Garden itself.

A monument to Frederick Graff stands in the South Garden, at first view perhaps, out of place in its style. Erected in 1848, one year after his death, it resembles The Albert Memorial in London, and represents the Gothic taste in American architecture. It celebrates, as one newspaper said earlier in his career, Frederick Graff's "taste in the design, and judgment in the arrangement of the works at Fair Mount, with his indefatigable zeal for the public interest in every department (*National Gazette*, February 24, 1823). Graff's memorial in Gothic style in the midst of the Greek architecture that he created for the Waterworks contributes an ironic contrast to Fairmount's complex history.

FAIRMOUNT BOTH STARTED and has mirrored the evolution of Fairmount Park. Fifty-nine years after its first reservoir was built, the *Inquirer* contrasted use with beauty in reporting the building of another reservoir: "The East Park reservoir will make a considerable inroad on the park, but it will occupy ground which possesses no feature of natural interest." It defines the features of "natural interest" that distinguish Fairmount Park's beauty: "The most picturesque portions of East Park are those near the Schuylkill. Here the ground retains most of its natural features; but little of it has been dedicated to cultivation. Forest trees and underwood still remain; ravines, glens, hill, precipices, bluffs and rocks still offer their diversified attraction to lovers of nature" (November 8, 1871). The author's assurance that the rugged beauties of the park "still remain" overlooks the most obvious exception: Fairmount itself had been "dedicated" to municipal water supply. He probably considered his statement about Fairmount Park as separate from Fairmount. The presence of Fairmount as the introduction to Fairmount Park and the source of its name can confuse visitors, and especially the natives. At the terminus of the Benjamin Franklin Parkway, they can see it as a fixture on the map of the city. For them, Fairmount stands,—as it has always stood in Philadelphia's topography and culture,—uniquely and grandly alone.

After the needs for a municipal water supply in the Waterworks had used much of Fair Mount in 1809, art appreciation in the Philadelphia Museum of Art used almost all the rest in 1925. Only the South Garden and the cliff above it have preserved some sense of the heyday of the Fair Mount, which Fanny Trollope called "one of the very prettiest spots the eye can look upon." In her description of the fountain with Rush's statue, she finds a special charm in the scene as a whole: "its dark, rocky background, the flowery catalpas which shadow it, and the bright shower through which it shows itself, altogether make the scene one of singular beauty." She sees charm in layers of nature and art "altogether."

Fairmount, in its layers,
Greek Doric on the river bank,
Gothic canopy honoring Frederick Graff on the garden terrace,
Victorian rustic and Greek classical gazebos on two terraces,
early American sculpture of William Rush on three terraces,
"altogether" with fountains, and sycamores shading the garden,
shaded in turn by craggy cliffs,
still charms Philadelphians as William Penn's first and foremost hill.

CHAPTER 20

Building an Acropolis on Fairmount

In 1694, Johannes Kelpius, a man of prophetic Biblical piety, and his congregation emigrated from Transylvania to Pennsylvania. They were on a special pilgrimage to meet the Woman of the Wilderness. *The Book of Revelation*, chapter XII, had revealed to them her fleeting radiance: "A woman clothed with the sun, and the moon under her feet . . . fled into the wilderness where she hath a place prepared of God." In the "wilderness" of the New World, they hoped to witness her millennial apocalypse.

After arriving in Philadelphia, Kelpius led them up the Schuylkill to settle on the Wissahickon Creek. Along its banks, his community kept a vigil for her arrival. Traveling up river, June 21, the day of the summer solstice, they stopped at Fairmount. At twilight, these children of God's creation lit a bonfire on the hill to celebrate the longest day of the sun's radiance. Against the darkening sky, Fairmount shone like a beacon.

Brockton Brown imagines another pilgrim emigrating from Germany to Pennsylvania to fulfill a duty of his faith. Hoping to bring the Gospel to aborigines, he builds no great temples, which may awe them by the presence of his god. American evangelists of the nineteenth century chose groves for their temples. He chooses "the top of a rock," on the Schuylkill above Fairmount. Like Fairmount, its sides were "steep, rugged, and encumbered with dwarf cedars and stony asperities." On its summit, sixty feet above the river, he builds "what to a common eye would have been a summer house," in a circle,

This picture illustrates the origin of the column as a tree trunk.
The Tuscan column suits primitive architecture in the wilderness.

twelve feet in diameter. To fix his circle in its classical roots, he surrounds it with twelve Tuscan columns, and caps it with a dome. Tuscan columns, simpler than the severe Doric, suit primitive structures in the wilderness.[110] "This was the temple of his Deity." With this concise dedication, Charles Brockden Brown, Philadelphian and the first American novelist, punctuates his description of a wilderness shrine in his novel, *Wieland or the Transformation* (1798).

Of these two stories, Brown's fiction seems more real than Kelpius' history, but both celebrate divinity on a hill above the Schuylkill. Rising from a coastal plain, hills like Faire Mount radiate numinous beauty, before they serve practical use. Brown's narrative also illustrates the evolution of the hill. After the death of the evangelist to the aborigines, his children redecorate their father's "temple of his Deity" with a bust of Cicero and a harpsichord. An Acropolis evolves from nature to religion to culture.

In its centuries, Fairmount has provided a home for temples,—first of sun worship, then of technology; and, finally, of culture. In the nineteenth century, most notably, technology joined with culture in equipping and decorating it as the Fairmount Waterworks. William Rush carved a statue of Mercury for the apex of the dome of a summer house atop Fairmount. Mercury celebrated the mercurial quick wits of American ingenuity. The keystone of the Market street bridge (1932) also celebrates Mercury as the eponymous god of the merchants on that street. In ancient Greece, Athenians built the Parthenon to house the statue of Athena Parthenos, their patron deity. They left the mercurial to merchants in their harbor, but Americans have always celebrated the market place.

The practical simplicity of Greek architecture suited Americans' mercurial practicality. With the exception of the engine house, which looks like a plain four-story dwelling, the buildings of the Waterworks have Greek facades of the Doric order, after the Tuscan, the simplest style of Greek architecture. They represent a continuity of a classical tradition passed on by Benjamin Latrobe (1764–1820) to his assistant, Frederick Graff (1774–1847), and, in turn, to Frederick Graff, Jr. (1817–1890). In 1869–1874, the younger Graff completed the plan for Fairmount. Basing his design on his father's drawings of 1820, he added an open-air pavilion between two Doric facades.

In the twenty-first century, we must use our imagination to picture tourists flocking to see the Fairmount Waterworks in 1835. Mark Twain said that the site resembled the Bay of Naples; because a man could see it and die,—it not only topped the bucket list, it set all other destinations aside! Both useful and beautiful, the Waterworks fulfills the Horatian definition of art that combines *utile dulci*, "the useful with the sweet." Americans had pragmatic aesthetics.

After the visitors enjoyed the breezes and charms of the Schuylkill, they marveled at the technology. In *Walden Pond*, Thoreau (1854) describes the awe which the power of technology could inspire:

> When I hear the iron horse make the hills echo with
> its snort-like thunder, shaking the earth with its feet,
> and breathing fire and smoke with its nostrils, it seems
> as if the earth got a race now worthy to inhabit it.

The Waterworks

The four-story engine house is on the far right, a large open-air pavilion in the center with six Doric columns, and two Greek facades with four Doric columns on either side.

> If all were as it seems and men made the elements
> their servants for noble ends! If the cloud that hangs
> over the engine were the perspiration of heroic deeds,
> or as beneficent as that which floats from the farmer's fields,
> then the elements and Nature herself would cheerfully
> accompany men on their errands and be their escort.

Thoreau's use of the subjunctive "were" indicates that he is expressing a wish and not a fact. If a steam locomotive "were" God's gift to mankind, it "would" perform heroic deeds; but, in fact, it was not God's gift and it was not using nature for "noble ends."

> How unfortunate his misunderstanding!
> He obviously had not visited the Philadelphia Waterworks!

If he had visited, he would have marveled at a steam engine unchaining "beneficent" nature by powering the pump that drew water from the Schuylkill to the reservoir on Fairmount. He could also have recognized that Rush's *Schuylkill Chained and Unchained* celebrated this noble liberation.

Fairmount was a public park, but it attracted the gentility, who enjoyed both aesthetic beauty, as romantic as Brown's temple above the Schuylkill; and useful engineering, triumphant for the public good. In contemporary illustrations, well dressed, genteel ladies and gentlemen promenade in the South Garden and the Doric pavilion nearby.

Dressed in finery, they arrived in carriages to enjoy their stroll. To provide even more for such genteel folk to enjoy, Graff designed nearby Lemon Hill with carriage drives. In 1875, one writer in the *Inquirer* commented on these trappings of wealth: "The display of handsome equipages on the drives adds variety to the scene, which is gratifying to all but the envious." Poor folk should appreciate wealth as an ornament to society. Lemon Hill drive, Fountain Green drive, and Strawberry Mansion drive, off of Kelly drive, still remind us of these old-fashioned pleasures of the park's carriage patrons. Most Philadelphians could not get to the Park easily. In the 1850's, for example, they considered the Academy of Music on Broad street far from the city,—how much farther would a Philadelphia pedestrian have considered Fairmount? He could only get there by shank's mare or by paying carfare.

In March, 1871, after Fairmount Park had left Fairmount far behind, an editorial voice in the Philadelphia *Inquirer* pointed out that New York City had designed Central Park especially for pedestrians: "The Mall and the Ramble were open to the public long before the drives were finished." By contrast, beyond the gardens around Fairmount and Lemon Hill, "the whole immense area of the Park" was "almost entirely devoted to drives and bridle paths." By contrast also, "the whole immense area of the Park" on both side of the Schuylkill was more than twice the size of Central Park. What could the poor pedestrians do? They had a long walk to the meetings of the Fairmount Park Planning Commission; and, after they arrived, their voices would have been too weary to be heard.

IN 1891, THE *INQUIRER* described Fairmount Park as the city's "great pleasure ground" (May, 1891), but by 1925 extraordinary urban development had elevated Fairmount itself as the city's great cultural acropolis. Philadelphia's commitment to the classical tradition in creating this acropolis put William Rush's sculptures in their place as early American craft. To set this lofty aspiration literally at the foundation, it hired Carl Paul Jennewein (1890–1978) to design two complementary arches and niches (*aedicula*) in the walls of the hill. To set this classicism at the top, it also hired him to design a pedimental sculpture for the museum.

Jennewein could draw on a long tradition for the decoration of the pediment, but he faced a challenge in decorating the encircling wall. Since the rocks of an acropolis stood in the foundations of man's first walls of defense, they reach back to elemental origins. Jennewein alluded to these origins by carving a personification of each one of the four elements,—earth, air, fire, and water,—on the keystones of the *aedicula* and the arches. (This classicism in the 1920's has received the label Greco Deco.) The arches complement each other: the north and south arches of the ground floor entrances represent fire and water, with appropriate quotations from Homer and Pindar, the great poets of the epic and lyric traditions:

> Homer's *Iliad* 12, line 441—
> ΘΕΣΠΙΔΑΕΣ ΠΥΡ (θεσπιδαὲς πῦρ),
> "God-kindled fire";
>
> Pindar's *Olympian Ode*, line 1—
> ΑΡΙΣΤΟΝ ΜΕΝ ΥΔΩΡ (ἄριστον μὲν ὕδωρ),
> "The very best, indeed, water."

The *aedicula* also complement each other: the purely decorative north and south *aedicula* represent air and earth, with appropriate quotations from the Presocratics, the first natural philosophers:

> Xenophanes of Colophon (570–478 BC), fragment 27—
> ΕΚ ΓΑΙΗΣ ΓΑΡ ΠΑΝΤΑ ΚΑΙ ΕΙΣ ΓΗΝ ΠΑΝΤΑ ΤΕΛΕΥΤΑ,
> "From earth, indeed, all things; and into earth all things end;"
>
> Anaximenes of Miletus (586–526 BC), fragment 2—
> Η ΨΥΧΗ Η ΗΜΕΤΕΡΑ ΑΗΡ ΟΥΣΑ ΣΥΚΡΑΤΕΙ ΗΜΑΣ
> "Our soul, being air, controls us."

To set these passages in chronological order: Homer, *Iliad* 12, 441, represents fire as "god-kindled" (θεσπιδαὲς): "Rouse, you horse-taming Trojans, break the wall of the Argives, and fling among the ships *god-kindled* fire." His epithet "god-kindled" originates in the myth of gods first possessing fire and Prometheus stealing it from them to benefit mankind. This myth takes us back to the days of gods and men.

The Presocratics abandoned Homer's theology for science. Xenophanes represented earth as the beginning and ending of all things (ΕΚ ΓΑΙΗΣ ΓΑΡ ΠΑΝΤΑ ΚΑΙ ΕΙΣ ΓΗΝ ΠΑΝΤΑ ΤΕΛΕΥΤΑ). *Genesis* 3, 9 also mentions this abiogenesis (without (a-) biogenesis) from dust: "In the sweat of thy face shalt thou eat bread, till thou return unto the ground; for out of it wast thou taken: for dust thou art, and unto dust shalt thou return."

Anaximenes represents air as soul and the nexus of creation (Η ΨΥΧΗ Η ΗΜΕΤΕΡΑ ΑΗΡ ΟΥΣΑ ΣΥΚΡΑΤΕΙ ΗΜΑΣ). Along with Xenophanes, he also gave a materialistic interpretation of creation. *Genesis* 2, 7 brings both earth and air together in God's creation of man: "Then the Lord God formed a man from the dust of the ground and breathed into his nostrils the breath of life, and the man became a living being." Both earth and air have their place in the Bible's story of origins.

Pindar has written the fourth act of this elemental drama. In 476 B.C., his "Olympian Ode" celebrated the victory of Hieron, Tyrant of Syracuse, in the single horse race of the Olympic Games. Pindar's priamel, his poetic device, weighs the relative worth of water, sun and fire. Its famous first line, ἄριστον μὲν ὕδωρ, "the very best, indeed, water," stands out as his most famous, and most enigmatic, lyric observation. (On the suggestion of Samuel Johnson, this line was inscribed on the pediment of the Pump Room in Bath.) The Presocratic philosopher Thales had also chosen water as the best, but Pindar at first confirms Thales' preference and then rejects it in celebrating a man's Olympic victory.

In four lines, Jennewein stages four acts of a Greek drama. In the first act, Homer attributes fire to the gods. In the second and third, Xenophanes and Anaximenes take the elements from the gods. Xenophanes brings all things down to earth, but Anazimenes exalts air as the soul that holds them all together. In the last act, Pindar at first celebrates water as best, and then exalts man's glory above it. This drama turns protagonists into antagonists! It sets up a contest between gods, elements, and man as the measure of all.

THE PATRONS AND PLANNERS of Fairmount's acropolis also appreciated its evocation of Greek culture in making connections on the city plan. In Athens, the Panathenaic Procession processed through the streets until it reached the Acropolis and the altar in front of the east end of the Parthenon. The Benjamin Franklin Parkway also links City Hall in Center Square with the east entrance of the Philadelphia Museum of Art. An architect pictured the Museum as the goal of a processing multitude. In both cases, the acropolis marks central points in the city.

Entering the Acropolis by the Propylaia, literally, the front gate, the Panathenaic Procession processed past Doric columns on the porch outside and Ionic columns in the passageway inside. Once within the *temenos*, the sacred enclosure (*cf.* its cognate, temple), it faced two buildings, the most important of which, the Parthenon, was peripteral, that is, it had thirty-four columns of the Doric order on its perimeter. The Erechtheum, north of the Parthenon, housing shrines to Athena, Poseidon and Erechtheus, a legendary king, had two porches of columns of the Ionic order.

In Athens, this variation joined the heavy, plain, native Doric order with the light, decorative, foreign Ionic order, both immediately obvious in the Propylaia; and, individually, in the Doric Parthenon and the Ionic Erechtheum. Athenian civilization found its unique expression in this variation. Commissioned to design the Philadelphia Art Museum, the architectural firm of Borie, Trumbauer and Zantzinger interpreted this variation of the orders.

This interpretation in Philadelphia challenged the architects. One plan in 1908, for example, showed a Propylaia at the base of Fairmount. The final design mediated a dispute between Horace Trumbauer, who wanted the museum to be one building, and his two colleagues, Charles Borie and C. Clark Zantzinger, who wanted a number of "temples," like those on the Athenian Acropolis. Their associate, Howell Lewis Shay, brought the two plans together by incorporating three facades into one building. Separate buildings suited

Greeks, Shay reasoned, because they enjoyed mild, dry weather; but one building would save Philadelphians from slogging through their wet weather that often made slush from rain and snow.

Shay, however, had no intention merely to reproduce an Athenian building. To begin with, for storage and display, the Museum needed a building four times the size of the Parthenon. As the terminus of a long vista, its columns also had to be much taller than the Parthenon's Doric columns. Shay knew that the tallest columns in the ancient world were the sixty-foot-high Corinthian columns of the Roman Temple of Zeus in Athens. For the museum in Philadelphia, he bettered the height of the Athenian columns by three feet. At sixty-three feet, these columns were almost twice the size of those of the Parthenon. Although the choice of huge Corinthian columns marked a departure from the Doric severity of the Parthenon, the length of the porch and its number of columns are similar: the facades of both the Parthenon and the Philadelphia Museum of Art are octostyle, that is, they have eight columns, and they are both 110 feet wide. In Philadelphia, the facing porticos of the wings on either side of the court have Ionic columns like those of the Erechtheum. The Ionic porticos in Athens and Philadelphia are both hexastyle, that is, they have six columns. The columns of the Erechtheum are twenty-two feet; those of the museum, thirty-four.

In size, the Philadelphia Museum of Art far surpasses the buildings of the Athenian Acropolis. Both, however, display a variation of the orders: in Athens, Doric and Ionic; in Philadelphia, Ionic and Corinthian. As a visitor approaches the museum in Philadelphia, he passes by two Ionic wings on either side toward a Corinthian entrance in the center. Passing through these two Ionic facades at right angles to a central Corinthian facade, he experiences diversity in the unity of a single building.

The most subtle element of this unity in diversity is so subtle that it can escape notice: the lines of the building have a slight variation. The Corinthian columns of the central facade, for example, would meet 2.5 miles above the earth, if they were extended. They also describe a circle which would have a radius of .4 of a mile. Even the stairs climbing the hill swell out toward the city. In Greek, ἔντασις (entasis in Latin and English), literally, stretching, an architectural term, describes this swelling. The Greeks employed entasis either to correct a trick that our eyes play on us when we see straight lines as curves, or to make the building seem bigger than it is, or to contradict what our eyes expect to see.

FAIRMOUNT HAS EVOLVED since 1694 when it first shone as Johannis Kelpius' beacon for the summer solstice. The classic variation of the orders,—Doric, Ionic, and Corinthian,—follows its evolution: the Doric fit its simple beginnings, as it decorated the Fairmount Waterworks. From the origin of this order in Center Square, Benjamin Latrobe passed it on to his assistant, Frederick Graff, and, in turn, to Graff's son. Doric simplicity also fit William Rush's early American sculpture and Carl Jennewein's elemental Greco Deco.

In the twentieth century, the union of Ionic and Corinthian on the porches of the Philadelphia Museum completed Fairmount's evolution. Sophisticated representations of nature in art and architecture have refined its first celebration in the Sacred Fire at the solstice. Elegantly dressed ladies and gentlemen no longer arrive at Fairmount in "handsome equipages," but this art represents their ambition which has elegantly clothed Philadelphia's acropolis.

CHAPTER 21

All One: Morris's Place on The Hills, Pratt's Gardens on Lemon Hill

IN 1875, THE *INQUIRER* pointed out one advantage that Philadelphians enjoyed in their life on the coastal plain beneath the Piedmont Plateau. On this lowland between the Delaware and Schuylkill Rivers, they had an "irresistible tendency" to "seek out pleasant places on the neighboring hills." "There is no more sensible way of securing advantages of a summer vacation," it explains, than staying in "a family hotel," a few miles up the Schuylkill. Up in these hills, families "enjoy rural recreations and healthful conditions of rustic life" (July 29, 1875).

By 1875, middle class Philadelphians were enjoying in country hotels what wealthy men in the eighteenth had enjoyed in their country estates. The *Inquirer* pointed to many family hotels in the airy hills above Philadelphia, but it would not have mentioned Fairmount, the first hill and the second, Lemon Hill on the Schuylkill, because they had already become the first two parts of Fairmount Park. With the exception of Fairmount's unique story told in the last two chapters, Lemon Hill's story evolved without such unique distinction. On the other hand, its story, has its own special place in the history of the city, because it, at least started to follow a typical evolution.

At first, this evolution followed a typical pattern, because it started with a country estate. Long after the Sheriff had sold Robert Morris' estate, The Hills, to pay his debts in 1799, the second hill directly above Fairmount, soon to become Lemon Hill, became the site of a hotel and garden in 1838. Its evolution between Morris' purchase in 1770, Henry Pratt's in 1799, and Philadelphia's in 1844 prepared for its place above Fairmount.

Further, in the history of Lemon Hill, its typical beginning has a distinctive ending: the country estate became, almost uniquely, a park. It became a park, because Mr. Pratt had turned Lemon Hill into a garden that many Philadelphians loved and wanted to preserve. This evolution stands out: most country estates have become neighborhoods in a usual pattern of urban development.

Early pictures of Lemon Hill give one obvious clue to its name: a *limonerie* on its slope looks as impressive as the mansion at the top. In 1770, before Robert Morris built this hothouse for lemons, he had invested in The Hills, as a working farm. A notice in *The Pennsylvania Packet*, June 9, 1790, offers its produce for sale:

For Sale, a large Quantity of
Good English Potatoes
For seed or Family use—Also
Good old Hay, Clover & Timothy,
At Robert Morris's Place, up Schuylkill, by Hills

Notices also appeared about retrieving a cow and a horse that had strayed onto the property or paying to pasture cattle on its fields. (Horses, one notice advised, might find pasture at Springettsbury, the Penns' neighboring farm to the east.) Morris could claim no special distinction for such earthy truck, but he built townhouses so sumptuously they did establish his reputation for panache. He built one so impressive that his friend George Washington rented it during his Presidency from 1790 to 1800; and he started to build another so extravagant that he could never finish it. Philadelphians called the first building The Executive Mansion and the other Morris' Folly. He also had ambitions for his rural retreat, even if he did name it The Hills, in a simple reference to its topography. One clue: he sold some exotic plants to Henry Pratt in 1799 for the impressive sum of $750.00,—no small potatoes, or even "Good English Potatoes," at that price!

In the nineteenth century, Henry Pratt (1761—1838), more than Robert Morris (1734–1806), laid the foundation for the fame of Lemon

Pratt's Gardens or Lemon Hill pictured around 1810

Hill. A much younger man, Pratt had done business with Morris, and visited him at The Hills, taking an interest in his exquisite hothouse horticulture, and paying handsomely for some of it. After his friend's bankruptcy, he had the good luck of being able to purchase a small part of the property, but the central one, at a Sheriff's Sale in 1799.

Pratt built on what The Hills had begun, but he first changed its name, for an obvious reason. Morris had named his estate simply for the hills on its three hundred acres. Pratt purchased only one of Morris' hills on forty-two, but he prefixed and entitled his one hill with "Lemon," both to commemorate and to cultivate his friend's *limonerie*. Lemon Hill's impressive greenhouse justified its name.

This sequence of names from The Hills to Lemon Hill establishes a continuity between the ambitions of the two men. The Sheriff's Sale of one lot of forty-two acres to Pratt had come close to decimating Morris' three hundred. The new name that Pratt gave to his property subtracted a single hill from hills, Lemon Hill from The Hills. He was figuring on more than arithmetic. Lemon Hill singularly mixed wit with humility and pride. It made a humorously subtractive tribute to the grand old days and the grand old man of The Hills. Morris, who had spread himself thin in many investments, might have appreciated Pratt's cultivation of *multum in parvo*, much in little.

Robert Morris' hills and Henry Pratt's hill represent the two sides of Philadelphia's history from the eighteenth into the nineteenth centuries. In his great profit and equal loss from the expansive life of the eighteenth century, Robert Morris has left a complicated legacy. Henry Pratt, settling into comfortable trade, domesticity, and gardening in the nineteenth, claims no such fame or its complications. He has gained fame by making his garden famous. Visitors to Lemon Hill called it Pratt's Gardens, which stood apart from the beautiful Federal mansion that Pratt built at their center. One English visitor in 1819 marveled at its "artful disposition of walks and waters, sun and shade, the elegance of the greenhouse and ornamental statuary." He summed up his praise in one phrase, "a little paradise" (*Selections from Letters of E. Howitt* in The Library Company). With an historical focus, another visitor, Andrew Jackson Downing (1815–1852), the father of American landscape design, called it "the most perfect specimen of the geometric mode in America." Most Philadelphians simply enjoyed this little paradise that Pratt generously shared with them. In 1828, for example, thanks to his "usual liberality," the students enrolled in a six week course in botany at the Jefferson Medical College toured Lemon Hill's grounds and green-house (*National Gazette*, April 21, 1828). Because of this sharing, Downing gave Pratt credit for greatly increasing popular taste (*A Treatise on the Theory and Practice of Landscape Gardening*, 1859).

Pratt sold Lemon Hill in 1836, two years before he died. After he sold the property, and before the City of Philadelphia bought it in 1844, Lemon Hill had eight years of precarious existence. Even its fame did not guarantee its immunity to "improvement." "Alas for 'improvement!,'" one observer soliloquized, as he observed Lemon Hill, "it drives its ploughshare fiercely over creation, leveling everything down to monotonous scenes of utility" (*National Gazette*, May 14, 1836). Of course, developers had their eyes on Lemon Hill as a choice tract of land, but Pratt had so firmly established its importance in his thirty-seven years of stewardship that Philadelphians had renamed it Pratt's Gardens. "Hooray for fame!", we can now exclaim; it has averted the fierce "ploughshare" of utility. This fame had not passed away, either with Pratt's passing or with his garden's passing into other hands. Philadelphians enjoyed this little paradise too much to lose it.

Pratt's liberality lived on,—but for a price of admission. Immediately after its sale, Lemon Hill opened its arms to charity: "Mr. Isaac S. Lloyd," the *National Gazette* reported, "who lately purchased Lemon Hill or Pratt's Garden, has generously tendered the use of that beautiful place to the Managers of several Infant School Societies of the city and Liberties, to be used for the benefit of those schools during the summer" (July 15, 1836). Admission cost 12 1/2 cents for one visitor, visiting once;[111] or $5.00 for one family, visiting the whole season. Picture the delighted children, whose parents purchased the season ticket. As they played about the flowers and fountains, they made this garden their "little paradise" for real, not just in poetic hyperbole. Children especially loved Lemon Hill.

In April of 1836, children's parents were not paying to see daisies: "The rich flowers and shrubbery are now coming forth in all their beauty, and the season is approaching when an elegant place of resort will be, as it ever has been, most ardently desired" (*National Gazette*, April 28, 1836). By the end of September, the garden had grown even more beautiful: "The garden at present is more beautiful than it has been this season. There are no less than 800 dahlias raised this year from seed, in full bloom . . . of every shade, size and hue, from the deepest purple to pure white (*United States Gazette*, September 21, 1836). (Mr. Pratt had retired from the garden, but its gardeners had not!) Lloyd provided refreshments appropriate for families: "fruits, ice cream, coffee, &c." This decorous enjoyment in an "elegant place of resort" became the stuff of both legend and nostalgia throughout the century.

But, Isaac Lloyd had a problem, the usual one: without the wealth of men like Morris and Pratt, he could not balance the books of paradise. In 1838, after only two years, he put all the plants of the greenhouse up for sale. The notice appeared in May with an appreciative retrospective, particularly appropriate after Henry Pratt had died in

February: "The collection was first commenced by the celebrated Robert Morris before the Revolutionary War; and has since been brought to perfection at immense cost and pains by the late Henry Pratt. It now embraces specimens of the most choice plants from every corner of the globe . . . many of them having been at Lemon Hill more than half a century and are supposed to be upwards of 100 years old . . . Entrance to the garden at the foot of Coates street" (*National Gazette*, May 23 & June 5, 1838). This adventurous venture in horticulture could not remain viable with patronage of 12 1/2 cent admissions.

Together, Morris extravagantly and Pratt conservatively had, in their turn, sown the seeds and fostered a golden age. The names of their gold,—The Hills, Lemon Hill, Pratt's Gardens—tell their own stories in turn. Pratt cut one Hill from The Hills; and with a wink, he called it a lemon. He developed, and shared his Lemon so enthusiastically that Philadelphians gave him special credit by calling it Pratt's Gardens. And yet, Morris, the Founding Father, created what Pratt watered and grew. These two men treasured their gold, whatever they or other people called it. Five months after Pratt died, thirty-nine years after Morris sold his plants to Pratt in 1799, and seventy-eight years after Morris first started to grow them in 1770, their spirits shared the nostalgia when Isaac Lloyd finally sold their plants in 1838,—*Sic transit gloria mundi*. With that sale, the essential glory of The Hills-Lemon Hill-Pratt's Gardens passed away. Eventually, the shrubbery died through neglect; and only "grand old tulip trees" remained, as Charles Keyser observed in 1856.

As children continued to play, this glory bathed the next epoch of Lemon Hill in its glow.

The first innkeeper at Lemon Hill, Anthony Wayne Olwine, started the democratic silver age of Lemon Hill. He was advertising his "delightful and highly cultivated establishment" in August, as Lloyd was clearing out the remains of the plant sale in June: "A. W. Olwine has taken this splendid establishment, which is now open for the reception of visitors . . . Boarders taken" (*National Gazette*, August 6 & 15, 1838). The manor was taking in boarders only months after the death of its lord! Olwine also introduced the middle class propriety that would characterize Lemon Hill for the rest of the nineteenth century: "To exclude from the premises as much as possible all improper company, and better to preserve from injury the improvements and valuable shrubbery, it has been found necessary to furnish at the gate, tickets of admission 12½ cents." If the middle class folk could not be gentry for 12½ cents, they might at least act with genteel decorum! Olwine had as little success in charging admission for hospitality as Lloyd had in charging it for charity, because he gave no public notice of this inn in 1839. His inn-keeping was short-lived, but Lemon Hill's life as a place of resort was only beginning.

Both before and even after the City of Philadelphia bought Lemon Hill in 1844, entrepreneurial innkeepers like A. W. Olwine ran the house and gardens as an elegant resort. They and especially the municipal government faced a perennial problem about the refreshment: should liquor be served? No one forgot that it had gained its fame as a genteel family resort. And yet, for a time,—proper or "improper company," who can say?,—German families, in Brewery Town across Pennsylvania Avenue, used Lemon Hill as their beer garden. Philadelphians joked that Lemon Hill had become Lager Hill. In those days, advocates of the Temperance Movement picked American resorts as a battle ground, but the German-Americans felt no conflict. They looked with scorn on those boring and brutish Anglophiles, who could not admit the superiority of Germanic recreation:

> Any person familiar with our German population knows how much superior its recreations are to those of native born Americans. . . . The grand pic-nic at Lemon Hill was the most striking proof of the superior civilization of the Germans in the matter of public amusements. The hilarity at that festival was almost entirely unaccompanied by intoxication. Everybody was in his or her happiest mood, yet very few were under the influence of drink. Could half the number of native-born Americans have met, for a similar celebration, without twice as much uproar? (*Public Ledger*, August 9, 1853).

Many "native born Americans," that is, the English speaking people, contradicted the Germans' boast that their "pic-nic" was "almost entirely unaccompanied by intoxication." They felt, one newspaper reported, that the city, in general, had "a duty to prevent the sale of liquor on Lemon Hill," which had become, they added with a xenophobic sneer, "the resort of half-drunken foreigners" (*Public Ledger*, July 27, 1855). "Half-drunken" contradicted the boast of *gemütlichkeit* "almost entirely unaccompanied by intoxication;" but the slur "foreigners" displayed linguistic parochialism, because Germans could not avoid the appearance of foreigners, since they spoke German. In any case, it might have seemed a waste that a site as historic as Lemon Hill should be leased for "no more lofty purpose than the sale of lager beer, pretzels and *Limeberger Kase*" (*Inquirer*, January 24, 1864). No matter, in any case, the T-totalers won the battle. When it became a city park, after a brief age of golden amber on Lager Hill, no one on Lemon Hill tasted anything stronger than lemonade.

Children continued to play and adults enjoyed music from the bandstand. The presence of children justified T-totaling refreshment. Newspapers often reported this activity: "The Sabbath School attached to the church in Race street below Fourth had a celebration on Lemon Hill; upwards of 400 children joined the excursion and partook of the pleasure and exercises of the day, which consisted of singing, prayers and innocent amusements" (*Public Ledger*, June 19, 1841). "Upwards of 400 children" may seem a lot, but this number would go double and up. For decades to come, these "innocent amusements" encouraged both decorum and piety. The children of those "half-drunken foreigners" got lessons in abstemious American life.

In 1854, ten years after the City of Philadelphia had acquired Lemon Hill, it incorporated many nearby towns; and one year after it incorporated these towns, it incorporated Lemon Hill into the park on Fairmount. By 1855, this consolidation started to create a beautiful park for the city. The Park Commission improved Henry Pratt's late Federal mansion by wrapping it in a two-story balcony. This "improvement" catered to Victorian taste, and brought the outside in with "a splendid view" of the river and the city from the house. It "handsomely" renovated its rooms "for the accommodation of ladies and children" (*Inquirer*, July 17, 1862). With the Lager Beer sign removed, Lemon Hill served lemonade.

In 1889, the city expanded its serve the public by building a large pavilion to give ample accommodation to the concerts that visitors had enjoyed since the early 1860's. Eventually, it accommodated the Lemon Hill Association, which institutionalized Lemon Hill's function as a playground by bringing in 800 to 1,000 children from poor,—its brochure said "congested,"—neighborhoods every Saturday during the summer. After enjoying an afternoon of "good, wholesome fun," and eating ice cream, they assembled in the pavilion for thirty minutes of singing songs and singing out Scripture verses. On Sunday, it advertised non-sectarian services of Christian worship, with talks that appealed to secular audiences:

LEMON HILL ASSOCIATION
"TRUE DEMOCRACY"
LEMON HILL OPENS
SUNDAY, 3 P. M.
ALL—WELCOME—ALL
(*Philadelphia Inquirer*, June 1, 1912)

How appropriate the theme of "True Democracy" in this place! By 1901, Lemon Hill had evolved to serve everyman,—and his children. No one heard the old complaint that the park only served as a "delightful and highly cultivated" resort for the well-to-do. Henry Pratt's benevolence had evolved.

This pavilion stood until May of 1933 when one of the "grand old tulip trees" fell on it in a storm. The *Inquirer* reported that it crushed the sounding shell "like an egg shell," and snapped one of its pillars "like a matchstick." The fall of the tulip poplar gave one sign that nature *was* taking over—and taking revenge! Thereafter, concerts moved up the river to Robin Hood Dell; and without the necessary upkeep by the city, the gardens were also falling to ruin

In 1925, the first two hills at the base of the Piedmont experienced the advent of high culture: the Philadelphia Art Museum came to Fairmount; and its director, Fiske Kimball came to Lemon Hill, where he lived until his death in 1955. As a restoration architect, Kimball removed its homey porch, restoring and even improving the building, inside and out. If anyone has ever complained that Lemon Hill served "no more lofty purpose" than drinking beer or eating ice cream, he has had his way. The Art Museum has virtually made the mansion an artifact in its collection.

We do not need to enter the mansion to see artifacts on Lemon Hill.
A grand old tulip poplar still soars above the fishpond and belvedere.
What history it has witnessed in aristocratic, democratic, and populist rituals!
After 250 years, it has seen Robert Morris' hill become a museum by itself.
It welcomes us to the gardens, where we can feel evocations of its past.

CHAPTER 22

William Coleman (1704–1769), at Home in Woodford (1756)

> I had form'd most of my ingenious acquaintance into a club of mutual improvement, which was called the Junto (Benjamin Franklin, *Autobiography*)

IN 1727, FOUR YEARS after Benjamin Franklin entered Philadelphia in his first and famous walk up Market street, he assembled "most" of his "ingenious acquaintance in a club," which he called the Junto.[112] Philadelphia had no institution of learning or even a bookshop, but Franklin asked his friends to pool their books so that, together, they could learn more about their many interests. For "mutual improvement" they met every Friday evening to discuss topics of "Morals, Politics or Natural Philosophy;" and each member wrote one essay every three months. With exuberant pride, he called the Junto "the best school of philosophy, morality, and politics that then existed in the province." At that point in its cultural life, young Philadelphia had little that could challenge Franklin's claim. He went on to organize his friends in founding other institutions for the improvement of their city.

Franklin lists ten members of the Junto, each one with something "ingenious" to recommend him. The first, "Joseph Breintnal, a copyer of deeds for the scriveners," loved poetry, and wrote "some that was tolerable." The last he saves as the best: William Coleman (1704–1769), "then a merchant's clerk, about my age, had the coolest, clearest head, the best heart, and the exactest morals of almost any man I ever met with." A year later, in 1728, Coleman proved himself a "true" friend by offering Franklin the money to free him from a partner in the *Pennsylvania Gazette*, whose alcoholism was threatening their business with bankruptcy. Coleman, Franklin concludes, "became afterwards a merchant of great note, and one of our provincial judges." Benjamin Franklin has become famous for his intelligence and initiative in projects like the Junto, but he could not have succeeded without good citizens like William Coleman. Starting as a "merchant's clerk" and ending as "one of our provincial judges," Coleman nurtured his own virtues, shared them with friends, and used them to serve the public good. His sharing with Benjamin Franklin traces a distinct thread through his life.

Twenty nine years after he had joined the Junto, Coleman, at age 52, built Woodford, as his country house, only four miles outside the city. In about twenty of these twenty-nine years, by using that "coolest, clearest head, best heart, and exactest morals" in the market place, he had generated enough profit as a merchant so that he might build his good life on a good living. In his good life, however, enough was just enough and not too much, because he built only one of the two stories of the building that we now know as Woodford. His maturity had so topped off his life with thrift and common sense that he refrained from topping off his country house with a second story.

This country retreat of one story crowned his life as a well-deserved reward. At Woodford, he might enjoy the leisure to continue the studies and the public service that he had started three decades before. Ben Franklin and some of the Junto's alumni, reuniting at Woodford on Friday evening, would bring together some of the best of William Coleman's life.

COLEMAN'S QUAKER PARENTS had prepared him for success in Philadelphia, where ambition and hard work found fertile fields for growth.[113] His mother Rebecca came to the city one year after William Penn had arrived in 1682. She remembered, Franklin wrote in her obituary, "when the famous Philadelphia consisted of but three

Houses, the rest of the Dwellings being Caves" (*Pennsylvania Gazette*, September 20, 1770).[114] "Thus," her eulogist continues, "has this worthy Person resided in this City almost from its first Foundation, and hath seen such a rapid Progress in its Increase, as perhaps no other Instance in the known World has fully equalled." The elder Colemans' lives represented Philadelphia's dynamic progress, even though membership in the conservative Quaker Meeting would eventually inhibit it. Their son William grew up in a city that would foster his talents. It even made him a judge because he was judicious.

Coleman's father, who had died in 1732, was one of the first members of the Carpenters' Company in Philadelphia, and had helped to increase the number of houses well beyond the first three that his wife first saw. By contrast with his parents, William Coleman and his friend Benjamin Franklin were come-lately's, but each man continued the first inhabitants' work enthusiastically. Coleman's father had built Philadelphia's buildings, and his son's first career built its trade.

In 1727, when Coleman joined the Junto at age 23, he was working as a "merchant's clerk." In the decade of the 1730's, he used his very cool, clear head to make himself a merchant out of the merchant's clerk. Like Franklin, he found some help. Throughout the 1730's, another man had also been advancing as a ship's captain bringing merchants like Coleman their stock. Captain John Hamilton commanded a ship in at least fourteen voyages from 1733 to 1739, to Lisbon, the capital of Portugal, to Madeira, one of its islands, and to Dublin, the capital of Ireland, with stops in Antigua, Barbados, and Jamaica. After he had completed these voyages by 1740, he stopped sailing to join Coleman in the market place.

Hamilton and Coleman planned a partnership for three years, from 1740 to 1743, advertising goods for sale, at their "Store near Carpenter's Wharf." From London and Bristol, they imported and sold "sundry sorts" of textiles, plus iron and steel ware, glass, pepper, loaf sugar, men's and women's hose, *etc., etc.* (*PG*, August 14, 1740; June 18, 1741; and December 20. 1743). In the three years of his partnership with Coleman, Hamilton kept close to home, with only one voyage to Boston in 1742 and another to Maryland in 1743 (*PG*, October 28, 1742; and September 22, 1743). December 20, 1743, a notice in the *Pennsylvania Gazette*, announcing "sundry sorts of English goods" for sale, also mentioned that the term of the partnership of Hamilton and Coleman was "very near expiring." The partners would "divide their Stock, and close their Company-Accounts in a short Time."

By the early summer of 1744, William Coleman announced his independent business:

> To be SOLD
> Very reasonable for Ready Money or on Six Months
> Credit, the following Goods (most
> of them just imported in the Warren,
> Captain Cox, from London)
> By WILLIAM COLEMAN
> (*PG*, June 24, 1744)

On his own, he was selling English goods, but of higher quality than Hamilton and Coleman's stock: "fine scarlet and white flannel . . . lamb and shammy gloves and mittens . . . men's silk hose . . . china bowls and dishes, chocolate cups . . . suits of superfine broad cloth," *etc.* Coleman's marriage and family were giving him incentive to generate more income: he had married Hannah Fitzwater in 1738, and adopted her orphan nephew, George Clymer (1739–1813), in 1746, after the child's father, a famous privateersman, had died at age 35. The Colemans' adopted son grew to great accomplishment, when he signed the Declaration of Independence, at age 37.

The mention of the ship Warren in this notice in the *Pennsylvania Gazette* gives a clue to an important current in Coleman's life that would carry him from trade to public service and bring him closer to Benjamin Franklin. The Warren was also called a galley or a snow. A snow, from the Dutch *snauw*, beak (*cf.* snout in English), had been derived from a three-masted ship, with two gaff sails, in place of the third mast. The two sails were attached to an extension of the bow that looked like a beak, a "snow" in Dutch. Fast and easy to handle, the Snow Warren could also serve in the navy.

Three years later, in 1747, Coleman, along with the Snow Warren, entered on a new venture. At the beginning of the year, he had joined with Benjamin Franklin and prominent merchants to sponsor a lottery. In announcing it in the *Pennsylvania Gazette*, Franklin does not mention that its profit would buy cannons to defend the city from the depredation of Spanish and French pirates in the Delaware Bay:

> TICKETS in the Philadelphia Lottery, are sold by William Allen, Joshua Maddox, William Masters, Samuel M'Call, senior, Edward Shippen, Thomas Leech, Charles Willing, John Kearsley, William Clymer, senior, Thomas Lawrence, junior, William Coleman, and Thomas Hopkinson, at their respective Dwellings, and by B. Franklin, at the Post Office (*PG*, January 26, 1747).

Thomas Hopkinson had set up his store next to Hamilton and Coleman's. They are now listed together in this venture. In this scheme for the defense of the city, Coleman was acting with the most prominent citizens of Philadelphia but outside the Quaker Meeting. Unable to condone such military activity, even though it was solely defensive, the Meeting dismissed Coleman from membership. Now he could join Philadelphia's most progressive citizens.

After piracy and the panic, the money from the lottery commissioned the Snow Warren as a Privateer for offense. Just a few months later, sailing in to lend a hand, it cruised unsuccessfully in the Spring: "Privateer Snow Warren of this place arrived here from a cruize, but without any further success" (*PG*, April 9, 1747). Out again, it returned in the early Summer with a prize of a French Privateer of 16 guns and about 130 men (*PG*, June 25, 1747).

COLEMAN WAS GROWING into a more complex civic life. In his last commercial venture at the end of the 1740's, he sold copper stills "of different sizes, from thirty to eighty-five gallons" (*PG*, August 24, 1749). In his work, positions of trust and public service were taking the place of trade, from which he had made enough money that he could work more for the public good. Over time, he made a gradual transition from his counting house to the school house and, finally, to the court house.

In his progress from counting house to school house, he continued his work with Benjamin Franklin. Four years after forming the Junto, which shared learning and books, Franklin turned it into the Library Company, which specifically shared books. He served as its Director;

and Coleman, with his head for numbers and business, as its Treasurer, from 1731 to 1734 and from 1742 to 1757 (*PG*, May 10, 1753). In 1741, with Benjamin Franklin, Philip Syng and Hugh Roberts, Coleman helped to prepare a catalogue of its books.

To widen the purposes of the Junto-Library Company throughout the Colonies, Coleman and Franklin helped to found the American Philosophical Society in 1743, and the Academy—the University of Pennsylvania—in 1749. The initiative for the Academy had started in the discussions of the Junto. As its clerk and treasurer until his death, Coleman also purchased some of the institution's first books and maps. In their bookish interests, they built on the "mutual improvement" of the Junto to establish the University of Pennsylvania.

Both men also worked to promote health and public safety in Philadelphia. Coleman supported Pennsylvania Hospital from 1751 until his death when he bequeathed the institution £50. Discussion in the Junto about the loss of homes by fire inspired a project to form "a company for the more ready extinguishing of fires, and mutual assistance in removing and securing of goods when in danger." In 1752, both he and Franklin served as Directors of the Philadelphia Contributionship for Insuring Houses, known as Hand in Hand (*PG*, April 12, 1753).

Unfortunately, some physical afflictions started to slow down his career. A decade later, kidney stones prevented him riding with Mason and Dixon on their expedition, but he wrote up their reports of the boundary dispute in 1761 and 1762 (Whitfield J. Bell, Jr., *Patriot Improvers: 1743–1768*).

The fire mark of The Philadelphia Contributionship

Coleman's progress in public service from 1727 to 1761 goes down the list of Philadelphia's classic institutions which first served its learning—Junto (1727), Library Company (1731), American Philosophical Society (1743), and the University of Pennsylvania (1749)—and then its practical needs—from Pennsylvania Hospital (1751), to the Contributionship (1752), and right along the Mason and Dixon Line (1761). The two clasped hands, which the Hand in Hand Company took as its logo, represented the spirit of mutual assistance that motivated all Franklin's and Coleman's projects for the benefit of their city.

In June of 1750, one important trust marked an epoch in his life. Benjamin Franklin assembled his most trusted friends as witnesses and executors of his will: "I desire my good friends William Coleman and Philip Syng, to give their advice from time to time where it may be needful in the settlement of my affairs" (Snyder, 29). Coleman also served as an executor to the estate of George Fitzwater, his father-in-law, Abraham Claypoole; and Samuel Powel, Jr. (*PG*, June 28, 1750; August 15, 1751; and August 22, 1761). In Franklin's life, however, his friend Coleman predeceased him by twenty-one years

HAVING BALANCED MAKING a good living as a merchant with a good life as a friend and public servant, William Coleman, in his early 50's, started thinking about a second home for his leisure. In 1756, he purchased a relatively modest plot of 12 acres for £96, at a "public vendue" directed to the Sheriff, Samuel Morris:

> BY virtue of a writ to me directed, will be exposed to sale, by publick vendue, about three o clock, on the 12th day of May next, at the house of John Biddle (Indian King Tavern), a piece or parcel of land, part of Shute's plantation, situate in the Northern Liberties township, about four miles from Philadelphia, bounded on two sides by the land of Thomas Hood, and by the Wissahickon road, and on other two sides by other land late of Thomas Shute deceased, containing 12 acres, late the estate of Thomas Shute deceased, taken in execution by Samuel Morris, late Sheriff (*PG*, May 6, 1756).

In the early years of the eighteenth century, the classic estates along the Schuylkill were taking shape. From the original property, "well known by the name of Shute's plantation," bordered by Mifflin's Lands, and by the River Schuylkill, Joseph Galloway had also purchased the 30 acres that would become Edward Burd's Ormiston (*PG*, June 7, 1759). From Mifflin's Lands, also known as the Fountain Green, John McPherson would purchase land for Mount Pleasant.

Coleman's modest purchase of 12 acres suited his moderation: in his career as a judge which he started in 1751, he exhibited the same judicious character. In Judge Coleman's passing through Woodford's classic Tuscan Doric portal in 1758, we might see a stereotypical image of well-earned dignity. The dignity of the man was dignifying his home, and *vice versa*. In their book about Woodford, the Snyders tip the balance in favor of the edifice. "Coleman was more than comfortable in his new surrounding, he was dignified and uplifted by them" (Snyder, 26). It is true: men build buildings and buildings, in turn, build men; but Coleman was bringing the dignity of an exemplary life to the Tuscan portal of his Georgian home. He did not need the Tuscan Doric to remind him of of the simple dignity of an American citizen.

The *Pennsylvania Gazette* published a full description of the estate after Coleman's demise in 1769:

> THE COUNTRY SEAT late of William Coleman, Esq.; within 4 Miles of the, City of Philadelphia, on the West Side of Wissahickon Road, will be sold by public Vendue; it contains about 12 Acres, with a House of Rooms on a Floor finished in a neat Manner; an Out-house suitable for a Tenant, built of Stone, with 4 Fire-places, 2 on each Floor, and a Cellar under the whole, a good Stone Chair-house and Stable, a handsome Garden, a thriving Orchard of good apple Trees, and other Fruit, and a Well of excellent Water. The whole Place being under good Post and Rail and Pallisadoe Fence (*PG*, May 11, 1769).

Woodford, the main house "of Rooms on a Floor," has only one story. Its being "finished in a neat Manner" refers to the elegant simplicity of the Tuscan Doric outside and wood and marble work inside. The "out-house," i.e., a farm house "suitable for a tenant," unlike Woodford, has two stories, "with 4 Fire-places, 2 on each Floor." The "good Stone Chair-house and Stable" probably occupy one building. On its own, a "chair-house" was a shed that housed two-wheeled horse-drawn, two passenger vehicles; but it made sense for Coleman to build storage for vehicles as part of his stable for horses, especially on such a relatively small estate. Like his neighbor, Joseph Galloway, he had "a handsome Garden, a thriving Orchard of good apple Trees, and other Fruit." He lived in this house from its completion in 1758 until his death in 1769.

BENJAMIN FRANKLIN WROTE Coleman's obituary after he died on January 11, 1769. He had the opportunity to bring his admiration for him, first expressed in his *Autobiography*, to a fitting conclusion:

> PHILADELPHIA, January 19. On Wednesday, the Eleventh Instant, died, at the Age of 64, The Honourable WILLIAM COLEMAN, Esq., an Assistant Judge of our Supreme Court. He was always esteemed a valuable and useful Citizen, and a Gentleman of great good Sense, and unblemished Virtue. Tho' much pleased with Study and Retirement, he possessed many social Virtues, and was ever fond of those Subjects, which were most likely to render him serviceable to his Neighbour. He was an able and an upright Judge, and in that Character gave the greatest Satisfaction to his Country. And we may say, with much Reason, that this Province has few such Men, and that few Men will be so much missed as Mr. Coleman (*PG*, January 19, 1769).

Franklin sets himself a high goal in depicting Coleman's quality of character. He does not mention his career as a merchant, but, with an eye toward the head, heart and morals of the man whom he had praised in his autobiography, he relates his private to his public virtue. Though Coleman was "much pleased with Study and Retirement," he was a "valuable and useful Citizen," who focused on "those Subjects, which were most likely to render him serviceable to his Neighbour." Franklin derived his insight into William Coleman as a man "much pleased with Study and Retirement" from his days in the Junto when he first got to know him as an eager young learner. Ability in mathematics made him "serviceable" as treasurer of the Library Company and the Academy.

Coleman's career as a judge also arose from this desire to study "serviceable" subjects. It started in the 1750's and culminated with his appointment in 1758 as an Assistant Judge of the Pennsylvania Supreme Court. The young man whom Franklin had first praised as a person of private distinction,—"the coolest, clearest head, the best heart, and the exactest morals,"—had grown to enjoy public distinction: "this Province has few such Men, and . . . few Men will be so much missed as Mr. Coleman."[115]

Also working for the public good, Coleman intended to free the young "negroe children" in his household, but only when they reached a certain age:

> SEVERAL young NEGROE CHILDREN
> are to be bound out to the Ages of 26 and 24, in Pursuance of the Will of William Coleman, Esq. Application to be made to Hugh Roberts, or George Clymer, Executors (*PG*, July 6, 1769).

After Coleman's wife had predeceased him, his death left no household in which his slave children could grow to maturity and freedom. Rather than freeing these young people in his will, Coleman "bound" them "out" to families, until they were 24 and 26 years old. Having come to adulthood in completing their term, they could set out as freedmen into the world safely.

Edward Burd described the large number of distinguished Philadelphians attending the obsequies following Coleman to his grave:

> Nearly two hundred of our principal men attended his corpse to the grave. I saw his coffin upon the shoulders of Mr. Chew, Mr. Tilghman, Uncles E.S. (Edward Shippen) and Mr. Gibson, this I believe is the Quaker custom. He has left an estate valued at £15,000, £6,000 of which he has devised to George Clymer and £3,000 to each of his sisters—his wife died shortly after his return from England (Burd, *Selections from the Letters*, January 16, 1769).

COLEMAN ENJOYED WOODFORD for eleven years from 1758 until his death in 1769. It gave him a retreat where he considered his cases before the State Supreme Court and shared with Franklin the care of the Philadelphia institutions that they had founded. Long before he had the luxury of a country residence, he expressed to a young man visiting England the pleasures of a "steady quiet mind" and a quiet life "at home:"

> As far as my experience goes, the greatest happiness arises, not so much from new scenes and entertainments, as from a steady quiet mind and the consciousness of doing right, and this happiness a man may find at home; and yet I believe it proper that a young man should see the world to be better convinced of the little it affords (letter to James Pemberton, November 18, 1748, in the HSP).

Writing this letter in 1748, just about the time when he was turning from his career in trade to civic duties at home, William Coleman pictures the "steady quiet mind" that would build and enjoy Woodford.[116] For a little more than a decade before his death, he enjoyed contentment at home in Woodford—the "greatest happiness . . . from . . . the consciousness of doing right."

CHAPTER 23

David Franks Adds Another Story to Woodford

WOODFORD, AS WE NOW KNOW IT, has two stories, but it started its life with only one. In 1756, William Coleman (1704–1769) built it as a home of one story. After buying the house in 1771, David Franks (1720–1794) had an obvious reason for adding the second: Coleman had one child; Franks had seven. These children, and especially their mother, needed more room. In addition, David, and especially his daughter Rebecca, also filled Woodford's two stories with dramatic stories of their day.

Coleman and Franks both engaged in trade, but their lives overlapped into different times. Born in 1704, Coleman sold his wares and practiced his virtues in the idyllic days of early Philadelphia. Franks, born in 1720, also worked hard at keeping store and living virtuously; but he, by contrast, suffered from the divided loyalties in Philadelphia during and after the American Revolution. In those days, a merchant's life depended on whether he put stock in the British or in the Americans.[117]

The national and religious complexion and division of David's story can start with his father, Jacob (1688–1769), who, at age twenty, emigrated from London to New York. He did not start a business by selling his wares from a pushcart, but by acting as an agent for his family's mercantile firm. In contrast with Jacob, many immigrants brought nothing but their work ethic and the hope that once planted in fertile soil, it might reap profit. Jacob had already profited from his family's business back in London. They had planted and reaped much; and young Jacob planned for more. He obviously gave his son David's life its start, but his life story, with its connection to his family back in London, can also give some clues for David's story in its course and in its ending.

Jacob Franks died in 1769, two years before his son David purchased Woodford at age 51. Benjamin Franklin published his obituary in the *Pennsylvania Gazette*, probably out of respect for his distinguished son in Philadelphia:

> NEW-YORK, January 23. Last Monday Morning died in an advanced Age, Mr. JACOB FRANKS, for many Years an eminent Merchant of this City: A Gentleman of a most amiable Character; in his Familv, a tender and kind Master; as a Merchant, upright and punctual in all his Dealings; as a Citizen, humane and benevolent; a Friend to the Poor of all Denominations, affable and friendly in his Behaviour to all. He is now gone to receive from the Supreme God, whom he adored, his Reward among the Faithful. The Memorial of the Righteous is Blessed. On Tuesday his Remains were decently interred in the Jews Burying Place, attended by a great Number of his Friends (*PG*, January 26, 1769).

Jacob was a good man of business—"upright and punctual in all his Dealings." He was also a good man—"humane and benevolent," a "friend to the Poor of all Denominations." In Judaism, the chosen denomination, his charity reached out to "all Denominations." In addition to his "Reward among the Faithful" before "The Supreme God," he has won a "blessed" memory among the living: the Memorial of the Righteous is Blessed," one of the sons of Solomon has declared in *Proverbs* 10.7. Jacob's trade, back and forth across the Atlantic; his family on either side; and his Judaism, with its roots and their spread, made him cosmopolitan. He passed on this life—and its fate in the American Revolution—to his son David.

In spreading the family's trade and influence, Jacob's younger sons, Moses and David, in their turn, left New York to seek new opportunities in Philadelphia with their maternal uncle, Nathan Levy (1704–

1753). David, age 20, with Moses, 22, advertised their stock, "Just Imported," in the *Pennsylvania Gazette*:

> JUST IMPORTED
> And to be sold by Moses and David Franks, at their store at the Widow Hannah Meredith's, in Front-street,
> CHOICE Bohea Tea, Callicoes, Cambricks, Pistol lawns, wide and narrow scarlet and cloth coloured camlets, hairpins, crapes, flowered damasks, tufted fustians, pewter, yard wide, seven eighths & three quarters garlix tandaens, fine glaized callicoe, fanoes, muslins, black and coloured taffities and persians, poises, camlettees, florrettas, buttons and mohair, London shalloons, buckram, check linnens, cotton romals, osnabrigs, and sundry other sorts of European goods cheap for ready money or four months credit (*PG*, May 7, 1741).[118]

Moses and David Franks' stock also spoke the languages of the world: camlets from an Arabic word for velvet, mohair from an Arabic word for wool, romals from a Hindi word for handkerchief, and taffities from a Persian word for woven silk or linen. The Franks brothers' stock took their customers on a world tour.

Customers appreciated the opportunity to choose from this variety. Before ready-made clothing became popular in the nineteenth century, tailors and the distaff side of families in the eighteenth made clothing from these various fabrics. Home-spun and their warp and woof got them down to basics, as ready-made clothing in the nineteenth and twentieth centuries did not. These goods originated from all over the world, but the Franks brothers only described them as "European."

David Franks could refer to his goods as "European," because they had passed through his family's connections in London, but he also referred to them more specifically as "East-India" (*PG*, February, 1756). As a young man, he aspired to visit India in the hope of admiring and getting a share of its fabled wealth. The British East India Company had been pouring India's goods—and its wealth—into London since 1600. He never fulfilled this dream, but he started to own the ships that might bring him its goods, even though he never sailed in them to get there.

His brother Moses went back to London and joined his father in shipping supplies to the British army in Georgia. This family business with the British government would eventually involve David in loyalties tragically divided. In the meantime, he joined with his uncle Nathan in 1743 in outfitting some ships. The next year, the firm of Levy and Franks shared ownership of the schooner *Drake* with Thomas Hopkinson. Hopkinson also shared business ventures with William Coleman, the first owner of Woodford. For five years, from 1748 to 1753, this firm advertised berths "for freight or passage" on four ships: the Brigantine Richa, named after one of his sisters and his daughter; the Snow Amphitrite, the ship London; and, most often, the ship Myrtilla. Levy and Franks' first notice in the *Pennsylvania Gazette* announced her maiden voyage from Philadelphia:

For L O N D O N,
The Ship M Y R T I L L A,
Richard Budden, Commander:
Will sail with all convenient speed, great part of her loading being ready; she is 250 tons burden, ten guns and twenty men. For freight or passage apply to Messieurs Levy and Franks, or said master on board his ship at Hamilton's wharf.
N. B. Said ship will certainly sail by the 15th of October; and as Mr. Levy goes in her, all that are indebted to, or have demands against, them, are desired to come and settle them betwixt and that Time
(*PG*, September 22, 1748).

"For London"—the four Franks' ships, advertised in the *Pennsylvania Gazette*, all sailed from Philadelphia "for London." This notice, in particular, announces that Uncle Nathan would be on board. In the future, notices would mention the ships of their fleet importing "an assortment of East-India and European goods to be sold by Levy and Franks." The firm of Levy and Franks advertised these voyages many times from 1748 to 1753.

In 1751, David and his uncle moved their business into the most significant house in Philadelphia. The *Pennsylvania Gazette* announced that the firm of "LEVY and FRANKS" had "Remov'd from their store in Front and Water-streets to the house of Isaac Norris, Esq.; wherein the Governor lately lived, in Second-street" (June 27, 1751). They were setting up shop in the Slate Roof House, in which William Penn had lived from 1699 until his final departure in 1701, and which Isaac Norris (1671–1735) had purchased in 1709. His son, Isaac Norris, Jr. (1701–1766) lived there until 1741, giving the name Norris' alley to its side street. From that year until 1864, the younger Norris and his heirs rented out the property.

In uniting with Thomas Hopkinson as co-owners of the *Drake* in 1744 and in leasing the Slate Roof House from Isaac Norris in 1751, David was associating with the best of Philadelphia's merchants. In 1743, the first year of his partnership with his uncle, he had joined the community in the most significant personal bond. On December 17, 1743, David took Margaret Evans (1720–1780) as his bride in Christ Church. He was not the first person in his family to marry a Gentile. His mother had already agonized over the marriage of his sister Phila (1722–1811) to Oliver Delancey (1718–1785). The relatively liberal atmosphere of the colonies along with its dearth of nubile women in the Jewish community could explain his breaking from orthodoxy. Joining the community even more, David became truly ecumenical: in addition to his regular attendance at services in Christ Church and baptizing his children at its font, he maintained membership in his family's synagogue in New York. Considering David's prominence in the community, it should be no surprise that in 1748 The Dancing Assembly, Philadelphia's most famous society, included David Franks in its first subscription.

David Franks was gaining connections in the community, as he unfortunately lost his important family connection with the death of his Uncle Nathan on December 23, 1753. Nathan was buried in a plot that had been waiting just for him. He had acquired its nine hundred square feet on Spruce street from Thomas Penn for the burial of his daughter in 1740. As he had requested, he was buried at its center. By acquiring this privileged place for his family, Nathan Levy also won a significant place in history. This cemetery has survived as the oldest evidence of a Jewish presence in Philadelphia; and Nathan Levy's grave, with its ledger stone on a rectangular box, as the oldest legible inscription in this hallowed ground. Mikveh Israel, Philadelphia's first synagogue, eventually made this cemetery its own.

Throughout 1754, David advertised the settlement of Uncle Nathan's estate:

> All those persons that have any demands against the late partnership of Levy and Franks, or the estate of Nathan Levy, are desired to bring them in for payment: And all those indebted to them are earnestly requested to be speedy in their payments, or they depend on being sued. David Franks.
>
> N. B. To be sold, exceeding cheap, at the late company store, in Second-street, in order to finish accounts, A very great assortment of European and India goods, cutlery ware, nails, Russia duck, Scotch and rappee snuff, &c.[119]

Franks follows up this assurance that merchants with debts over-due "may depend on being sued" with an aggrieved complaint that people would pay "little regard" to his request—

> Little regard being paid to the above advertisement, this is to assure those that are backward in their payments, that they may depend on being sued, and that very soon, without further notice (*PG*, January 15, 1754, and fourteen more times throughout the year).

—and an assurance that they would not get away with it. Merchants "backward in their payments" could depend on being pushed forward into court. Franks gives all his creditors in arrears no more warning of a lawsuit than this general one in the *Gazette*. With this peremptory attitude, it is no surprise that he was consistently bringing lawsuits to court.

Having sold off much of the stock of Levy and Franks to settle his uncle's estate, David made a fresh start in 1754. He fitted out "the ship *New-Myrtilla*, Richard Budden, Commander" and adverted the readers of the *Gazette* to her "*extraordinary accommodation for Passengers*" (December 12, 1754). After his uncle's demise, with the exception of launching the *New-Myrtilla*, Franks was pulling in his sails. *Viribus Unitis*—he had profited from a strength in union with his family that he no longer enjoyed. During the French and Indian War (1754–1763), he formed a new partnership for his family business of victualizing

British troops: "By the general's Command, WILLIAM PLUMSTED and DAVlD FRANKS, contractors for supplying the army with Provisions and Carriages (*PG*, October 30, 1760). Having made many connections in three terms as mayor of the city, William Plumsted put David on even firmer ground.

David gave up his store's historic location in the Slate Roof House, relocating to Water street, also known as King street.[120] He bought his stock from what other merchants' brought into the harbor, but he spared no expense in buying. In a notice in the *Gazette*, he advertised a huge stock, "too tedious to mention" in its entirety, like that of a department store (*PG*, March 11, 1755). The next year, he contented himself with a brief notice:

> Just imported in the last vessels from London, and to be sold by
> DAVID FRANKS,
> At his store, in the house where the late Thomas Lawrence, Esq.
> lived in Water street, very reasonable,
> A NEAT assortment of European and East-India goods, suitable for the
> season (*PG*, September 25, 1756).

On his own, David expanded his business into the larger community. In 1751, his old ship the *Myrtilla* delivered eight bells from London for Christ Church. In a turnabout, he had not helped to pay for their casting, but his old employee, Captain Budden of the *Myrtilla*, delivered them without charge.

A family connection took him out to Woodford. In 1759, his sister-in-law, Rebecca Evans married Alexander Barclay (1713–1771) in Christ Church. Barclay, like Franks, was a member of a mercantile family in London, eventually the founders of Barclay's Bank; and, like Franks, he also came to Philadelphia as an agent for his family's business in representing the interests of the Crown. Ten years later, in 1769, Barclay purchased Woodford at the public auction dictated by William Coleman's will. He made the winning bid of 745£. Coleman had made it attractive by adding "a handsome Garden, a thriving Orchard of good apple Trees, and other Fruit, and a Well of excellent Water" (*PG*, May 11, 1769). Barclay added a porch along the length of its back wall.

Alexander Barclay lived to enjoy his country retreat for only two years. In the violent protest against His Majesty's Stamp Act, his employee received death threats and he so suffered from his divided loyalties that he died of a stroke in 1771. As he visited Woodford, David Franks must have sympathized with his brother-in-law's plight. He must also have liked the place, because he attended the sheriff's sale, which sold it by an auction:

> BY virtue of a writ to me directed, will be exposed to public sale, on the premises, on Saturday, the 22d of June instant, precisely at 3 o'clock in the afternoon, a certain brick messuage and tract of land, situate in the Northern Liberties of the city of Philadelphia, about 4 miles from said city, containing 12 acres an 4 perches of land, bounded by the Wissahickon road, and lands of Joseph Shute, Thomas Hood, and others; late the estate of Alexander Barclay, Esq.; deceased; to be sold by Judah Foulke, Sheriff (*PG*, June 20, 1771).

Barclay's demise left his family in financial straights that made this Sheriff's sale inevitable. David made the winning bid of £880.

David Franks both increased the frame of the house and its fame. Like its two previous owners, Franks bought it in his early 50's to crown his life of hard work. He could see a cautionary tale in the tragic fate of his brother-in-law's divided loyalties, but he continued to victualize His Majesty's army. In the occupation of Philadelphia, September, 1777, General William Howe visited David Franks at Woodford to discuss, among other things, maintaining the supply lines that David managed.

The "other things" gave Woodford its most colorful chapter in the history of Philadelphia. Franks' youngest daughter, Rebecca (1760–1823), to whom her mother had given the name of her aunt, Rebecca Evans Barclay, was seventeen, and "the belle of Philadelphia," "handsome and witty," as Winfield Scott later described her. General Howe brought along his staff, including the handsome and talented Major John André (1750–1780), who met Rebecca, nicknamed Becky, and her friends in their visits to Woodford. Handsome young men meeting beautiful young women—two forces of nature! Those "other things" became very important things. The young peo-

John André

ple nourished these sparks by almost daily commutes on the Wissahickon road out to Woodford. Major André also visited the Franks at their townhouse on Second street between Chestnut and Walnut. His friend and Becky's cousin, Captain Oliver DeLancey, Jr. joined the company. André's brush portrayed the ladies' beauty and his pen praised it. "We have no evidence of how Mr. and Mrs. Franks liked the situation," Mark Stern has observed, "but there was nothing wrong with finding a way to please your best customer," who was also, unfortunately, the patriots' worst enemy.

Just before the British left Philadelphia for New York City, André used his artistic talents to design the triumphal arches, the decorations, and even the invitations for General Howe's farewell party, The Mischianza, May 18, 1778. This grand social event, probably the grandest in the history of Philadelphia, recreated medieval pageantry. Soldiers, as Knights of the Blended Rose or the Knights of the Burning Mountain, jousted for the favor of their ladies. Mr. and Franks were among the guests; but Becky led the procession of the Ladies of the Burning Mountain. André and his messmates were having some fun in the make-believe, but Becky's was glorying in her own unique victory.

Once the British departed, and left their American friends alone and unprotected, American patriots returned to Philadelphia on a vindictive hunt for traitors. Their hunt sparked painful prosecutions of David Franks, from 1778 until his death in 1793. His biographer, Mark Stern, has observed that much historiography of the American Revolution has "idolized and elevated to the status of demigods" founding fathers like Washington and Adams (Stern, xi). No patriot, certainly, had any reason to burn votive candles to David Franks. If for nothing else, radical patriots might persecute him for his attendance at the Mischianza and its celebration of his daughter Becky. (How dearly should a man pay for having a beautiful and charming daughter!?) With the radicals in power, he was finally caught in "the tangled web of personal relationships" (Stern, 35) that he had been weaving all his life. By asking him to supply both British and American armies, Congress "had placed him in an impossible position" (Stern, 149), and it now left him to pay the price.

Two trials acquitted Franks of charges of treason or complicity with the enemy, but the radicals, implacably pursuing revenge, questioned the validity of the juries' verdicts. Franks had his defenders. One of them, in an anonymous letter to *Dunlap's Pennsylvania Packet*, ascribed a "wicked intent" to those who would attack "the bulwark of our liberties, Trial by Jury, as well as . . . the safety of every citizen, who may hereafter be acquitted by the laws of his country, and the judgement of his peers" (May 13, 1779). Chief among his enemies, Joseph Reed (1741–1785) had secured the Presidency of the Supreme Executive Council of the Commonwealth of Pennsylvania, the governing body formed after the Declaration of Independence. With his influence and that of his fellow radicals on the Council, the state had "forfeited and seized the tract of land on the Schuylkill" of 45 acres (*Aurora General Advertiser*, June 17, 1780) belonging to Franks' neighbor, Joseph Galloway. (Edward Burd would acquire this estate and name it Ormiston.)

Foiled in prosecution, radicals did the next best thing. In October of 1780, without a trial, it sent David Franks and William Hamilton into exile. William Hamilton, who later became the well-known lord of the manor at the Woodlands, was the brother of Andrew Hamilton, who, in 1768, had married Abigail Franks (1744–1798), David's oldest daughter. This exile sent the two men behind enemy lines in New York City (Stern, 155). David's wife Margaret had died just days before his exile. He left his two daughters in Philadelphia to bury her in the cemetery of Christ Church. Having owed money to Thomas Paschall, among his many creditors, since 1775, Franks transferred Woodford to him in November, 1780.

Arriving in London, July 2, 1782, David could at least find some consolation in reuniting with his brothers and his two sons, who welcomed him in an unfortunately inconvenient homecoming. Virtually destitute and relying on his family's charity, as his life in Philadelphia lay in ruins, he could have taken little pleasure in the reunion. Dogged by creditors in England, he returned in 1789, hoping to salvage some of his investments. He died in Philadelphia during the yellow fever epidemic of 1793.

Rebecca Franks married a British officer and spend her later years comfortably in Bath, England. And yet, her life was never as colorful as it had been at Woodford. After the British left Philadelphia in 1778, Becky Franks' star passed its zenith. Writing to Betsy Shippen from Woodford, she wistfully reported the "news": "News you ask for, alas where is there any that we call good. For my part I have given up the thoughts of hearing any more. What's become of all the beaux? I'm afraid they've quite deserted this road." "This road," the Wissahickon road that led to Woodford, never again saw the cavalcade of belles and beaux. No more handsome British officers with whom to flirt! Her star passed its zenith after her triumphant cavalcade at the Michianza, but her father's sank to its nadir.

Woodford's star has also declined, although its bricks and woodwork have survived David Franks and his daughter Becky. Prominent houses on their hills above the east banks of the Schuylkill, like Hamilton's Bush Hill, Morris' The Hills, and even the eccentric Captain McPherson's Mount Pleasant, upstage Woodford, behind them on the Wissahickon road. They shine as American icons, "idolized and elevated," but no one of them can surpass the drama of Woodford's human story.

Woodford

CHAPTER 24

The Experiences of Laurel Hill Mansion

BINDING BRICKS WITH MORTAR in Flemish bond has strengthened Laurel Hill Mansion, just as the mores of its two families have bound it to history: solid Philadelphia building material—the Rawles bonding with the Shoemakers, and the Physicks with the Randolphs. At the foundation, Francis Rawle (1660–1727) emigrated from Plymouth, England, to Philadelphia in 1686. From William Penn, he purchased 2500 acres, which he named after his home back in England. Like the founders of the Plymouth Colony in Massachusetts, Rawle, as a Quaker, was seeking religious refuge that he found in Penn's Holy Experiment. Immigrants like him, "better educated and broader-minded" than the average,[121] were giving Pennsylvania the head-start that made it a radiant temple on a hill in the eighteenth century.

Widening his focus, Francis Rawle soon moved from his country estate, eventually known as Plymouth Meeting, into Philadelphia. In the city, he bonded with an important Quaker family by marrying Martha, the daughter of Robert Turner (1635–1700). Francis and Martha widened their focus quite a bit by raising ten children.

Of this brood, their son William (1694–1741) passed on his father's heritage to his son Francis (1729–1761). Francis eventually acquired the 31 acres on which his wife would build Laurel Hill Mansion. Grandfather Francis, who had been the master of 2500 acres, had paved the way for his grandson Francis to establish this relatively small estate.

Even more solidly than in the vast estate of Plymouth Meeting, however, this founding family bound up its mores with Laurel Hill.

William Rawle died in 1741, when his son Francis was 12 years old. At this point, the second family, the Shoemakers, Germans from Kresheim in the Palatinate—Isaac (1669–1732), his son Benjamin (1704–1767), his grandson Samuel (1725–1800) and his great-grandson Benjamin (1747–1808)—added another course to the fabric of Laurel Hill. Like many wealthy families in Philadelphia, the Rawles and the Shoemakers had gained their prominence as merchants. Each family owned a store and a wharf on the Delaware River. Benjamin Shoemaker and his son Samuel also served as the city's mayors. On William's demise in 1741, Benjamin served as an executor of his estate:

> ALL Persons indebted to the Estate of William Rawle, late of the City of Philadelphia, Merchant, deceased, are desired to pay the same unto His Executors; and those who have any Demands against the said Estate, are desired to bring in their Accounts, that they may be adjusted, by Benjamin Shoemaker, William Cooper <Mary Rawle's husband>, Rebecca and Elizabeth Rawle, Executors.
> Note. There is to be let by the said Executors, the late Dwelling House of the said William Rawle, deceased, with a Wharf, and very good convenient new stores (*Pennsylvania Gazette*, March 3, 1742).

The executors of William's estate from his own family—his sisters, Rebecca and Elizabeth Rawle, and his sister Mary's husband, William Cooper—had special confidence in Benjamin Shoemaker, since they included him, the only non-family member—but, soon to become one—in settling their brother's estate.

Although William's father, Francis Rawle, the elder, had ten children—perhaps, because he had had ten children!—his son William and his wife, Margaret Hodge Rawle, had only one. Their only son Francis, the younger, therefore, profited particularly from his family's wealth and cultivation. In 1748, at age 19, he spent a year in Rome; and, in 1755, he toured Ireland for a year. When he returned in 1756, he married Rebecca Warner (1730–1819)—the single most important person in the history of Laurel Hill. Rebecca's grandfather had served as an executor of William Rawle's estate. Her sister Katherine (1737–1810) further connected Francis to her family. She married Joshua Howell (1726–1797), who owned an estate of 76 acres on the Schuylkill, which he called Edgely. From his brother-in-law Joshua, Francis purchased 31 acres, in 1761, a little less than half of Howell's property. He was purchasing the land on which his wife Rebecca would build Laurel Hill Mansion.

After his return from Ireland, Francis sold stock from his store on the Delaware River and real estate along its banks. He advertised his first offering of goods for sale in the *Pennsylvania Gazette*, October 26, 1758:

> Just imported in the Speedwell. Capt. Robinson, from London and to be sold by
> FRANCIS RAWLE,
> At his Store, almost opposite the Ferry-house, in Water street, near Arch street, an Assortment of Woolen and other Goods, which he will sell cheap for ready Money, or six Months Credit at furthest.

Francis Rawle was probably living and working at his father's house, but the addresses are different. William advertised his goods to be sold "at his House in King street near Mulberry (commonly called Arch) street" (*Pennsylvania Gazette*, March 4, 1731). He had referred to "Water street" as "King street," so called, because all goods passing from the river over that street paid duty into the coffers of the King. Francis also did not explain that Arch street was originally called Mulberry. It would have made sense for him to live and work in his father's home, since the executors of William Rawle's estate had kept his "late Dwelling House with a Wharf, and very good convenient new stores" to be "let."

Like many of his contemporaries, Francis' father had offered tracts of land for sale: for example, 60 acres along Duck Creek, a tributary of the Delaware, developed with a grist mill and a cooper shop; and 407 acres on Frankford Creek, another tributary of the Delaware, closer to a state of nature, with meadows and a quarry (*Pennsylvania Gazette*, May 18, 1732 and May 29, 1735). Francis did not advertise any such sales. Instead, he represented the Pennsylvania Land Company, which four English merchants had established in 1699 by investing £2000 in leases from William Penn. Fifty years later, its holdings were being liquidated. Francis' aunts, Rebecca and Elizabeth, having served as executors of his father's estate, worked with Ebenezer Hopkins to collect back payments before and during their nephew's visit to Ireland:

> WHEREAS all persons indebted to the Pennsylvania Land Company in London, have been, from time to time, delaying coming to pay their respective dues, which they have neglected to comply with; this is to acquaint them, that if they do do not attend at the house of Rebecca and Elizabeth Rawle, in Water street Philadelphia, on the 27th, 28th, and 29th of the 5th Month (May) next and discharge the same, they will be proceeded against, without further Notice, by Ebenezer Hopkins (*Pennsylvania Gazette*, April 18, 1754).

Back from Ireland and just married, Francis also took up their work; but, by 1758, he was representing "Ebenezer Hopkins deceased":

> THE Subscriber, appointed Agent for the Pennsylvania Land Company of London, in the Place of Ebenezer Hopkins deceased, gives this public Notice to all Persons indebted to said Company for Arrearages of Rent, that if they do not discharge the same on or before the first Day of March next, he will be obliged to sue all delinquents . . . Attendance to receive Rents, or transact any Part of the Company Business, will be constantly given at my House, almost opposite the Ferry House, in Water street near Arch street, by FRANCIS RAWLE (*Pennsylvania Gazette*, January 5, 1758).

Francis adds one detail to his address: his house is "almost opposite the Ferry." He and his aunts must have been working, at least in part, for charity, because the money from this settlement was to be donated to the Pennsylvania Hospital. In 1755, before he left for Ireland, Francis had contributed £12 for its construction to "encourage the Establishing of an Hospital for the Relief of the Sick Poor of this Province and for the Reception and Cure of Lunaticks (*Pennsylvania Gazette*, May 29, 1755).

Unlike his father, Francis Rawle did not sell real estate along the Delaware, but he had cut out a piece of it for his own estate, Point-no-Point, at the mouth of Frankford Creek. On June 7, 1761, he accidentally shot and killed himself while hunting on this estate. His demise brought some of his family connections together:

> ALL Persons indebted to the Estate of Francis Rawle, deceased, are requested to make speedy Payment; and those who have any Demands against said Estate, are desired to bring in their Accounts, that they may be adjusted and paid, by Rebecca Rawle, Samuel Shoemaker, Joshua Howell, Execut.
> N. B. There remains on Hand, at the Store of the Deceased, opposite the old Ferry-House, An Assortment of dry Goods, to be sold reasonably for Cash, or short Credit (*Pennsylvania Gazette*, August 27, 1761).

Joshua Howell appears here as an executor. Howell, Francis' brother-in-law, had sold him 31 acres of his Schuylkill property. More significantly—and bringing all these connections together—Samuel Shoemaker (1725–1800), another executor, would marry Francis' widow Rebecca, in 1767, six years after he had helped her to settle her husband's estate. When Rebecca and Samuel Shoemaker eventually built Laurel Hill Mansion on her late husband's property, they were living next to her sister and brother-in-law, Katherine and Joshua Howell. (Joshua Howell's house does not survive, but Laurel Hill on Edgeley Drive pays tribute to Howell's property, from which their property was derived.)[122]

Francis Rawle, the younger, died young, but he has a special distinction: his son William (1759–1836) did honor to the family. He became a distinguished lawyer and, in 1783, a founding partner of Rawle & Henderson, the oldest law firm in the United States. His biographer gives his parents special credit: "their proudest distinction, I say with no disparagement, was in giving birth to such a son."[123] His distinguished life also brought his grandfather and great-grandfather's excellence to a special fruition. The senior Francis Rawle (1660–1727) had brought that excellence from England, passed it on to his son William (1694–1741), his grandson Francis (1729–1761), and, finally, to his great-grandson William. Those mores of this family have brought special distinction to the bricks and mortar of Laurel Hill.

The widow Rebecca Warner Rawle married Samuel Shoemaker in 1767. She had inherited Point-no-Point on the Delaware, but her husband's death motivated her to make a new start by building Laurel Hill on the Schuylkill. She built a small house; in fact, she called it her "little country house" (Eberlein and Hubbard, 299). It had one room on the first floor, 30 feet wide by 20 feet deep, and two rooms on the second. With its three bays, it resembled Woodford, built ten years earlier. In both houses, the center bay gives a suggestion of a pavilion,—Laurel Hill, by extending 9 inches; Woodford, by 5—with a pediment above Doric columns that frame the front door, and another pediment above the second floor window. Distinctively, Laurel Hill has a frieze, with triglyphs and metopes of the Doric Order, above its door; and jack arches, with keystones, above its four windows. Joseph Galloway, the Shoemakers' neighbor across the Ormiston Glen, called it "a very pretty place."[124]

Laurel Hill

The year 1767 marked the beginning of the Shoemakers' pleasant life at Laurel Hill. Rebecca's youngest daughter, Peggy, reminisced that she had enjoyed "some of the most agreeable parts of my life there." Ten years later, the year 1777, unfortunately, marked the beginning of the most unpleasant part of their life. They were not alone in their suffering: many others like them maintained a loyalty to King George III that made them traitors in 1776. "They were, as a class, the best people in the province," one historian has observed, "people of wealth, education, culture and refinement" (Eberlein and Hubbard, 294). In Philadelphia, their loyalty came to a crisis in 1777, when General Howe and his troops occupied the city. He asked the two neighbors, Joseph Galloway and Samuel Shoemaker to manage the government of Philadelphia. William Brooke Rawle (1843–1915), the great grandson of William Rawle, the lawyer, has pictured these two neighbors on either side of the glen separating their homes:

> Mr. Galloway was an intimate friend of Mr. Shoemaker. Their country places, <Laurel Hill and Belleville,> adjoined each other, and we can picture to ourselves these two old cronies wandering or sitting on the banks of the Schuylkill, or in the glen separating the places, or among these lovely old trees, admiring the beautiful landscape and condoling with each other upon the sad state of affairs which, as they thought, their misguided countrymen had brought to pass.[125]

From its refuge out in Lancaster, the Continental Congress considered these two loyal subjects traitors and threatened to charge them with high treason, if they continued to aid the British invaders. The two Loyalists stood their ground. When the British retreated to New York, Shoemaker and his stepson William Rawle went with them. His stepdaughter Anna lamented, "Those joyful days when all was peace and prosperity are gone" (October 26, 1781, Rawle, 403).

Worse was yet to come. After the surrender of Cornwallis at Yorktown in 1781, Joseph Reed (1741–1785), chief among the enemies of the Loyalists, used his power as President of "the Supreme Executive Council of the Commonwealth of Pennsylvania," to seize the property of Galloway, Shoemaker, and other loyal subjects of the King. Even before the final victory in 1781, with his influence and that of his fellow radicals on the Council, the state had "forfeited and seized "a lot of ground on Poplar Lane containing about five acres, late of Samuel Shoemaker" (*Aurora General Advertiser*, June 17, 1780). By one report, Reed lived in Laurel Hill, as soon as he took possession of it (Rawle, p 400). When his wife died during this time, September 18, 1780, some whispered that she had gotten her just deserts after gorging herself on peaches from Rebecca Shoemaker's orchard! After Reed enjoyed the sweet fruit of his victory at Laurel Hill, Major James Parr purchased it from the state in 1779 and leased it to French Minister, *Monsieur Chevalier de la Luzerne.*

The Minister understood Rebecca's claim to be a legitimate owner, and he agreed to let her take the lease. In a letter to her daughter, May 12, 1784, she describes his *noblesse oblige* with a bit of irony:

> I believe I mentioned that the Minister of France was going home soon; it is fixed for next month, and I have had a specimen of French generosity in an Ambassador bargaining with the owner of a little country house for the remainder of a lease. Nothing less than the rent he gave will do, and I must agree to that or not have it. I suppose he will think he has been extremely liberal and genteel in agreeing to be paid yearly as rent, and not insisting upon the money down as he paid it. He keeps possession until the 10th of June (Rawle, p 406).

What else could Rebecca do?!—"I must agree or not have it." She paid His Excellency £100 *per annum* for a three-year lease. On June 16, 1784, she returned to Laurel Hill for the first time since 1779. In 1787, three years and £300 later, it was again advertised "to be sold or let":

To be Sold or Let,
(And may he entered upon immediately)
THAT elegant COUNTRY SEAT, situate on the Banks of Schuylkill, in the Northern Liberties, below the Falls; together with a Coach house, stables, and a Large Garden with excellent fruit trees. For terms apply to
PETER MILLER.
N. B. This Place was formerly occupied by his Excellency
the Chevalier Luzerne
(*Dunlap and Claypoole's American Daily Advertiser*, May 31, 1787).

Nota Bene, indeed!—the *éclat* of "his Excellency the Chevalier Luzerne" lent the property a special glow. By 1787, Joseph Reed had died and resentments had cooled. After Rebecca's husband had returned from England, April 21, 1786, she was finally able to purchase Laurel Hill, which had rightfully been hers from the beginning. Eight years after her daughter's lamenting that "those joyful days . . . are gone," Rebecca and her family had paid the price of again finding some joy in their days.

Samuel Shoemaker's loyalty to King George III had caused him hardship and financial loss, but it also had its rewards. In England, he got some help from Benjamin West, whom he had helped in the first years of his career as an artist. West, who had charge of the King's paintings, arranged for him to meet His Royal Highness. Shoemaker recorded his favorable impression in a letter:

> I cannot say but I wished some of my violent Countrymen could have such an opportunity as I have had. I think that would be convinced that George the third has not one grain of tyranny in his Composition, and that he is not, he cannot be that bloody minded man they have so repeatedly and so illiberally called him. It is impossible; a man of his fine feelings, so good a husband, so kind a father *cannot be a Tyrant*.[126]

The King also had a favorable impression of Samuel Shoemaker: His Majesty sent him a rare print as a memento of the visit; and his Parliament voted him a special compensation.

Samuel Shoemaker lived his last days in Laurel Hill and in Pomona, his home in Germantown, until his death in 1800. His obituary, passing over his politics, praised his character: "Few have distinguished themselves more than he has done in private life, by an affable, courteous and obliging behavior to all his neighbors, and none has sustained with greater propriety in his family the amiable character of an affectionate husband, father and friend" (Rawle, 412).

A widow for nineteen years, from 1800 to 1819, Rebecca suffered from the isolation and debilities of age. Her son William, while engaged in his legal career, asked his sisters to "divert" their mother "by some conversation."[127] Her death in 1819 marked the end of two important chapters in the history of Laurel Hill and Philadelphia, before and after the American Revolution—the first as idyllic as the second was turbulent. The year 1819 also marked the beginning of the Waterworks at Fairmount—a marvel of technology for the public good, but the end of pastoral simplicity on the river.

Laurel Hill Mansion has remained to bear witness to these different epochs of the life of Rebecca and her city. In material progress, its idyl before the war and its straightened circumstances during and after witnessed the foundation of a public project like the Waterworks at Fairmount. The Fairmount dam benefited the health of the city by doing harm to the ecology of its river. In moral progress, the final days of Rebecca's life also witnessed significant steps in bringing together the loyalist with the patriot allegiances of William Penn's Holy Experiment. At Laurel Hill, Rebecca Warner Rawle Shoemaker's life reflected the conflicts of American life.

After Rebecca's death, her son William Rawle kept the house in the family for nine years, but he sold it in 1828 to Dr. Philip Syng Physick (1768–1837). The Rawle-Shoemaker family had owned the property for sixty-seven years.

PHILIP SYNG PHYSICK grew up on the Schuylkill. His parents, Edmund Physick and Abigail Syng managed Lansdowne, John's Penn's estate on the banks of the Schuylkill. When Philip attended the Quaker school and boarded in town, he visited them on weekends and walked back on Monday morning.[128] He was in class and learning, as the ten o'clock scholars hurried in. After he received his AB degree at the University of Pennsylvania in 1785, he went to London for his medical education. By 1792, he was back in Philadelphia, in time to treat victims of the yellow fever epidemic in the hospital at Bush Hill on the Schuylkill. In 1797, after contracting a case of the fever, he convalesced at his brother's home on the banks of the Susquehanna. He so enjoyed this estate that he eventually purchased it as a summer residence.

In adulthood, Philip Physick's work as a physician did not allow him much time to return to the idyl of his youth on the Schuylkill. His commitment resembled that of William Rawle as a lawyer. "I doubt very much," his son-in-law Jacob Randolph reflected, "whether history could show an example of a more pure and absolute devotion to professional pursuits than he exhibited" (110). On the other hand, he did make room for another love: "as the tender and affectionate parent," Randolph continued, "he never appeared so happy as when surrounded by his children and family" (111–112). Hoping at age 60 that his family might enjoy a home like the one he had enjoyed as a boy, this "tender and affectionate parent" purchased Laurel Hill in 1828.

By 1828, however, as Dr. Physick was entering his seventh decade, life on the banks of the Schuylkill had changed. The same year that he purchased Laurel Hill, his neighbor, Samuel Breck, suffered from one unfortunate consequence of this change. Breck's daughter Lucy (1807–1828) died from typhoid fever at Sweetbriar, his home on the west bank of the river. Ever since 1819, the dam at Fairmount had caused the river, which young Physick had seen in its rapid, free-flow, to back up in stagnant pools. Stagnation, in turn, bred the typhoid, from which Lucy Breck had died. For her father, Lucy's death turned his "beautifully situated" estate and its "fine gardens" into an "irksome and gloomy" place. This danger did not discourage Physick's purchase, but it did encourage his caution.

Dr. Physick's caution made more room in Laurel Hill for nostalgia than for family. His daughter, Sarah Emlen Physick (1801–1873), who had married Dr. Jacob Randolph (1796–1848) in 1822, would make the most of this property. The Physick-Randolph family visited this house, but they did not live there. On the other hand, their caution did allow conviviality. In the 1830's, Sarah's younger brother, Philip Physick, Jr. (1807–1848), joined the Quoit Club. Sarah and Jacob made Laurel Hill available as its club house. "They could not live on the grounds on account of the malaria," one member of the club recalled, "so they <the Randolphs> allowed us to use them" (*Inquirer*, December 26, 1889). In 1911, William Brooke Rawle found some humor in reminiscing that the members of the Quoit Club had more inclination to hang out than to work out. In this "mildly athletic association," he observed, "our fathers and grandfathers . . . found the exercise of pitching quoits such a thirst creating one as to require them to indulge in a plentiful consumption of the fluids with which they stocked the house; this they did with much conviviality" (Rawle, p 414). Fifty years later, the last surviving member confirmed this "plentiful consumption of liquids":

> There was no lager beer in those days. But the wine! Ah, that was wine worth tasting. We had it imported direct from Howard Marsh & Co., at Madeira, and it was of the finest brand. It only cost us $2.75 or $3.00 a gallon, but you could not buy such wine as that to-day for less than $25 or $30 a gallon. Champagne was tabooed; we never allowed it on our festal board. . . . Long after dinner we would sit under the protecting shade of the mighty oaks, sip our Madeira and smoke our cigars. The warbling of birds and the rustling of leaves were the only accompaniments to the sounds of our own voices, while now and then the bugles of the boatman signaling to open the locks down at Fairmount added a musical charm to the rugged beauty of the scenery

The Quoit Clubmen savored the "finest" wine in shade of "mighty oaks," atop the "rugged beauty" of the Ormiston vale opening on the Schuylkill valley. Wine and sport made their hangout, with its "mildly athletic" workout, into an idyl. When the Quoit Club disbanded, most of these young men, it was said, joined the Philadelphia Club. They seem to have been settling into—or settling **with**—a comfortable and sedate middle age.

Before his death in 1837, Dr. Physick had reason to remain happily at home, while his son socialized with the Quoit Club on Laurel Hill. His house on Fourth street had a large garden that William Penn encouraged throughout his Green Country Towne. Right in his own backyard, he could enjoy "cooling breezes" from the Delaware River, wafting the "perfume" of "roses and many old-time flowers" into his window (*Philadelphia Times*, January 24, 1892).

While their father was enjoying his beautiful garden in town, Dr. Physick's family, some time in the late 1830's, made a major architectural addition to Rebecca Rawle's "little country house." It seems unlikely that the good doctor himself would have undertaken this project, except for their enjoyment. This addition, an octagonal wing, with a large room on the first floor, seems inappropriate for the modest style of an elderly gentleman, but very appropriate for the social aspirations of young people. It provided people like the members of the Quoit Club with social space. Its last member called Laurel Hill "one of the grandest club houses in the State."

The two wings, the one on the north, built by the Rawle-Shoemakers about 1800 and the octagonal wing on the south, built by the Physick-Randolphs about 1839, have two different purposes. The one-story south wing added space for a growing family. For the same reason, David Franks built a second story for Woodford to give his wife and children more space. Forty years later, the Physick-Randolphs built the octagonal wing for the enjoyment of guests like the members of the Quoit Club. Also with social aspirations, the Hemphills, a decade earlier, had built a large room in the south wing of Strawberry Mansion. Most people just live in their homes, but others want social presence, and build accordingly, usually by additions. Laurel Hill, at first, provided a beautiful eminence for a home when the Rawles built a small house and moved in. Laurel Hill Mansion offered a grand place to entertain when the Physick family took possession, but never moved in. From south to north, the two wings of Laurel Hill follow a sequence of living space for family in one generation and social space for guests in the next—progress in space, in time, and in purpose.

Throughout the nineteenth century, Laurel Hill hosted social events and picnics. One advertisement for an excursion of the Philadelphia Lyceum indicates the dignity of these rentals, "kindly granted by the family":

> THE TWENTY EIGHTH ANNIVERSARY EXCURSION
> OF THE
> PHILADELPHIA LYCEUM,
>
> Will take place on SATURDAY, the 21st of July, leaving the Depot of the READING RAILROAD, at the corner of THIRTEENTH AND WILLOW, at EIGHT o'clock, in cars ESPECIALLY CHARTERED FOR THE EXCURSION, and proceed to the mansion of the late Dr. Jacob Randolph, (on the banks of the river Schuylkill), several rooms of which, including a cool cellar for depositing baskets of provisions, and the use of the surrounding grounds, have been kindly granted by the family. The usual routine of LITERARY EXERCISES will be presented, and every arrangement has been made for the accommodation of the company. Return by a SPECIAL TRAIN, at half-past seven o'clock in the evening.

> Tickets, Thirty-five cents; Children, Twenty cents.
> To be procured of
> JACOB M ELLIS, S. E. cor. Ninth and Spring Garden.
> JOSEPH M. TRUMAN, No. 413 Franklin street.
> REHN & HURN. No. 1819 Chesnut street.
> SAMUEL II. CARTLEY, No. 129 S. Fourth street.
> Or at the Depot on the morning of the excursion.
> As the grounds are strictly private, no person admitted without a ticket (*Inquirer*, June 19, 1862).

Established in 1829, the Philadelphia Lyceum provided "the instruction of young gentlemen" in Latin, Greek, French, German, Spanish, English, and mathematics as preparation for college, service academies or counting houses (*Inquirer*, December 29, 1829). By 1862, it had made almost thirty summer excursions that enjoyed papers and speeches—"the usual routine of LITERARY EXERCISES"—and then the "baskets of provisions" deposited in the cellar. The "several rooms . . . granted" by the family doubtless included the octagonal room on the first floor, ideal for the "literary exercises," especially if it rained. This "strictly private" venue made their party as special as it had been for the Quoit Club, even though their membership was not as strictly exclusive.

In 1869, seven years after the Philadelphia Lyceum visited Laurel Hill, forty-one years after Dr. Physick acquired it, and one hundred-and-two years after the Rawle-Shoemaker family built it, Physick's daughter, Sarah Emlen Physick Randolph, three years before her death, sold it to the city. From 1900 until 1915 the Colonial Dames of America maintained Laurel Hill. The Dames painted it white on the exterior, divided its large front room to receive visitors, and opened it as the first house museum in Fairmount Park. In the octagonal room, William Brooke Rawle read his address to them in 1911.

The last surviving member of the Quoit Club started to reminisce about his youthful idyl under the boughs of "mighty oaks" in the "rugged beauty of the scenery" by saying first that "the Park was quite a different place" back then. "There were no steamboats to plow the Schuylkill," he explained, "and no railroads to disturb the natural beauty of the land. The Schuylkill was then used by the Schuylkill

Navigation Company to tow down coal barges of seventy-five or a hundred tons each." The presence of the railroad predated Fairmount Park by more that three decades. In the early days of the park, the "steamboats," plowing the Schuylkill as excursion boats, dropped off passengers at several landings along the river. Laurel Hill certainly was "quite a different place." When he visited in 1835, it was not a park house in the city, but a private home in the country.

In every epoch of Laurel Hill, Philadelphians have enjoyed their own experience. In 1790, the Rawle-Shoemaker family enjoyed a pastoral idyl; in 1835, the Quoit Clubmen, an idyllic clubhouse; and, in 1880, the picnicers off the steam boats, a beautiful grove with a view. We can bring all these experiences together. Francis Rawle (1660–1727) and his grandson Francis (1729–1761) have given all of us a good start.

CHAPTER 25

Strawberry Mansion

EACH ONE OF THE three notable masters of the hill and the mansion now called Strawberry has contributed to the American pursuit of liberty. These three men—

> Charles Thomson, born in 1729,
> William Lewis, born in 1752,
> Joseph Hemphill, born in 1770

—were born about twenty years apart and worked in a span of about sixty years, from 1770 until 1830. They all advanced the work of making America free: Thomson in the 1770's, Lewis in the 1790's, and Hemphill in the 1820's. Charles Thomson took the first step. He counter-signed the Declaration of Independence, and served its cause for fifteen years. The deed to his property, which he called Somerton, seemed to pass on a patriotic duty to William Lewis and Joseph Hemphill.

Lewis and Hemphill called their home Summerville, but the eventual name of the property, Strawberry Mansion, has also forged another link, as the fragrant *Fragaria* has imprinted the fame of these three men with its own special prestige.[129] It's quite natural! The strawberry plant, laden with fruit of Mother Nature's bounty, graces this station in the history of man's natural birthright. Many visitors to Strawberry Mansion have enjoyed this American story and topped it off with a bowl of strawberries and cream. Daniel Webster celebrated his enjoyment—why shouldn't we?

STRAWBERRY'S NAME AND FAME started with humble beginnings. After his father died on the passage across the Atlantic, Charles Thomson (1729–1824), a Presbyterian of Scots-Irish ancestry, arrived in America, a young, penniless orphan. He took to the study of language and taught Latin at the William Penn Charter School and the University of Pennsylvania, then called the Academy. When the Continental Congress first met in Carpenters' Hall in September of 1774, the delegates appointed this man of letters as their secretary. *Dunlap and Claypoole's American Advertiser* briefly reported his appointment on September 12, 1774:

> On Monday last the gentlemen delegated by the several provinces to represent them in CONGRESS met in this citv for that purpose, when the Hon. Peyton Randolph, Esq. was chosen chairman, and Charles Thompson, Secretary.

John Trumbull, *Declaration of Independence* (1819) with Charles Thomson standing above John Hancock, the chairman

Charles Thomson recorded minutes and wrote the correspondence of the Congress for fifteen years. When John Trumbull represented the signing of the *Declaration of Independence*, he placed Thomson standing above and a little to the left of John Hancock.

Thomson had this privileged place because he had stepped forward to attest the document. When the printer John Dunlap first issued the *Declaration of Independence* on July 5, Thomson's signature attests that of John Hancock, subscribing the final and famous "pledge" of the "lives," "fortunes" and "sacred honor" of the Founding Fathers signing the Declaration:

> . . . we mutually pledge to each other our lives,
> our fortunes and our sacred honor.
> Signed by order and in behalf of Congress,
> John Hancock, President.
>
> Attested,
> Charles Thompson, Secretary.

All the signers sacrificed for their pledge, but some suffered obviously. For his "sacred honor," Thomson,—who was, strictly speaking, a counter-signer,—sacrificed a significant piece of his "fortunes." In the Fall and Winter of 1777 and 1778, three years after he attested John Hancock's signature, the British occupied Philadelphia. Although, in general, they demonstrated restraint,—for example, they did not burn down Carpenters' Hall or Independence Hall,—they did burn down Thomson's Somerton. In contrast to this unusual revenge, they did no damage to the Founding Fathers' neighboring houses, like Richard Peters' Belmont or Robert Morris' The Hills.[130] Twelve years later, William Lewis rebuilt Somerton and renamed it Summerville.

Thomson served as Secretary, while thirteen men served as presidents of the two Continental Congresses, in the Revolution, and of the Confederation Congress in the 1780's. After he had "pledged " his fortune in 1776, sacrificed a piece of it in 1777, and weathered the storms of controversy during the Constitutional Convention in 1787, the *Inquirer* praised him as a "venerable patriot" when it announced his resignation on July 25, 1789. In September 24, 1774, by contrast, a matter of fact beginning had briefly announced Thompson "chosen" for office; but a sense for momentous closure grandiloquently announced him resigning it:

> On Thursday last that venerable patriot CHARLES THOMPSON, Esq. resigned to THE PRESIDENT of the United States his office of Secretary to Congress—a post which he has filled for nearly Fifteen Years with reputation to himself and advantage to his country.
>
> When Heav'n propitious smil'd upon our arms,
> Or scenes adverse spread terror and alarms
> Thro' every change the Patriot was the same—
> And FAITH and HOPE attended THOMPSON's NAME.
> NEW YORK, July 25, 1789.

At age 60, after fifteen years as America's first Secretary of State, Charles Thompson had won the title, "that venerable patriot." He had lived through "scenes adverse" spreading "terror and alarms" of revolution that had destroyed his home on the banks of the Schuylkill. This violence had followed the second Continental Congress of 1776. He had given his time and concern throughout the "scenes adverse" of politics that threatened to dissolve the American Union during the Constitutional Convention of 1787. Having endured all this turmoil, he deserved the homage of his fellow citizens.

As part of his service in the cause of freedom and as consolation in his own travail, Thomson put his knowledge of antiquity to a dynamic use. As his country faced adversity during the political turmoil in the 1780's, he confirmed his "FAITH and HOPE" in the great experiment. Drawing from the language of ancient epic, he endowed the new nation's Great Seal with the confidence that God was smiling on its Union. By his suggestion, the motto, *Annuit Cœptis*, "He (God) has given the nod to the things that have been begun," adapted from Vergil's prayer in the first book of his *Georgics*, stood above the eye of Providence on the reverse of the Great Seal.

Writing to Thomas Jefferson in 1785, Charles Thomson declared his own protest for independence: Slavery, he declared, was "a cancer that we must get rid of. It is a blot in our character that must be wiped out." If not by "religion, reason and philosophy, confident I am," he concluded with ominous foresight, "that it will one day be by blood." In his personal life, he took independence seriously. As he managed Harriton, his wife's family home and his home in retirement, he hired laborers, instead of owning them. His most faithful servant, Page H. Swan, one of his father-in-law's slaves, maintained a separate city residence on Moyamensing avenue. He worked as a free man at Harriton, until Thomson's death in 1826.

The reverse of the Great Seal of the United States of America

Charles Thomson never rebuilt his home that the "terror and alarms" of war had destroyed. Although few, even of the Founding Fathers, could surpass his patriotism in the pursuit of "life, liberty and the pursuit of happiness," William Lewis (1752–1819) did work that made him worthy as the next owner of Thomson's property. Rising from a humble Quaker farm in Delaware County, Lewis became a distinguished lawyer and helped to draft "An Act for the Gradual Abolition of Slavery in Pennsylvania," which became law in 1780. This act, the work of the famous abolitionist, Anthony Benezet (1713–1784), stands out preeminently as America's first law abolishing slavery.

In 1783, Lewis purchased the site of Thomson's house, thirteen acres off the Wissahickon Road, for £1,700 in gold and silver. By one tradition, George Washington visited him at Woodford, which Lewis rented while he was building over the ruins of Thomson's house (Lawrie, 40–41). President Washington came to respect his character. In 1791, appointing him to the District Court of Pennsylvania, he expressed "special trust and confidence" in his "wisdom, uprightness, and learning."

In contrast to McPherson's grandly Georgian Mount Pleasant or Coleman's sedately classical Woodford nearby, Lewis' home, "simple, and small, had almost the aspect of a farmer's house." As an old farm boy, a Quaker, and a lawyer, intensely devoted to his practice of defending justice, he had little time or inclination for a pretentious home. "There was nothing grand about it; it did not impose," one historian has said, "it welcomed." "He had so closely pursued the solid and the useful," said a friend, "that he had no leisure to attain the beautiful."[131] This observation actually referred to his legal briefs. Though not grand, Lewis' home was spacious: it had a wide hall, with a parlor on the left, a dining room on the right, and steep stairs leading to three bedrooms. He had built it, like the farmhouse of his youth, for year-long residence, "more cozy" than his townhouse, with "fireplaces" in the basement "to heat the floors of the rooms above" (Lowrie, 77 and 85).

In his "cozy" parlor, Lewis shed his professional manner and played the genial host, "pleasant and facetious in social conversation" (Primrose). When a neighbor, William Rawle of Laurel Hill, dined at Lewis' "villa," as he called it, he wrote in his diary that "one would not from the conversation have taken <it> for Tusculum" (McFarland, 52). With a wink, his allusion to Tusculum puts his host in classical company. In his villa at Tusculum, just south of Rome, Cicero had serious conversations about wisdom, which he published as his *Tusculan Disputations*. Rawle's ironic allusion to his friend's banter as unequal to this philosophy draws the parallel by the single word Tusculum. By this reference, he invites us to bring Rome to Philadelphia, and Tusculum to the banks of the Schuylkill. Tusculum and the Schuylkill offered beautiful views, particularly to those who could afford to build a villa on their heights.[132] William Lewis resembled Cicero, but without the *gravitas* of Ciceronian philosophy associated with the *Tusculan Disputations*. That evening, Rawle enjoyed "pleasant and facetious" conversation with Lewis. Their light hearts "would not" equal the serious tone of Cicero's *Disputations*, even though everything else in their lives "would."

By the time of his death in 1819, Lewis had built, in addition to the main house, a stone kitchen, a tenant's house, a floored stable for four horses and a cow; barns stables for other animals, a coach house, milk house, smoke house; along with a quarry, fishery, and ice house on the Schuylkill.[133] Two years later, in 1821, Joseph Hemphill (1770–1842) purchased the estate. As the third owner of the property, he filled out this important "inter-twining network of Philadelphians"—in this case, a network of patriotic duty—that has woven the fabric of Strawberry Mansion.[134] Like Thomson, significantly, he came from Scots-Irish ancestry; like Lewis, more significantly, he had been raised on a farm in Chester County; and, most significantly, like both Thomson and Lewis, he worked to make America a land of freedom.

As a young man, Hemphill joined the Pennsylvania Abolition Society at the age of 26. This humane impulse motivated much of his career. In three terms as a member of the United States' House of Representatives, from 1819 to 1823, he opposed the extension of slavery into Missouri, co-authoring a report on the slave trade trade, which described it as unconstitutional and inhumane. He also opposed Jackson's proposal to remove the Cherokee people from their lands in a deportation that became infamous as the Trail of Tears. Still a conservative, on the other hand, he opposed the abolition of slavery in the District of Columbia and he supported the Society for the Colonization of Free People of Color of America, that eventually proved to be benevolent racism, which, at first, even Abraham Lincoln supported.

In 1827, to provide a proper venue for the entertaining necessary in his political career, he and his son, Robert Coleman Hemphill, added the south wing, with "a really noble room" for parties; and, a few years later, the north wing. Hemphill and Lewis had called their home Summerville, but his son Robert did the spadework for a change in name when he planted strawberry plants imported from Chile, *Fragaria chilœnsis* (Lowrie, 130). Strawberries would find their place in Summerville's history.

One story about Summerville and its strawberries has a ring of truth, even if it only survives as a bit of family lore. Hemphill gave a party for Daniel Webster (1782–1852) in the hope that the godlike Daniel would make a significant after-dinner speech in support of Andrew Jackson. The Great Orator did speak, but he compromised, as he so often did, by toasting the delicious strawberries that he had just enjoyed for dessert (Lowrie, 143). Homage to hospitality did not help Hemphill's politics, but it accomplished something even better by

Strawberry Mansion with two wings added by Joseph Hemphill

bringing nature into his home. Strawberries made it so famous that it took their name.

After Joseph Hemphill died on May 29, 1842, his son Robert, who wasted too much money at the Robin Hood Tavern, down the road at East Falls, and at the race track on his father's property, had to sell his father's estate in April, 1844:

> FOR SALE—And immediate Possession given.—The FARM, situate on the West side of the Ridge Road, nearly opposite the third milestone, (known as the late "Judge Hemphill's Place,") containing thirty-two Acres, on which are erected a large Mansion House, a Tenant House, stone barn, stabling, spacious Ice Houses, &c., with two quarries of good Stone opened on the Schuylkill. It is offered low, and terms will be made to suit the purchaser. For further particulars, apply to Charles Shaw, No. 229 Spruce street (*Public Ledger*, February 23, 1844).

In late Spring, another realtor advertised this property for a seasonal rental as "a delightful and convenient summer residence" (*Public Ledger*, June 19, 1844). Next year, a third realtor appealed to entrepreneurs:

> TO RENT—The handsome and spacious COUNTRY SEAT of the late Judge Hemphill, dec'd., with the Lawn in front and Stables attached

> thereto, situate on west side of the RIDGE ROAD, next below the Robin Hood Tavern, three miles from the city. The premises may be advantageously used, it is believed, for a Summer Boarding House. Apply to THOS. WILLIAMSON, 150 Arch street (*Public Ledger*, June 28, 1845).

"A Summer Boarding House"?! Within a year, the fate of this historic property slipped from being for a sale, to a seasonal rental, to a boarding house! In 1846, George Crock, accepted the challenge. A farmer in the neighborhood, he purchased the property and rented it out for the next twenty years.[135]

In 1847, William Latham hosted a picnic at Strawberry Mansion,—with apparent success: the Western Social Assembly gave him "their sincere thanks" for his hospitality:

> The managers of the Western Social Assembly Third Annual Picnic, held at Strawberry Mansion, on Tuesday August 17, 1847, take this method to return their sincere thanks to Mr. Wm. Latham, for the handsome and superior manner in which he prepared dinner and supper, and for his indefatigable exertions to please us in every way, and would recommend him to other managers. Also to Mr. George Coleman and his band, for their unremitting exertions to please the party in every way (*Public Ledger*, August 23, 1847).

A "social assembly" represented fraternal organizations that flourished in American democracy of the nineteenth century. Other "managers" must have taken this recommendation. Liberty Assembly announced its "Second Annual Picnic to be given at Strawberry Mansion, on Tuesday, September 18" (*Public Ledger*, September 17, 1849); and the Norma Assembly announced its "First Grand Picnic to be given at Strawberry Mansion—coaches from the Odd Fellows' Hall (*Public Ledger*, June 21, 1851). Strawberry Mansion maintained a good reputation, because Sunday schools also chose it as a venue for their excursions:

> Sunday School Excursion—The pupils and teachers connected with St. Francis Xavier Sunday School, will make an excursion to the Strawberry Mansion on Thursday next. Extensive arrangements are being made to render this a delightful affair (*Public Ledger*, August 19, 1857).

The "extensive arrangements" might include games on "the lawn in front," an organ grinder with his monkey instead of "Mr. George Coleman" with his band, pony rides from the stable, feeding ducks on the river, and, of course, lots of strawberries, ice cream and cake—after prayers and grace, of course. Philadelphians made Strawberry Hill their favorite resort for picnics. Through the nineteenth and into the twentieth centuries, on any nice day in the Spring or Summer, groups of children could be seen strolling about through the groves or resting "in unconventional attitudes under shady trees and in quiet nooks" (*Times*, July 27, 1891).

Strawberry Mansion did more than host picnics. From the eighteenth century, inns and taverns often served as the meeting places for clubs. The Penn Township Lodge of the International Order of Odd Fellows rented Strawberry Mansion for its meetings, until the lodge announced that it was moving to its own own hall:

> I. O. O. F. — The Members of PENN TOWNSHIP LODGE, No. 319, and the Order in general, are particularly requested to meet at their Hall, STRAWBERRY MANSION, on THURSDAY MORNING, the 27th inst. at 8 o'clock, to proceed to the Dedication of the New Hall, at Manayunk. A splendid band of music will be in attendance By Order of the N.G. — no. 25-21-68 Attest, G.W.B. Felton, Sec. (*Public Ledger*, November 25, 1851).

In the Spring of 1861, the first shots of the Civil War closed the doors of Strawberry Mansion. Later in the summer, it "revived":

> STRAWBERRY MANSION REVIVED—A select Soiree will be given at this old favorite place of resort, on WEDNESDAY AFTERNOON, August 14, 1861. A powerful Orchestra has been engaged, which will produce the most fashionable Quadrilles, Waltzes, &c., commencing at 2 o'clock. The Cars of the Ridge Avenue Passenger Railroad, connecting with many other Roads of the city, pass every few minutes. Tickets, 25 cents (*Public Ledger*, August 15, 1861).

Other activities during the war, reflected the military life in the city: a picnic for the benefit of "the Volunteer Refreshment Committee" (*Inquirer*, September 14, 1861). The lawn also served as a parade ground: "Company D, First Regiment, Girard Home Guard, will parade for target practice this afternoon, to Strawberry Mansion" (*Inquirer*, August 5, 1861).

Twenty-five years after George Crock purchased Strawberry Mansion, he sold it for $102,375 to the City of Philadelphia, which incorporated its acres into Fairmount Park. At the same time, however, the Fairmount Park Commission paid him for damages and gave him "immediate possession" (*Inquirer*, April 17, 1871). Apparently, he was leasing it from the city. As a manager, no one else could have claimed more experience.

In 1871, Strawberry Mansion took its first step into the modern life of the city. As one of the many places of resort in the Park, it continued to be popular, in fact, even more popular, because its inclusion in the park made it commonly, and not exclusively, available. An appreciation of its charms in 1883 marks a highpoint in Philadelphians' enjoyment of the Park:

> **Strawberry Mansion.** Since the opening of the regular season Strawberry Mansion on the Schuykill is crowded daily by the swarms of hot and thirsty humanity that flock there from the dusty city. A pleasanter place could scarcely be wished for; certainly, it could not be found. It is situated on the most beautiful and commanding spot in Fairmount Park and easily accessible by street cars or Fairmount steamers. While the ear is charmed by the sweet strains from Simon Hassler's noted orchestra, the eye of the pleasure seeker is delighted by the splendid view of the river and West Park, both being made doubly enjoyable by the cool breezes that blow so delightfully cool nowhere else within easy reach of the city. Its varied attractions render it a most desirable resort for family parties, picnics and excursions (*Philadelphia Times*, June 23, 1883).

Strawberry's attractions had a special appeal: like visitors in the eighteenth century, who arrived by the Schuylkill or by the Wissahickon road, "the swarms" of humanity in 1883 also arrived by the road or by the river, but more conveniently on "street cars or Fairmount steamers." Once there, they also enjoyed this "most beautiful and commanding spot" with a "splendid view of the river" from its lofty eminence. Perhaps the managers of Lemon Hill down the river might have questioned whether "cool breezes . . . blow so delightfully cool nowhere else within easy reach of the city," since Lemon Hill was perhaps within easier reach of the city, although it had a less commanding view. On the other hand, Lemon Hill was so close to the dock at Fairmount that the swarms of visitors to Strawberry Mansion might also enjoy getting there on one of the "Fairmount steamers." It really was a destination!

After the pleasant trip on the river and the splendid view over the river had charmed the eye, "the sweet strains from Simon Hassler's noted orchestra," particularly, delighted the ear. One attraction, which would have, so to speak, accompanied the music, is missing: there is no mention of dancing. What would Euterpe, the Muse of music, prefer more than twirling with her sister Terpsichore? Another facet of this enjoyment does get an oblique mention: describing the "swarms" as "hot and thirsty" suggests that they needed refreshments. Of course! What would better complement Euterpe's embracing Terpsichore than a little refreshment, especially appreciated by the hot and bothered father who brought his brood on the excursion? Also, without profit from a bar and restaurant, how else could managers like Mr. Crock have paid the pipers? In this sense, the sale of food and drink made the music possible. And if not a vintage or a brewage, at least a strawberry float might sweeten the experience.[136]

Strawberry Hill and Mansion became classic parts of life in Philadelphia. In 1896, the Park Theatre, at Broad and Fairmount, hosted a musical comedy, "Miss Philadelphia"—"a dream of William Penn's visit to modern Philadelphia . . . introducing every feature of Philadelphia life that is familiar to the eyes of the every day promenader." One scene pictured "a very clever burlesque on trolley parties <at> Strawberry Mansion, . . . displaying children indulging in summer games and a bicycle parade" (*Philadelphia Times*, April 14, 1896). The article in the *Philadelphia Times* of 1883 could elaborate the scene.

Philadelphians' enjoyment of Strawberry Hill as a resort marks a golden epoch in the history of the city. In the twentieth century, custodians of the historic houses in Fairmount Park developed more appreciation for the history of their houses than the recreational pastime in and around them. The women of the Committee of 1926 continued the work which they had done in the Sesquicentennial by transferring it to the maintenance of Strawberry Mansion. These ladies brought history together with nature by serving strawberries and ice cream after their lectures.

A Note on Strawberries with Cream, Either Chilled or Iced

In 1846, Philadelphia's *Public Ledger* kept its readership abreast of what New Yorkers were doing by "Things in New York," a column that quoted from their newspapers. When the first fruits of Spring had come to market, the Gothamites announced the fruit of an early harvest: "Strawberries and cream, the first of the season, are being served at some of our refectories today" (*Public Ledger*, May 19, 1846). (Strawberries in "refectories"?—a little hyperbole—but leave it to Gothamites to gild the lily!) Although many Philadelphians might have thought that refectories could only exist in sophisticated Manhattan, they were right up with its citizens in enjoying strawberries and cream, wherever they could find them. Back home on the Schuylkill, for example, the Point Breeze Hotel advertised this dish, confident, apparently, that it, and nothing else, would attract patronage:

> STRAWBERRIES and CREAM at the POINT BREEZE HOTEL, on the banks of Schuylkill. JAMES C. LAFFERTY, Proprietor, is prepared to furnish visitors with this delicious fruit, larger and finer than they have been for years past (*Public Ledger*, June 5, 1845).

What Philadelphians or New Yorkers, whether devoted to fashions, old or new, would not join in this chorus?

> Strawberry shortcake, huckleberry pie—
> How sweet they cán be—my, oh my!

The strawberries that gave the hill and the mansion their names have claimed a special place in this story. At first, confectioners did not flavor their ice cream, but local gardeners offered a solution when they started to cultivate strawberries. This fruit topped it off nicely. Of the several garden-spots known for their strawberries and ice cream, Strawberry Hill stood out as one of the best. It could boast of serving this dish since 1808 (*Philadelphia Times*, August 24, 1891; *Inquirer*, April 12, 1896, p 33).

CHAPTER 26

The Versatile John McPherson (1726–1792) of Mount Pleasant (1761)

The Very American Tale of His "Race Fairly Won"

FOR BARBADOS directly,
The Brigantine ADDISON,
JOHN M'PHERSON
Commander;

New lying at Oswald Peele's wharf; and having best part of her cargo already engag'd, will certainly sail in about two weeks. For freight or passage apply to John Durborow, or said commander on board.

N. B. She has good accommodations for passengers, and is a prime sailor (*Pennsylvania Gazette*, December 6, 1750).

IN 1750, JOHN MCPHERSON (1726–1792), at age 24, notified Philadelphians that he would command a voyage on "The Brigantine Addison," bound "directly" for Barbados. By a very circuitous path, he had come a long way, both from his birthplace and from the perverse humors of his youth. Born in Scotland, he was one of six sons of the second son of the Laird of Cluny. In his teens, he had sailed from Scotland to escape the consequences of his youth, which had pumped hot young blood into the cliché wild and misspent. Now in his twenties, he was sailing from Philadelphia as an entrepreneurial commander. "The Brigantine ADDISON" launched the career of this man, whom one historian has called, a "progressive, versatile and constructive genius." Looking for some saving grace for the disgrace of his youth,

Jack McPherson's uncle had said that the wild colt might sometimes make a good horse.[137]

From 1751 until 1758, he advertised no further voyages from Philadelphia, but he was setting up a store for its lucrative trade. In this trade, he was joining the ranks of merchants, safe and snugly ashore, like John Durborow, in his store on Third street, who had signed up a crew for the voyage to Barbados.

Eight years later, at age 32, McPherson was advertising a cruise, as a privateer against "His Majesty's Enemies":

> Now fitting out for a Cruize against His Majesty's Enemies,
> and will sail by the Tenth of September,
> The Privateer SHIP
> BRITANNIA
> John M'Pherson Commander,
> Mounts 16 Guns, 9 pounders, and carries 150 Men.
>
> All Gentlemen Sailors, and others that are inclined to enter on board the said Ship, may see the Articles at Mr. M'Intire's, at the Sign of the Ship Pennsylvania, in Front Street (*Pennsylvania Gazette*, August 17, 1758).

Unlike The Addison, bound to a port of call, sailing "directly" on a voyage for cargo, The Britannia was bound to nowhere in particular, cruising crosswise, on a chase for prizes. Cruising for plunder seized from "His Majesty's Enemies" steered McPherson into blood-soaked waters. From profit on "The Brigantine Addison" to plunder on "The Privateer Ship Britannia," he was chasing the bubble of reputation and riches, even in the cannon's mouth. If the wild colt can make a good horse, his own wild youth had also steeled him to seek a fortune by the spoils of war.

Two years later, having returned to Philadelphia richly laden with spoils, and acting as an "agent" in their distribution, he shared them with "all Gentlemen Sailors, and others," who had been "inclined,"—that is, bold enough—to join him in the adventure:

> Philadelphia, May 8, 1760. JOHN M'PHERSON, agent for the ship Britannia's company, having recovered some money, at a Court of Admi-

> ralty, for those that were in said ship, last cruize, is now ready to pay the same at his store, near the Drawbridge (*Pennsylvania Gazette*, May 22, 1760).

Back in Philadelphia, and no longer on an adventure as a privateer, McPherson has settled into business "at his store, near the Drawbridge" that arches over Arch street at Front on the Delaware. The "Court of Admiralty" is taking time to unravel its red tape, because McPherson advertises a final distribution five years later:

> THE Officers, Mariners, &c., who belonged to the private Ship of War Britannia, JOHN M'PHERSON Commander, that Cruize which commenced in October 1760 are desired to meet at Michael M'Intire's, Tavern-keeper, in Walnut street, on Monday, the 13 of December, at 9 o'Clock in the Forenoon, to receive the last Payment for said Cruize, from the above mentioned John M'Pherson, Agent (*Pennsylvania Gazette*, December 5, 1765).

Michael McIntire, Tavern-keeper, at "the Sign of the Ship Pennsylvania"—the corner of Pewter Platter Alley and Front street—had seen the crew sign up in 1758; and, in 1765, sign off with their "last payment." What stories mine host could have told after observing them starting and ending their adventure! Most obviously, he saw what price Commander McPherson had paid for his fortune—wounded nine times and one arm shot off twice. (Anything left after the first shot had been blown off by the second.) The brutal experience of war must have tamed the wild colt.

THE SPIRITED HORSE, however, had not left the wild colt very far behind. In 1761, at age 35, McPherson had not received the final distribution of the prize money but he had enough to build a beautiful country house. For a little while, at least, his impulsive nature had the money to do nothing by halves.

First, he bought 31+ acres of Fountain Green, the Mifflins' estate on the Schuylkill. They had settled in the area before the arrival of William Penn. For the impressive sum of 4£'s, he purchased a copy of Abraham Swan's *A Collection of Designs in Architecture* (London,

1757); and pointed out its first plate to the carpenter Thomas Nevell (1721–1797). He might carefully have perused the book, but the first house he saw he liked. From whatever design, his house was to be picture-perfect, right off a fashion plate of design.

Nevell built the mansion that has endured as the most splendid on the Schuylkill. In the entrance pavilion, he surrounded the door with the Doric order, beneath a pediment and a Palladian window, similar to the door and window in the tower of the State House, which he had helped to build eight years before in 1753. Both buildings articulate classic elements of Georgian architecture, but the State House had not extended its door with a pediment. Nevell was improving on the design of the State House: the triangular pediment filled out the door and made a smooth transition between it and the window above. Without knowing that the State House would enjoy great fame when it took the name Independence Hall, Thomas Nevell was creating another building that would take a distinguished place in the epoch of Georgian architecture. Each building, one public and the other domestic, has become a classic in its own category.

To extend the mansion to perfect Palladian balance, Nevell built matching outbuildings on either side, a kitchen on the left and an office on the right. With the help of this craftsman, John McPherson had created a masterpiece. "The whole impressive grouping," one historian has observed, eloquently announces "the state maintained by the Colonial occupants of this truly noble seat" (Eberlein and Hubbard, *Portrait of a Colonial City*, page 341). By financing such a "truly noble seat," McPherson had paid his way to "the state," to which he had aspired, but for which he could not pay for very long.

At first, he named his home Cluny after the ancestral seat of his clan back in Scotland, but he later changed its name to Mount Pleasant. In contrast, his neighbor, Edward Burd called his house Ormiston after his ancestral seat in Scotland, and felt no need to change the name. Burd was preserving family ties; McPherson was reaching beyond them. His first wife, Margaret Rogers McPherson (1732–1770), without any connection to his clan back in Scotland, perhaps suggested the new name. This was America, we can hear her saying; and in America, it made sense to celebrate its beautiful places, and not one that was distant and irrelevant.

An anonymous watercolor on ivory of John McPherson (Philadelphia Museum of Art)

Consider the portrait of the master of Mount Pleasant. It does not swagger, but it portrays a man who does. With a sharp eye and a penetrating glance, John McPherson looks not only active, but aggressive and even volatile. We see the spirited horse that the wild colt had sired. On September 18, 1775, he displayed some of this wild spirit when he visited John Adams:

> This Morning John McPherson Esq. came to my Lodging, and requested to speak with me in Private. He is the Owner of a very handsome Country Seat, about five Miles out of this City: is the Father of Mr. McPherson, an Aid de Camp to General Schuyler. He has been a Captain of a Privateer, and made a Fortune in that Way the last War. Is reputed to be well skilled in naval Affairs.—He proposes great Things. Is sanguine, confident, positive, that he can take or burn every Man of War in America.—It is a Secret he says. But he will communicate it to any one Member of Congress upon Condition, that it be not divulged during his Life at all, nor after his Death but for the Service of this Country. He says it is as certain as that he shall die, that he can burn any Ship.

Adams assigns Mcpherson, even at age 39, to a previous generation. The old captain has a fortune from "the last war" and a son, John McPherson, Jr., age 21. "Sanguine, confident, positive, that he can take or burn every Man of War in America," he has a secret so secret that it requires a private meeting and must never, in his life or after his death, be "divulged," although "he will communicate it to any one Member of Congress." Whatever the secret that he may be guarding, "he can burn any ship in America." "Sanguine" confidence, proposing "great things," but veiling them in secrecy—no wonder that some people thought he was insane!

McPherson, hoping to keep Adams on the hook, invited him to dinner at Mount Pleasant the following week. For the sake of seeing Mr. McPherson's "elegant seat," Adams is happy enough to stay on the hook a little while longer. He mentions the "seat," the family and the renewed "proposals:"

> Monday, September 25, 1775—Rode out of town and dined with Mr. McPherson. He has the most elegant seat in Pennsylvania, a clever Scotch wife, and two pretty daughters. His Seat is on the Banks of Schuylkill. He has been Nine Times wounded in Battle. An old Sea Commander, made a Fortune by Privateering. An Arm twice shot off, shot thro the Leg &c.—He renews his Proposals of taking or burning Ships.

"Clever Scotch wife" refers to McPherson's second wife, Mary Ann McNeal McPherson (1747–1828); the "two pretty daughters" were Margaret (1763–1785) and Mary (1765–1832), twelve- and ten-years-old when Adams visited.[138]

This "old Sea Commander," as Adams calls him, has not invited him, a delegate to the Continental Congress, merely to socialize and admire his home and its furnishings. Adams, after tipping his hat to McPherson's beautiful home and attractive family, gets down to the reason why he had been invited to dinner. His host was making the same "proposals" that he had heard the week before: "He renews his proposals to taking or burning ships." "Taking or burning" echoes some of McPherson's "sanguine, confident, positive" manner and Adams' amusement in reporting it. This "old Sea Commander" either needed more adventure or more money,—very probably, more money. (One may ask now,—and even more then,—an obvious question: Is Jack Mcpherson so crazy as to run the risk of having his other arm shot off?) Throughout the Revolutionary War, he continued unsuccessfully to offer Congress his services as a privateer.

McPherson also ran his plantation with a little swagger. After the inevitability of a horse straying onto his property, he published the following notice in the *Pennsylvania Gazette*:

> Came to M'Pherson's Plantation, near Philadelphia, on the River Schuylkill, on the 22d inst. November, a dark bay Horse about 14 Hands

> high, a small white Spot in his Forehead, black Feet, Mane and switch Tail. The Owner is desired to prove his Property, pay Charges, and take him away, otherwise he will be sold for the same (*Pennsylvania Gazette*, December 5, 1765).

William Hamilton and William Bingham published similar notices after a horse or cow strayed onto their properties, but they did not threaten to sell the animal if its owner did not claim it. Captain McPherson had learned a peremptory tone in his years of commanding his own ship and commandeering the enemy's.

Mount Pleasant's spendthrift master needed money long before he proposed to resume privateering. January 12, 1769, only eight years after he had built Mount Pleasant, he put it up for rent or sale. The *Pennsylvania Gazette* published his fullest description of the property. Its lines flow forth with an exuberance that resembles its "constant springs":

> To be LETT or SOLD, by
> JOHN MACPHERSON
> (Who expects soon to go abroad),
>
> A PLANTATION, in the Northern Liberties (with great propriety called MOUNT PLEASANT) on the river Schuylkill, about four miles from Philadelphia, containing 160 acres of land, about 68 acres of which are in good grass, great part whereof is well watered by constant springs, and from which were cut last year, at least 80 tons of the best hay, and it is thought it will produce much more next year, as 12 acres of the 68 were put last year in red clover, and not mowed.

The Mifflins' name for their estate, Fountain Green, from which he had derived his first acres, indicated that Mount Pleasant, in addition to being pleasant with a view from its mount, also had green fields, "well watered by constant springs." These spring-watered fields produced 80 tons of "the best hay" with a promise of more from the next harvest. The notice goes on to enumerate orchards and livestock:

> There are a great number and variety of the best inoculated and grafted fruit-trees, viz. apples, apricots, cherries, peaches, pears, plumbs,

> quinces, and a number of chestnut and shell-bark trees. The kitchen garden is large and within a stone wall; it contains a variety of fine fruit trees, above 50 beds of asparagus, as many of strawberries, and one of artichokes; there are three covered dung pits, with sundrv other conveniences for collecting manure, a large covered fold for sheep and a very convenient moveable pen for manuring the land by cattle.

McPherson finds superlatives even for his orchards: "the best inoculated and grafted fruit trees." To the fruit in the orchard, he add chestnuts and shell-bark <hickories> in the grove, vegetables in the kitchen garden, sheep in the fold and cattle in pens. Of course, this gentleman farmer does not pass over fertilizing his fields with dung, with three pits and "sundry other conveniences" for collecting it.

In concluding, McPherson brings his superlatives to a peroration. As if Adams' ranking Mount Pleasant as "the most elegant seat in Pennsylvania" has been inadequate, McPherson sets his sights on surpassing anything in North America. He pulls out all the stops both in praise for health and in potential for wealth:

> It is needless to mention the many genteel, regular and convenient buildings on it, as they are so well known; they at least equal if not surpass anything of the kind in North-America; the situation is remarkably healthy and beautiful, and the conveniences for fishing and fowling are excellent. The plantation may easily be divided into five small ones, on three of which are already built houses, &c. for tenants. It will be left with or without the principal or mansion house, as can be agreed on (*Pennsylvania Gazette*, January 12, 1769).[139]

The fame of Mount Pleasant makes it "needless to mention" its "genteel" buildings, but McPherson mentions them anyway in a *praeteritio* that "surpasses anything" already said. The buildings are as "regular and convenient" as the dung pits and the "very convenient moveable pen for manuring the land by cattle." In addition to describing Mount Pleasant as a plantation perfectly fit for the gentleman farmer, fisher, and fowler, with a location "remarkably healthy and beautiful," McPherson appends an incentive to the investor: Mount Pleasant will generate income by itself and, especially, by its possible subdivision into five properties.

In 1770, to reduce the burden of his debt, he rented his house for the summer, to Mr. Alvaro Deornelles for 70£'s, a considerable amount, and then to Don Juan de Miramilles (1713–1780), the Spanish envoy, and arms dealer, who occupied it until his death in 1780. In 1778, the final notice of sale by auction, "public Vendue," has none of the appreciative details that McPherson had elaborated nine years before:

> To be SOLD by public Vendue, On Saturday the seventeenth instant, at Six o'clock in the evening, at the Coffee-house, the very healthy and elegant seat called Mount-Pleasant, containing about one hundred and twenty acres of land, in the Northern Liberties, upon the river Schuylkill. There is on the place every necessary building, (besides a tenant's dwelling-house and spring-house at a distance from the other improvements) several stone quarries, some of free stone, a considerable quantity of watered meadow, and a mineral spring near the mansion house. On a part of the land it is believed there is a coal pit: The Gentleman from whom Mr. Macpherson purchased that part, reserved to himself and his heirs one quarter of the profits of the coal, should the pit ever be worked (*Pennsylvania Packet*, October 12, 1778).

The notice follows its most expansive assertion, "the very healthy and elegant seat called Mount-Pleasant" with a bare statement that it has "every necessary building" and quarries with "free stone," already excavated. Long before the bonanza of coal in the nineteenth century, the possibility of finding it next door seemed promising investment, which the Mifflins, from whom McPherson purchased the first tract of land, had reserved for their benefit. His auction was not final, because no one wanted to pay the price either of the purchase or of dealing with the encumbrances of the mortgage and lease.

After ten years of advertising, McPherson finally found a buyer. On March 22, 1779, he sold Mount Pleasant to his old commander, Major General Benedict Arnold. By that time, the sale could not have given him any profit. It was subject to the lease of Don Juan de Miralles and to a mortgage of £70,000. Benedict Arnold never occupied the house, but his "later notoriety" gave it the dubious honor of being called The Arnold Mansion (*American Daily Advertiser*, January 28, 1795).

John M'Pherson continued to make a living as a "Broker." In 1782, he published a notice for the sale of "two new vessels on the stocks in this city . . . His office is in Chestnut street four doors from Second, where he has stores for the reception of goods, and he may be seen every day at the coffee-house from eleven to one (*Independent Gazetteer*, November 5, 1782).

In the nineteenth century, the infamy of Benedict Arnold's treason and the sad fate of his wife, Peggy Shippen, to whom he had given Mount Pleasant as a wedding present, overshadowed the story of John McPherson. Arnold did not deserve this credit, since he neither built the house, nor even lived there. In the late nineteenth century, a city councilman tried in vain to pay for a plaque attributing the house to John McPherson.

McPherson's later life deserves more notice than Benedict Arnold's, even though he no longer lived in Mount Pleasant, and, in fact, had failed to maintain it. He could have claimed greater distinction than Benedict Arnold, because he, at least, maintained and certainly improved his moral life. Freed from the burden of maintaining the extravagance that had preoccupied his youth and burdened his age, this "spirited horse" turned his attention, quite literally, to virtue.

In 1789, he took the first step in his philosophical introspection by publishing his autobiography with a very ambitious title, *A History of the Life, Very Strange Adventures, and Works of Captain John McPherson; Which Will, in Many Parts, Appear Like an Eastern Tale.* Of course, he first laments the trouble he had caused his mother—"Dear woman, many a tear she shed on my account." She had hoped that he would have a career as a Presbyterian minister and sent him to school where he might learn Latin. The young Jack, he reflected, "wild, stubborn, drunken boy" that he was, "could not learn it—indeed I said I would not." Jack's teacher confirmed that he was "the most stubborn child" he had ever known. As his wild and outrageous rascality burst beyond the grove of academe, he so disgraced his family that he eventually ran away to sea. In the interim, before he settled in Philadelphia about the year 1746, he gained so much hard-won experience as a sailor that we can see why John Adams had said that he was "reputed to be well skilled in naval Affairs."

In the last ten years of his life, from 1782 to 1792, he took the second step in his philosophical career. "For the benefit of mankind," as he announced, he taught and published his lectures, first about "Natural Philosophy" and then about "Moral Philosophy." In the footsteps of Aristotle, he considered meta-physics after (meta-) physics. At first, he lectured "at his own house, near Pool's bridge." North of the city, Pool's bridge crossed Cohoquinoque Creek, later known as Pegg's Run, at Front street, just a little above Callowhill. Pegg's Run flowed from the spring of Spring Garden. Along its banks, the tanneries and slaughterhouses dumping their effluvia into the stream did not create a desirable neighborhood. McPherson might well have taken Juvenal's observation, *Virtus laudatur et alget* ("Virtue is praised and is out in the cold.") as a text for one of his lectures.

With the payment of a guinea for all the lectures or a half dollar for one, a philosophical inquirer could attend his class "on Mondays, Wednesday and Saturdays, at 12 noon and at 7 in the evening"—one class convenient for those free during the day; and the other for those free in the evening. McPherson found a kindred spirit in Joseph Sharpless, a fellow merchant, who, in 1789, had opened a "Morning School" for girls and an "Evening School" for "young gentlemen," opposite Coombs' Alley on Second street (*Pennsylvania Packet*, May 18, 1789 and October 11, 1790). He taught English grammar, without the aid of Latin, and geography from a globe. At Mr. Sharpless's academy, McPherson delivered a special "lecture on Bigotry" in the Spring of 1791 (*Aurora General Advertiser*, April 14, 1791).

In February, eight months before his death on September 6, 1792, he notified the public of the final step in his philosophical career:

> WHEN JOHN M'PHERSON lectured on Moral Philosophy, his audience begged he would publish them as soon as possible, for the benefit of mankind. The three full are now printed, viz. one on the Divine Legislation of Christ; one on Benevolence, and one on Discretion. They are sold by Mr. William Woodhouse and the said M'Pherson, for one quar-

> ter of a dollar. His Lectures on Bigotry, and one on Seduction, he will soon get printed (*The Freeman's Journal* or *The North-American Intelligencer*, February 1, 1792).

Three years after publishing his autobiography that tells about the *Very Strange Adventures . . . Like an Eastern Tale* of his profligate youth, he has come full circle. He paid no attention to his mother when she begged him to be good; now he does pay attention to "his audience," when they have "begged" him to teach them to be good. His foolish youth had its spark of conscience and benevolence; and his age could appreciate how easily he had stifled it. We can imagine his eloquence in explaining and expounding how "discretion" might resist "seduction." He hoped to help youth chart a straight course through the seething straits of young blood.

IN 1926, THE PHILADELPHIA MUSEUM OF ART opened Mount Pleasant as a showcase for some of its collection. Fiske Kimball, the Director of the Museum, described this house as uniting "beauty and historical interest to a degree very rare in America" ("Mount Pleasant," *Bulletin of the Pennsylvania Museum*, v. 22, #105, September, 1926). To pinpoint this "historical interest," Eberlein and Hubbard suggested that its Colonial occupants lived as nobly as its Palladian refinement might suggest. "The whole impressive grouping" eloquently announces "the state maintained by the Colonial occupants of this truly noble seat."

John McPherson's history at Mount Pleasant is "impressive," without being as formally "noble" as its Palladian proportions. The crazy quilt of his life creates this interest. He wrote a play—*Tragic comedy, Hodge Podge Improved; or, the Race Fairly Won*—that sounds like a theatrical version of his autobiography. His own dramatic style would pick fragments of his tragedy and comedy for the hodgepodge of an American stew. The title of his autobiography compared his life to an "Eastern Tale," but his life tells a western tale, even though 'western' did not strike him as evocative of romance as 'eastern.' His very American tale demonstrates romance enough in his "race fairly won."

IN 1869, THE CITY OF PHILADELPHIA purchased Mount Pleasant and made it part of Fairmount Park. Fifty-seven years would pass between its purchase by the city and its transfer, in 1926, to the Philadelphia Museum of Art. The city first provided recreation; and then gradually the museum made it part of its edification. For recreation, Mount Pleasant came to be known as The Dairy, where one of its Palladian out-buildings served milk and ice cream, especially to children and their families. A merry-go-round also entertained them (*Times*, October 13, 1899). An article in the *Inquirer* in the 1880's showed just how much people can forget about edification when they're havin' fun. The writer thought that its Palladian "cubes" looked like a picture from a story book:

> . . . a collection of picturesque buildings which seem, in the distance, to have been taken out of a child's box of playthings, set up on the grass and forgotten. There are two blue barns with red tops, matching each other at equal distances on the nearer side of a magnificent green circle, and beyond, at equal distances, two hollow cubes of white houses with red roofs.

As he was enjoying some ice cream in front of one of the "two hollow cubes," he contemplated the scene "in the middle of the great circle:"

> In the middle of the great circle probably the most superb buttonwood tree in Pennsylvania hides, in the view from this point of the avenue, a still stately mansion that reminds you at once of a gentleman of the old school, venerable but erect and dignified, under his eighty years.

The reporter admires "the most superb buttonwood tree in Pennsylvania," now no longer there for those who admire the many beautiful trees in the park. When he creates a past for the house, his imagination conjures up "a gentleman of the old school, venerable but erect and dignified." Another article pictured him as "a quaint old sea captain" (*Inquirer*, June 1, 1894). These images may please a reader's penchant for melodrama, even though the reality of the "progressive, versatile and constructive," but manic, "genius" could please him more. McPherson's idiosyncrasy offer us more interest than a stereotype. He then creates another stereotype about the architecture of the building that has its own interest:

> The first feeling on looking at the formal dignified exterior of the house is that something is wanting. Reflexion discovers it to be porches. If built they have been removed. Possibly the owners thought there was shade enough about the place, and the Italian accessory might be dispensed with; but its absence imparts a city-like appearance to the mansion (*Inquirer*, August 10, 1882).

A porch, "the Italian accessory," Victorian architecture's great gift to American domesticity in the nineteenth century, would have defaced the facade of this Palladian edifice in the eighteenth. This writer, however, had expectations. Not far down the river, a porch had defaced the facade of Lemon Hill, a Federal building of about 1800. Such architectural intrusions had made Philadelphians feel that the houses in the park had been built,—and then rebuilt,—for their enjoyment. And what could they enjoy more on a Summer afternoon than a porch?

Many might not have understood Mount Pleasant's architecture and history, but some had enough understanding to prevent the addition of a porch. By the 1890's, Miss Charlotte Pendleton, a Philadelphia socialite, presented the plans of Fairmount Park Art Association to give the public free access to Mount Pleasant as "a true example of the colonial mansion." Only recreation stood in the way: "the mansion with restaurant and dairy is a great accommodation to the public" (*Inquirer*, May 11, 1893). Edification was starting to win its battle with recreation

Before edification won, there was a compromise of edifying recreation:

> A notable feature of the society women's club life in Philadelphia is the Moviganta Klubo, which is an exclusive motor club for women who drive their own cards. This club, with the exception of one in London, is the only organization of its kind. The Club owes its existence to Miss Margaret F. Corlies, daughter of Mrs. S. Fisher Corlies. Every convenience has been added to the clubhouse which seemed necessary to bring it to the state of comfort demanded by the modern club woman. The old Arnold Mansion has been entirely renovated. The interior has been planned by Miss Corlies. The tea room in the early spring and

> early summer is remarkably pretty, with its color harmonies with which the bright gowns of the matrons blend (*Inquirer*, March 13, 1913).

Before Fiske Kimball, "the new director of the Pennsylvania Museum of Art," started to live in Lemon Hill, and he had permission from the Fairmount Park Commission to make that historic residence, <Mount Pleasant,> his home" (*Inquirer*, October 20, 1925). Three decades before, it had been considered as a residence for the mayor of the city (*Times*, May 24, 1896). Mount Pleasant survived either bid to use it as a perk for municipal office-holders.

John McPherson lived an impressive life, because he lived it in excess. In his undisciplined youth, Jack infused it with outrageous genius, but, with the wisdom of years, he translated his wild youth into spirited maturity. Even when he seemed to have settled into the moderation of a mature life in trade, he was planning something spirited. In balancing his disgraceful youth with his virtuous old age, he maximized his virtue by giving lectures to recommend a remedy for its disgrace. He aspired consistently to great things: in titling his autobiography, he tipped the balance with extravagant hyperbole: *Very Strange Adventures . . . Like an Eastern Tale.* Even his virtue broke into excess!

Out of this confusion, he left one clear, unforgettable legacy. In his maturity, his extravagance gave the city its finest residence of Georgian architecture. He could not afford to maintain it, but his wild spirits could not have afforded to miss the pleasure of building it. Jack took these Palladian blocks out of his toy chest, set them up on a pleasant mount above the Schuylkill, and left them as a memento of a panache not to be forgotten.

CHAPTER 27

Edward Burd (1749–1833), at Home in the Peace and Beauty of Ormiston Glen (1795)

ESTATES AND THEIR MANSIONS on the Schuylkill from the eighteenth century survived in Fairmount Park through the nineteenth as hotels, restaurants, playgrounds, and beer or ice cream gardens. In the twenty-first century, the lives of their first owners only just echo among the sounds of children at play and adults at their picnics. George Washington, for example, would not have the pleasure in visiting Belmont today that he had when he went there to visit Richard Peters. In Peters, he found both a kindred spirit and a fellow horticulturalist, who cultivated his garden at Belmont as he and Martha cultivated theirs at Mount Vernon. One notable exception—Washington would enjoy visiting Bartram's Garden today, because it still reflects the love of nature that he shared with John Bartram.

Ormiston survives as another exception, although not as remarkable as Bartram's Garden. On a hill above the Schuylkill River, it still overlooks the same wild glen that spread beneath it in the eighteenth century. Philadelphians in the twentieth-first century can still have an appreciation for it like that of its owners, Edward Burd (1749–1833) and his son, Edward Shippen Burd (1779–1848). The Burds were lawyers and not students of botany and horticulture like the Bartrams, but Ormiston continues to reflect the natural peace and beauty that they loved. Its wooded glen and fresh air can please visitors today as they pleased the Burds two hundred years ago. If Washington visited

Ormiston, its glen would still welcome him, even though he would miss talking with Edward Burd and his son under its lofty canopy of trees.

Before Edward Burd owned this property in 1793, Joseph Galloway (1731–1803) had owned and improved it as an investment. He might have appreciated its beauty, but he improved its use. In a similar investment, Galloway had also owned land on the Schuylkill River near its confluence with the Delaware: "one hundred and five acres, being one third on Hog Island; twenty-eight acres at the mouth of the Schuylkill" (*Pennsylvania Packet*, August 5, 1779). He started to improve these acres by advertising for men who understood "grubbing and clearing of low grounds and cripple" (*Pennsylvania Gazette*, June 26, 1760). According to the root of its adjective, "low ground" is cripple, because, in the marsh, its cripple creeks creep. The men he employed would grub, that is, dig up and clear, the land around the crippled creeks so that he might use it in breeding and raising "cattle, horses and hogs" (*Pennsylvania Gazette*, July 18, 1754). The hogs on Hog Island eventually served Philadelphians by eating their garbage. (Much later, men working on Hog Island ate "hoggies" for lunch. Landfill has made this island part of the city, but Philadelphians still eat the same sandwich, which they call a hoagie,)

On higher ground up river, Galloway acquired the future site of Ormiston: "a tract of land on the Schuylkill, in the Northern Liberties" that contained "about 45 acres, with a good house, Belleville, and other valuable improvements" (*Pennsylvania Packet*, June 17, 1780). He described this property a little more carefully when he advertised it for rent:

> TO BE LETT—A Messuage and Plantation, lying between the Country Seats of Samuel Shoemaker, Esq.; and Captain McPherson, bounded on Schuylkill, a good orchard, of the best chosen fruit, Quarries of Stone, and a Shad and Herring Fishery. Enquire of JOSEPH GALLOWAY (*Pennsylvania Gazette*, February 17, 1773).

Galloway names his two neighbors. To the north, Samuel Shoemaker had married Rebecca, the widow of Francis Rawle, the first owner.

On this property, Samuel and Rebecca built Laurel Hill Mansion in 1767. To the south, Captain John McPherson had built Mount Pleasant Mansion in 1761.

Enhancing his investment by "valuable improvements," Galloway got stone from a quarry on the hill and caught fish from the river. Quarries and fisheries characterized the early industrial history of the Schuylkill. Before the Schuylkill Navigation Company built the dam at Fairmount in 1819, "shad and herring" came up river with the tides. In the season of three months for catching shad, fishermen could make enough money to support their families for the year. The quarries supplied stone for jetties from which they could cast their nets. Off Galloway's property, in particular, there was an island (see the map), from which fishermen might have 'thrown out' these jetties (*cf. jeter*, to throw in French). The fishery could not operate after 1819, because the water, which the dam at Fairmount had backed up, inundated the island, leaving, in its backflow, no island, no jetties, no tides, and not enough fish to make an industry. Fishing had had such importance in local economy that the fishermen brought a case against the Navigation Company when its dam swept away their livelihood.

Galloway's quarry supplied local builders. To supply construction in the area, quarrymen mined granite from Fairmount and the hills on the riverbanks above it. Up river, the hill above East Falls, for example, provided the granite that raised the huge stone pile of Eastern State Penitentiary (*Inquirer*, July 16, 1893). On the hill at Ormiston, rocky outcroppings indicate vestiges of a quarry. On the land around it, "a good orchard" offered the "best chosen fruit"—peaches and apples, not average but, Galloway boasted, choice. From his quarry, fishery and orchard, he aimed to make a profit by letting it out on lease, after making improvements. Luckily, he left the glen alone.

Fate had plans for Joseph Galloway. He had been a delegate to the First Continental Congress, but he remained loyal to the Crown. Some Patriots considered him so diabolically loyal that they devised a banner, picturing him on a small pony, driven by the devil, blowing on a trumpet and shouting encouragement: "Push on, my brave Galloway" (*Aurora General Advertiser*, December 26, 1798). As a consequence of his picking the losing loyalty, the state "forfeited and seized" his

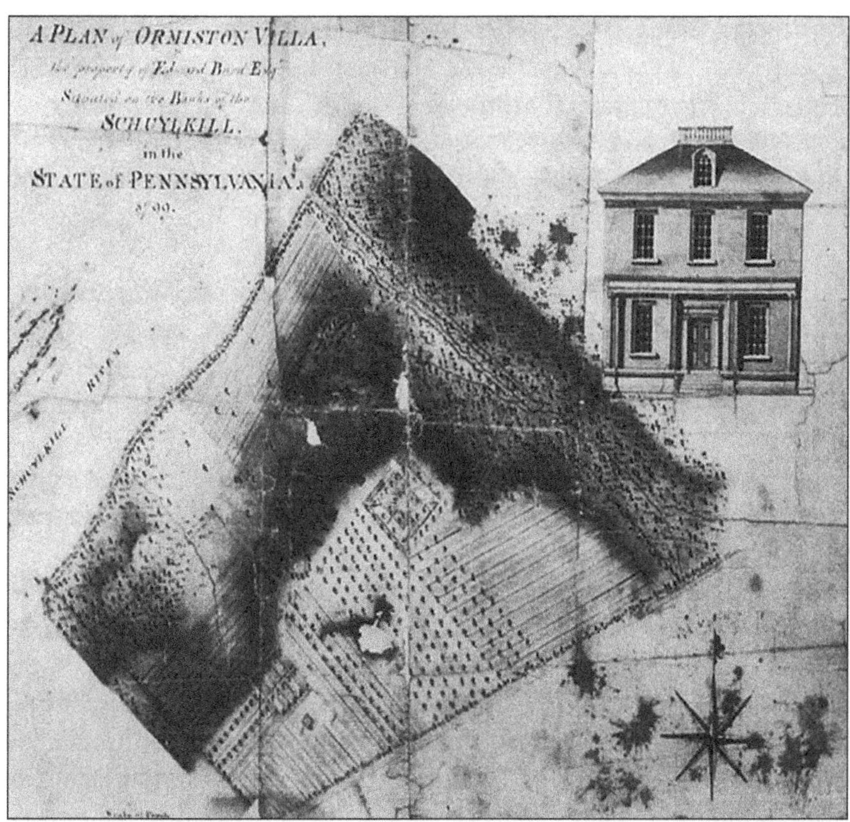

Map of Ormiston

This map shows orchards, and a wooded glen with its stream flowing into the river, in which there is an island. The elevation of its mansion shows three bays, a front porch of four Tuscan columns and pilasters, perhaps Ionic, never put in place, surrounding the door. (The back porch has two Tuscan columns supporting a classical pediment.)

estates, in particular, the "tract of land on the Schuylkill" of 45 acres (*op. cit.*, June 17, 1780); and, in addition, eleven city lots on Market street (*Pennsylvania Packet*, January 26, 1786).

Edward Burd bought Galloway's 45 acres on the Schuylkill through Joseph Reed (1741–1785), the President of the Supreme Executive Council. Reed, a special foe of Loyalists like Galloway, would have enjoyed seeing him pilloried as the devil's disciple.

Almost as soon as he purchased this property, Burd put Galloway's "good house" to a very good use. He took his family there to escape the yellow fever epidemic in the summer of 1793; but, almost just as soon, he found it not good enough for his family's needs. He moved them almost immediately to the Falls of the Schuylkill, where Mr. Lawrence's house was "larger and more convenient" (*Letters*, September 19, 1793).

Five years later in 1798, during another outbreak of yellow fever, he wrote to his sister about the house that he was building. He describes it as "good," but it must have been better than Galloway's "good house," because he had torn that one down: "I have built myself a good house at Schuylkill, which I expect to raise in a few days . . ." (*Letters*, October 10, 1798). Galloway had built a house good enough for his workers; Burd was building a better one for his family. 'Building' can be synonymous with 'raising,' but Burd implies that his raising completes his building. He built the house with brick and then perhaps raised its roof with a wood frame. Whatever his word choice, "building" does not at first make obvious good sense with "raising."

Whether building and then raising or doing both at the same time, Burd makes very good sense in choosing a name for his home: "<I expect to> call it Ormiston after the name of our Grandfather's seat near Edinburgh." He establishes continuity in his family history by calling his new home Ormiston, "after the name of our Grandfather's seat near Edinburgh." In Scotland, Ormiston, a town ten miles east of Edinburgh, had ancient origins, which no Scot could claim uniquely as his heritage. On the other hand, Ormiston on the Schuylkill can claim a unique heritage from the "seat" of the Burds' grandfather. In Scotland, many took Ormiston as a surname. In Philadelphia, Edward Burd's home has given it a special name.

The Burd family was continuing a family tradition by spending their summers in a house of the same name as their ancestor's. By contrast with other estates along the Schuylkill, Ormiston is a family home and nothing else. Next door, Captain John McPherson had built Mount Pleasant Mansion to flaunt wealth and impress the gentry. Edward Burd had no pretensions. He focused his "world" and "happiness" on his family, for whose "ease and comfort" he spared no "exertion" (*Letters*, May 5, 1812).

Burd anticipated the place of Ormiston in his family's life: "I am very fond of the country in summer and intend to keep my family there hereafter in that season." He makes no mention of any building, because the joys of "the country in summer" were all important. He got his priorities straight: Mother Nature would enhance his home; his home could not possibly enhance her. In a higher elevation above the coastal plain, he enjoyed "rising early in the Summer and enjoying the bracing cool of the morning and taking exercise every day" (*Letters*, June 2, 1801). On the seashore at Long Branch, he also enjoyed "a constant coolness in the air which was very refreshing. This was owing to a Sea Breeze . . ." (*Letters*, August 6, 1788). He appreciated sea breezes, but he preferred mountain air as healthier and more reliable.

In preference to life beside the sea, Burd advocates the virtues of life in the country: "I expected to have been before this time at Long Branch to have joined the female Branch of my family, but the sea shore not agreeing with my daughter Peggy, Mrs. Burd returned with her after being there about eight or nine days." "The female Branch" of the family had gone off to Long Branch, a place of fashionable resort. High fashion did not change the fact that the sea air was not agreeable to his daughter's health. "Our dear invalid," as he called his daughter Peggy, would enjoy better health at Ormiston: "I believe, the shower bath and air of Ormiston with exercise every day, will do her more service than traveling about the country" (*Letters*, July 18, 1801; and August 1, 1803). Showers from the Schuylkill and exercise in the glen would do his daughter better "service" than salt air and sea-bathing that were too bracing for someone of her delicate health. Who needs to go to the spa at Saratoga Springs, when Ormiston Spring, right at home, may serve the same purpose? "The female branch" of the family could get a taste of the fashionable life of Saratoga or Long Branch by attending parties at Mount Pleasant and Laurel Hill or in the city. Mr. Burd would, as he said, "keep my family" in the summer home that he had built for them.

Two years later, Burd persevered in advocating the virtue of country air: "I am this day taking her <Peggy> out to Ormiston in order to have the country air till the summer season shall be past" (*Letters*, August 27, 1803). The *paterfamilias*, whose benevolence we can discern in Charles Wilson Peale's portrait, knew what was best for his

Charles Wilson Peale's portrait of Edward Burd (1820) at the age of 70

daughter. In a letter to his daughter Sarah, he advocated the old bromide, "East, West, Home's Best."

> Notwithstanding the gay scenes through which you have passed or may yet enjoy, you will be sensible that the most solid comfort is to be found at home. This truth is universally acknowledged and is wisely so ordained by the Ruler of the Universe, who causes the Hollander to be satisfied with his unhealthy marshes and the Swiss with his bleak and barren mountains (*Letters*, September 28, 1810).

The Christian humanist Erasmus reasoned similarly in *The Praise of Folly*: there's no accounting for a man's foolish attachment to his home, except to attribute it to his benevolent Creator. Burd's children "have passed" through and "may yet enjoy" fashionable resorts like Long Branch or Saratoga, but God has meant their hearts to find their home in Ormiston. "The Ruler of the Universe"—what better authority!—has ordained Burd's deepest love.

Edward Burd could not preserve Ormiston's "bracing cool of the morning" for his grandchildren, but he could and did preserve its glen where they could enjoy it. In his will, he ordered that none of its trees be cut down, except those in decay. "So faithfully" the *Inquirer* reported on July 25, 1876, "was this request observed that when Ormiston became the property of the city it was one of the wildest and most beautiful spots in the Park." Philadelphians can also thank him for requiring that Ormiston Glen retain its sylvan charm. In 1876, one citizen, Earl Shinn (1838–1886), under the pen name of Edward Strahan, praised its beauties grandiloquently:

> The grand ravine, which runs between Ormiston and Edgeley, is perhaps the most striking feature in Fairmount. Look into and along its depths, up its sloping hilly sides, and through its long ranks of trees—is it not a majestic and impressive scene? An aisle of God's forest-temple, it dwarfs all the cathedrals that man has reared; it is worthy of its boundless dome—the sky. The moonlight, which is so intense here, loses its brightness, as it struggles through the multitudinous foliage, and goes wandering through the trees and slopes. Here and there at the hither end a tree stands out strong, distinguishable from its leafy companions, but as we advance, we find ourselves in what is neither light nor darkness, but a tender twilight shade hovering above the greenery which surrounds us, and of which we may almost be said to be a part, so deeply has it interpenetrated our thoughts and feelings. We stand among these gigantic forest fathers like one of themselves. That magnificent tulip poplar on the other side of the brook, and this grand old fellow here—they have strengthened and enlarged us, lesser and weaker children of nature. We should like to embrace them, but our arms are too short. The lowest branch is full sixty feet above our head. We would like to shake hands with them, but we can not reach high enough. This is not tall talking by any means, but short talking—it is so far below the magnitude of these old forest kings. They wait their poets, who to largeness of imagination will add a greater knowledge of nature than most poets possess. . . . We city folk feel its manifold beauty, however,

its grandeur, its magnificence, and nowhere more deeply than in this noble ravine (*A Century After*, 128).

Shinn praises Ormiston's "grand ravine" as the most striking feature in Fairmount." It has remained the park's "most striking" ravine, because it is the only one that has survived without any modern intrusion,—except for the river drive that cuts off the confluence of its stream with the Schuylkill. The "magnificent tulip poplar on the other side of the brook" has not survived, but its descendants have, in addition to stands of oaks and beeches. "Majestic and impressive," dwarfing "all the cathedrals that man has reared," "gigantic forest fathers . . . old forest kings" in "this noble ravine"—Shinn's superlatives rise to poetic hyperbole, but we can not deny his premise that forests have their own special "grandeur and magnificence," and that Ormiston Glen has survived as the "most striking" example in the park—particularly striking for us, simply because it has survived. After we have walked through this "noble ravine," we can feel that it has "strengthened and enlarged us;" and that it has brought us, either literally closer to home, or metaphorically closer to the "Ruler of the Universe."

Edward Burd's son, Edward Shippen Burd (1779–1848), married Eliza Howard Sims (1793–1860) in 1810, a few years after Rembrandt Peale had painted his portrait. (Imagine the man in Charles Wilson Peale's portrait smiling benevolently on his son, as Rembrandt Peale has represented him. How benevolent the father; how handsome and carefree the son, on whom he smiles!) This second generation of his family continued in their ownership of Ormiston, but fate eventually removed Edward and Eliza's children from any possibility of enjoying for long its bucolic scene. Of their eight children, five died in infancy. Their surviving daughters, Elizabeth and Margaret lived to young womanhood; but Elizabeth (1815–45) died at the age of twenty-nine, and Margaret (1819–1844), at the age of twenty-five. One boy, Woodrop (1822–1837), named after his maternal grandfather, died at the age of fifteen. Sadly, all eight children predeceased their parents. Fortunately, perhaps, Edward Burd, Sr. predeceased the three surviving grandchildren when he died at the age of 84, in 1833. He did not

Rembrandt Peale's portrait (1806–1808) of Edward Shippen Burd at the age of 26, four years before his marriage

live to see his son bereft of the "world" and "happiness" of his eight children.

Edward Shippen Burd and his wife Eliza lived in luxury, but in addition to respecting Edward Burd's intention that they preserve the glen, they also preserved Ormiston as the unpretentious family home as he had intended it to be. After their bereavement, instead of developing properties that they could not pass on to children, they redirected their interests and their considerable wealth to charitable and religious institutions. Three years after his last surviving child's death, Edward Shippen Burd died in 1848, aged sixty-nine years. Along with a successful career in law and business, he was a founder of St. Stephen's Protestant Episcopal Church and a life-long member of its vestry. In his will, he left it a generous bequest. His widow survived him for twelve years, dying in 1860, at the age of sixty-seven. By her will, she founded an orphanage for girls, which she had first built in her backyard.

Edward Shippen Burd's canopy tomb in St. Stephen's Church

In addition to establishing the orphanage and working for St. Stephen's, she consulted with its clergy and vestry in the creation of a remarkable work of art. In 1849, a year after her husband's death, she contracted with the sculptor Henry Kirke Brown (1814–1886) to create a marble canopy tomb for her husband, not free-standing but along a wall. On the wall above the recumbent statue of her husband, the Burd's family crest celebrates his Scottish heritage. The family's motto in the tomb's inscription, *In croce spes mea* (In the cross, my hope), also celebrates this ancestry back home in Scotland. In its representation of blessed repose, the handsome effigy of Edward Shippen Burd awaits the union of body and soul at the resurrection.

Each generation of the Burd family has left a legacy, one in the natural beauty of Ormiston Glen, and the other in the artistic beauty of Edward Shippen Burd's tomb. In either one, nature and art speak well for their lives. Ormiston Glen connects us to them by beauty without words. The tomb in St. Stephen's connects us by words and by images. They speak eloquently, one in nature and the other in art; but both proclaim Edward Burd's faith that the "Ruler of the Universe" brings all men back home.

The Royal Heritage Society took charge of Ormiston in 1982. In a letter to the *Inquirer*, one citizen welcomed their caring for this property, but she lamented that a camp for children with cerebral palsy, which had operated there, could no longer use its house and grounds. This camp had offered "sports, hikes, games, nature study, arts and crafts" to these children for a few weeks in the summer (*Inquirer*, November 6, 1982 and July 31, 1960). One summer, sixty-three young people had volunteered to serve as counselors (*Inquirer*, August 10, 1964). Either project might reflect the Burds' interests, because they had both celebrated their heritage and contributed generously to help children in need.

On the other hand, Edward Burd, Sr. would have no problem in solving the dilemma between history and health that this citizen posed in her letter. In picking a home for the Royal Heritage Society, any one of the many historical buildings in the park could serve as a home for an historical society. Ormiston's "noble ravine" would better give to needy children the fresh air and beauty that Edward Burd, Sr. had considered most useful to his children. In the present, Ormiston, by its name, celebrates his family's heritage; by itself, it benefited his children's health in their time; but, in our time, it has made his family's heritage of benefiting other children's health a thing of the past.

WEST PARK

CHAPTER 28

Girard Avenue Bridge

OUT IN PHILADELPHIA'S SUBURBS, and off the Ridge road that headed north from the city, Stephen Girard's college opened its doors in 1833. At the same time, it also opened Girard's avenue from the Ridge to bring the new students to its doors. The City of Philadelphia called this new road Girard avenue, naturally, because it led to Girard College. Once this avenue had served its first, important purpose of bringing the college students to their teachers, it literally evolved,—it rolled out, as any road does in connecting the life of its neighborhood. It connected with the Columbia railroad along the Schuylkill river in 1847. Seven years after that, the city appropriated $7,500.00 for a bridge to carry the avenue across the river (*Public Ledger*, October 24, 1854). Finally, in 1855, twenty-two years after 1833, when it had first served as the avenue to Girard College, Girard avenue's bridge took off to take an important place in the history of Philadelphia.

Philadelphians had high hopes for the future of this bridge. In the 1850's and 60's, they had marveled at the new neighborhood between Girard College and the east bank of the Schuylkill, laid out, built up, and consolidated into their city in 1854. Consequently, they also had high hopes when they saw the Girard avenue bridge connecting it to the neighborhood on the west bank of the river, also newly consolidated. A notice in the *Inquirer* of the sale of an ice cream saloon, across the street from the College, gave promise of this avenue joining refinement with good business: "The Girard Avenue bridge being now nearly completed, the trade from the west will make this a great thoroughfare and a good location for business" (*Public Ledger*, November 8, 1855 & April 24, 1860). The Schuylkill has always separated its city by a bi-coastal mentality between those living on either its east or west bank, but a bridge like this one stretches hands across the river.

Mixing the past with the future, this bridge brought together,—eventually, it separated,—an antithetical pair: mad bulls and merry children. Both might rampage over the bridge, but not safely at the same time. Livestock were a familiar sight, since the stockyards to the west sent droves of them into the city to the east. Adults in their right mind kept their distance, but children might not be wise enough to keep it. Imagine a few mischievous urchins spooking a herd to a stampede! Eventually, the city ordered that drovers could not drive their herds over the bridge after 8AM (*Inquirer*, November 15, 1872).

Children had a special place on the bridge, which, by the 1860's connected, one newspaper editor said, "the two shores of our magnificent park." They would have called this park "our magnificent" playground. The Park Commission estimated that 50,000 of them crossed the bridge on holiday in 1870 (*Inquirer*, March 4, 1870). They might have been heading from West to East Park, where 1000 children sometimes visited Lemon Hill on Saturdays. For example, the city, to serve them, made the park available to public schools for a picnic on September 12, 1871. This public service popularized the park among Philadelphians, who would have appreciated their tax dollars rewarded with pleasant, healthful influences, especially for children of their urban poor (*Inquirer*, May 26, 1871). On that special day, no drovers and their herds were allowed on the bridge (*Inquirer*, September 12, 1871).

Once the bulls were kept at bay, the bridge held a promise of connecting good business with healthful pleasure from either one of its banks; but, unfortunately, the freshly consolidated city had failed to do good business when it built it in 1854. Within ten years, city engineers declared its flimsy trusses "unsafe for travel," and set up barriers to prevent the passage of vehicles,—pedestrians might cross at their own risk (*Inquirer*, March 18, 1864). This thoroughfare seemed fated for thorough humiliation, but no one could have known then how proudly the Girard avenue bridge would eventually fare.

For eight years between 1864 and 1872, repairs to the bridge kept throwing good money after bad. Bad building and maintenance sharpened the editorial voice of the *Philadelphia Inquirer* to a sarcastic edge: "If Philadelphia is not altogether the worst governed city in the country, it is, at least, the one whose rate of taxation is the highest." Even the notorious political bosses in New York City should look to Philadelphia for lessons in "plunder and misrule." Right beside this jeremiad, an article lamented the condition of the Girard avenue bridge as an "unsightly and dangerous rattle trap that should be immediately toppled over" (*Inquirer*, June 25, 1869). A year later, the edge sharpened: "a shell, a sham, and a death-trap" (*Inquirer*, January 25, 1870). Two more years passed before the city planned a new one.

And yet, Philadelphia might yet shine even in its humiliation. This deathtrap particularly stuck out as an egregious disgrace because it linked the two shores of a beautiful park,—a rusty chain linking two beautiful jewels. But how could anyone enjoy such beauty when he had to risk his life to get to it? "The new park will soon be in splendid condition for driving," the *Inquirer* boasted, "but," it lamented, "the tremor in passing over this bridge spoils the pleasure for man; while others, not willing to run the risk, are debarred from the pleasure of a drive through that really charming spot" (*Inquirer*, April 2, 1870). Even young Phaethons should prudently buy life insurance before passing over the river, just in case, like their namesake, they pass away by a fall.

In 1872, the City Fathers finally responded to this crying need, but they had a special reason for doing so. Philadelphia, as the Cradle of Liberty, had won the right to celebrate the centennial of the signing of the Declaration of Independence. It chose its new park as the site of this celebration. The park, originating around the reservoir on Fairmount and then including Lemon Hill, made up East Park, located just south of Girard avenue. Across the river, West Park, with its entrance by Lansdowne Drive, right off the bridge, would be the site of the celebration. Its two broad plateaus, Lansdowne and Belmont, spread out amply for the fairgrounds. In 1872, the city had four years to become the cynosure of all eyes as the Cradle of Liberty from back in 1776 and the showplace of American technology in 1876. Building the Girard avenue bridge as the gateway to Lansdowne Drive brought the first challenge in the preparation.

What a change in the almost forty years since 1833!
At first, this avenue was bringing students to Girard's college.
Now, it was bringing the world to America's centennial.

The eighteen years since the building of the first bridge in 1854 also brought a practical challenge: Philadelphia now needed to make much more significant choices about the material and design of this gateway. Another wooden bridge, no matter how well constructed, would not suit the place or the time. Romans had built triumphal arches for their gateways. Americans were building triumphal technology. To begin with, which building material should be chosen for this technology: iron or stone? The Romans had built with stone and their buildings had lasted for centuries; but, one newspaper article suggested, it did not seem imperative that the bridge be made of stone.

Modern technology of iron had appeal, but one question did still seem imperative: can an iron bridge last as long as one built of stone? The best engineers in London seemed to think that it could: Westminster and Blackfriars' bridge, made of stone in the eighteenth century, were replaced by iron in the nineteenth. An iron bridge cost less money and took less time to build. A small part of the money saved would pay for repainting (*Inquirer*, November 1, 1872). And yet, before the vote in City Council, Councilman Wagner expressed his doubts. Iron bridges, he said, require a great deal of looking after, and, in the end, they do not prove as durable or as economical as stone bridges. His observation did not convince his fellow councilmen,—their final vote: stone, 5; iron, 12. Iron carried the day. The city boasted that after it had taken a loan of $1,500,000.00 for the bridge, it would save from $200,000.00 to $300,000.00 by building with iron (*Inquirer*, May 28 & October 28, 1872).

In fourteen months, the bridge went up like an erector set. July 4, 1874, Philadelphia marked a significant epoch in its history, when, on the same day, it laid the corner stone of its City Hall and dedicated the Girard avenue bridge. Both events marked great beginnings. Building City Hall was starting to fulfill William Penn's plan that Center Square be the true center of his city. Building the bridge fulfilled his city's plan to start the celebration of the centennial of the United States of America by opening its gateway. Philadelphians proudly watched their City Hall bringing together William Penn's east and west boundaries. More marvelously, their new bridge would bring together their country and even their world from the farthest reaches of the East and the West. Could William Penn have ever even imagined that his town would have such a reach?!

After the *Inquirer* had issued complaints,—long, loud and lordly,—about the instability of the old bridge, it breathed a sigh of relief in celebrating the stability of the new one: ". . . there is no reason why this bridge should not be a valuable legacy to the great-great-great grandchildren of the youngest City Father present at the dedication" (*Inquirer*, July 3, 1874). It predicated this happy future, however, on one condition: "If the iron is not painted, it will rust." Councilman Wagner was right: iron does need "looking after." Americans, take note! A "valuable legacy" needs to be preserved.

Philadelphians were not worrying about the future. Right then and there, their bridge was a marvel. First of all, it was the widest in the world, 96 feet wide, its roadway, 67 feet; and its two sidewalks, 16 feet each (*Inquirer*, April 11, 1874). The carriages of city officials drove eight abreast to meet the officials of the Phoenix Iron Company for the dedication in the middle; as citizens thronged the sidewalks to observe. Back in England, the Blackfriars' and Westminster bridges were only 70 and 80 feet wide. When a Brit approached the Centennial by the Girard avenue bridge in 1876, he would marvel at what Philadelphia engineers could design and what Philadelphia mechanics could build,

Currier and Ives: Girard Avenue Bridge

even before he saw a single building. Americans crossing the bridge in 1874 would see that Philadelphians had set a standard: would the Centennial buildings prove aesthetically and architecturally as great a success as that "colossal yet graceful structure" (*Inquirer*, July 7, 1874)?

After enthusiasm for the Centennial had cooled, some Philadelphians started to take a cold, hard look at their bridge. To begin with, they regretted that City Council, choosing between iron and stone, had chosen iron. Instead of a graceful stone arch, it had built a rectangular iron box, "too low and monotonous in line to contribute any beauty to the park" (*The Times*, July 19, 1885). They granted that it might have met the needs of business on Market street but not those of beauty in Fairmount Park. Beauty aside, the *Inquirer* revealed that the bridge had been built at 40% over cost; and that some inequity between the three contracting parties,—the builders, the Phoenix Iron Company, and Philadelphia,—bordered on iniquity. "Extravagance and jobbery ruled, and the city was robbed" (*The Times*, July 19, 1885). The reporter, who had written a lament in 1864 about the 1854 bridge, could be writing the same lament in 1885 about the 1874 bridge. In both cases, the passing of a decade had allowed some objectivity.

And yet, even if experienced, sharp eyes considered the bridge unattractive, it was still connecting "the two shores of our magnificent park." In fact, it connected them even better after the lower deck, at the bottom of the rectangular iron box, opened in 1887 (*Inquirer*, November 12, 1887). This deck, serving as a pedestrian and equestrian walkway, especially provided a safe passage for horse and rider, when equestrians had to compete with motor cars at the beginning of the twentieth century. After the park had accepted the reality of automobile traffic by 1920, some old die-hards met in a cavalcade of more than 100 horsemen on Belmont Plateau, inspected bridle paths in the Park and then crossed the river by the equestrian walkway under the bridge (*Inquirer*, April 28, 1929). People like these were enjoying the park enough that they did not consider the aesthetics of the link between its east and west banks. After all, bridges mainly serve people by getting them to where they want to go.

Consider, for example, Alice and Kate's experience. What were they thinking after they opened the *Inquirer* on Wednesday morning, August 28, 1895 and read this notice in the personal column?

ALICE AND KATE — IF AGREEABLE WE
would be pleased to meet you this afternoon,
2 o'clock. Girard avenue bridge. DUDES.

In a picture in *Harper's Weekly*, one young lady crossing the bridge on her wheel, passes two "dudes" with theirs on the sidewalk. If the ice cream saloon, advertised in 1855, was not still making sundaes, the dudes could have found other suitable parlors, before or after visiting beautiful bowers and paths in the park. The bridge only just connected their fun.

Sixteen years after the bridge had welcomed visitors to the Centennial, and while it was connecting the Dudes with Alice and Kate, one 'if' rose from the past to threaten its life: "If the iron is not painted, it will rust." It was rusting, because it had not been painted. The city had hired painters for $5,500.00, for which, one inspector reported, no one could have done any "proper job at all" (*The Times*, October 12, 1882). Even without close inspection, the inspector could see that its bolts had not been painted and its rusty joists, never touched. "In some places," he continued, "I was able to turn up rust with my knife and take off large pieces intact" (*Inquirer*, October 19, 1882). By 1924, the *Inquirer* had reported that the city was using 200 tons of steel to replace its massive beams that had corroded to "wafer-like thinness" (*Inquirer*, September 23, 1924 & August 21, 1927).

The Girard avenue bridge had started its life as the link between "the two shores of our magnificent park." Pictures from the Centennial give an impression that the bridge only led to Lansdowne drive; but, by the twentieth century, it served mainly as the extension of Girard avenue from east to west. In extending Girard avenue, the bridge bore more traffic than it ever had: on the average eight hour day in 1933, it handled two times more cars than the Delaware River Bridge (*Inquirer*, August 26, 1933). Without proper maintenance, however, it became less able to bear this load. By the 1960's, the city had to limit it at 20 tons, even though the state limit was 36 (*Inquirer*, February 25, 1968). It pulled down the old bridge in 1968, and dedicated the new one on December 1, 1971.

Before the old Girard avenue bridge had finished its life, it had lived to its 94th year. In the first year of the new bridge in Philadelphia,

Blackfriars Bridge (1869) in London was passing its 101st. year, and Westminster (1862), its 108th. Thanks to the stewardship of the City of London, these bridges have survived to count many more years as legacies of the technology and life of 19th century London. The comparatively short life and slow death of the Girard avenue bridge tells an obvious, cautionary tale. In 1854, Philadelphia built a bad bridge, not worth maintaining; in 1874 it built a good bridge but maintained it so poorly that in a few decades it finished its life as disgracefully decrepit as the first one. Philadelphians might have been able to teach Londoners something about construction, but they could have and should have learned much from them about respecting and maintaining it. They were proud of their magnificent bridge, but their city did not respect their pride by making sure that this legacy could endure. In 1971, Philadelphia built a third bridge across the Schuylkill at Girard avenue, after it had neglected the legacy of the second bridge as the entrance to the Centennial.

Even while it was rusting away, the Girard Avenue bridge enjoyed its fame in the pictures. In 1893, the Eleventh Street Opera House provided the venue for "Slocum's Bright Extravaganza." The pictures illustrated scenes of some exciting activity in the city:

> Scene 1, "Chestnut street by Electric Light."
> Scene 2, "Girard Avenue Bridge."
> Scene 3, "P.R.R. Lightning train"
> (*Inquirer*, March 26, 1893).

Before the movies animated pictures by making them move, people flocked to picture shows just to watch attractive stills, hoping that bright lights might animate the scenes. In Scene 2, Slocum probably chose to picture the bridge when the city illuminated it with fireworks on the Fourth of July or with bright red and green at Christmas. In 1893, the Girard Avenue Bridge focused Philadelphians' happy celebrations in the center of their park. They enjoyed these celebrations like happy children at home, unaware that the rotting floor underneath them might collapse.

CHAPTER 29

Sweetbriar and the Strong Holds of Samuel Breck

THE STORY OF SAMUEL BRECK (1771–1862), the academic young man from Boston, and, eventually, the father of the family at Sweetbriar Farm, can start with that of his father-in-law, John Ross of Philadelphia. John's history can explain the origin of Samuel's ambitions in Philadelphia. As a father-in-law, John Ross set a high standard. Breck's family life at Sweetbriar would shape and test his hold on both the property and on what he and his wife called their "philosophy."

On December 8, 1768, John Ross (1729–1800) married Clementina Cruickshank (1745–1828). In 1773, Clementina gave birth to a daughter, Jean (1773–1858). Before and after the American Revolution, Ross had such success in trade with the East Indies that he both purchased his father-in-law's estate on Cobbs Creek, seven miles outside the city, and expanded it to six hundred acres. He renamed it The Grange after his friend's, the Marquis de Lafayette's, ancestral home, *Château La Grange*.[140] As he acquired the trappings of wealth, he built a town house in 1789, at Pine and Second street. After two years, he also purchased a farm of thirty acres on the west bank of the Schuylkill, only a mile northwest of the city.[141] John Ross was rising in the ranks of Philadelphia merchants. Living a life that reflected his good fortune, he attained a standard of living not easy to match.

SAMUEL BRECK MARRIED John Ross' daughter on Christmas Eve, 1795. One year after that, Ross relived a chapter in his own history when he passed down his property on the Schuylkill to his daughter and son-in-law. In this case, however, he was wealthy enough that he gave it to Jean and Samuel as a wedding present. Their thirty acres stood in marked contrast to his six hundred. Their thirty acres, however, had distinction: on the west bank of the Schuylkill, their property stood closer to the city and its urbane life than those vast fields of The Grange, off on the banks of Cobbs Creek.

Before Samuel, Jr. withdrew from mercantile trade, and retired, so to speak,—at age 26,—to Sweetbriar, he closed down the business that he had shared with Lewis Deblois. In June, 1797, he advertised his stock for the last time: "A quantity of the best Boston beef in whole and half barrels, fit for ship's use; ditto Pork ditto; A quantity of Sherry Wine; A few Pipes Oil Proof Brandy, just landed from Bordeaux; chocolate in boxes; Rice, Cotton, Castile Soap; and four or five barrels large Orange Peels, &c." (*Inquirer*, June 5).[142] His business partner and their stock reflected his father's and his father-in-law's connections with France.

Breck was withdrawing from trade to live the life of a gentleman. Building an estate, overseeing its management, and also cultivating his interests in history and literature would more than fill his time. He kept good records of his academic work, which the Historical Society of Pennsylvania has preserved in an archive. The introduction to this archive anticipates the work that he was undertaking in 1797: "Breck's worldly interests were truly vast and are well preserved. The materials in this collection represent a staggering amount of subject interests and a near-lifetime's worth of documentation."

In 1797, Samuel Breck built a house on his thirty acres property as his permanent home. Taking the name of one of the wild flowers, he named it Sweetbriar after the Sweet Briar Rose. His wife had enjoyed beautiful roses in her childhood, since her father's estate had an extensive garden with hothouses and greenhouses. "No roses," exclaimed one of Ross's granddaughters, "were so beautiful as those from The Grange" (Eberlein and Hubbard, 52). In the language of flowers, the Sweet Briar Rose teaches a lesson in balanced contradiction: the briar wounds, but its rose makes that wound sweet.[143]

In choosing Sweetbriar as the name for his home, Breck celebrated its simplicity in nature. In his diary, on the other hand, he also boasted about its "elegance": "It is a fine stone house, rough-cast, fifty-three feet long, thirty-eight broad, and three stories high, having out-buildings of every kind suitable for elegance and comfort."[144] In his entry for August 2, 1828, he lists the appurtenances of his "elegance and comfort": "fine gardens, greenhouses and every necessary appendage, such as barns, stables, coach house, farm house etc." In naming his home Sweetbriar, Breck set up a poetic contradiction of its elegance in the midst of simplicity, but he was also joining the best of two worlds by joining "elegance" with "comfort." Sweetbriar's "comfort" and simplicity made its "elegance" livable.

Samuel and Jean were anticipating a life of balanced contradiction. They were espousing the oxymoron in the Epicurean philosophy of *aurea mediocritas*, the golden mean, literally, "golden mediocrity," between extremes. This insight fit Samuel's Breck education and literary interest. He could see it in a translation of one of Horace's poems in a local newspaper:

The man who loves the golden mean,
His house is warm and neat and clean,
He sighs not to be great;
He envies not the pompous hill,
But wise, despises, laughs at all
The tinsel toys of state
(Horace *Odes* II, 10, in the
Pennsylvania Packet, December 25, 1781).

Breck's father-in-law had set him a high standard, but balancing simplicity, elegance, and comfort in a golden mean set an even higher one. In his thirty-nine years at Sweetbriar, Breck would weigh the price he had to pay to maintain this Epicurean philosophy.

Breck's decision to make Sweetbriar his permanent home set him apart from the elegant *façon de vivre*. Many wealthy families of his day, like his in-laws, John and Clementina Ross used country estates for fashionable entertaining and summer retreat. John Ross, for example, had a reputation for treating his guests to excellent claret, a French wine from Bordeaux, from his wine cellar at The Grange. His daughter Jean had lived in both the country and the city. She

"Sweetbriar Mansion in 1843"

In Samuel Breck's words, the "beautiful sloping lawn, terminating at the river, [is] now nearly four hundred yards wide opposite the Portico." In this chromolithograph by Augustus Kollner (1813–1906), the portico occupies four bays on the right of the house. Kollner dated this lithograph five years after Breck sold Sweetbriar.

had grown up with her family at The Grange, until she was sixteen years old, at which time her father had built his town house. She could have encouraged her husband to espouse the simplicity of her early upbringing in the country, especially after his retirement from trade made it both possible and perhaps a necessity.

Jean also knew that her father's lavish lifestyle had brought him close to bankruptcy. It hit her and her husband not just close to home, but literally at home. They were living on a property that her father perhaps should not have purchased, but certainly one that he should not have given away. Their decision,—motivated by virtuous thrift or cautious necessity,—set a very different course for their lives.

Other aspects of Breck's life had already set him apart. He was born in Boston, not in Philadelphia, but like many wealthy Americans of the eighteenth century, Bostonians or Philadelphians, he and his father had made their fortunes as merchants. Samuel first attended the Boston Latin School. After his father had become acquainted with

Frenchmen in America by serving as the agent to their Royal Army and Navy during the American Revolution, he sent young Samuel for four years of schooling by Benedictine monks in France. Graduating in 1787, Samuel returned, educated in the Classics, fluent in French, filled with enlightened philosophy, and well prepared for his life of learning. Five years after his return from France, his father moved the family to Philadelphia. Philadelphia appealed to Samuel Breck, Sr. (1747–1809) because he wanted to escape the heavy taxation in Boston, and also because French culture in the 1790's had found its home in Philadelphia. Before his daughter's marriage, John Ross had also played a prominent part in this francophile culture, when he had served as the agent of the American Congress in Paris. Ross had visited his friend Lafayette outside of Paris, at *Château La Grange*.

IN 1808, TEN YEARS after his retirement to Sweetbriar, Breck reflected on his life: "I found myself at twenty-six years of age, . . . confined to a sober, solitary country life . . . my fortune . . . reduced to the standard of a decent subsistence . . . placed alone with Mrs. Breck to exercise our philosophy and learn to laugh at that world which we could not enjoy." After he sold off his stock in trade, he lived the life of a gentleman on his estate, modest both in land and in profit. Although some clouds, he continued, "have darkened my hermitage," "that measure of happiness which it is proper for us to taste" filled their lives. Samuel and Jean's "philosophy" probably gave them an enlightened life instead of a "sober" consolation in the face of necessity. They laughed at "that world which we could not enjoy," as Horace laughed "at all / The tinsel toys of state." In the company of Horace, their "warm and neat and clean" house, nestled among wild sweet briar roses, made this "decent subsistence" a welcome alternative to luxurious urbanity.

With his eyes on the sweet rose instead of its briar, Breck has also described "decent subsistence" enjoying "elegance and comfort" in "sober, solitary country life." Perhaps he was contrasting this "decent subsistence" on thirty acres to his father-in-law's luxury on six hundred. Perhaps he also called subsistence "decent," because his father-in-law's luxury had caused some indecent—to stretch the word—financial embarrassment upon his demise in 1800 and the sale of The Grange in 1810. Jean and Samuel's "philosophy" profited from the lesson that they had learned from the financial embarrassment of Mr. Ross's demise. His success and consequent excess, though generous and well-meant, motivated, or perhaps even forced, his daughter's and son-in-law's "sober" life in the country. John Ross enjoyed cultivated roses, but Jean Ross Breck and her husband found contentment in the wild sweet briar.

To PROVIDE HIS FAMILY with "elegance and comfort," Breck employed servants, three in the house and two in the stable, garden and field,—five, at the least, but sometimes nine or ten. These servants could not enjoy elegance, but they certainly did enjoy comfort, with the "greatest abundance," Breck boasted, "commonly seventy pounds of fresh butcher's meat, poultry and fish a week" (*Diary*, April 10, 1822). In addition to room and board, his cook received six dollars per month, in weekly installments of one dollar and fifty cents; and chambermaid, five dollars per month, in weekly installments of one dollar and twenty-five cents. His gardener received one monthly payment of eleven dollars; the waiter and the farmer, ten each. (In this account, he does not mention a stableboy or coachman.)

These salaries may reflect some inequities. By the week, he paid the cook and the chambermaid a comparatively modest wage; by the month, he paid the waiter more. When he complained later that he had six cooks in twelve months, he might have stopped to think that he had not been paying them enough! The gardener received the highest wage. Since the property was relatively small, Breck regularly employed only one gardener and one farmer. He estimated the sum of these wages as $600.00 a year, in a grand total of $3300.00 to $3500.00 for the maintenance of the whole estate (August 2, 1828)—adjusted for inflation in 2021, about $80,000. His expenses did indeed reflect "a modest subsistence" for a gentleman of his class.

According to the needs of the season, however, Breck hired extra hands. For planting, May 14, 1822, he hired four men to remove his "greenhouse plants from the conservatory to the new garden." For harvesting, July 15, 1817, he hired twelve men to reap five acres of rye, during, he comments, "excessive fine harvest weather." In a later year, he harvested wheat (August 23, 1833). In winter, he intended to harvest ice on the Schuylkill, when he "called at the house of a mason, who lived in the neighborhood, to hire him and his two boys to assist in filling the ice house" (January 20, 1808). Masons who cut stone could also cut ice. Breck was doing the job of an overseer, whom he could have hired to oversee Sweetbriar's maintenance. In this oversight, he faced challenges every season.

Breck faced a special challenge in providing for the education of his daughter Lucy (1807–1828): "A country residence," he reflected, "is peculiarly inconvenient for the education of children (October 13, 1820). Three days a week, he took her into the city for "dancing from 10 to noon, drawing from 11 to 12, and music from 12 to one." At home, a "private tutor" spent two and one half hours attending to the basics of "grammar, cyphering, writing, reading, geography, history, etc." The simplicity and elegance of Sweetbriar's "solitary country life" could suit the Brecks, but not their daughter's need for refined tutelage. His father had sent him to school in France. He, at least, could arrange for his daughter's education in Philadelphia.

Nature offered one challenge that proved insurmountable. When Breck built Sweetbriar in 1797, he enjoyed his view on its hill above the Schuylkill. In 1797, the river, by the flux and reflux of its tides, was in constant motion. He could not have imagined the changes that would come within two decades. By 1819, "the corporation of Philadelphia" was building a dam at Fairmount to draw water for a reservoir on the hill. In anticipation, Mr. Elliott visited, September 2, 1819, to survey "my island, meadow and ground in front of the house, all which I shall probably lose by the construction of the water dam now erecting about one mile below me." The dam at Fairmount would back up the water to cover about 15 or 16 acres of Sweetbriar's river bank. The next year, Breck and his daughter Lucy visited this dam, just one mile down river:

> *August 18, 1820* I walked with my daughter to the canal & dam now constructing by the corporation of Philadelphia. It is upon a stupendous plan and will cost between one & two hundred thousand dollars. These works are for the publick benefit, and must of course be executed, altho' to the great detriment of individuals, particularly myself, as my estate here (at Sweetbriar) will be deprived of 16 acres of its best meadow land, and all my alluvial pasture will be drowned.

Water backing up behind the dam, he observed, became "apparently stagnant and must alter the character of the atmosphere hereabouts which for 23 years (that I have resided here) has been of the most salubrious kind." Did Breck anticipate the danger? This "dam at Fairmount," a project renowned for its "public benefit," which he admired with Lucy in 1820, was threatening his "family" with disease in the following year:

> *September 27, 1821* Our young lad, Henry McConnell, took sick, and as I have had one of my family sick before, and feel somewhat timid about the effects of the dam lately erected at Fairmount, just below me. Indeed, I felt some concern upon that head long ago, and am still apprehensive that it will throw us into fever & agues, intermittent, remittent or bilious fever.

These "fevers and agues" took a sad toll on his family in the summer of 1828:

> *July 25, 1828* This will ever be to me a day of the most sorrowful recollection. At midnight of this day my strongest hold on earth, my only child and much beloved daughter Lucy, breathed her last.

Losing his daughter, his "strongest hold on earth," loosened his hold on much else. In the next entry in his diary, August 2, 1828, he starts to take the toll of Sweetbriar for its sale right after he heard the tolling of his daughter's death. He and his wife, he records, have held on to Sweetbriar principally on his "daughter's account." In bereavement, he sharpens the bitter edge of his sorrow by tracing its causes and effects. The dam at Fairmount, he reasons, has caused the stagnation of the Schuylkill, which, in turn, has caused the typhoid fever, from which his daughter has died. Death has made his once "beautifully situated" estate with its "fine gardens" now "irksome and gloomy." In 1837, almost ten years after his daughter's death, he offered his estate for sale. He was moving the furniture into his new home on Arch street, west of Broad, by September of 1839.

In the next twenty-three years before Samuel Breck died in 1862, he filled his life with political, civic and literary projects. After he sold

Sweetbriar, he had time to expand them, because he did not have to oversee its maintenance. In his term as a state senator, 1832–1835, for example, he championed the cause of public education:

> The bill for General Education by common schools has passed the House of Representatives at Harrisburg, by a very large majority. This bill is due in great part to the enlightened zeal of our estimable fellow citizen. The Hon. Samuel Breck's whole public life has been a uniform effort for the public good (*National Gazette*, March 1, 1834).

"Enlightened zeal" and "uniform effort for the public good" characterized Samuel Breck's life. This gentleman would grace any home.

Before Fairmount Park incorporated Sweetbriar into West Park, William Torr lived there and ran his business, The Sweetbrier Ice Company, on the river. Torr lived in the house until 1844, at which time he leased it to an innkeeper. The innkeeper took advantage of its "beautifully situated" location and its "fine gardens" to advertise its use for "Pic-Nics—this spot can not be surpassed if equalled in the County of Philadelphia. There is a grove of silver pines; beneath their delightful shade, two hundred persons could dine. It is the fourth farm on the banks of the Schuylkill above the wire bridge, next above the Egglesfield Farm" (*Public Ledger*, May 26, 1846). Other estates on the Schuylkill like Lemon Hill and Belmont also opened their gates to school and Sunday School outings:

> Formal Opening in the Park.—The formal opening of the play-ground and the restaurant connected therewith, at the Sweet Briar Farm, at Fairmount Park, took place yesterday afternoon. This will be a favorite resort with citizens during the summer months, as various innocent plays may be indulged in; and refreshments are obtainable at all hours throughout the day. The spot is delightfully situated on the west bank of the Schuylkill, a short distance from the Girard Avenue Bridge (*Inquirer*, June, 4, 1870).

By its association with Sunday Schools and evangelism, children enjoy "innocent plays" around Sweetbriar, and their parents worship

Fillmyre's Beer Garden, Benjamin Ridgway Evans (1834–1891), 1880

on its front lawn: "On the lawn before Sweetbriar, the laymen of the Evangelical Alliance held their open air service" (*Inquirer*, August 17, 1891). After its pious first years, going from spirituality to spirits, Sweetbriar also hosted Fillmyre's Beer Garden in 1880. For either its beer or root beer, Sweetbriar, as the first property of Fairmount Park off the Girard Avenue Bridge, became "a favorite resort for pedestrians, drivers and cyclers. Its many shaded nooks afforded safe retreats from the sun's hot bolts" (*Inquirer*, May 11, 1891).

"Shaded nooks," as an aspect Sweetbriar's topography, played a part in another chapter of its history. Eventually, the city suffered from improper drainage in its valley, from which Breck's family had suffered. One of the city's neighborhoods in West Philadelphia gradually grew up around the "Glen": **Sweetbriar Glen, The Place Had Become a Source of Disease**, announced a headline in the Philadelphia *Inquirer* on March 30, 1896. This "glen," the article reported, was "fast being filled up and will be made level with the street. Thirty-ninth street and Girard avenue will entirely disappear. Earth is being dumped into the place at the rate of 250 to 300 loads daily, filling up what was one of the deepest glens in all the park with 200,000 loads of dirt." Seventy years after Lucy's death, the city was remedying the source of her father's heartbreak.

In the years since the Brecks moved out, two very different roads roads from different times have swept past Sweetbriar. In the 1860's, the Fairmount Park Commission united the various properties of West Park by a carriage drive. Right at the entrance off the Girard Avenue Bridge, the base of Sweetbriar's front lawn served as the beginning of Lansdowne Drive, which the Commission "formally opened on the 24th of June, 1869" (*Evening Telegraph*). Lansdowne Drive, heading first to Lansdowne, the famous estate of John Penn, swept over its plateau and up George's Hill in a graceful circuit of West Park.

Lansdowne drive served the exclusive carriage trade of Philadelphia's upper class. Newspaper editorials often commented on this special privilege of wealthy citizens and their fancy equipages: "The wants of pedestrians," the *Inquirer* grumbled, "seem to be of secondary importance" (*Inquirer*, March, 1871). When the Park Commission sewed together the estates on the west bank of the Schuylkill to unite West Park, Sweetbriar was only one patch, and a less important one, in the quilt. Philadelphia's wealthiest, like Fairman Rogers and Alexander Cassatt, on four-in-hand carriages, were sweeping through Breck's property in the showiest trappings of their wealth. Imagine Samuel and Jean sitting on their front porch, laughing at the trappings of "that world" that they "could not enjoy."

In the 1950's, the Park Commission sacrificed the most beautiful part of Sweetbriar's property,—its lawn slopping down to the river,—when it voted to allow the Schuylkill Expressway through West Park. This highway cuts a steep cliff no more than twenty yard in back of the house. With Lansdowne Drive on the west side and the Schuylkill Expressway on the east, Sweetbriar has witnessed the intrusions of both carriages and automobiles. The *Inquirer*'s lament in 1871 may apply even more to the intrusion of the Expressway: "The wants of pedestrians seem to be of secondary importance."

If Samuel Breck could have foreseen the dire consequences, he would not have built Sweetbriar as his family home. He did build it because his father-in-law had given him the property, with its opportunity of being a lord of the manor, but he spent thirty-nine years realizing that the role did not really suit him. Most of his neighbors, on the other hand, in generations of their families, had been to their manors born: the Bartrams to their gardens, the Hamiltons to the Woodlands, and the Peters to Belmont, had a commitment to their properties. For Breck, Sweetbriar was his family home, not his family business or legacy. As a consequence, after living there for less than half of his life, he did not pass it on to another generation. His "hermitage" resonates with his own special story, because he occupied it thoughtfully,—sometimes, very happily,—and described in his diary the ways in which it did and did not suit him.

From the beginning, Breck's "philosophy" synthesized more philosophy than reality. It required simplicity, but he made simplicity elegant, although elegant in the same way that Horace, the Epicurean, called his relatively elegant habits simple. In his "decent subsistence," he enjoyed "elegance and comfort;" and in his sober "solitary country life," he enjoyed visiting interesting neighbors like the Peters and the Hamiltons. He could have raised his daughter in this "country life," but he busied himself taking her into Philadelphia to acquire refinement in dance, art, and music. His philosophy and his life in the world did not harmonize. Sweetbriar, his name for the house, highlights contradiction; and his life there embodied it.

Death had turned Breck's harmony into dissonance. In facing it, he realized that Sweetbriar had been his family's home, not his life. Lucy's life, not his life of intellect or property or public service, held him in his "strongest hold on earth." He knew, however, when to attune his life to new holds. At age 26, for example, after closing down his business, he had retired to find contentment at Sweetbriar. At age 66, finally, after his daughter's death, he again retired to find contentment on Arch street. This philosopher adjusted and found contentment wherever he lived.

CHAPTER 30

Fairman Rogers on Lansdowne Drive

IN 1876, PICTURES OF the Girard Avenue Bridge gave an impression that it led straight to Lansdowne drive as the entrance to the Centennial Grounds. After 1876, the bridge and the drive no longer enjoyed this prestige, but they continued to lead to West Park. Even without the Centennial, West Park was worth the trip, especially for equestrians. On their trip from the city to the park, they passed by the promenades of Fairmount and Lemon Hill to the East River Drive and its panoramas of the Schuylkill. After they crossed the bridge, Lansdowne drive took them up country, traversing the beautiful hills, dales and plateaus of West Park. Pedestrians, of course, could also enjoy this beauty, but they had to take a long walk to see it.

In 1880, Thomas Eakins put Fairman Rogers (1833–1900) in the front rank of equestrians by making him the subject of his painting, "The Fairman Rogers Four-in-Hand." He pictured Rogers' coach passing through the gardens on Lansdowne drive. This drive enjoyed its own special prestige, but when a swell like Fairman Rogers drove on it to take his thoroughbreds through their paces, it glowed even brighter. His distinguished life clarifies its distinction.

WHEN FAIRMAN ROGERS DIED in Vienna in 1900, he had been living in Europe, actually in Paris, for ten years. Mary Cassatt (1844–1926), was also living in Paris. She was the sister of Alexander Cassatt (1839–1906), the man to whom he sold his house on Rittenhouse Square and to whom he passed on the presidency of the Four-in-Hand Club.

Thomas Eakins, "The Fairman Rogers Four-in-Hand" (1880)
In the original, the parasol is red, as are the wheels of the London coach.

Mary, at the beginning of her career in 1866, had gone to Paris at age 22, because it offered her the education in art that she could not find at the Pennsylvania Academy of Fine Arts in Philadelphia. Fairman, at the beginning of his full retirement in 1890, had gone to Paris at age 57, because it offered him another facet of the refined leisure that he always cultivated. She was painting paintings that made Paris a cultural capital where he would enjoy the good life. Although they may seem very different, Mary Cassatt and Fairman Rogers shared an interest in art and respect for excellence. Even at leisure in Paris, Rogers was writing *A Manual of Coaching* (1900) that would make a lasting contribution to the art of the four-in-hand.

Fairman must have disappointed his friends in Philadelphia when he finally retired to Paris, because his good life had done them a lot of good. After he graduated from the University of Pennsylvania in 1853, he taught Civil Engineering at the Franklin Institute for eleven years and at his *alma mater* for sixteen. He also shared his learning outside the classroom. To the public, he delivered a "splendid," "graphic and absorbing" lecture on glaciers at the West Philadelphia Institute (*Evening Telegraph*, March 28; *Inquirer*, April 7, 1866); and "admirable lectures" at the Academy of Music (*Inquirer*, April 6, 1868). In his retirement from his professorial duties in 1871, at age 36, he did Philadelphia a valuable service as the chairman of the building committee of the new home of the Pennsylvania Academy, designed by the firm of Furness and Hewitt (*Inquirer*, December 9, 1872). He had a connection by marriage to Frank Furness: his sister had married Frank's brother Howard in 1860.

Rogers' career in engineering had built only a part of his good life. Upon their father's demise in 1870, he and his sister inherited his estate (*Inquirer*, October 24, 1870). He then set out on a career as a gentleman. To punctuate his departure from professorial duties, he donated his professional library of 4,500 volumes to the University of Pennsylvania (*Inquirer*, March 14, 1873). After his service as its Dean of Faculty, the university asked him to be its Provost (*Inquirer*, February 27, 1880), but he declined. He was setting his sights on a life made good by his own avocations.

By 1870, the newly laid out Lansdowne drive, "the grand drive" stretching five miles from the Girard avenue bridge to George's Hill, provided the best course for Fairman's horses (*Inquirer*, July 1, 1869). "He had enjoyed sports as a young man," his brother-in-law, Henry Howard Furness, reminisced after Fairman's death, but "of everything pertaining to Riding, Driving, and Hunting, Professor Rogers was unfeignedly fond." He had a passion for horsemanship and, especially, for the four-in-hand, which represented driving at its "highest perfection." Toward the end of his life he praised its thrill in his *Manual of Coaching*: "There is something so exhilarating in the motion behind four horses, through the fresh air, that even stupid people wake up, and for once make themselves agreeable."

Cultivating the "thrill" as an art, Rogers revived this old custom and practiced it with the same precision that he applied to civil engineering. He spared no expense in the pursuit: the *Inquirer* reported his purchase of "an unusually stylish and valuable set of four-in-hand harness" crafted by Messrs. Henry G. Haedrick and Son, 15th and Locust. "In workmanship, finish, mounting and material," the report boasted, "it surpassed any of this kind produced in America"

(*Inquirer*, June 20, 1871). When Fairman Rogers cracked the whip, his exquisite equipage made no empty show. He gave dignity to what others regarded as the frivolous pretensions of the idle rich.

Having purchased the best that America had to offer, Rogers ideally did not,—and, pragmatically, he could not,—limit his activities to any one place. Naturally, a happy inevitability took him back to England, as an important home of equestrian arts. There, he rode with the Pytchley and the Quorn Hunt, and he was also a member of the North Warwickshire Hunt. Back home, since, at first, he drove the only amateur four-in-hand in Philadelphia, he sought out New York City for a run with kindred coaches. He joined the New York Coaching Club as its only Philadelphia member (*Inquirer*, Feb 6, 1877); and in its Spring Parade, he drove a team of bays in a red-wheeled London coach, probably the one that he is driving in Eakins' painting (*The Times*, May 28, 1877). His friend Frank Furness designed a home, Ochre Point, for him in Newport, from which he sailed his yacht Magnolia. He also drove his four-in-hand on its Ten Mile Drive, although, as time passed, he could no longer bask in the glory of being the only whip of a four-in-hand in this exclusive resort (*The Times*, July 31, 1879), although he was still probably the best,—he would have loved the friendly rivalry. Make way for Tally-Ho and the gentleman from Philadelphia tooting his horn!

In any coaching expedition, the guard of his four-in-hand literally did toot its horn. Bringing Philadelphia and New York together, Rogers organized a special trip of the four-in-hand coach from the one city to the other. "Although the occasion was that of a private pleasure trip of twelve gentlemen," the *Inquirer* reported, "it was very generally made a public matter of, the novelty of the affair provoking a large degree of public interest." Rogers was also bringing the past and the present together in a spectacle worthy of the theatre: his guard Fowndes in the box blew "tantivy" loud and clear, sounding a "merry and melodious greeting in prolonged notes on his horn" (*The Times*, May 7, 1878).[145] The journey concluded at the St. George Hotel on Broad Street below Walnut (*The Times*, May 4, 1878). The New York crowd must have been glad they had admitted Rogers as a member, especially after he dined them at his mansion on west Rittenhouse Square. The *Inquirer* enthusiastically traced their route and called the trip a "splendid success" as a "healthful recreation for ladies and gentlemen."

In ever more democratic America, Fairman Rogers was turning back the clock by making a recreation of the leisure class worthy of respect. In reviving the sport of four-in-hand coaching, he was old-fashioned and proud of it! For anyone of any class, he provided a model of how to live life. A writer in the *Inquirer* hoped that his genteel avocation might raise the low classes from their low tastes. It drew this moral from its account of Rogers' coaching adventure: "Perhaps this taste for open air amusement will elbow lower classes of sporting out of their great and demoralizing influence upon society (*Inquirer*, May 6, 1878). With Rogers' example, the perennial Yankee glorification of work could make concessions to intelligent leisure for its own sake (*The Times*, October 22, 1899).

With the exception of Alexander Cassatt, on whose six-hundred acre farm an overseer and eighteen stable boys trained more than seventy-five thoroughbreds, no whip in Philadelphia could rival Fairman Rogers. Many, however, happily followed him, literally following him as he led them in the first parade of the Four-in-Hand Club in 1890. Rogers was leaving Philadelphia with a refined bang: "Never before in the history of Philadelphia socialdom was such a spectacle witnessed as that presented yesterday on the south side of Rittenhouse Square" by the very cream of Philadelphia society. (*Inquirer*, May, 1890). "Never before," the *Inquirer* boasted,—and 'never after,' the historian may add,—did the swells of Rittenhouse Square so strut their stuff.

After Rogers had left for Paris, this "ultra swell organization," announced its second annual parade in the Spring of 1892. The swells sported the panache of their club: green cutaway coat, with brass buttons, light pantaloons, striped buff vests, and high light hats. Just a private affair, but the newspapers delighted in covering it. Everyone, it seemed, came out to watch or to follow the parade in "carriages, phaetons, tandems and victorias," wherever they could find room. Alexander Cassatt, the second president of the club, cracked his long whip at 4 in the afternoon. The procession then drove down the smooth surface of Locust street to the Belgian blocks of Broad street, west down Spring Garden and north through East Park, over the Girard Avenue Bridge to Lansdowne drive. On Lansdowne, it galloped up

"The Coaching Club," *Harper's Weekly*, May 1881

the hill and viewed the beauty of the park in all its glory. The "coachers" exclaimed in pleasure at the work of the gardeners as they passed through the gardens near Horticultural Hall (*Inquirer*, May 15, 1894). (Thomas Eakins had pictured Fairman Rogers' four-in-hand in this most beautiful part of the park.) After Lansdowne ended at George's Hill and Belmont, Cassatt reviewed the cavalcade.

This pomp and circumstance, the *Philadelphia Times* explained, "gave less fortunate mortals the opportunity to gaze upon a ravishing display of fine horse flesh, gayly caparisoned and brave men and fair women in all the beauty of Spring attire. He would be a jealous churl indeed, if any of the more highly favored class would lead him to accuse it of ostentation" (*The Times*, May 3, 1896). A slice of medieval romance in Rittenhouse Square! Romantic hyperbole, reminiscent of the novels of Sir Walter Scott, puts an ironic edge on this effusion. Mark Twain had joked that Scott, by his glorification of brave knights and fair ladies, had started the Civil War. Scott's novels did inspire Southern gallantry; and some people took pride in calling Philadelphia the northernmost southern city. "Philadelphia," *The Times* boasted, "rightfully boasts of having a larger following of the four-in-hand than any other city in the country" (*The Times*, May 12, 1895). By a stretch of this reasoning, more people in Philadelphia read Sir Walter Scott than in any other Northern city and fewer jealous churls objected to his celebration of gallantry.

When Fairman Rogers arrived in Paris in 1890, he had the opportunity to reunite with Mary Cassatt (1844–1926), two Philadelphians with a common heritage. Beyond the family connections, like that of Alexander Cassatt, her brother and Fairman's fellow clubman, their interest in art gave them a broad common ground. Mary had left Philadelphia, because the Pennsylvania Academy of Fine Arts had offered women little opportunity for instruction. Back in Philadelphia, Fairman had become a trustee of the Academy; and, in 1876, after he chaired its building committee and opened its doors on North Broad street, he also opened them to women as the equals of men. He left a place better for his having been there. When, for example, he left Newport for an extended trip to Europe, neighbors continued to visit his gardens at Ochre Point to see the perfection of his art of "ribbon gardening" (*The Times*, July 27, 1880).

Public institutions, like the Pennsylvania Academy were opening their facilities to public access. Local newspapers for example, exuded enthusiasm about the pomp of the Four-in-Hand Club, but they also spoke up for the greater public interest: "With a rather curious unanimity," the *Inquirer* observed in 1872, people were complaining that the city was laying out a "A Rich Man's Park" with little concern for the poor pedestrian beyond Fairmount and Lemon Hill (January 27, 1872). In 1888, for example, it reported that the city spent $60,000 for a new carriage drive but only $1,000 to provide storm shelters in the old mansions. Doubtless, Rogers' fellow coachmen had been lobbying for better access to West Park.

Rogers and his friends represented an oligarchy, in which, literally, a few men ruled. The *polloi*, literally, the many, pled their case with polyglot eloquence: "Are not the necessities of the poorer people more pressing and should they not be provided for first" (*Inquirer*, August, 1888)? In the design of Fairmount Park, the obvious answer to this plea had been 'no.' In cultivating their passion for horsemanship, Fairman Rogers' Four-in-Hand Club had not opened the park to the needs of poor pedestrians. (Few pedestrians, in any age, would turn off the Girard Avenue Bridge and up Lansdowne drive to walk about six miles to Belmont.) Equestrians were having their day; and at its high noon, Rogers' cavalcade whirled their panache up to Lansdowne Drive. Especially from our day, in which the automobile has ridden roughshod over all competition, we can understand his plea: Should not the ideals of this genteel equestrian move even churlish minds to allow him his time in the sun?[146]

CHAPTER 31

Belmont

The citizens of Philadelphia gathered on July 4, 1788 to celebrate the Constitution of the United States that had been ratified the year before. To welcome and confirm their new federal union, chosen members of all their city's trades and professions led a Grand Federal Procession. At the head of the twenty-seventh contingent, the Agricultural Society had unfurled its flag, depicting Industry by a man ploughing, and Plenty by a woman holding a sickle and a horn of plenty. Following behind, Richard Peters, president of the society, led the farmers (*Pennsylvania Gazette*, July 9, 1788).

Until his death forty years later, Peters continued to lead this society as its beloved president. The Agricultural Society helped farmers in more than agriculture. In addition to its help for "agriculture," it added service to "manufactures" (*Pennsylvania Gazette*, August 27, 1788). The one gave an incentives to the other. Why invent a better mousetrap, for example, except to prevent vermin from eating all the grain in the silo? Stone from the quarry on Belmont, for a specific example, was advertised as "fire-stone," used to contain copper vats in Peters' brewery (*Pennsylvania Gazette*, August 11, 1784). Richard and his son, Richard, Jr., cultivated manufactures in various aspects of technology. Much modern technology can trace its origins back to the farm.

Peters lived all his life on his family's farm, where he was born in 1744 and where he died in 1828. His father, William, had named it Belmont, to celebrate its beautiful hill rising above the Schuylkill, just a few miles Northwest of the city. Aside from his managing Belmont, Richard Peters served as a judge during the epoch of America's Founding Fathers. They all knew him; and when they visited him at Belmont, they always enjoyed his company.

George Washington visited often. He had relied on Peters as his Secretary of War during the American Revolution and appointed him to the bench after it. When Philadelphia served as the nation's capital from 1790 to 1800, our beleaguered *Pater Patriae* visited Belmont as respite from the burdens of his office: "There," a friend observed, "sequestered from the world, and the torments and cares of business, Washington would enjoy a vivacious, recreative, and wholly unceremonious intercourse with the Judge; walking for hours, side by side, in the beautiful gardens of Belmont, beneath the dark shade of lofty hemlocks" (Samuel Breck, *Address Delivered before the Blockley and Merion Agricultural Society*, 1828). Deborah Norris Logan described this avenue of hemlocks, in back of the house, as "planted close and arched above." At the end of the avenue, an obelisk marked the boundary of the property, at the farthest distance from the Schuylkill River. On the other side of the house, an avenue of cherry trees led from the front door down to a Chinese Temple, as a summer house along the river.

While strolling and showing off his gardens, "the Judge" loved to talk. His engaging personality made him a legendarily vivacious and loquacious host. His chat so charmed even Indians at a pow-wow that they adopted him into their tribe and named him *Tegohtias*, Talking Bird. The Peters family could speak seriously, however, when the conversation came round to their estate: even Thomas Penn, proprietor of Springettsbury, the first important estate on the Schuylkill, looked to them for advice. Their life on Belmont, in the golden age of American history, made it legendary.

Three generations of the Peters family,—William (1702–1786), Richard (1744–1828), and Richard, Jr. (1780–1848),—got tenants to maintain the property. Their advertisements in the city's gazettes from 1764 to 1845 trace its evolution. At first, in 1764 and 1771, William Peters described Belmont as a farm: "a good House, Barn, Stables and Milk-house, all of stone, Barrack, Cider-Mill and Press under cover, and almost every other convenience for a Tenant." He divided the land into 90 acres of "cleared land," "a sufficient quantity of woodland," 15 acres of "watered meadow," an orchard of 150 grafted apple trees "bearing fruit of the best quality," and another of 200 cherry trees "of various sorts." By 1771, he had increased the number of trees in his two orchards. Arboriculture brought use together with beauty. For beauty, the "lofty hemlocks" in the gardens would shade George Washington's walk twenty years later.

In 1771, also, William reserved for his family's use "the principal dwelling-house, gardens, *etc.*," because he still wanted them to enjoy the beautiful hill, even if they did not live there to cultivate it. On the other hand, he had the good sense to look for a tenant with a family: "A man with a small family will be most agreeable" (*Pennsylvania Gazette*, January 31, 1771). Hirelings, he feared, might not take good care of the property.

After William died in 1786, his son Richard expanded his 15 acres of "watered meadow" to 60 or 80 acres. "A large dairy is the principal object," he announced in the *Pennsylvania Gazette* in 1803. In the first decades of the century, Richard, whom Andrew Jackson Downing called a "scientific agriculturalist," improved his management of the property. As the president of the Agricultural Society, he had been doing some research; and by 1803, he advertised "upland clover in its prime." He had also learned to require family values: his father had considered them "agreeable;" for him, they were a must: "The tenant must be competent, in his own family, to do the greater part of the work of the farm and dairy." Character had also became a must: "Good temper and sobriety are as necessary as integrity, in the plan on which this farm has been (beneficially to tenants) usually leased." "Usually" hints at some exception that gave him unusual trouble

The man hired in 1803 had a wife who probably had not passed inspection, since Peters' notice in 1813 also hints at some disappointment: "The tenant must be married, and his wife industrious, and intelligent in the business of the dairy, and marketing." Any prospective tenant should have had enough sense to marry a canny woman of business and not a simple milk maid. Just in case an applicant might not have been paying attention, he added a final warning: "No application need be made by persons not of the above description." Judge

As a Founding Father, Richard Peters had the honor of his picture on a cigar label.

Peters issuing sentences from his bench had learned to speak forcefully. He was saving jokes and jollities for his guests (*Pennsylvania Gazette*, January 19, 1803; December 15, 1813).

Judge Peters had succeeded in hiring a good gardener, because Andrew Jackson Downing admired his work. In *A Treatise on the Theory and Practice of Landscape Gardening, Adapted to North America* (1841), Downing described the excellence of Judge Peters' garden as it was thirty years earlier:

> The seat of the late Judge Peters . . . was, 30 years ago, a noted specimen of the ancient school of landscape gardening. Its proprietor . . . was also no less remarkable for the design and culture of its pleasure grounds than for the excellence of its farm. Long and stately avenues, with vistas terminated by obelisks, a garden adorned with marble vases, busts and statues and pleasure grounds, filled with the rarest trees and shrubs, were conspicuous features here. Some of the latter are now so remarkable as to attract strongly the attention of the visitor. Among them, is the chestnut planted by Washington which produces the largest and fin-

> est fruit; very large hollies; and a curious old box tree much higher than the mansion near which it stands. But the most striking feature now, is the still remaining grand old avenue of hemlocks (*Abies canadensis.*) Many of these trees, which were planted 100 years ago, are now venerable specimens, ninety feet high, whose huge trunks and wide spread branches, are in many cases densely wreathed and draped with masses of English Ivy, forming the most picturesque, sylvan objects we ever beheld. . . .

Richard Peters, Jr. maintained his father's property after he had died, since much of the garden, "still remaining," continued "remarkable," but Richard Peters, Sr. got the credit. On the other hand, he did sell his father's lemon and orange trees (*National Gazette*, September 27, 1828). The aspiration to the *Orangerie* had died out with the past generation.

The Peters' interests extended from agriculture to manufacturing and to industry itself. Three years before Richard Peters died, he and his son advertised to bring the work of the textile industry from the village of Manayunk down river to Belmont: "To Weavers and Manufacturers—To Let, a large frame house and four acres of ground . . . The house and ground may be used for a weaving establishment and bleach green, or for any other Manufactory" (*National Gazette*, January 24, 1825). For "a bleach green," some of four acres would serve as a greensward on which to spread products of the "weaving establishment" so that the sun might bleach them the old-fashioned way. Inviting "any other Manufactory" sounds like an ominous invitation to a Devil's workshop of industrial effluvia that the founders of Fairmount Park wanted to keep up the river, and away from the city's water supply. The Peters family, most likely the younger Richard, was listening to the siren call of modern technology.

In the first years of the nineteenth century, industry was inevitably moving up and down the Schuylkill, as the old orders of the eighteenth century were passing away. Two years after Jefferson and Adams died on the Fourth of July, 1826, the death of their friend Richard Peters, in 1828, inscribed one more name on the memorial of the American Revolution. Richard Peters, Sr., distinguished as "Judge Peters," had established the fame of Belmont by the end of the eighteenth century, but Richard, Jr. gave it a name in industry by the middle of the nineteenth. At first, he invited some eco-friendly industries like quarrying ice or stone (*National Gazette*, April 23, 1833 & November 25, 1843). As the president of the Philadelphia Ice Company, he advertised for a design of an improved ice house (*National Gazette*, October 16 and 25, 1833).[147]

Bleaching cloth on the green, and quarrying ice from the river or stone from the hill looked back to old skills, but Richard Jr., was looking forward to the new technology of the railroad. With other citizens, he met at the Merchants' Coffee House, where his father's generation had also met. Richard and they were also planning a revolution with an 'r' in the upper case,—the Industrial Revolution. "No one of the internal improvements," a newspaper reported of the first railroads in this new revolution, "will more extensively and efficiently promote the prosperity of the Commonwealth and of the city of Philadelphia" (*National Gazette*, December 18, 1830). This new epoch would leave its indelible mark on Belmont.

Peters served on the acting committee of the Pennsylvania Society for the Promotion of Internal Improvement in the Commonwealth (*US Gazette*, March 22, 1825). By the end of the decade, the Columbia Railroad ran up the Main Line of Public Works in Pennsylvania, now shortened to Pennsylvania Avenue. By his plan, the rails crossed a bridge, just across from Belmont, and climbed its steep hill by a specially engineered "Inclined Plane," a funicular railway (*US Gazette*, November 28, 1835).

Peters was engineering, so to speak, a *coup* that many entrepreneurs throughout the nineteenth century dreamed of. As rails stretched west across the continent, some of them fulfilled this dream by getting the rail companies to set up stations on their land. Richard Peters, Jr. did not need luck; he was on the committee that took the Columbia Railroad right across his property, with a station nearby.

A railroad station also makes no sense if the stop offers passengers nowhere to stay and nothing to see while they're staying. Peters saw to it that his railroad station had a railroad hotel near the Inclined Plane: "Belmont Cottage Hotel," the *National Gazette* announced, "to be rented . . . situated on the west side of the river Schuylkill, near the eastern termination of the Columbia Railroad Bridge . . . The location

The Inclined Plane rising above the Schuylkill to Belmont.

The cable between the tracks pulled the train up the hill.

for public entertainment is equal if not superior to any in the neighborhood of Philadelphia. The certainty that the railroad bridge will be completed before the month of February will secure a large portion of public patronage to this establishment" (*National Gazette*, November 22, 1833). As his father and grandfather had done, Peters advertised for a tenants to manage his property, but his tenants were no longer merely tending crops and cows.

The Columbia Railroad bridge crossed the Schuylkill in February of 1834, but the Belmont Cottage Hotel was already open for business in March of 1831. "Erected expressly for a hotel," it had "seven rooms, four garrets, two kitchens, a large piazza in front, and another in the rear of the main house" (*US Gazette*, March 25, 1831). The "piazza" refers to a porch. (A piazza also surrounded Pratt's mansion on Lemon Hill.) The reference to the "main house" can explain the use of three nouns to describe one place. Peters referred to his father and grandfather's Belmont Mansion as "the main house," to which he was adding a hotel that he called a cottage to distinguish it from his family home. Together with all that his father and grandfather had built, his resort had impressive, "if not superior," attractions "for public entertainment:" "there is also large ice house, and large convenient stables and sheds. . . . a large fish pond more than four feet deep, 80 in length and 30 in width." Could William Peters have anticipated that his work on the property was taking the first steps in building a resort?

Like Peters, many others were developing resorts up and down the Schuylkill. Down river, for example, tourists might also admire the beauty and technology of Fairmount and stay at one of the hotels nearby. They had more to see if they took the short train ride up river, across the bridge, and up the Inclined Plane to Belmont. On the hill, the spectacular view of the city alone was worth the trip. Some could even see boats on the Delaware River from that height,—they must have had eagle eyes!

In 1834, the Columbia Rail Road and its Inclined Plane itself were the new attractions: they made Belmont "of increased interest and resort," and—quite extraordinarily—a rival of Fairmount. Add to that cutting edge of modern technology, the "active business of the Schuylkill Navigation Company" that offered endless "animation and interest" along the river. For amusement, guests at the hotel could play on a ten pin alley, a shuffle board, and, in special matches during the season for pigeon shooting, with clay birds shot from a spring trap (*Public Ledger*, February 20, 1838). The neighborhoods of Fairmount and Belmont enjoyed healthy lives as resorts before they became tracts in the patchwork of Philadelphia's park.

With such interesting attractions, how could the Belmont Cottage Hotel not have succeeded? After the advertisement in 1833, a similar one appeared in 1840, but this time offering "a great public resort" for sale or lease (*Public Ledger*, October 2, 1840), by the "agent for

View from Belmont (1874)

Judge Peters' estate" (*Public Ledger*, March 29, 1851). The property was appreciating in historical value and capitalizing on "the famous Judge Peters' " distinction:

> Delightful summer resort—The famous Judge Peters' farm, at the head of the Inclined Plane, Columbia bridge, three miles from Philadelphia. This fine old estate, now belonging to the Belmont Company, has been fitted up, and will be open by the first of May, for Society excursions and Pic-Nic parties. There will be a large dancing floor erected in the grove, expressly for dancing parties. The farm will be open to receive parties and schools every day during the season, except Sundays . . . Ice cream and other refreshments can be had at all times, except on the Sabbath" (*Public Ledger*, April 20, 1855).

This notice in 1855 made no mention of the third generation of the Peters family. The glorious past had as much significance as the present. For that glory, imagine the edification of the Sunday school students as they gazed upon George Washington's chestnut tree, "cherished at Belmont, as a precious evidence of the intimacy that subsisted between those distinguished men." After the Inclined Plane had been abandoned as impractical by 1850, the railroad passed by the estate and left it to its glorious history of our Founding Fathers.

After 1855, the "Belmont Company" might have survived for a few years by making its hotel a popular resort, but the Sheriff was selling it by 1862. Notice of its sale in 1863 appealed mostly to romantic nostalgia: "To Capitalists—will be sold . . . the hotel well known as "Belmont Cottage," one of the most romantic and picturesque spots on the banks of the Schuylkill, commanding an expansive and varied view of the river. No situation has greater advantages either for public or private parties or for retired enjoyments" (*Inquirer*, July 4, 1863). Sometime after Belmont became part of Fairmount Park, the commissioners of the park razed the Belmont Cottage Hotel, and preserved Belmont Mansion for its historical significance.

After the third and last member of the Peters family had opened his farm as a hotel and resort, there seemed to be little change between his property in 1845, that of the "Belmont Company" in 1855, and of the Fairmount Park Commission in 1870: "The Park Commissioners are now prepared to lease Belmont Mansion to proper parties for the establishment of a well conducted restaurant" (*Inquirer*, March 31, 1870). All three were leasing a resort. Like Lemon Hill, Belmont also went through a period between the death of its owner, and its incorporation into Fairmount Park, but the transition seemed easier, because of Belmont's continuity through these three owners. After Fairmount Park razed the Belmont Cottage Hotel, the property became known simply as Belmont Mansion (*Inquirer*, August 10, 1870). The rails and river that made Belmont "of increased interest and resort" in 1835 had gradually lost their appeal.

Belmont Mansion now stands in splendid isolation above its plateau. In 1869, the incorporation of Belmont into the Philadelphia park system removed divisions within and between properties and all but the most significant buildings. In 1876, the celebration of the Centennial of the United States of America put its Agricultural Building, fittingly, on Belmont Plateau. Displaying the accomplishments of American farmers would have delighted the Peters family, but the necessity of removing their own accomplishment to do it would have saddened them. Advances in agriculture had made Belmont attractive in 1836, but their celebration at the Centennial destroyed any remnants of that attraction in 1876.

Besides agriculture, industry has also left no monument on Belmont. The Fairmount Waterworks closed in 1909, but the facility opened as a museum by the end of the century. The Columbia Railroad abandoned its funicular on Belmont in 1850, and visitors must try to imagine it climbing the hill. Belmont Plateau is now the scene of baseball games and cross country races. As a site for these activities, it serves the public. Belmont Mansion, on the other hand, remains a part for the whole of its history. As Alexander Pope has suggested, we can "consult the genius of the place," when its hill and river tell us their human stories.

Notes

1. Similarly, the country estate of the Francis family, which they at first built up as a neighborhood of wood frame houses, has become a city neighborhood with only one of their original houses surviving—see chapter 16, "The Family Ties of Francisville."
2. Howard W. Jenkins, *The Family of William Penn, Founder of Pennsylvania* (Philadelphia, 1899), p. 59
3. Also in recognition of the Springetts, Sir William Keith, the lieutenant-governor, laid out a tract of land, 6 miles wide, 15 miles long, near present-day York and also called it Springettsbury Manor.
4. Jenkins, p. 134, from a description of a tourist in 1755, who visited the estate when it was left in a little neglect.
5. See Reinberger and McLean, *The Philadelphia Country House*, pp. 232–236
6. The development of the estate to the east, Bush Hill, was called "Bush Hill Improvement."

   The etymology of 'improvement' or 'to improve' has nothing to do with that of 'to prove' or 'to approve'.

   It derives from the Latin verb *prodest*, "it is of use," "it is profitable."

   Proving something tests its value, improving something makes it valuable.
7. On the extension of Callowhill street from the Delaware River to the Schuylkill, see Robert I. Alotta, *Mermaids, Monasteries, Cherokees and Custer: The Stories behind Philadelphia Street Names* (Chicago, 1990), 42–43: it was first confirmed as the name of the street in 1770. Since it was the first street outside of Philadelphia, William Penn wanted to name it New street. Callowhill was also a town projected by the Penns between Vine street and Pegg's Run in Northern Liberties (Joseph Jackson, *Encyclopedia of Philadelphia* [Harrisburg, 1931] v. 2, 363).
8. At some point when Springettsbury Farm was giving way—or already had given way—to "improvement," a mapmaker drew a map of the old Springettsbury Farm in the context of the new neighborhood. He put on the map the street that was eventually called Fairmount Avenue in 1871, and he anticipates the extension of Callowhill.
9. Charles E. Peterson, *Carpenters' Hall* (Philadelphia, 1953), p. 101
10. The essay in this book, "Edward Burd (1749–1833), at Home in the Peace and Beauty of Ormiston Glen (1795)," gives background for the life of Joseph Galloway.
11. Richard K. Betts, *Carpenters' Hall and its Historic Memories* (1896), p. 15

12. Charles J. Cohen, *The Origins of Carpenters' Hall, Philadelphia, with Incidents of the Neighborhood* (read at a meeting of the Numismatic and Antiquarian Society held at Carpenters' Hall, September 19, 1917), p. 7
13. "The Old Penn Mansion. Its Appearance Today and a Century Ago. Its Interesting History. The Uses to Which it has Been Put" (*Evening Telegraph*, November 24, 1866). This article gives a thorough history of the Slate-Roof House.
14. Eberlein and Hubbard, *Portrait of a Colonial City* (1939), and others have given a later date for the construction.
15. Alexander Graydon (1752–1818), *Memoirs of his own time*
16. John F. Watson, *Annals of Philadelphia* (1855), vol. 1, p. 165
17. In Pennsylvania, in 1698, "Carpenters will get between Five and Six Shillings every day" (*Labor Review*, v. 30, no 1, January, 1930, p. 7).
18. In this book, see "David Franks Adds Another Story to Woodford," for more details about the family.
19. After visitors drive across the Benjamin Franklin Bridge to visit Franklin Court, up the Benjamin Franklin Parkway to visit his National Memorial in the Franklin Institute, and north to Franklin Town past the silhouetted bust of Benjamin Franklin on the overpass of I-676, they may think that Philadelphia has had no other citizen more worthy of memory. What an injustice! Penn weighs in the balance with Franklin, as Yahweh with one of His prophets. At least, Penn's statue surmounts the tower of City Hall.
20. Literal translation:
    Naturam optimam ducem, (Naturę, the best guide,)
    tamquam deum sequimur, (as though a god, we follow,)
    eique paremus (and we are obedient to her).
21. Similarly, Brian Charles Burke, *Beneath the Surface to the Heart, A Life of Theodore Roosevelt*, writes a biography on the basis of TR's reading in his youth. The Roosevelts and the Logans enjoyed the luxury of a profound literary culture.
22. Frederick B. Tolles, *George Logan of Philadelphia* (Oxford, 1953), p. 51
23. Literal translation:
    Nec vero dubitat agricola, (Nor, indeed, does the farmer hesitate,)
    quamvis sit senex, (although he may be an old man,)
    quaerenti, cui serat respondere: (to respond to the man asking him for whom he sows:)
    'Dis immortalibus, ('For the immortal gods,)
    qui me non accipere modo haec a maioribus voluerunt,
    (who wanted me not only to receive these things from ancestors,)
    sed etiam posteris prodere' (but also to hand them down to posterity').
24. Latin *stercus stercoris*, dung, manure (*cf.* the Germanic cognate dreck)
25. Deborah Norris Logan, *Memoir of Dr. George Logan of Stenton* (1899), p. 43
26. "There is another method, discovered by the provinces of Britain and those of Gaul, the method of feeding the earth by means of itself, and the kind of soil called marl: this is understood to contain a more closely packed quality of richness and a kind of earthy fatness, and growths corresponding to the glands in the body" (*Alia est ratio, quam Britanniae et Galliae invenere, alendi eam ipsa, genusque, quod vacant margam. Spissior ubertas in eā intelligitur et quid adipes ac velut glandia in corporibus*—Pliny, *Historia Naturalis*, book 17).

27. Literal translation:
    By my opinion, indeed, I hardly know (*Meā, quidem, sententiā, haud scio*)
    whether any <life> is able to be more blessed (*an nulla beatior possit esse*).
28. *Victum*, the fourth principal part of *vivo*, I live, is the root of English victual, food that a man needs to live.
29. Literal translation:
    Not only by duty, (*Neque solum officio,*)
    because, to the universal race of men, (*quod hominum generi universo*)
    culture of fields is essential (*cultura agrorum est salutaris*),
    but also, both by the delight, which I have mentioned, (*sed et delectatione, quam dixi,*)
    and by the fulness and supply of all things, (*et saturitate copiāque rerum omnium,*)
    which, to the sustenance of men, (*quae ad victum hominum*),
    and also to the cult of the gods, pertain (*ad cultum etiam deorum pertinent*).
30. Serjeant/sergeant, the Old French form of Latin *servientem*, is a doublet of servant. A sergeant, like a sergeant at arms, is an official of a court who enforces its will.
31. Literal translation:
    In agris erant tum senatores, id est senes,
    (The senators, that is, the old men, were then in the fields,)
    siquidem aranti L. Quinctio Cincinnato nuntiatum est
    (if indeed it was announced to Lucius Quinctius Cincinnatus)
    eum dictatorem esse factum . . . ;
    (that he had been made a dictator. . . .)
    A villā in senatum arcessebatur
    (From the farm into the senate, were summoned)
    et Curius et ceteri senes,
    (both Curius and other old men,)
    ex quo, qui eos arcessebant viatores, nominati sunt.
    (from which fact, those, who summoned them, were named travelers.)
32. Letter of Roberts Vaux to John Binns, quoted on p. 42 of Kenneth W. Milano, *The History of Penn Treaty Park*
33. At about the same time also, Thomas Jefferson was reported to have suggested that his tomb be "a granite obelisk of small dimensions" (*The National Gazette*, November 23, 1826); and the citizens of Boston proposed to erect a large obelisk over the grave of Benjamin Franklin's parents (ibid., June 22, 1827).
34. In 1869, Monument Cemetery preserved the pairing of Lafayette with Washington when it honored the two with a 70 foot high obelisk. It had hired John Sartain to design it. In 1956, Temple University bought the cemetery for an athletic field and a parking lot. On a monument in Lawnview Memorial Park, it preserved the bronze profiles of the two men from the base of the obelisk, but it threw the shaft, along with many other tombstones and monuments, into the Delaware River to serve as riprap.
35. Berthold Daun, *Siemering* (*Künstlermonographien* LXXX), 1906, pictures the sculptor's monuments throughout his book.
36. A pedestrian bridge across the Schuylkill at Valley Forge bears Sullivan's name, because Washington ordered him to build a bridge across the Schuylkill during the Continental Army's encampment there.

37. Martin I. J. Griffin, *History of "Old St. Joseph's," Philadelphia* (1882), and Eleanor C. Donnelly, *Life of Father Barbelin SJ* (1886), have written detailed histories of the church.
38. Rev. Jacob Duché took Tamoc Caspinina as an acrostic of his title: The assistant minister of Christ Church and St. Peters in Philadelphia in North America (*The Times*, November 17, 1895).
39. *Te Deum* are the first two words and the title of the hymn. The full sentence is *Te Deum laudamus*, "We praise you God." In place of a title, the first two words of a text are its *incipit*, "here begins."
40. Donnelly includes a reference to Washington: "The immortal Washington said to a priest (afterwards the Archbishop of Baltimore, Rev. Ambrose Marechal) in allusion to a full length picture of the Blessed Virgin Mary, which hung at the head of his bed: 'I cannot love the Son without honoring the Mother.'"
41. Deborah Mathias Gough, in the first chapter of her book, *Christ Church, Philadelphia, The Nation's Church in a Changing City*, treats the initial hostility between Quakers and Anglicans.
42. On the Doric Order in Philadelphia, see its mention in three chapters of this book: "Carpenters' Hall, 'The Nation's Birthplace,'" "Benjamin Chew's Family in the City and in the Country," and "Nicholas Biddle's Greek Facade on John Craig's Spanish Andalusia."
43. By a long tradition from Roman antiquity, 'd' represented *denarius* that became a penny in the Middle Ages.
44. Numinous, full of divine power, from *numen*, divine power, and *nuere*, to nod, expresses the work of divinity in the most general sense.
45. A portrait of his father, George II, in a wooden relief, removed during the Revolution, was restored to its place on the east facade of the church, just above the chancel window, on January 31, 1894 (*Inquirer*, February 25, 1894).
46. "The Poetry of Steeples" in *Harper's New Monthly*, January, 1876
47. Later evidence contradicts William's assurance. In the chaos of the epidemic, Bush Hill was used as a potter's field: "Hundreds of victims were buried in the neighborhood at that time, and many of the houses thereabouts are built over their graves" (*The Times*, October 6, 1889).
48. In his diary, January 14, 1814, Samuel Breck mentions James Hamilton's sale of Bush-hill, containing 187 1/2 acres. In his will, James intended to perpetuate his estate and a square bearing the family name. After William's death, his heirs went to court and successfully barred this entail, March 5, 1814, at which time the estate was broken up (*The Times*, June 14, 1891).
49. Mythmakers love stories; historians love facts: Bartram, in letters, gives the bare fact that he first became aware of the study of botany at age 10 or 12 (Thomas Slaughter, *The Natures of John and William Bartram* [1996], p. 47).
50. Carl and Jessica Bridenbaugh, *Rebels and Gentlemen* (1942), in their chapter, "Gentlemen of Leisure and Capacity," give some background for the Powels, especially in the third generation.
51. Two other chapters in this book present the evolution of similar Philadelphia families:

James Logan (1674–1751)	Andrew Hamilton (circa 1676–1741)
James Logan, Jr. (1718–1776)	James Hamilton (1710–1783)
George Logan (1753–1821)	William Hamilton (1745–1813), nephew,

52. George B. Tatum in his book, *Philadelphia Georgian, The City House of Samuel Powel and Some of its Eighteenth-Century Neighbors* (1976), pp. 6–25, gives details about the lives of the three Samuel Powels, grandfather, father, and the grandson, whose house he is describing.
53. Stephen Brobeck, "Revolutionary Change in Colonial Philadelphia: The Brief Life of the Proprietary Gentry," *William and Mary Quarterly*, vol. 33, 410–434, July, 1976
54. A chapter in this book, "Benjamin Chew's Family in the City and in the Country," gives a summary of Thomas Willing's enclave bringing together a number of Philadelphia families.
55. The title "esquire" designated the status of aldermen (Brobeck, p. 413).
56. Simon Baatz, *Venerate the Plow: A History of the Philadelphia Society for Promoting Agriculture, 1785–1985* (Philadelphia: 1985), p. 8
57. David W. Maxey, "A Portrait of Elizabeth Willing Powel (1743–1830)" in *Transactions of the American Philosophical Society*, New Series, Vol. 96, No. 4 (2006), p. 30
58. Henry Simpson, *The Lives of Eminent Philadelphians, Now Deceased* (1859), is quoted *passim* in this essay.
59. The Pennsylvania Agricultural Society encouraged good work in a broad range of farm products: "A bonnet of grass gathered on the banks of the Schuylkill, prepared, withered and fabricated entirely by female pupils of the Deaf and Dumb Asylum, received the premium lately awarded by the Pennsylvania Agricultural Society. The specimen is so perfect as not to be distinguished from the celebrated grass straw of Leghorn" (*United States Gazette*, January 14, 1825).
60. John Hare Powel, *Reply to Colonel Pickering's Attack upon a Pennsylvania Farmer* (Philadelphia, 1825)
61. Samuel Powel, "Sketch of the Life of John Hare Powel," 1893, Powel Papers, HSP
62. Charles Wood, "Powelton, An Unrecorded Building by William Strickland," *Pennsylvania Magazine of History and Biography*. v. 91 (2), 1967: 150, gives Powel a less noble motivation: "His incentive for erecting an imposing portico in 1825–1826 is perhaps not difficult to determine; he was a vain, rich, and socially important man whose prestige would be enhanced by such a monumental addition to his country seat." Wood finds it "not difficult" to pass over the possibility that Powel was discriminating in his choice of a classical order.
63. In his diary entry for February 20, 1839, Samuel Breck mentions Powel's work to open the bridge "free of toll" and thereby deprive its investors of their ownership for less than half of their investment. In one visit to their office, Powel spoke with "rage in his eye, and passion in his gestures." "This man," Breck concludes, "is generally disliked, but nevertheless possesses influence."
64. Nicholas B. Wainwright, *A Philadelphia Perspective: The Diary of Sidney George Fisher Covering the Years 1834–1871* (Philadelphia, 1967), quoted by Charles Wood, *loc. cit.*
65. A Philadelphian established his social prominence by his townhouse and then made his mark in the country. "Everybody of note has a residence in town," observed Lord Adam Gordon, after his visit in 1765 (Nancy E. Richards, *The City Home of Benjamin Chew, Sr., and His Family: A case study of the textures of life* [Philadelphia, PA: Cliveden of the National Trust, 1996], 3). Unfortunately, many a "residence in town," like Chew's on Third street, has disappeared.

66. Marion Harland, *The Homemaker* (1889), 429. Harland (1830–1922) wrote one of the first essays in a popular magazine about Cliveden. With her roots in Virginia, she described at length Benjamin Chew's ancestry.
67. Even more correctly, William Strickland, in 1825, built Powelton with a severe representation of the Doric from Stuart and Revett's *Antiquities of Athens* (1762). Such precise representation became the style six decades later in the neoclassicism of the early nineteenth century.
68. The Carpenters' Company had inherited the attribution by Vitruvius (*floruit* 1st century BC) of *virtus* to the Doric. By contrast, other architects in antiquity had attributed it to the taller, therefore, the loftier, Ionic or Corinthian (John Onions, *Bearers of Meaning, The Classical Orders* [Princeton, 1990], 39).
69. Margaret B. Tinkcom, "Cliveden: The Building of a Philadelphia Countryseat, 1763–1767," in *The Pennsylvania Magazine of History and Biography*, January, 1964, 31
70. In 1926, the Philadelphia Museum of Art opened Mount Pleasant as a showcase for some of its collection. Fiske Kimball, Director of the Museum, described it as uniting "beauty and historical interest to a degree very rare in America" ("Mount Pleasant," *Bulletin of the Pennsylvania Museum*, v. 22, #105, September, 1926). Eberlein and Hubbard imagined its occupants living lives worthy of its Palladian refinement: "The whole impressive grouping" announced "the state maintained by the Colonial occupants of this truly noble seat." An essay in the present book, "The Versatile John McPherson (1726–1792) of Mount Pleasant (1761)" gives some background for these occupants.
71. Hamilton's successful defense of the free speech of John Peter Zenger in New York City had made him the prototype of the "Philadelphia lawyer."
72. Although not uniquely significant at the time, this house has survived, in the twentieth and twenty-first centuries, as the sole remnant of the Willing compound. Consequently, it enjoys name and fame as the Powel House (see George B. Tatum, *Philadelphia Georgian: The City House of Samuel Powel and Some of Its 18th Century Neighbors*, Wesleyan, 1976).
73. When John Penn returned to Philadelphia, he built Lansdowne on the banks of the Schuylkill in 1777, a house considered the finest Palladian villa in the country. William Bingham (1752–1804), who built his mansion on the remaining three acres of the Willing compound, south of the Powel House, for his wife Ann Willing (1764–1801), eventually rented Lansdowne in 1789.
74. The farthest point in the Birch print, "View in Third Street, from Spruce Street (1800)," shows just a bit of the willows at the north end of the street—specifically, between the lowest branches of the farthest tree and the soldier's black helmet. A large and elegant weeping willow rises alongside the Bingham mansion on the left.
75. Brian Hanley, "Slavery, Consumption, and Social Class: A Biography of Chief Justice Benjamin Chew (1722–1810)," *Lehigh Review*, 2013, p. 31
76. On Ann and William Bingham, see chapter 15 in this book, "The Epoch of Ann and William Bingham."
77. Jennifer L. Green, *Cliveden: Legacy of the Chew Women of Germantown* (West Chester University, 2004), tells the story of three women of the Chew family who preserved Cliveden through the nineteenth and twentieth centuries.
78. Robert C. Alberts, in his excellent book, *The Golden Voyage: The Life and Times of William Bingham* (1969), explains this superlative.

79. November 4, 1780, a month after the wedding, Rebecca Shoemaker commented on the match: "Speaking of handsome women brings Nancy Willing to my mind. She might set for the Queen of Beauty, and is lately married to Bingham, who returned from the West Indies with an immense fortune. They have set out in highest style; nobody here will be able to make the figure they do; equipage, house, clothes, are all the newest taste,—and yet some people wonder at the match. She but sixteen and such a perfect form. His appearance is less amiable" (*Pennsylvania Magazine*, vol. 35 (1911), 398).
80. Most famously, Ann's profile appears on the American draped bust dollar of 1796, probably from the inspiration of her portrait by the American artist Gilbert Stuart.
81. William Bingham's obituary bears witness to the legacy of character, which he passed on to his son: "On Thursday morning last departed this life, in the 46th year of his life, Mr. William Bingham, merchant of this city, a Gentleman, whose disinterested Good-Nature and Kindness endeared him to all his acquaintance. His death was that of a Christian, resigned, serene and happy" (*Pennsylvania Gazette*, February 23, 1769).
82. As a gift of friendship, Bingham paid for Gilbert Stuart's portrait of George Washington, in the last year of his presidency, and sent it to Lord Lansdowne, the Prime Minister of England at that time. In 2001, the National Gallery in Washington, DC, finally acquired this iconic "Lansdowne" portrait and brought it back from England.
83. An entry in Samuel Breck's diary mentions Thomas Bones: *July 29,1816* Joseph Buonaparte returned to Lansdowne yesterday. He shook Mr. Bones, the tenant, most cordially by the hand. He is devoid of pride and very sociable.
84. Margaret Brown, "Mr. and Mrs. William Bingham of Philadelphia, Rulers of the Republican Court," *Pennsylvania Magazine of History and Biography*, vol. LXI (1937), pp. 301–305
85. Powell, with double 'l', reflects the Welsh spelling of the name; Powel, with one 'l', its English spelling.
86. Long before this portrait, both families had significant histories in Philadelphia. Mrs. Samuel Mifflin's grandfather-in-law had arrived in Philadelphia in 1679, three years before William Penn. Rebecca Mifflin Francis' grandfather had been attorney general in the state of Pennsylvania. Her uncle Tench would celebrate the ratification of the Constitution on July 4, 1788 by riding with eight other citizens "of the Union" on the Grand Federal Edifice, drawn by ten horses.
87. Similarly, John Powel Hare became Samuel Powel's heir by flipping his middle and last name to John Hare Powel (see the chapter, *John Hare Powel—Balancing Beauty with Use at Powelton*, in this book).
88. Refugees constructed a similar vault on the south side of Walnut street above Tenth (*Inquirer*, November 29, 1896).
89. In 1800, William Hamilton had also advertised Hamiltonville. North of Hamiltonville, John Hare Powel's sale of his estate in 1851 would create Powelton, a similarly fashionable community. Hamiltonville (1800) and Powelton (1851) represent two significant neighborhoods in West Philadelphia.
90. John Bach McMaster, *The Life and Times of Stephen Girard, Mariner and Merchant* (1918), II, p. 451
91. Peripteral,—Greek *peri*, around + *pteron*, wing,—describes a temple with "wings" of columns all "around." A pterodactyl, for example, had a wing finger (dactyl).

92. The 93 square miles of the islands of *Saint Pierre* and *Miquelon*, in the Gulf of Saint Lawrence, survive as last possessions of the French empire, whose inhabitants are citizens of France.
93. Plato gave classic expression to this truth: "But, do you give this knowledge indeed to doctors or to any other creative talent (demiurge) except to the man having understanding of things dreadful and not dreadful, the man whom I call courageous?" (ἀλλὰ τοῦτο δὴ σὺ δίδως τοῖς ἰατροῖς γιγνώσκειν ἢ ἄλλῳ τινὶ δημιουργῷ πλὴν τῷ τῶν δεινῶν καὶ μὴ δεινῶν ἐπιστήμονι, ὃν ἐγὼ ἀνδρεῖον καλῶ;—Plato, *Laches*, 195D)
94. Literally, "lost their Latin," (*perdu leur latin*). In French idiom, a man "loses his Latin," when he no longer has enough knowledge to deal with a problem.
95. William Francis Zeil (ed.), *The Diary of Peter Seguin, a Young House Guest of Stephen Girard* (1984)
96. Perhaps Girard got more publicity than he deserved. A Mr. Oliver wrote the *Gazette* to inform the public that he was growing in his backyard "in New Fourth street above Poplar lane, two stalks one fifteen feet high and 4 inches and a quarter in circumference, the other thirteen feet high and 5 inches in circumference" (*US Gazette*, August 22, 1828).
97. Corned beef, aka salted beef, is so called because "corns," i.e. grains, of salt have preserved it. Corn, from Latin *cornu*, horn, can also refer to the grains of either British wheat or American Indian maize.
98. *The Place—Stephen Girard's House, Historic Structure Report* (2005), unpublished monograph in the archive of Fairmount Park
99. Nicholas Biddle Wainwright, *Andalusia, Countryseat of the Craig Family and of Nicholas Biddle and his Descendants*, 20
100. R.A. McNeal (ed.), *Nicholas Biddle in Greece, the Journal and Letters* (1993), 201 & 206
101. Roger G. Kennedy, *Greek Revival in America* (1989), 93 and 195
102. See "Nicholas Biddle and the Beauty of Banking," chapter 4, 131–165, in Jeffrey Sklansky's *Sovereign of the Market, the Money Question in Early America.*
103. The history of Andalusia and of the Second Bank of the United States involves the succession of three famous early American architects, related as teacher and student, and separated in birth by about twenty years:
    Benjamin Latrobe (1764–1820) designed Andalusia's north facade.
    William Strickland (1788–1854) designed the Second Bank.
    Thomas U. Walter (1804–1887) designed Andalusia's south facade.
104. "An Eclogue on the Plough" appeared in the only agricultural journal published in the country:
    All hail, ye farmers, young and old!
    Push on your plough with courage bold,
    Your wealth arises from your clod,
    Your independence from your God.
    If then the plough supports the nation,
    Let Kings to farmers make a bow,
    And every man procure a plough
    (*American Farmer*, April 8, 1825).
105. Nathan Schachner, *Thomas Jefferson: A Biography* (1951), p. 568

106. Biddle, *An Address Delivered Before the Alumni Association of Nassau-Hall* (1835)
107. Sklansky, 152, probably derived from Conyers Middleton's *Life of Marcus Tullius Cicero*
108. A month after its first report, the *Public Ledger* complained that the city had not completed the repair: "Is it not time that the hole at the north end of Fairmount was filled up, and that part of the ground restored to something like its proper condition? The reckless mutilation, above ground of the beautiful point of rocks, through quarrying operations of Engineer Birkenbine, with the silent acquiescence of the late councils, is of course past remedy; but it is to be hoped that our new Council will show a little more interest" (*Public Ledger*, May 18, 1860).
109. "The Chief Engineer proposed to remove the steps up to Fairmount and construct a roadway, which will be permanent, less laborious to ascend, and more conformable to the natural beauty of the scene" (*Public Ledger*, January 31, 1860).
110. A Doric column is thick and without a base; but a Tuscan column is thin and with a base. A Tuscan column has a smooth shaft, but a Doric column has flutes (grooves).
111. In 1836, 12½ cents represented the old custom of dividing the Spanish dollar into eight pieces, that is, pieces of eight or bits. Two bits bought a shave and a haircut.
112. Junto, from Spanish *junta* and Latin *junctus* (cf. English junction), originally referred to a 'joining together' of men for some secretive political purpose. Franklin used the word, because he kept the names of its members secret.
113. Chapter 2, pp. 24–31 of *The Story of the Naomi Wood Collection and Woodford Mansion in Philadelphia's Fairmount Park*, 1981), by June and Martin Snyder, offers the best account of Coleman's life.
114. Since William Coleman's mother died in her 92nd year in 1770 and William died in his 64th in 1769, she lived about two years longer than her son. This sequence allowed Franklin to praise his friend and his friend's family twice.
115. Compare the conclusion of William's obituary: "He was an able and an upright Judge, and in that Character gave the greatest Satisfaction to his Country. And we may say, with much Reason, that this Province has few such Men, and that few Men will be so much missed as Mr. Coleman" (*PG*, January 19, 1769), with that of his mother, two years later: "She was Mother of WILLIAM COLEMAN, Esq.; lately deceased; — a Gentleman, whose Character and Abilities have done Honour to this Province, of which he was a Native" (*PG*, September 20, 1770). Franklin has turned the narrative of his friend's obituary in 1769 into the monumentality of an epitaph by 1770.
116. By contrast, his neighbor, John McPherson, who built Mount Pleasant in 1761, had just the opposite of "a steady quiet mind." In his old age, McPherson brought his life into balance by writing and teaching about virtue.
117. Mark Abbott Stern has written a full biography of Franks, *David Franks, Colonial Merchant* (2010).
118. In the eighteenth century, merchants imported a stock that would make a cosmopolitan reminisce: the Bohea Tea came from the Bohea Hills in China; and looms from all around the world had woven the textiles: in France, lawn from Laon, cambricks from Cambrai, and shallots from Châlons-sur-Marne; in Germany, garlix from Goerlitz, and osnabrigs from Osnabrück; in the East, damask from Damascus in Syria, calico from Calicut in India, muslin from Mosul in Iraq, and buckram from Bokhara in Uzbekistan.

119. Russian duck (*cf.* German *Tuch*, cloth) is strong cloth. Rappee, from French *râpé*, grated, from Latin *raspare*, to scrape, grate, rasp, refers to a coarse snuff made from dark tobacco.
120. A notice in the *Gazette* describes the neighborhood of Franks' store: "Lost in the middle of last month, a Gold Thimble, with fleer top, marked M. K. supposed to be dropped in walking from the house of Thomas Lawrence, Esq. up the stone steps that leads from thence into Front-street, and from thence to Morgan's corner, in Market-street, opposite the Jersey Market. Whoever can give intelligence thereof at the New-Printing-Office, so as it may be had again, shall have Five Shillings reward" (*PG*, August 13, 1752). Only one example of the "stone steps" from Water street to Front has survived.
121. See Rawle's biography in *Dictionary of National Biography*, 1885–1900.
122. The son of Samuel Shoemaker, Benjamin (1747–1808), twelve years later, would marry Rebecca Warner Rawle's younger sister Elizabeth (?–1823) in 1773. This marriage would bring three of the Warner girls into the Howell-Rawle-Shoemaker constellation.
123. Henry Simpson, *The Lives of Eminent Philadelphians, Now Deceased* (1859)
124. Reinberger and McLean, *The Philadelphia Country House* (2015), p. 309
125. William Brooke Rawle, "Laurel Hill and Some Colonial Dames Who Once Lived There," *Pennsylvania Magazine of Biography and History*, v. 35 (1911), pp. 385–414. To avoid some understandable confusion in his family tree, William Brooke Rawle (1843–1915), the great grandson of William Rawle (1759–1836), changed his name from William Rawle Brooke to William Brooke Rawle. He continued the fame of his family by distinguished service at Gettysburg in the Civil War. He has given a special authenticity to this account of his ancestors during and after the American Revolution, which he first wrote as an address to the Colonial Dames.
126. *Pennsylvania Magazine of History and Biography*, "A Pennsylvania Loyalist's Interview with George III," vol. II (1878), pp. 35–39
127. Martha Crary Halpern, *Laurel Hill, a Country Property along the Banks of the Schuylkill* (unpublished, 1985), p. 39
128. Jacob Randolph, *A memoir on the life and character of Philip Syng Physick, M.D.* (1839)
129. *Fragaria*, strawberry in Latin (*cf.* French *fraise* and Spanish *fresa*), shares its root with fragrant in English.
130. Sarah Dickson Lowrie, *Strawberry Mansion, First Known as Somerton, The House of Many Masters* (1941), p. 37
131. William Primrose, *Biography of William Lewis* (1820)
132. "The view towards Rome, looking from the Tusculan citadel, embraces the Campagna—on the left is the sea, and on the other side the whole Alban valley, with its beautiful undulations, and covered with a luxuriance of verdure that renders it a charming scene" (*The Crayon*, 1858, v. 5, No. 3). This description could also be made of the Schuylkill valley.
133. Esther Ann McFarland, *William Lewis, Esquire, Enlightened Statesman, Profound Lawyer, and Useful Citizen* (2012), pp. 94–95
134. C. Dallett Hemphill, *Philadelphia Stories: People and their Places in Early America* (2021)

135. In September of 1853, George Crock posted this notice in the *Ledger*: "RED STEER strayed—apply to George Crock above the third milestone on the Ridge road" (*Public Ledger*, September, 28, 1853).
136. Nine years later, the *Times* published a more practical appreciation of Strawberry Mansion:
"AT STRAWBERRY MANSION. The grounds around Strawberry Mansion were thronged with pleasure-seekers from early until late, and many a weary toiler and tired business man with wife or sweetheart with him found yesterday rest and enjoyment in listening to the music of the Keystone Military Band, which played at intervals from 4 to 10 P. M. Great as was the crowd there was ample accommodation for all on the numerous benches placed on the lawn and in the rooms of the mansion. Altogether it was an ideal day in the Park, and the thousands who went out to the city's grand breathing spot attested the appreciation in which it is held in their hearts. The religious needs of the Park visitors were catered to by the Evangelical Alliance, whose service on the children's playground was well attended. The address was by Isaac Naylor, a well-known English evangelist" (*Philadelphia Times*, June 22, 1892).
137. McPherson described his violent youth in his autobiography, *A History of the Life, Very Strange Adventures, and Works of Captain John McPherson; Which Will, in Many Parts, Appear Like an Eastern Tale* (1789).
138. In all, McPherson had nine children, born over a span of thirty years, between 1754 and 1784, by two wives. The first, Margaret Rogers, gave birth to four children, the two "pretty daughters," Margaret and Mary, and two boys, before she died in 1770; the second, Mary Ann McNeal, twenty-one years younger than he, gave birth to five children, three boys and two girls. Mary Ann McNeal survived her husband by thirty-six years.
139. The notice continued with a list of the estate's stock, staff, and paraphernalia: "ALSO for sale, with or without the plantation, 100 sheep, 12 cows, 3 steers, one bull, three horses, and several stout healthy negroes, one of which is a coachman, carter and plough man; one a gardener; and one a cook and dairy maid, which 3 may be lett with the place. To be sold also a scow, a battoe, carts, ploughs, harrows, rollers, and all sorts of utensils for the plantation, garden, quarry and dairy. There are several quarries of very good stone, which a tenant may work, as can be agreed on. The place is under good post and rail fence, great part of which is ditched. If it is lett, the tenant may have all the hay and straw left upon it at a reasonable value; for the said Macpherson is determined not to permit either cf these articles to be sent from the place, while it is his property, which is mentioned to prevent trouble."
140. The root of grange is *villa granica*, farmhouse for grain. Grange and granary are doublets.
141. Breck's notice for the sale of this property, which he eventually called Sweetbriar, in the *National Gazette*, 1837, gives its size as thirty acres. In his diary entry of August 2, 1828, he states that it "has 24 acres of good land." In either case, he may be counting or discounting "good land" above the flood plain from that which he can not call "good," because it was subject to flood. In 1819, for example, he estimated that fifteen or sixteen acres of his property would be covered by water rising above the dam at Fairmount.

142. "Five barrels" of orange peels may seem odd, but the peel of the orange was easy to preserve and best preserved its flavor. Orange marmalade preserves it best.
143. The Eglantine Rose, another name for the Sweet Briar Rose, derived from the Latin *aculeus*, needle, also refers to the Sweet Briar as a briar. The Sweet Briar Rose pricks, but it also heals.
144. In 1877, H. E. Scudder edited *Recollections of Samuel Breck with Passages from his note-books* (1771–1862). In 1978 and 1979, Nicholas B. Wainwright edited "The Diary of Samuel Breck" in four installments of *The Pennsylvania Magazine of History and Biography*: 1814–1822, in the issue of October, 1978 (469–508); 1823–1827, in January, 1979 (85–113); 1827–1833, in April, 1979 (222–251); and 1839–1840, in October, 1979 (479–527).
145. Tantivy, a folk form of *tantara*, from Latin *taratantara*, an onomatopoetic word, evoked the frightening sound of the war-trumpet. By the sixteenth century in England, tantara evoked a merry sound like that of a fanfare.
146. In the glory days of the Four-in-Hand Club, Fairman Rogers could not have anticipated the threat that automobiles would eventually pose. Each vying for his place, the equestrian argued his case with the motorist long after Rogers' death in 1900. In retrospect, an equestrian arguing a case may seem to be holding up a feather against the wind. Indeed, by the 1920's, equestrians saw the handwriting on the wall. After the park had accepted the reality of automobile traffic by end of the decade, some old die-hards met in a cavalcade of more than 100 horsemen on Belmont Plateau. They inspected bridle paths in the Park and then crossed the river by the equestrian span under the bridge (*Inquirer*, April 28, 1929). See chapter 28 in this book for the evolution of the Girard Avenue Bridge.
147. See chapter 5 in this book for George Logan also gaining financial independence by relying on industry: "A pleasant Country Seat," a farm that he put up for sale in 1802, also included a "Water Mill . . . conveniently situated for the Manufacture of Snuff, Chocolate or the Spinning of Cotton" (*Aurora General Advertiser*, March 18, 1802). A farmer on this property could became an industrialist.